THE NEW MONEY MASTERS

THE *NEW*
MONEY MASTERS

Winning Investment Strategies of
Soros • *Lynch* • *Steinhardt* • *Rogers* • *Neff*
• *Wanger* • *Michaelis* • *Carret*

JOHN TRAIN

1817

An Edward Burlingame Book

HARPER & ROW, PUBLISHERS, New York
Grand Rapids, Philadelphia, St. Louis, San Francisco
London, Singapore, Sydney, Tokyo, Toronto

FIRST EDITION

Designed by Sidney Feinberg

Library of Congress Cataloging-in-Publication Data
Train, John.
  The new money masters / John Train.—1st ed.
    p.   cm.
  "An Edward Burlingame book."
  ISBN 0-06-015966-9
  1. Capitalists and financiers—United States—Biography.
2. Investments—United States.   I. Title.
HG172.A2T73   1989
332.6'092'2—dc20
[B]   89-45071

89 90 91 92 93 AT/RRD 10 9 8 7 6 5 4 3 2 1

Contents

Acknowledgments

I am grateful to Kenneth Lubbock for advice and administration, to Virginia Armat for editorial help, to Helen Train, Sara Perkins, Barbara Phillips, Jane Vaughan, Piers Dixon, and Charles Phipps for reading the manuscript, and to Claudette Teen and Diane Scarborough for their patience with messy handwriting and mumbled dictation.

Part of "Managing Old Money" appeared in the *New York Times*; another part appeared in *Harvard* magazine, as did "Managing Harvard's Money" and the sections on Philip Carret and Michael Steinhardt.

Foreword

Ten years ago I wrote a foreword to the first *Money Masters*. Thanks to that boost—and perhaps the merit of the work itself— the book became a bestseller and has been in print continuously since. Now comes the sequel, and I wish it equal success.

By way of *glasnost*, I should confess to being John Train's cousin as well as his client. That noted, it can also be said that the stocks run by his firm have provided a total annual return of 19 percent compounded over the past decade, putting him in the same league as his subjects. So he knows whereof he speaks!

Claiborne Pell

Introduction

The New Money Masters

This book is intended to complement the studies of nine great investors in *The Money Masters*, which was first published in 1980.

A decade has passed, a number of the original masters have left the scene, and new masters have appeared—practitioners, in some cases, of novel or unfamiliar techniques.

So it seemed time for another sweep around the horizon. For variety, I have also looked at how some famous institutions and wealthy families handle their investments. I hope readers enjoy an X-ray view of the complicated and sometimes tortured machinery behind the bland public exteriors. And I have included one eminent subject, Philip Carret, whose perspective of more than sixty years in the business makes him far from "new" but all the more instructive.

After examining the cases that follow, I will try to sum up what can be learned from them in the Conclusions section: how these masters differ from their predecessors, and how one can profit from their discoveries.

J. T.

THE NEW MONEY MASTERS

1

Jim Rogers

Top-down Investor

Highly successful investors sometimes devise novel investment approaches, and Jim Rogers falls in that category: He bets on whole countries. He determines that a country is more promising than is generally believed, and then places his bets there before other investors even realize that the transaction is mechanically possible.

For instance, Portugal. After a takeover by the far left in 1974, the country had hovered close to civil war. The situation resembled Chile under Salvador Allende. The government imported professional activists to help prepare a communist takeover: several thousand from Cuba in the case of Chile, and many hundreds from the Soviet Union in the case of Portugal. Capital fled abroad and business slumped. Then the Portuguese anticommunist faction fought its way back to power and displaced the radical left. The risk of a communist takeover faded. The country began to breathe again. Gradually confidence returned. Tourism and business picked up, although to nothing approaching the previous level. Some substantial foreign industrial investments began to appear, but the stock market, a very modest affair in any event, remained closed to foreigners.

In 1984 Rogers felt that the time might be ripe. He approached the Portuguese financial authorities about investing there. In 1985, after six months, he received permission to reconvert into dollars the proceeds of transactions he might make on the local stock exchange. The leading investment firm in Lisbon told him that it was not recommending Portuguese stocks. Rogers nevertheless instructed them to buy all twenty-four stocks on the Lisbon exchange, and thereafter to buy every new issue that came out. He eventually had a total of thirty-five holdings. Portugal has been looking better and better ever since; his bold stroke succeeded brilliantly.

Another Rogers coup in 1984 was Austria. The Austrian stock market had stagnated at barely over half its level of 1961, twenty-three years earlier. A number of European countries had passed investment incentives to encourage their capital markets, including the French, whose economy and currency had collapsed under the socialist government of President François Mitterrand. Rogers saw that the Austrian government was preparing to follow suit. He was sure that European money managers, looking around for whatever hadn't moved yet, would in due course fasten on Austria. He inquired at the New York branch of the principal Austrian bank how a foreigner could invest in Austrian stocks. The bank didn't know: There had been virtually no investment interest in this largely socialist, yet stable and successful, country. So little information was available outside Austria that Rogers went to Vienna himself to inquire. At the Ministry of Finance he asked what political factions or other interests were *against* the idea of liberalizing the stock market and encouraging foreign investment. When the answer came back that there were none, he felt he couldn't miss.

One problem did emerge: Morgan Stanley's International Index showed Austrian stocks selling at sixty-seven times earnings, an appallingly high figure. Upon investigation, though, Rogers discovered that this was a completely misleading statistic, since the index consisted of only nine companies, three of which were losing money. Morgan Stanley also said that the Austrian market had inadequate liquidity. That, however, turned out only to be so because most transactions took place off the exchange: The banks traded actively among one another. "Morgan Stanley should be shot," is Rogers's charitable judgment. On the other hand, thanks to Morgan Stanley's dismal figures and, probably, the intellectual laziness of foreign investors, there was almost no other interest in Austria from abroad. So Rogers placed his bets, and in the very next year the Creditanstalt Share Index rose 145 percent.

During this period Rogers became convinced that the German market was ready for a boom. It had been quiet for fifteen years, and the pressures were building for the country to liberalize its capital markets. As he said at the time, "The German market is going to be wildly profitable in the next three years. They are about to have a speculative boom that will boggle their minds." He called a German broker and announced that he wanted to buy a list of stocks. The broker asked if he should send Rogers recommendations, reports, news items, daily prices. "No," Rogers replied. "Germany is about to have an incredible explosion. If I see the prices on a regular basis, I might sell the stocks." He made his purchases, the market advanced. In the summer of 1986, after the market had doubled in eighteen months, he sold again.

Rogers is just as happy to be short a market as long—that is, to sell stocks he doesn't own, in the hope of covering (repurchasing) them more cheaply later. "It's a lot of fun finding a country nobody knows about," he says. "The only thing better is finding a country everybody's bullish on and shorting it." In the same year as his Austrian flier, he bet on a drop in the Swedish market, which had risen nearly sixfold in four years. The sag in the Swedish market was only 10 percent or so over the ensuing year, but the particular speculative favorites that Rogers shorted, including Ericsson, ASEA, Pharmacia, and Gambro, fell by 40 to 60 percent.

In 1986, he tried again on the short side, this time in Norway. As he explained, "They had enormous oil revenues and they thought things would go on forever. Since then, the price of oil collapsed. And that was a market that was, earlier this year, at an all-time high. It seems an obvious place to be short." The Norwegian market rose, but fell in the 1987 crash. Rogers covered Norway, with all his other shorts, in November 1987.

In 1985 Rogers tried the Malay Peninsula. At that time Singapore had a 42-percent savings rate. Prime Minister Lee Kuan Yew ran an exceedingly tight ship, economically speaking. He required that both employers and employees contribute to a central retirement fund. Then he permitted some of that money to be used to buy blue-chip stocks. Then he also cut taxes on investment. This created the conditions for a leap in demand for stocks, but did not actually trigger the event since there was general weakness in the economy and the markets. Growth had plunged from 8.2 percent in 1984 to a negative 1.4 percent in the second quarter of 1985. The government thereupon introduced a number of emergency measures to stimulate the economy. But a major Singapore-based holding company, Pan Electric, which had dozens of subsidiaries in Hong Kong, Malaysia, Bermuda, Brunei, and Britain, went bankrupt. The government panicked, and on December 2 the Singapore and Kuala Lumpur stock exchanges were closed.

Rogers told his friends in the government that this was a ghastly mistake, and indeed, when the two exchanges reopened a few days later, prices dropped by as much as a quarter. However, to Rogers this signaled the bottom, and he moved in. Malaysia barred new public issues of securities until order was restored in the market; Singapore passed a similar ban. This cutback of supply, coupled with the growth in demand from the tax cuts, finally propelled stocks upward. Both markets doubled in the next eighteen months. Rogers feels that because they are basically natural-resource economies, the countries should continue to do well, if one can assume that commodity prices could rise even slightly.

Rogers also likes Brazil, where he has a certain amount of money invested, even though the currency is not convertible. He had entered Brazil in the early 1970s. A stock exchange official had told him that it was impossible for foreigners to invest there openly; it had to be done through the black market.

"Well, where is the black market?" Rogers had asked.

"*I* am the black market," the official replied.

Rogers arranged for a bank account in the name of a Brazilian he never met, used it to buy stocks, paid the bank charges, and made a bundle. "The entire market went up ten or fifteen times within a few years. Not just one stock, the whole market! That's like the Dow Jones jumping to 23,000!" he says.

Rogers is not ordinarily interested in making an investment in a country using a local straw man to dodge exchange controls. What if the man dies? John Templeton has told Rogers that he is buying into Korea, but since this is in theory not legally possible, Rogers does not know how he is doing it mechanically.

Rogers's policy has always been to keep his holdings in his own name in the largest bank in each country, preferably one with an office in New York. He reasons that the largest bank will be the last to go bankrupt if there is a national crisis.

Key Tests of a Good Country

Rogers's four tests of a good country to invest in are:

1. The country must be doing much better than it had been.
2. It must also be better off than is generally realized.
3. The currency must be convertible. Currency convertibility is an interesting question. Basically, he finds it best to wait until the currency already *has* become convertible. If it is going to become convertible a month ahead, then he will wait a month. The key conception is that there is plenty of time to invest after the currency has become convertible.
4. There must be liquidity for the investor. (In the same spirit, he won't buy "investment letter" stocks.) "I always like to be able to get out of something if I'm wrong," he says.

Aside from anything else, it is useless to buy if no other foreigner can. So Rogers wants to enter a country through conventional channels, to see what the experience is going to be like for those who come after him. People sometimes say that they are getting an introduction to the chairman of the board of the Central Bank, or whatever. However, that dignitary may, in Rogers's words, be "foaming at the mouth" to attract investors. Other, less well introduced investors may not receive the same welcome.

Rogers says that he considers Indonesia a buying candidate. In 1988 it made its currency convertible. The Pacific rim is booming, Indonesia is rich in natural resources, and its large and able population is getting used to the benefits of capitalism. A commission to encourage foreigners to invest has been created. The authorities determined that they should start a stock market, because the other countries in the region had. Twenty-four stocks were listed (only some available for foreigners). All these measures were successful. Then they asked, "Since we've succeeded in getting foreigners to buy, how can we encourage the local population to buy?" The whole investment process there, says

Rogers, is just starting, and if he's right, it will develop much further. He is bullish on the agricultural products that underpin the economy, and foresees an upturn in its oil. "Five years from now, Merrill Lynch and James Capel will have offices there. Seven years from now the commodities will be booming, even Bache will have an office, and that will be the top. Anyway, today an investor willing to accept risk should contact an Indonesian broker and buy all the shares available and every new one that is issued."

The other day, Rogers said, John Templeton called him and said that things seemed extraordinarily cheap in a particular country. Rogers replied that he wants to know *why* things are cheap. There are lots of countries where things are cheap and will stay cheap, so he wants to see reasons for change. When he bought into Austria and Portugal, investors did not even know how to perform the mechanics of making an investment in those countries. So when he learned that this information was going to become available, he could foresee a better investment outlook there, based on rising demand from abroad.

Raw Land

I described to Rogers my own experiences looking for a way to take advantage of new oil strikes in foreign countries. I have found that parking lots in a provincial or national capital are an interesting approach. They aren't subject to rent control, and one doesn't have to put in massive amounts of capital for improvements. In the end, much of the benefit of any mineral strike flows to the government, which invariably taxes the oil profits. It then expands the ministries involved, meaning more government workers, more offices, and more housing. So there's a big pickup in the capital city. Even in Scotland, during the North Sea oil strike, this was a much easier solution than figuring out which exploration companies had the best territories, or which service enterprises were ahead in selling pipe or providing helicopter services to the oil rigs. Raw land in the capital will eventually soar, and give one a relatively trouble-free existence in the meanwhile.

Rogers agreed, but pointed out that if things go wrong, raw

land might not sell. A stock market may collapse to half or even a quarter of what it was, but at least you can always get out. I answered that not infrequently a market can also be closed down or become hopelessly illiquid—as indeed had happened previously in many of the countries whose recoveries he participated in later. In France there is usually a flight out of financial assets into real property when things get very sticky. And it can be an advantage not to be able—and thus tempted—to sell: A very long term approach to holding raw land has probably been the most profitable of all investment strategies. Rogers doesn't disagree, but for himself still prefers liquidity.

Jumping the Gun

Sometimes Rogers tries his hand in an undiscovered market too early in the game. In 1985, troubles in Iran and Afghanistan had severely curtailed the supply of Oriental carpets to the West. Encouraged by a story that the Nepalese economy was booming, thanks to a surge in demand for carpets there, Rogers journeyed to Katmandu. The head of the Nepalese stock exchange was more than a little taken aback by the interest of this lone American. It turned out that the market had only nine stocks, thinly traded. Rogers remembers reflecting, as he peered into the tiny shops on main-street Katmandu, "This is a *really* primitive society. It's too far away and too complicated, and the lines of communication just don't exist." He decided that a motorcycle trip into the Himalayas was likely to be a better idea than investing there.

Background

How does one get a sense of the risks and opportunities in different countries? Through travel, and by reading in history and philosophy—not in business school. Rogers says his own success has come from discovering things that others haven't bothered with, places where others haven't gone yet but are about to go. Rogers quotes Kipling: "What can he know of England who only England knows?" He says he got a perspective on England in the United States and on the United States in England.

He was conscious of international currency and investment

movements even as a student. While on a scholarship in the early 1960s at Oxford, where he went after graduating from Yale, he became convinced that the pound sterling was about to cave in. As a result, he walked around day after day with only a few shillings in his pocket, hoping to be able to exchange his dollars at a more favorable rate after the inevitable devaluation. Inevitable it may have been, but Rogers had gone home to the United States before the British government finally let the pound fall.

A self-styled "poor boy from Alabama," Rogers was raised in Demopolis (population 7,800), where his family's telephone bore the easily remembered designation of Number 5. The nearest big city, Selma, with a vast population of 19,000, was fifty miles away. His father, a member of an old Alabama family, managed a plant for the Borden Chemical Company, which produced Elmer's Glue and formaldehyde.

Rogers attended Yale, graduating in 1964. Confused about what he wanted to do in life, he applied to several graduate schools and had interviews on campus with several company recruiters. One of the interviewers, from Dominick & Dominick, had grown up in Hell's Kitchen in New York City. Rogers and the interviewer liked each other, and a job offer resulted. By that time, Rogers explained, he had decided to go to Oxford in the fall; he asked his interviewer friend if he could work just for the summer. This was unusual, but in the end arranged. At the time, Rogers did not know a stock from a bond. But he fell in love with the securities business almost at once.

"What I liked about it was not so much investing money, because at that time I didn't have any, but that if you were smart, used your wits, and paid attention to the world it was all you had to do. At that time I was extremely interested in what was going on in the world and used to read voraciously. You didn't have to wear the right tie,* you didn't have to join the country club, you didn't have to join the PTA. You could do what you wanted to do, and they would pay you to do it. I thought that was the most exciting thing I'd ever seen." That autumn he went to Oxford, where, being a small man, he earned

*He now always wears a bow tie.

a rowing blue as a cox. (John Templeton, curiously enough, also grew up in a small southern town and went to both Yale and Oxford. He and Rogers were introduced by the Master of Balliol.)

Rogers speaks in a modest, almost shy, way—but rapidly and exactly to the point. He invariably wears a sport jacket with nonmatching trousers and no overcoat, even in New York's bitter winter weather. By the time he came home to the United States, he realized that his keenest interest was in international finance. He wanted to be a "gnome of Zurich," who invested everywhere and in everything. In the summer of 1965 he returned to Dominick & Dominick to work at the firm's over-the-counter trading desk. Then came two years in the Army, where he ran his commanding officer's portfolio and developed a growing determination to make money. "I wanted to make enough so that I would never have to worry about working again," he says.

Right after the Army, Rogers worked at Bache, and then for Dick Gilder, where, as he puts it, he learned that "you'd better understand the numbers. So many people in the 1960s didn't know what they were doing. As far as that goes, lots of people right now are making money, but don't know why." Subsequently, he went to Neuberger & Berman.

While working at Arnhold and S. Bleichroeder in 1970 he met George Soros. They formed the most successful twin-star investment team in the business. While they were together they never had a down year, and from December 31, 1969, to December 31, 1980, the Soros Fund chalked up a gain of 3,365 percent while the Standard & Poor's composite index advanced about 47 percent. When they began there were just the two of them and a secretary. Soros was the trader, and Rogers specialized in research.

The fund was characterized by independence of thought: Neither Rogers nor Soros has much time for Wall Street research analysts. "They all follow the herd. Nobody gets rich doing that," says Rogers. "It's a fast way to bankruptcy." But Rogers does not think of himself as merely a contrarian, whom he defines as someone who would have bought U.S. Steel, now USX, every year since 1959 and lost money. You have to be right as well as different.

The fund's greatest successes came from an ability to foresee large and general changes—secular, as opposed to cyclical. Rogers, who still follows this orientation in his own investing, explained at the time: "We aren't as much interested in what a company is going to earn next quarter, or what 1975 aluminum shipments are going to be, as we are in how broad social, economic, and political factors will alter the destiny of an industry or stock group for some time to come. If there is a wide difference between what we see and the market price of a stock, all the better, because then we can make money." This is what Wall Street calls the top-down approach.

A decade after inception Soros and Rogers were still the only thinkers in the firm, although the staff had grown to thirteen. In the same period, starting with $12 million dollars under management the fund had grown to $250 million—one of the factors that prompted Rogers to leave in 1980: He thinks large funds become unmanageable. His share of the profits on leaving came to $14 million.

Rogers describes himself as "very much a loner, a maverick, a misanthrope." He has a somewhat bohemian point of view, and has motorcycled through Latin America. He says he doesn't like people in general, although he is happy to teach security analysis at Columbia's Graduate School of Business. He traded the teaching fee for his first course for a lifetime membership at the Columbia gymnasium facilities. Warren Buffet, who attended one of Rogers's classes, said it was "absolutely sensational. . . . Rogers is doing the same thing that Ben Graham was doing thirty years ago—bringing the realities of the investment world to the classroom."

He is planning to leave most of his money to Oxford and Yale for travel fellowships, to let others have the same broadening exposure that he had. Students will receive $18,000 a year if they agree to spend 75 percent of the succeeding two years out of their own country. Otherwise there will be no restrictions. To his Columbia students he says, "Study history and philosophy. Do anything in preference to going to business school: Wait on tables, hitchhike in the Far East." Only thus, he emphasizes, can they develop a rounded perspective on life.

Rogers once considered getting an MBA himself. However, a senior partner at Dominick & Dominick told him: "Go short some beans and you'll learn more in just one trade than you would in two years at 'B-School.' " Rogers didn't go, and indeed soon learned how to lose money. He began as a speculator in 1968. In January of 1970 he felt that a bear market was coming, and with all his money bought puts on machine-tool companies. On May 26, 1970, he sold his puts: "I got it to the day," he says. Many of them had tripled in value in three or four months. Then the market rallied for a few months, and Rogers went short all over again. After that, the market advanced strongly for two years. Rogers lost all the money he had. It wasn't much, but what he had, he lost. He feels that the Dominick partner was right: It was a most useful experience, which he is glad to have undergone in a fashion that cost him $5,000 rather than $50 million.

By this time he had decided the best way for him to make a fortune was by running a hedge fund, where he could buy, sell, and also sell short. He has never stopped shorting since, and he has made a fortune. "It grates on me to this day when people say that I've been lucky," he says. "It's worse on the short side: I tell them that something is going to go badly, that they'd better sell their stock. I tell them that I am going to go short myself. Then they answer that Morgan Guaranty has a bullish story on the industry. Then the companies do start getting into trouble, and the stocks go down. Then people blame it on me. They've even blamed lower oil prices on me. I didn't understand the story of 'kill the messenger' until it happened to me!"

Pursuing his international bent, Rogers opened an official, tax-paying Swiss bank account in 1971 and started buying one-ounce gold bars in Canada, before ownership of gold bullion by individuals had again become legal in the United States. He was struck by a Cartier-Bresson photograph he owns of mobs seething outside the National Bank of China in 1949, waiting to switch paper money into gold. He brought one or two bars at a time into the United States, so that if he were caught he would not get into too much trouble. He keeps substantial amounts of gold as an "insurance policy," although he does not believe that the price will rise soon: As things get worse in South Africa, the government, corporations, and individuals there will sell the gold they hold abroad, since that is all they have to sell. This will hold the price down.

He maintains further "insurance" in Swiss francs, together with large holdings in German marks. As an alternative, Rogers considers the Dutch guilder, the Austrian schilling, and the Singapore dollar satisfactory. In 1987 he felt that the dollar would decline heavily against the yen, but observed that the Tokyo market is a rigged game. He is puzzled that after all these years most U.S. investors still do not understand the need for foreign currency and bond holdings as a hedge against a decline in the dollar and the U.S. market.

Now "retired" and running his own money, Rogers says, "Everybody dreams of making a lot of money, but let me tell you it isn't easy." He ascribes much of his success simply to industriousness. He says that when he was a full-time money manager, "The most important thing in my life was my work. I didn't do anything else until my work was done." When he joined George Soros he moved into a handsome beaux-arts–style house on Riverside Drive. He rode his bicycle every day to the office on Columbus Circle, where he worked nonstop—taking not a single vacation in a ten-year period. He still lives in the house, which he has furnished in the style of a British club. "At the time I worked most intensely," he says, "I really knew an enormous amount about what was going on in the world, just about everything that any single human could." He says he never felt anxiety about whether he was right when his views differed from everybody else's. "Other people can't sleep at night. I hit the pillow asleep."

The Outlook

The U.S. government has lost control: The currency has been debased faster than at almost any time in history. The debasement of the currency took 300 years in Rome, a century or more in Spain, and 50 years in nineteenth-century England, whereas in the last twelve years the U.S. deficit has risen more than in all the years of the country's history. In the eighteenth and nineteenth centuries the United States was a net debtor, but the money was applied to productive assets. Now it is borrowing to finance military expenditures and transfer payments. Within two or three years the U.S. external debt will exceed that of all the rest of the world. There has been no case in history, says Rogers, of the world's reserve currency being debased that fast, and this revolution has not yet been fully reflected in the financial markets.

Next Steps

Whatever happens next has to be bad, says Rogers. Soon those abroad lending to the United States will stop doing so, recognizing that conditions here are out of control. At that point the government must do one of three things:

1. Sit tight, and let the U.S. public finance the deficit. But we have only a 3-percent savings rate, so interest rates will go to 18 percent or 20 percent. At that point the bond market will disappear, and exchange controls will be imposed (not, however, on money that is already abroad, only on money that is still here).
2. Try to encourage savings through fiscal policy.
3. Cut spending.

Any of these alternatives will hurt the economy. Thus, there will inevitably be a financial crisis. Financial companies will experience extensive bankruptcies. Many Wall Street and Tokyo firms will go out of business. Whether there is a depression at this juncture will be up to the politicians: In all likelihood, though, they will do the wrong thing. But in any event, by 1992 the Republicans will be swept away.

To forestall disaster, Rogers believes a number of steps would be required.

First, the capital-gains tax should be eliminated. Then, taxes on savings should be reduced, such as by bringing back generous provisions for IRAs and Keogh Plans. The elimination of these encouragements in 1986 was a serious mistake.

However, Rogers believes that the basic problem is not taxes, but spending. For example, the U.S. government spends $5 billion a year to support 16,600 sugar farmers. We pay 22¢ a pound, while the world price is 9¢ a pound. This has a lamentable effect in Latin America, which cannot sell sugar at a decent price. Instead of this, according to Rogers, one would be better advised to pay the U.S. sugar farmers a substantial sum simply to get out of the market altogether.

Investing in Stocks

In domestic portfolio investment, Rogers bets on whole industries in the same way as, when investing abroad, he bets on countries. First he develops a massive investment concept. He then buys every stock available in an industry that he thinks is set for a turnaround, the way he buys every stock in a country. How does he select the industries? *He looks for a major secular change*, ignoring fluctuating business conditions. "The way you find things to buy low and sell high is to look for unrecognized or undiscovered concepts or changes. Whenever you see something, don't look at it and say, 'That's a brown rug'; say, 'How can that rug change, or is that rug going to change? What's happening in the world that may make it different two or three years from now?' If you look at a company that's bankrupt, it is not necessarily always going to be bankrupt. If you look at a company that is growing by leaps and bounds, it is not necessarily always going to grow by leaps and bounds. So look for change. And by change I mean secular change, not just business-cycle change. I'm looking for companies that are going to have good performance even when the economy is going down. Examples would be things like the oil industry in the seventies. It didn't matter what happened in the economy. The oil industry and oil stocks did very well. In fact one of the reasons the economy didn't do well was because oil stocks did so well, because they were all booming. But that's what I mean by a secular change. A major ten-year change took place in the oil industry."

Rogers looks for four principal types of changes:

1. *Disasters.* Examples include Lockheed, Chrysler, International Harvester. Company crises of this magnitude imply that the whole industry of which the company is a part is in a catastrophic situation. Usually, *when an entire industry is in a crisis, with two or three major companies bankrupt or on the verge of it, the whole industry is ready for a bounce, as long as there is something in the situation that should change the funda-*

mentals. As one instance of a sector in need of a catalyst for change, Rogers cites the steel industry: It has been bankrupt for years, but nothing has happened to bail it out.

2. *Changes for the worse.* These usually fall into the "trees do not grow up to the sky" paradigm. When an industry is so popular that investing institutions own 80 percent of the shares of its top companies, one can be reasonably confident that the stocks are overvalued in the market. In this situation, Rogers will go short many of the stocks in the industry, not just one. Here one must be particularly careful. Just because something is high does not mean that it cannot go a lot higher. So he tries to chart precisely when the major change for the worse is about to take place.

3. *New trends.* The "natural look" was an example. When in the seventies women began to turn away from overdone makeup, and indeed any makeup, Rogers studied Avon Products and decided that at over seventy times earnings, it was due for a fall. He shorted at $130, and covered a year later under $25.

Some of these have included day-care centers, manufactured housing (alias mobile homes), hospital chains, and the garbage business. Rogers recalls attending a garbage convention in 1969, when new competition was taking the business out of the hands of the municipality/Mafia duopoly. The other delegates, some of whom were very rough characters indeed, were stunned: Someone from Wall Street had actually turned up at a garbage convention! However, many of these same rough characters now have houses in Palm Beach, and some of their companies are on the New York Stock Exchange. Currently, he sees growth in the gardening suppliers—nursery centers, and so on—because of the increased number of retirees and their need for leisure activities.

Another example is the motorcycle. In the 1950s, "motor-cycle" meant (as he says) "trashy," "low-rent." By the 1960s, however, Honda could advertise, "You meet the nicest people on a Honda," perhaps including Malcolm Forbes. Rogers didn't happen to spot this conception in time, but he says that if he had been smart enough he could have worked out that Honda was a buy, along with Japan in general.

Other major trend changes include hospitals, which a generation or two ago were run by municipalities and by charitable foundations, and today are more and more run by profit-making companies; alcohol-treatment and mental-health centers; and mobile homes, which were considered an atrocity when Rogers was a boy—his mother didn't want him consorting with people who lived in them, whom she called "trailer trash."

Somewhat similar are hotel chains. Rogers points out that Hilton has gone up 100 times in the market in the last thirty years. In the old days there were hotels in different cities, even very fine hotels, but all differently owned and run. Then it was realized that there could be high efficiencies of scale and improvements in quality control by running them as chains under the same banner.

Another secular change occurred in the 1970s when the nursery school was succeeded by the day-care center. "When I was growing up I went to nursery school. And nursery school was just a little lady down the street who took in all the kids on the block and looked after us while our mothers went to the beach or did whatever mothers did in those days. But that really wasn't very organized or efficient or economic. In the seventies something developed called day-care centers. They developed for a lot of reasons: one, because it was more efficient and it was more organized and it was cheaper for people to send their kids to day-care centers. But also they changed the tax laws so that they gave you tax incentives for giving your children care while you went to work. And we had the whole phenomenon of working women. I mean, mothers went back to work or went to work or wanted to work. So it was a whole new concept, a whole new market to develop and some very clever lads got together and developed chains of day-care centers. Now, Kindercare in fact went public in 1972. It was just an obscure Alabama company that you could have bought all you wanted of in a public offering. I remember because I was the only institutional investor at the time. Now, of course, it is a very dynamic industry."

4. *When the government decides to act.* It then throws money at a problem. Rogers became the largest outside shareholder of Lockheed in 1974, when the company was a rumored bankruptcy candidate. Rogers noticed that in the Arab-Israeli War of 1973 the Egyptian Air Force enjoyed an extraordinarily high degree of success against the Israelis, even though the Israelis had far

superior aircraft and pilots. Rogers discovered that the Egyptians had been supplied with Soviet electronic devices that the United States was unable to supply to the Israelis, because during the Vietnam War our defense effort had concentrated on day-to-day supplies at the expense of long-range technological development. On learning this, Rogers reasoned that the United States would have to catch up with the Soviets in defense electronics. Lockheed had some of the best. The stock went from $2 a share to $120, Loral went from $0.35 to $31, and E-Systems went from $0.50 to $45. At that time E-Systems was little known, but Rogers discovered it by asking Lockheed and Northrop who their most effective competitors were, along with reading trade journals and consulting defense experts. When E-Systems had advanced to $8, Rogers discussed it with a banker, who liked the story but said he couldn't buy it for his bank until it rose to at least $10, because that was the cutoff point that the institution's policy imposed. People have different "crazy criteria," says Rogers, such as that a company must have a market capitalization of $50 million, or whatever.

Contemplating governmental trends, Rogers also spotted collection agencies, an interesting bit of reasoning that might elude most of us. The government lends to students, small businesses, and a great many others. For decades it made little attempt to collect this money when due. In the late 1970s it decided to hand over the job to private collection agencies. Moving a billion dollars around means little to the government, but any significant fraction of that can mean an immense change in the fortunes of a small company, which collection agencies usually are.

Another discovery was dredges. In 1975 the Army Corps of Engineers, which has the chore of keeping inland waterways navigable, realized that its aging dredges were obsolete. The corps had three choices: Buy newer dredges, recondition the old ones, or leave the business and contract it out. The corps determined on the last course, pruning its inventory of dredges from forty-four to eight. (Before that time all independent dredging companies together had owned twenty-four dredges.) One company, Great Lakes Dredging, then advanced 1,000 percent in the market.

Another occasion on which government intervention changed an industry was nursing homes. Until the 1960s young people used to look after their parents, but then the government increased its involvement, with Medicaid, Medicare, and support for nursing homes. Nursing-home companies began floating large public issues. When one of the largest, Four Seasons, went bankrupt, it was found to have been using fraudulent accounting, and many other companies proved to be overextended, not really making money. Other scandals followed. So the whole industry collapsed in the market. After a while Rogers noticed that some of the companies had tightened up their operations, were selling off marginal divisions and money-losing operations, and were turning profitable. So he visited a number of them and in due course realized that although very few homes had been built in recent years because of the notorious problems of the industry, the American population was still inexorably aging. So he invested in one of the companies, Beverly Enterprises, which made a large advance.

The dredge example illustrates another central Rogers principle: the importance of supply and demand. Rogers says *the trick to getting rich is correctly sizing up supply and demand.* Neither the communists, nor Washington, nor anybody else has been able to repeal that law, he observes. I think it is one of the most useful ideas in this book.

As an instance of the principle he cites the oil industry. Why, Rogers asks, did the price of oil soar in the 1970s? The general perception is that OPEC did it. However, he retorts, OPEC had tried every year since 1960 to lift the price of crude, but was never successful: The price always went down again. The real reason goes back much earlier. In the 1950s the Supreme Court determined that the U.S. government could regulate the price of natural gas. The government thereupon did so, at an extremely low rate; so low, in fact, that by degrees it became unprofitable to produce gas at all. It was often simply burned off—flared—when it was produced along with oil. So for the rest of the 1950s and through the 1960s there was very little drilling for gas. At the same time, though, consumers woke up to the excellence of gas as a fuel: It is cheaper and cleaner than oil or coal. Increasingly, householders converted to gas, at the very time that exploration was winding down. So by the early 1970s many of the gas-pipeline companies were running out of supply. Rogers remembers noticing that prospectuses for pipeline bonds had stopped promising that there would be a sufficient supply of gas to pay the interest on the bonds. From an annual report of Helmerich & Payne, a drilling-rig supplier, he learned that the number of rigs in use in America was steadily declining, simply because people were not keeping up the exploration required to maintain the national oil and gas supply.

Rogers went to Tulsa and visited a series of drilling companies. All reported dreadful business conditions. He decided that it was unimaginable that the pipelines would be allowed to go bankrupt and thus cut off gas to stoves around the country. So starting with the onshore drilling companies, which were suffering the most, he bought oil drilling stocks, oil shale company stocks, everything in the industry. Not long after, OPEC's fourfold price hike and the oil embargo gave the market a tremendous boost. Yet in 1971, Rogers had already determined that the gas industry *had* to undergo dramatic improvement, two years before OPEC finally succeeded in raising prices in 1973. The fundamentals were already in place. OPEC merely provided what is called in physics the "exciting cause."

Then, however, came the "trees do not grow up to the sky" sequel. When oil rose from $2.80 to over $40 a barrel the whole country went on an energy-conservation binge: insulation for buildings, smaller cars, efficient appliances. And at the same time there was an enormous step-up in oil exploration. As a result of these two factors the supply-demand equation reversed and has stayed reversed. Oil and gas prices—and stocks—plunged.

A similar play currently, he says, is public-utility stocks. Rogers perceives an important government-based change coming for the industry: These companies, he feels, are sure candidates for deregulation. It would be hard for them to be regulated more unfavorably than they have been, so things are bound to improve. There's even a chance of full deregulation. Thus far there have been no takeovers, no leveraged buyouts, and only one merger. Some of the companies have an immense positive cash flow. Rogers probably owns thirty different utility-company stocks, which he began buying in 1981. He doesn't expect to sell before the 1990s, if then, and he would probably sell the entire group more or less at one time. To him they are essentially one stock, or at least one conception.

Specifically, he likes General Public Utilities and Dominion Resources, formerly Virginia Electric. Dominion had been constructing a number of nuclear-power plants. It finally abandoned one, leaving it uncompleted. When Rogers started buying, the stock was yielding 13 percent to 14 percent. With the end of the company's capital spending program, and falling oil and gas costs, Dominion's situation improved dramatically. Rogers points out that in the utility business a growing territory can be a disadvantage—you have to build plants to keep up with the demand. He feels, incidentally, that it would be much better for the health of the business to permit competition between different companies in different territories, across jurisdictional lines.

Other utility companies he favors are Northern Indiana and Public Service of Indiana. Rogers bought the latter's 9.60 cumulative preferred, which has a sinking fund, at $62. It soon advanced over $90. The stock had $20 of cumulative dividends, which it will pay off in time. At that point Rogers's stock will have cost him $42, on which cost it will be yielding almost 20 percent. Rogers said he might sell the stock when it started paying a dividend. The company can certainly earn $4 a common share in the 1990s. It is able to buy excess power capacity from neighboring territories, and if necessary can convert its atomic plant to a gas-fired plant.

Techniques and Strategies

What are Rogers's techniques in stock selection? One has been mentioned: He never talks to brokers or security analysts. "You've got to *sell* to those people." Their ideas don't work out, he claims—they follow the herd: "Even when you tell them that things are changing, they not only do not believe you, but will pooh-pooh any evidence you care to point out."

The important thing, in his view, is "*develop a way to think independently*," as he and George Soros did so profitably. He says: "I have always found it much better just to sit and do your own reading. I wasn't very smart, so when I talked to people it would muddy up my thinking. I was much more successful just sitting back, reading and figuring things out, and coming up with absurdities, no matter how absurd they were. I found it much easier and more profitable if I just stayed with what I knew very well, not what somebody else told me."

He says that *he has never been able to make money from inside information*, even if legal and ethical. Nine times out of ten it is wrong, according to Rogers, because it is factually incorrect, or because it has been garbled en route. "If you get inside information from the president of the company, you will probably lose half your money. If you get it from the chairman of the board, you will lose all of your money. So stay away," he counsels.

While working as a money manager full-time, he used to read newspapers from at least five different countries, some forty periodicals, and about eighty trade journals, including *Variety*, *Publishers Weekly*, *Iron Age*, and the like. Most of these are deadly dull, and indeed full of fluff provided by public relations agents. But sometimes there is a suggestive article or advertisement. He also read hundreds of annual reports and followed insider trading figures for lots of companies. He still reads a great deal, but less than before.

Many of Rogers's investment ideas come from observing the everyday world around us. A typical discovery was Banc One. His broker at Merrill Lynch said that he would appreciate it if Rogers opened a cash-management account, which would gain him some points with the firm. Rogers noticed that the checks for his CMA were drawn on Banc One, which he had never heard of. He looked into the company and found that it had a computer system that was primed to participate in the growth of check and credit-card processing for the rest of the big brokers. The more he studied the situation the more he liked it. In due course he became a shareholder. The stock went from 6 in mid-1980 to 30 in mid-1986.

Look Down Before You Look Up

One of his key ideas in buying stocks is to insist that the stock must be so cheap that even if everything goes wrong the worst that can happen is that your capital will be sterile for a while. "I look down before I look up," says Rogers. An example would be buying stock in a company in bankruptcy at the time. Still, one can never be sure on the short side: However right you are, the market may move against you and cost you a great deal of money.

He makes no attempt to avoid taxes. As he says, when he came north he "aspired to a tax problem." He has never availed himself of tax shelters. Most of them are economically disastrous, he points out.

True to his principle of trading anything that can make him money, Rogers is active in commodities. He has traded orange juice, rapeseed oil, and potatoes, and he even bought a seat on the Sugar Exchange as an indirect way of betting on higher sugar prices.

He also makes a point of having short positions along with long positions. There is always someone doing things better, and somewhere things are going wrong.

The Investing Cycle

One of his primary rules is, *Don't lose money. If you don't know the facts, don't play.* Take your money, put it in Treasury bills or a money-market fund. Just sit back, go to the beach, go to the movies, play checkers, do whatever you want to.

"Then something will come along where you know it's right. Take all your money out of the money-market fund, put it in whatever it happens to be, and stay with it for three or four or five or ten years, whatever it is.

"You'll know when to sell it again, because you'll know more about it than everybody else. Take your money out, put it back in the money-market fund, and wait for the next thing to come along. When it does again, you'll make a whole lot of money.

"So my basic advice is don't lose money. Stay with what you

know, and then find something that you can make a lot of money in."

Spread Sheets

Rogers loves accounting spread sheets: They are his chief analytical tool. "Thousands of spread sheets, lots of numbers." He does not use computers, but has the work done by hand. He used to have three people at this task and is now down to one. He does not have access to any computerized data bases, because he cannot know whether their facts are reliable. He says that it is better to have no information than to have wrong information: If the basic facts are wrong, a geometric pileup of errors will follow, probably leading to a wrong conclusion. Specifically, one should avoid such secondhand figures as those in Standard & Poor's, Value Line, or brokerage-house reports. It is essential to go back to the annual reports and 10 Ks—a more detailed version required by the SEC.

Rogers says that when he writes to a company he always asks them for *any* filings they have with *any* regulatory authorities. There are sometimes filings of which he is unaware. He points out that for foreign companies on American exchanges, notably the American depositary receipts, one can request the U.S. form 20 K, corresponding to the 10 K that an American company files in addition to its annual reports. It is particularly important to get the 20 K, because the annual reports of foreign companies are extraordinarily uninformative.

Within the financial statements, Rogers says that the balance sheet is much more important than the income statement. He also gives great weight to the depreciation account. He likes to buy companies that are on the verge of bankruptcy. The cash available from depreciation may tell him if the company will survive in spite of reported losses. Depreciation and amortization are bookkeeping, not, he says, "cash going out the door."

He has developed his own spread-sheet format over the years. When he makes a serious mistake, he may add a line to his basic spread sheet to reflect what he has overlooked before: the trend of a company's receivables, or whatever. He finds that it is essential to have very long term spread sheets—ten to fifteen years—

to provide the historical perspective necessary to understand a company. (For an example, see Appendix I.)

He looks, for instance, at profitability over the years: When the results were good, *why* were they good? When the results were bad, *why* were they bad? Rogers likes to buy when things are bad, but just about to get better—not when they already are getting better. So he needs to know how bad things *can* get, as well as how good things can get.

Rogers says he knows that the 1987 bear market has not run its course because he never meets other people doing spread sheets by hand. In booming times anything works, but in hard times you learn to be careful.

Some of the ratios he tracks with care are the following:

1. Capital expenditures:
   a. In absolute terms,
   b. As a percentage of depreciation,
   c. As a percentage of gross plant and equipment, and
   d. As a percentage of net plant and equipment.

The ratio of capital expenditures to depreciation is not a scientific figure but, spread over many years, it gives an instructive insight. When it is very high, then you are likely to be at a top; when it is very low—that is, when no one is spending money—the outlook is good, since the supply of what the industry produces will be drying up.

2. Then he looks at the ratios of sales to receivables, debt to equity, and the others. *When there is almost no inventory, when receivables are low*, when the profit margin is 20 percent and the pretax return on equity is 25 percent, when capital expenditures are growing at 40 percent to 50 percent a year, then *Rogers begins to smell a classic top*, and a promising time to go short.

He notes that everything has been considered a growth stock at one time or another. Even aluminum was considered a growth industry in the 1940s and 1950s. Most former growth industries have had recoveries at some time. That does not truly turn them into growth stocks all over again. But when they are being *thought* of as growth stocks . . . *then* you have a shorting opportunity!

Spotting Tops

As an example of how an industry looks when it is ready to take a turn for the worse, Rogers cites financial services, such as investment bankers and stockbrokers. They hire huge staffs, expand their services, and raise money in the marketplace. You read that most graduates of the Harvard Business School have announced that they wish to become investment bankers. At that point, the end is near. For instance, in 1980 Atari hired 5 percent of the graduates of the Harvard Business School. Three years later, Atari was bust. In 1986, Goldman Sachs in turn hired 5 percent of them and within two years got into a terrible crunch, with massive layoffs, cancellation of building plans, and the like.

Toward the end of 1986 Rogers announced in *Barron's* that he expected one more big rally in the stock market, followed by a collapse, and that he was already shorting some of the invest-ment-banking and brokerage stocks, based on their getting over-extended, hiring on a massive scale, opening new offices, and the other characteristics of a cyclical top. Virtually all of them did in fact decline severely in 1987.

Spotting Bottoms

Rogers likes to look at his tried-and-true ratios to see how bad things can get; and when they reach the lower limit, he assumes they will start going the other way. For instance, when three or four of the big companies in an industry are losing money, as the autos were in the late 1970s, either there will be no auto industry at all—most unlikely!—or else conditions will improve. And in fact, this industry, which was grossly overregulated in the 1960s,* had a relaxation of regulations in the 1970s, and its capital needs were reduced. So he bought Ford, General Motors, and American Motors (not Chrysler, unfortunately). A similar turnaround, as already mentioned, is ahead for nuclear utilities today. They have endless problems, and yet there has to be such an industry. So Rogers foresees a buying point. *When he sees several major*

---

*I figured out during that period that the capital requirements of General Motors to cope with regulation and modernization exceeded the then market value of the corporation!

companies losing money, and capital expenditures coming to a stop, then he looks for an industry recovery.

Benjamin Graham's great rule was that one should buy when a stock is so cheap that you can't lose. Rogers's variation is that you should *buy when there is reason for change for the better.*

Here is how the turn comes in the market, he says: The situation of a company or an industry is a disaster, but the stock is still holding its own. Then a few people buy because their grandfathers worked in the plant, or some such reason. Then the Grahamites buy. About this time the supply of whatever the industry produces starts to dry up: supply and demand, a key tip-off! Then the outlook begins to lift, and a wider circle starts to buy. Then the stock goes up and up, and the Wall Street brokers turn positive, so their customers start to buy. Then, after a five-year recovery, the company is acclaimed as a growth stock (which it is not), and still more people buy.

But just when the curve of the stock price is rising the most steeply, the ratios often start approaching their worst levels. At the end, people are buying just because it is the thing to do. Rogers says that about then his mother will call to say *she* wants to buy the stock.

"Why do you want to buy, Mother?" Rogers asks.

"Because the stock has tripled," his mother answers.

"No, Mother, you're not supposed to do it that way," Rogers will say. "This is the most dangerous stage in the market."

Then the stock goes down, and the entire sequence operates in reverse. Finally, Rogers's mother calls again.

"I want to sell the stock."

"Why?"

"Because it's down 90 percent."

"No, Mother, you're not supposed to do it that way."

In March 1987 Rogers was anticipating a steep drop in the stock market. He said the early 1987 rally in the financial markets was fueled by paper money—essentially, the monetization of the federal deficit. This is what I wrote after our talk in that month:

> When it goes it will go quickly: the Dow could be down 300 points in a day, although it might be from as high a level as 3,000. We may see very high prices first, but he doubts we'll make it to

1988. ("Maybe in six days, maybe in six months . . .") In every real panic, people eventually sell because selling is the thing to do. When the decline comes, Rogers expects that index options will disappear, along with stock options and indeed junk bonds. He considers it indescribable "lunacy" to buy junk bonds today. He himself only owns bonds guaranteed by the U.S. government, or of equivalent quality. He thinks we are headed for very hard times because of the budget deficit and also the latest tax reform act, which he says history will judge as the 1986 version of the Smoot-Hawley Act. Rogers feels that the reform, in boosting consumption at the expense of investment and savings, takes us in exactly the wrong direction, and that the next market decline will be the worst since 1937. He does not expect, however, that there will be a general business depression, but that the damage will be mostly confined to Wall Street and the financial world. He predicts that several major firms in Wall Street, Tokyo, and London will go bankrupt.

Advice

A year after the October crash he was no more optimistic than before. The new president will announce some measures, Rogers said in November 1988, whereupon the stock market will have one last rally. But whether George Bush in fact does something or nothing, there will be a catastrophe, and he won't be reelected in 1992. The bear market in fact started in April 1987. Federal Reserve Chairman Alan Greenspan pumped a lot of newly printed money into the economy and saved the situation for a time. But that was just a prop, not a cure. Nobody realizes how bad things are.

In bear markets, things first decline to reasonable prices, then they fall to cheap prices, and then they reach unbelievable giveaway prices. After that, things get *really* bad, and everybody gets cleaned out. In the U.S., the next step will be real pain and suffering. The unraveling process has already begun.

Many of the last two years' leveraged buy-outs have already started to come unstuck. A number of companies are having trouble selling the bonds required to pay off the bank loans used for their recent acquisitions. The prices being paid for companies in acquisitions assume that there will be no recession for the next fifteen years. In fact, however, Rogers confidently guarantees a recession well within that time!

Wall Street is still crazy: Irrational things continue, such as the Nabisco takeover. And Wall Street ethics are deplorable. One of Rogers's students applied for a job at a famous company. The firm called him to inquire about the candidate. Rogers said that he was able, but of dubious ethics. "That's not important," said the interviewer. "Will he make money for us?" Another company called to ask about another one of his students who was looking for a job. Rogers replied that he was very, very bright, but without integrity or morality. He was hired anyway. Rogers is confident that this would have happened at many other firms as well.

A year ago he expected that the impending financial catastrophe would not necessarily affect the overall economy. Now, however, because of all the overborrowing, he fears that it will indeed spill over into the general economy. He does not know if there will then be deflation or inflation. Probably deflation followed by inflation. He expects to play the downside via financial instruments, rather than by going short. He hopes he will have sharp enough wits to figure out the appropriate response to whatever comes.

Fallout

Donald Trump is bust although he does not know it yet, says Rogers. New York real estate has been supported by the Wall Street boom. That, however, is over. Also, cooperative apartments are being created very rapidly. At some point, many of the largest New York apartments will again be given away for the assumption of the maintenance payments. Rogers is convinced that the art market is also going to collapse, and the way to take advantage of that event is to short Sotheby's stock.

Don't think the decline is over before it's over. One of Rogers's friends, "Bill," was the head of the petroleum group at one of the major banks. Rogers used to tell him that oil was going to collapse. Bill scoffed at this: "It's going to $100 a barrel," he would answer. By 1985, however, Bill had become a convert; he conducted appropriate hedging operations so that the bank would be safe even if oil got as low as $21 a barrel. By 1986, oil had hit $8 a barrel, and Bill was out as head of the petroleum group. And where did he go after this disaster? He became a head of the bank's Personal Asset Management Division, setting policy for their largest portfolios.

And gold? Gold has been a traditional store of value for thousands of years, but it can get behind the cost of living for considerable periods at a time. It should hold its own in the event of a return of hyperinflation, but it is not undervalued today the way it was in the 1970s. There may be some other good store of value for the 1990s, but Rogers has not figured out what it will be.

The Dollar

Rogers says he is sure of the dollar's continued fall. And indeed, since the government seems to believe that it is best for the country that the dollar should decline, he argues that it is patriotic to take money abroad, as he has done through purchases of foreign currencies. It is all too likely that the drop of the dollar could get out of control. He is sure that exchange controls are inevitable; only after that will come the "killer wave," the final collapse of the dollar. After that, one can bring one's money back.

Other Countries

Rogers is no more sanguine about the rest of the world. The Japanese market stopped going up in 1987, he says. He started shorting that market in 1988, and has made a profit in every stock he has gone short, even though the Nikkei average is making new highs. If that's the case, it can only mean that Japan is in a bear market. And now Taiwan and Korea are beginning to cave in. The United Kingdom has very high interest rates, and an inverted yield curve. What's more, Nigel Lawson, Britain's Chancellor of the Exchequer, has said that he will do nothing to stimulate the economy.

Rogers considers the two most remarkable things happening in the world to be the opening of China and the uniting of Europe in 1992. The latter, however, is not necessarily beneficial for the rest of us. Europe will be blocking out foreign imports. This may exacerbate America's problem, even though it apparently helps Europe, at least temporarily.

The twenty-first century will, in any event, be the century of China. The Chinese like to work very hard; they think entrepreneurially; they are extremely well motivated; they are prepared to delay today's gratification for tomorrow's benefit. And they have before them the overseas Chinese as an example of how to prosper. So, says Rogers, teach your children Chinese!

Specific Suggestions

In the midst of all this gloom, though, there are attractive situations. Some public utilities are a bargain, particularly nuclear utilities. Things can't get worse. He likes Northern Indiana, Public Service of Indiana, General Public Utilities, and Dominion Resources. He likes steel companies, some banks, and some agriculture-based companies.

Among countries, try Indonesia.

And on the short side, there's always Sotheby's.

2

Michael Steinhardt

Strategic Trader

Michael Steinhardt has had one of the greatest twenty-year runs in investment history. If you'd put $10,000 into his hedge fund, Steinhardt Partners, at its inception in July 1967, twenty years later you would have had over a million, thanks to an annual compound growth rate, net of his own fees, of 27 percent. How does one invest so successfully?

One answer is that Steinhardt pays about $35 million a year in commissions to Wall Street brokers. That kind of money can buy masses of Wall Street research, if that's what you want: 100-page analyses of companies, economic projections, studies of the outlook for foreign countries. Indeed, Steinhardt himself at one time purveyed such financial intelligence—as a writer for *Financial World* and an analyst at Loeb Rhoades & Co.

And yet deep Wall Street research is one thing that Michael Steinhardt has almost no interest in. On the desks of most investment people you see stacks of annual reports and studies from brokers projecting companies' prospects out for years into the future. But if you look around Steinhardt's office there is scarcely a scrap of paper to be seen. So what does the $35 million buy? The answer is that for this enormous outlay Steinhardt does not get the same kinds of prophecies that he used to produce himself when he was on the "sell side," as Wall Street calls it; rather, he hopes that it gives him a little edge in each of innumerable profit-making transactions.

On the other hand, small incremental gains alone would not fully explain his overwhelming success. He has reaped his major rewards from betting on "directional moves." As he says, "If we get involved in bonds, it's because we expect interest rates to go in a certain direction. . . . I look first at the big picture of where the market is going and then try to find stocks to fit a portfolio that reflects my generalized view of things. That contrasts with focusing first on companies that have terrific value regardless of the market."

Steinhardt could be called a strategic trader. First, he forms a large and general conception like those that we all derive from reading the papers: The yen will go up; inflation will get worse; it's time for a recovery in oil stocks. Having established his conceptual framework, he looks for the specific. Thanks to his commission dollars, he gets incessant calls with fragments of news that suggest profitable trades. "We're lowering our estimate on General Electric's earnings next quarter!" "The Citi is putting Brazil on a cash basis!" Some Wall Street houses have so much influence that when they change an opinion they can move the market by themselves. Steinhardt wants to get the "first call" when the key analyst of such a firm changes his mind.* Not because the analyst is necessarily right, rather because the people he calls after Steinhardt will *think* he'll be right. So if you read in the papers tomorrow that some wizard believes that prospects are improving for Texas Instruments, don't be surprised if the stock has already moved up: Steinhardt (and the other Steinhardts) probably heard it first.

From the broker's standpoint, a great advantage in dealing with Steinhardt is that he will give you an immediate order if he trusts you, without referring the idea to a committee or waiting to think about it. For one urgent telephone call, you can get a 100,000-share order. For that, you give him your very best attention! Steinhardt can also help a broker by purchasing an unusually large position in some stock he's interested in if the

---

*The "first call" is no longer as much of an advantage as it was. It was extremely helpful in the rapturous days of the "nifty fifty" in 1970 and 1971, or at other times when everybody in Wall Street was thinking the same way. What it means now is, rather, that Steinhardt is among the first to be shown merchandise. A very active trader who makes quick decisions tends to receive the earliest notification from a brokerage-house trading desk. That's what tens of millions a year in commissions buys you. Another benefit is oversize allotments of occasional hot underwritings. In a Wall Street feeding frenzy, that's money in the bank.

broker is stuck with it . . . at a price concession, to be sure. In return, if Steinhardt gets a piece of news that he thinks will knock a stock down, he may be able to twist a broker's arm to take it off his hands before the word gets out widely.

For Steinhardt, as for a racetrack bettor, the short term, the here and now, is reality. The long term, and Wall Street research that tells you about the long term, is the hereafter—a world of dreams. As a trader, Steinhardt feels much more comfortable carving out little gains—5 percent, 10 percent, 15 percent—over and over again than he would buying a stock and salting it away to await distant events that, as far as he is concerned, may never materialize. In 1983, for example, he bought 800,000 shares of IBM at $117. The stock had a modest move, advancing fifteen points. Most investors would look in the papers, note the advance, give a little grunt, and leave it at that. Then the stock dropped back to $120, giving up most of its gain. Oh, well! The difference is that Steinhardt had borrowed a hundred million dollars to buy his stock at $117, and sold out at approximately $132—making over $10 million! Then, to top it off, he went short a quarter of a million shares, covering as the price dropped back toward $120: another few million.

"I do an enormous amount of trading," says Steinhardt, who whirls his portfolio around every month or two in a good year, "not necessarily just for the profit, but also because it opens up other opportunities. I get a chance to smell a lot of things. Trading is a catalyst. How I envy the multi-year, long-term investor who fixes on a distant objective and can just wait and wait! No successful investor in the history of the universe can have had fewer doubles and triples than me. I'm always just making small moves. But still, most of the money I make is in holdings that I keep for more than a year." That is also about the length of time Steinhardt allows for his "directional" bets, which can be somewhat longer term than the bulk of his trading.

But there is more to Steinhardt's success than short-term stock trading. He is also prepared to speculate temporarily on the direction of the general market. He will go long on leverage, and even move to a net short position. "I have five or six security analysts, three to four traders, and one economist who look for what sectors of the economy are going to undergo important changes. What I hope that I can find using the economist's ideas is the difference between the consensus perception and a variant perception."

Some consider Steinhardt to be quite a conservative manager, given his avoidance of long-term commitments. George Keane, president of the Common Fund, an endowment client, says that despite the high annual turnover in his account—between 500 and 1,000 percent—"We view Steinhardt as a low-risk manager. He deals in short-term horizons all the time."

He runs three pools. One, for domestic taxpaying investors, uses extensive leverage—borrowed money; one, which uses less leverage, is for tax-exempt domestic institutions; and the third is for foreigners. Their holdings are almost identical; the difference between them is the category of investor. Steinhardt is limited to a maximum of ninety-nine participants in each pool; any more participants, and he would have to register the pools as investment companies. For several years he has been at that limit. Once a year the partnerships open for changes. Depending on how many withdraw, he may have one or two openings, but there is a long waiting list.

His oldest vehicle, Steinhardt Partners, may employ leverage when Steinhardt has a lot of confidence in a particular holding. There have been a few instances of this. One, his IBM coup in 1983, I just described. Another arose in 1981, when he became convinced that medium-term Treasury notes would have a big move. Steinhardt's economist-partner, George Henry, who had previously been a Federal Reserve Bank official, agreed that interest rates, then in the 14-percent area, had to decline. So he invested $50 million of his fund's cash and borrowed $200 million more to buy a quarter of a billion dollars' worth of five-year U.S. Treasury Bonds. Then he had to endure the agonizing wait for rates to drop. (At one point, the fund suffered a $10-million paper loss.) He lost some clients in that period, but eventually the gamble paid off: On his bond investment of $250 million, of which the fund had only put up $50 million in equity, he made a profit of $40 million. Steinhardt Partners was able to post a 10-percent gain in fiscal 1981, compared with a decline of 3.4 percent for the S&P 500. The following year, his leveraged

investment in intermediate government paper pulled the partnership up to a gain of 97 percent.

Not three years later, Steinhardt was back in the bond game.
In late 1984 he took a $400 million position, largely with bor-
rowed money, in intermediate government bonds, again betting that interest rates would decline. And once more the bet
was spectacularly successful. Rates were then near their record
high: The prime was around 15 percent, and longer rates were
about 13 percent. In July 1985, he dumped the bonds for a $25-
million profit.

As one associate has observed, "There's nothing timid about
the man": He likes massive moves. For instance, Steinhardt's
plunge into IBM was triggered by a recommendation from a
colleague who had the impression that Steinhardt might buy
20,000 or 50,000 shares. In fact, he bought several hundred
thousand.

Steinhardt spends the day behind a big wooden console shaped
like a ship's bow, full of screens, buttons, and blinking lights. He
feels that he isn't being paid to wear a particular uniform, so a
typical getup might be a black shirt open at the neck, with dark
trousers. He is plump; his round, mustached head with a thinning
cover rises like a seal's from a cylindrical abdomen. In repose, he
has a soft, husky voice and an amiable, gentle manner. He talks
in a subtle and literate way, closer to one's image of a book editor
than of a Wall Street trader. He admits he is overweight: He once
went to Canyon Ranch, an Arizona spa, to slim down, but the
portfolio wasn't doing well, so he came back in four days instead
of seven.

Like most great investors, Steinhardt started poor. He was
born in Brooklyn, the son of a jeweler. Steinhardt's parents were
divorced when he was one year old. For his bar mitzvah, his
father gave him 100 shares of Penn Dixie Cement and 100 shares
of Columbia Gas System instead of cash. When Steinhardt was
thirteen in Brooklyn, he says, "I knew nothing about the stock
market, and nobody I knew knew anything about the stock
market." He took to studying brokers' reports and following the
prices of his stocks in the *World Telegram*. He started frequenting
a Merrill Lynch office, with "the old men smoking their cigars

and watching the tape. It became a fascination for me." Soon he was buying and selling stocks.

An exceptional IQ enabled Steinhardt to finish high school at sixteen. He attended the University of Pennsylvania's Wharton School of Finance, from which he graduated at nineteen. He had no doubts as to his choice of career and, in 1960, went to work doing research for the Calvin Bullock mutual fund organization, at $80 a week. He was not a success, says Bullock. He then served in the U.S. Army Reserves, before writing, briefly, for *Financial World*. His restless brilliance could not be made to focus on such subscriber queries as "What is your view of General Motors," much less answer them, and eventually, he was fired. "It was awful," he says. "I thought my career on Wall Street was over."

Next, Steinhardt worked as a research analyst at Loeb, Rhoades & Co. One of his first recommendations was Gulf & Western Industries, which tripled. In a short time, Steinhardt was known as one of the top special-situations analysts. He also began exchanging information with another researcher, Howard Berkowitz, at A. G. Becker, who introduced Steinhardt to a fraternity brother, Jerrold Fine, then managing the partners' capital at Dominick & Dominick. (All three had attended the Wharton School at the same time.) On July 10, 1967, Steinhardt, Fine, and Berkowitz opened its doors, with an initial capital of about $7.7 million. The firm scored a 30-percent gain in its first year, and 84 percent in its second, compared with 6.5 percent and 9.3 percent for the S&P 500. They were off to the races. Steinhardt never looked back.

"It was a euphoric period," Steinhardt recalls. By the end of fiscal 1969, the firm had almost $30 million in capital, making all three of its under-thirty founders millionaires.

Steinhardt became the chief trader, while Fine and Berkowitz concentrated on research. The firm added staff in the 1970s, but the pace was always—as now—frenetic. It meant "not going to lunch, and making trades that involved fourteen conversations," says Steinhardt. The decade of intense, almost monomaniacal, dedication to investing left Steinhardt feeling that his outlook was too narrow. He yearned for a break.

"I've always focused on the question of purpose. Am I doing the best for my family? What are we doing in the world? Is this

the best thing to do in this life?" Puzzled by such questions, and
exhausted by ten years in the investment business, Steinhardt took
a sabbatical in 1978. He left $4 million of his $6 million net
worth in the care of Steinhardt Partners, which at that time was
running $110 million, and retired. As he said, he was smoking
too much, overweight (at 210 pounds), and felt that he "had quit
for good. I didn't want to come back." Few of his circle, knowing
his obsessive dedication to his work, believed he could keep away.

He did not get in touch with the office. Nor, he claims, did
he keep up with newspapers or the stock market. After brief
consideration of a stint in the Carter administration and then
with the City of New York, he started pursuing other interests,
including more time with his family in their Fifth Avenue duplex
overlooking Central Park and their twenty-four-acre retreat in
Mt. Kisco, north of New York City. There, he grew raspberries,
made jam, took piano and tennis lessons, read the Old Testament
with a rabbi, studied horticulture and yoga, tried jogging and
gave it up, restored a house, and visited Israel several times. After
a year, though, he returned to "this glorious business of ours."

The problem was that in his year off Steinhardt did not find
any other occupation that was uplifting and rewarding. "I was
trying to learn to deal with my life without the discipline imposed
by a career," he says. "The sabbatical allowed me to come back
and do largely the same thing that I had done before, but with
a broader perspective and fewer questions about the purpose of
my work." In any event, it's no longer money that keeps him on
the job. His wealth is estimated at over $100 million.

As for his partners, Fine left in 1976 to start his own private
investment partnership, Charter Oak Partners, in Connecticut.
(We will see him later running some funds for Harvard.)
Berkowitz followed in 1979 to set up HPB Associates, also a
private partnership. Since then, Steinhardt has managed it alone,
and done exceedingly well. He owns over 50 percent of his firm.

Steinhardt and his wife Judy spend weekends on a handsome
mini-estate outside of Mt. Kisco, New York. It includes an artificial pond, a tennis court, and a swimming pool. One of the days
we met, Steinhardt was wearing a blue sweatsuit with blue-and-
gray Nike sneakers, and white socks. The architecture is contem-

porary throughout. Two horses browse in a new paddock. There is a modern house for the caretaker and a cottage originally built as a cabana for the pool, for guests to change their clothes for swimming. They rarely used it for its original purpose, so Steinhardt converted the cottage into a separate office for himself. It now contains computers, telephones, and a fax machine. Sometimes Steinhardt announces that he is taking a day off and invites friends to stop by. Invariably, however, he remains in the cabana-office, glued to his computer screens and telephones, without returning to the house even for a moment to see his guests.

Along with his wife, Steinhardt once owned a commercial greenhouse in Queens, New York, that grew nine or ten different varieties of herbs that were marketed under the title of "Herbs Alive." "It's always just about to make money," he used to say. It never did, though, so he liquidated it. He is a valued trustee of the Brooklyn Botanic Garden. Of late he has started backing films.

He is fascinated by the Holocaust and has read most of the books on the subject. Keenly interested in the history of the Jewish people, he has visited Israel dozens of times and has business interests there. He observes that his attachment to the place is for him a substitute for adherence to its religion. He has a ladder of values, he says, in which money management, where he is now, is by no means the top rung. He likes to think that he might someday be able to take the next step up. I asked him how he proposed to save the next generation (his son was listening to our conversation) from the perils of excessive wealth. Steinhardt thought a moment, and then said that he hoped to accomplish this by transmitting the traditional values of his people— not his religion, but his *people*—to his children.

Not everyone can take Steinhardt's pace, or his sometimes savage impatience with investing mistakes. Those who have worked for him agree that he is in fact harder on himself than he is on others. "Whether he has picked the stock or not," says Harris Associates' Peter Foreman, "he blames himself." Steinhardt admits: "I tend to be a bit of a perfectionist. The demands

I put on people, the expectations, are probably at times unrealistic."

A *Wall Street Journal* article quoted some of his former employees: "It's a productive experience. It's just incredibly painful while you're there." Steinhardt "watches every stock you own like a hawk," the analyst added. "He wants answers. He won't let you slide by without answering his questions about each stock. It's a good way to run money. It's just a little too intense for some people."

Under these unrelenting—perhaps self-imposed—pressures, some think Michael Steinhardt may drop out again. As he says, "At times, I think about leaving the business. There is a repetitive quality to many of the things I've done. . . . I've always felt that there are more altruistic ways of spending my time."

For instance, one of the notions that came to him during his sabbatical year was that it would be useful to engage in a business activity in Israel, which has an abominable environment for enterprise—high inflation, a grossly excessive and meddlesome bureaucracy, and a Levantine business mentality. So, with an Israeli partner, he started a real estate and construction business in the so-called development towns. He was defeated by Israel's wretched business atmosphere. But he didn't give up. He bought an interest in the country's largest box manufacturer, and brought Merrill Lynch to Israel (MSC Ltd.).

Trading Techniques

"I have no positions in my partnerships that I don't understand myself," Steinhardt says. "If the analyst comes in and makes a case, I'll study it for five minutes and then do it. He'll have a story about better quarterly earnings, a management change, or whatever. I tend to manage passively—giving a good deal of latitude to the analysts whose ideas are working out. But if things *aren't* working out, I go over the story again and again. My principal role is general guidance, determining our overall exposure and deciding what level of risk we can accept.

"I see my role as trying to achieve the best possible return on capital, using the full range of techniques that will allow me to attain that goal, without commitment to any particular style.

Every day I ask myself where the risk-reward ratio seems right. Our first concern is long-term investment positions. Second, new issues, when they are attractive: We demand and receive large allotments. Third, we lend stocks to brokers to cover short sales, on which we demand the maximum interest. The brokers used to keep all the income, but in recent years one has been able to keep 40 to 90 percent of it. Fourth, we have people doing arbitrage, including buying into bankrupt companies and buying trade claims. Fifth, we avail ourselves of the full range of modern gimmickry: index futures, and the rest of it. I have four or five traders who deal with eighty or ninety brokers, in large measure to open doors. I couldn't achieve these results with long-term investing alone."

Wasn't this like the theory of A. W. Jones, I asked: Hire a collection of whizzes, give them their heads, and hang on? (The A. W. Jones partnership crashed and burned in 1974.)

"No," replied Steinhardt. "I devote a great deal of time to market analysis." The original A. W. Jones idea was that he wasn't able to analyze markets, but that he was able to determine relative values, so he could be long the good stocks and short the bad stocks. That never worked, of course. His managers, who had a piece of Jones's share of capital gains, egged each other on to take more and more aggressive positions. His partnership called itself a hedge fund, but basically it didn't reduce risk that way. "It's very rare, but I actually have been net short in my funds, to the tune of about 30 to 40 percent of their capital," says Steinhardt.

Steinhardt holds in contempt investors who want to buy cheap—that is, when a stock is selling at a low price in terms of its historic price range: That's much too simple. You must consider price-earnings ratios, industry developments, competitive developments, and many other factors.

We talked about Robert Wilson, a notable speculator, now retired. "He doesn't do any research," said Steinhardt, shaking his head in disbelief. "He relies on brokers and reads company reports. He's one of a kind." He plays the images, I observed.

"Most of my long positions are chosen on the basis of their long-term fundamental prospects—not that I necessarily actually do hold them for very long. I often say to my people, *make your choices on a long-term basis, even though what you're betting on will probably not happen.* I figure out how the market will respond to a long-term prospect, at least for a minimum period."

People often ask Steinhardt what the common thread is in his funds. He says it varies: "In 1982, it was the interest-rate play. In 1985, half the gain was in Montedison, an Italian company that we bought at 50 cents and sold at $3. In 1973 and 1974, we were up 30 and 40 percent in down markets."

Among several stocks in the same category, Steinhardt *greatly prefers to invest in one that has a repurchase program in its own shares.* Such a program gives an additional boost to its upward movement, and also gives the investor a better chance to sell when the time comes.

Looking at his portfolio, one finds no intellectual or philosophical thread. It's a hodgepodge. Still, in most years two or three holdings make most of the money. By being very active in the market, he is exposed to endless opportunities and is forced to focus on whatever areas of the markets are moving at the time. He is, in a word, eclectic.

"I started as a securities analyst myself—visited managements, studied the relative attractiveness of different industries, and so forth. That was in 1967. People were comfortable thinking in a long-term way. The best minds looked for companies which had the most promising secular growth characteristics. That, of course, led to the 'nifty fifty' heresy: People were willing to pay much too much for stocks that met those criteria. The search was on for baby-blue chips, in mariculture, or whatever, often ending in -onics. Everyone was looking for the new concept, the new service. They became insensitive to value, to the price-earnings multiples. The idea was to find the prospect of ten- or fifteen-year compound growth. The entrance fee didn't matter. It was possible to make projections of extraordinary growth forever. All that led to the debacle of 1973–74.

"Today the emphasis is overwhelmingly short term, on trading techniques and computerization. We're now getting equally exaggerated in that direction. How is it all going to end? I expect we'll go back to long-term thinking sooner or later.

"More and more money managers now believe they need a

variety of skills: They have to be able to handle Japan, the outlook for gold, fixed-income securities. For instance, suppose the market has a sudden movement. Why? It usually turns out that it's a breakout in a computerized index fund. So you have to understand how those programs work.

"I'm fascinated with the S&P futures," he has said. "They are a good measure of the essence of the market. There is an arithmetically correct price, called the premium, for an index future: the price that exactly expresses the value you are giving up in not owning the stocks, minus what you are saving by being able to use your capital for something else—the opportunity value. An excessive premium during the period from 11 to 11:15 A.M. is bullish, since it means that there is a powerful current of optimism out there. But if the overvaluation of the premium lasts for days and weeks, that is a more and more bearish sign. The number of programs that are carried out when the premiums are over fair valuation continues to rise, so at the end there are no new bettors left.

"Very few market participants understand the motivation for program trading. The chief one is that tens of billions of dollars in institutional hands have to remain liquid for weeks and months, since the institutions are going to have demands on the money—for working capital, or to pay insurance claims, or whatever. In other words, it's really short-term money. So if a broker offers the institution a higher riskless return over a short period than it could get in cash equivalents, that's attractive.

"Here's how it's done. When the S&P futures premium reaches a certain level, the computer says to sell the future and buy the underlying stocks. One doesn't need to buy all 500 stocks. It has been figured out that one can do it with fewer than 400 of them. So you have these sudden, very large scale trades. It's been simply astonishing how much this technique has added to the business of some of the big firms, such as Salomon."

The Short Side

Steinhardt has commented that for most people, himself included, selling short requires a psychological adjustment to overcome the idea that one is opposing America, motherhood, and apple pie, of being on the side of evil; also, it is hard to adjust to the idea that on the short side one can have infinite losses, compared with going long where one can only lose 100 percent.

However, Steinhardt's own investment principle is that *"you never make big money in the market without getting in the way of danger."* He went out on a limb in 1972 by shorting big-name growth stocks or "vestal virgins"—Polaroid, Xerox, Avon Products, and the like—at 30 to 35 times earnings, and with dismay then watched the same stocks hit 40 to 45 times earnings before they topped out and produced a sharp gain when the market collapsed in 1973. There was also the black January of 1976, when the firm had one of its biggest short positions ever and the market soared. Fortunately, such losses have been the exception. In 1973, Steinhardt sold short over 100,000 shares of Kaufman & Broad, the nation's largest home-builder, in the high 40s. The Steinhardt group made a packet when the stock collapsed in response to spiraling interest rates and inflation—first to the low 20s, where the group covered its shorts, and later down to 4.

I asked what sorts of stocks he went short, observing that most good speculators' experience was that one did not make money on the short side, but used the shorts as a balance against a larger long position.

"On the long side, I'm looking for lower-multiple dull stocks, laggards, with a recovery potential. *On the short side, I want to be in the best-known companies in America, the areas of speculative focus. I'm usually short the Who's Who of the market,* stocks in the institutional universe. The stocks I'm short tend to be the reverse of my longs. They're high-multiple, popular stocks with big institutional expectations built into the prices, which I think will be a disappointment. My perennial problem is the difficulty of timing the breakdown of those speculative expectations.

"Financial expectations of a speculative nature are a good thing to bet against, but you need the patience to hang in there, to suffer. I do tend to short too soon. I'm short Genentech, which has a $5 billion market capitalization, and really only one product, to which Lilly has just introduced a competitor, plus one potential product, a heart-attack remedy. It only has $200 million of book value. My short there has been giving me nothing but pain."*

He mentioned a firm on the West Coast made up of several brothers. They are money managers and brokers. They seek companies in which they can go short and make 80 or 90 percent or even 100 percent, through bankruptcy. They love to run down frauds and hyped situations. This is a superb area in which to put a modest amount—also a scary one. For example, for about a year Steinhardt was short a very large position in Cannon Group. The company was taken over by two Israelis in the early 1980s and showed a continuous gain in earnings per share until last year. They make movies and then profit by sale of the ancillary rights. They raised hundreds of millions of dollars from the market based on wondrous earnings reports. Steinhardt said he started going short Cannon at $19 and saw the stock rise to $46. (At the time we talked, Cannon had dropped below $6.)

Steinhardt's single best stock was King Resources.‡ He made seven or eight times his cost in the year 1968, before the company went bankrupt. "*We* were the greater fools," he says. "We really believed the story. We only sold because it went up so much.

"I went short some Japanese stocks—and lost money. I didn't yet understand the relationship between the yields on Japanese fixed-income instruments and the price-earnings multiples of their stocks. Obviously, the lower bond yields are, the higher the stock price-earnings multiple that you can justify." At that time, he told me, he was short 24 stocks and long 40.

Steinhardt normally reviews decisions intensively. He goes over his portfolio many times each day. He tends to focus on problems, not on successes. If a stock is acting well that day, relative to the market, fine. If not, he starts asking questions. Something may be wrong. It may be a random movement, but he wants to concentrate on it until he can establish that it is merely random.

He likes his portfolio to hold the companies that should get attention next from the arbitrageurs. Thus, he is often found at the front of current trends.

---

*It collapsed in due course.

‡The company, headed by John King, sold tax-oriented oil-drilling deals. It conducted a series of fraudulent transactions with Bernie Cornfeld's Fund of Funds before they both collapsed.

In the 1960s and the 1970s, he says, the intellectual quality was found in the merger-and-acquisition area—where it still is today—and research. Very few able men went into trading. But because of the philosophical shift of the last twenty years that's no longer true. It's no longer the Warren Buffetts that are the heroes, but the raiders: Asher Adelman, Carl Icahn, and Jimmy Goldsmith.

Before 1975 there was no reporting of trades that did not take place on an exchange. So an arbitrage was possible between the third market and an exchange. Steinhardt remembers being offered 700,000 shares of Penn Central when the stock was quoted at 6⅞–7⅛. Later Jeffries, a third-market firm, called him offering seven or eight hundred thousand shares over-the-counter. Steinhardt instantly checked the size on the floor and found that there was a huge, strong market. He bid for and bought the entire block at $6.15 a share. Forty minutes later he sold it on the floor, making over $4 million: a well-spent hour! This was essentially Jeffries's client's fault. He should have checked the floor of the New York Stock Exchange himself to determine the depth of the market. In any event, for a moment Steinhardt Partners became a block-trading firm. A window of opportunity existed then, which has since closed with the consolidated tape. Now there are very few such windows.

Investment Aids

Are there any good brokers? Steinhardt says he gets massive amounts of information on a regular basis, but has virtually never found a brokerage house or subscription service consistently superior over a long period of time. He says he perhaps has had one or two exceptions. He has had "love affairs," such as paying $1,000 to Tim Holt, a Chinese-American investment-letter writer, to visit his office and lecture, which he found useless. "I was singularly underwhelmed," he says.

People whose first interest is in commissions, he observes, are rarely the great stock-pickers. If someone is really great, it will make no sense for him to sell his ideas: The rate of return will be too low. The less able may find it economically worthwhile to sell their ideas. Most brokers "won't even come to bat, or hold an opinion for more than a few days if the tide goes against them," says Steinhardt. As for himself, he says everything he does is catch as catch can.

In his studies at the Wharton School of Finance one course he found worthwhile was on the philosophy of probability. It made him comfortable dealing with incomplete and inaccurate data. The probability course opened his eyes to a way of dealing with a variety of issues, even program trading; it enabled him to understand how much can be understood. Taking the probability approach to decision-making renders the whole process homoge-neous, he says, and allows one to make judgments on matters relating to technology, for instance, while knowing little about the actual technology in question. Steinhardt says he doesn't know what a 256K RAM is, but if there's an important change in that industry he can ask the right questions in order to focus on the issue, perhaps better than someone who really knows all about the subject.

By homogeneous, he means that different subjects can be handled similarly, such as the impact of a new computer on the other computers in a given market, or translating what he thinks the trade balance is going to look like into a view on inflation and its impact on the bond market—or, indeed, a view on when the Japanese are going to invest in the Dow stocks.

Steinhardt meets annually with a distinguished economist who each year is astounded that the world has not fallen apart since their last meeting. All the statistics—debt compared with savings, debt compared with GNP, debt compared with third-world earnings—are worse than ever. For his part, Steinhardt says, "One cannot help marveling at a system that has coped with the petrodollar shock, with higher and then lower inflation, and the other gyrations that we have seen. There's always something. In the 1960s people talked of the insolvency of the Federal National Mortgage Association (FNMA)—now they're wondering how to dispose of bad loans in the Texas panhandle.

"You know that awful feeling in a bear market that you don't want to look at the quotes: Your favorite stock is down six points, or it hasn't even opened. There are many people now dealing in these strange instruments—CATS and the like—who have never seen a crushing bear market. Lots of the participants are going to be in for a horrible surprise, particularly since the volatility has increased so.

"I remember a big down day in 1974 when the market was off sixty points. I put in an order, on a scale down, with a Chicago brokerage house I was dealing with. Then the system broke down! They couldn't handle the order. The result was a $2 million error, the largest in the firm's history. Lots of things are untested. On the other hand, to the extent that we have had tests, the system has survived fairly well. Petrodollars, the New York City crisis, the third-world debt. Still . . . still. . . ."

Advice

"The historic inhibitors of volatility have been muted," Steinhardt has said. "Things like portfolio insurance, program trading, internationalization of markets, the increasing of institutional investment have all made things worse. Specialists used to have a book to make markets, which is their role. Now their capital isn't nearly adequate for their job. They can only facilitate markets.

"The worst is that the institutional brokerage houses have not built up their capital to correspond to the growth of the market, so they can't really take positions. With the deregulation of commissions, the market-making function is being progressively abandoned by the big firms." I pointed out that this was the opposite of what had been expected: The theory had been that the institutional investors would stabilize the market. "That hasn't happened at all," said Steinhardt. "They all run around in a pack."

So what about the stock market in the coming period?

Some time ago he told a Columbia Business School panel that the two main reasons for the rise in the stock market were lower interest rates and the leveraging of America—leveraging the whole industrial base of the country. The result was a supply of stocks sharply reduced through leveraged buyouts, corporate repurchase plans, and, on the demand side, a feeling among corporations that it was cheaper to buy than to build. This phenomenon became a dominant factor in the American market.

As long as it remained intact, neither corporate earnings nor anything else mattered.

The new dominant factor is debt. It "will perhaps be the key to the economic future of the Western world," Steinhardt said, adding that debt is being used differently now from ten or fifteen years ago: "The ethics surrounding debt are different. I doubt if anybody in this room could have imagined six or so years ago that a President with the conservative stripes of Ronald Reagan would have allowed and encouraged deficits and have run deficits for six years, doubling the national debt. The ethics with which he grew up were anathema to that, and yet he did it and it's been an important part of the economic scene. Debt questions related to quality, to the Third World, municipal debt, consumer debt (which has grown to extraordinary proportions)—all have changed so much as to put a different pattern in our life. The growth in stock prices since 1983 relates more than anything else to a new use of debt.

"There has been an enormous growth of debt in the world, as compared to earnings or assets or anything else. It amounts to an economic leaning tower that will eventually topple. It cannot be sustained. The debt will eventually be repudiated and turned to equity, resulting in inflation."

Steinhardt predicts that we are entering a period of very great risk, owing largely to a new round of inflation. He points to rising prices for oil, paper, chemicals, and many commodities. He also cites the weak dollar as a trigger for increased import costs. He felt in early 1988 that inflation could more than double to 4 percent by the end of the year, which it did. He expected the economy to outdo most forecasts, helped by continued consumer spending and an improved trade balance; he also foresaw a tightening of credit, higher interest rates, and long-term T-bill rates up one or two percentage points—all of which came about. As a precaution, he cut back on equities.

When he thinks about markets, Steinhardt asks himself, what will change? If he had to guess—and maybe it is happening now, he adds—maybe stable interest rates are breaking down—rising—because of inflation. If there is an increase in inflation, which is likely, an early result will be higher corporate profits, because of greater demand. People will have more money to spend. If the inflation is demand induced, then companies producing steel, oil, aluminum, and such basic products will increase their profits. Later, however, the Federal Reserve will apply pressure, and the economy will start to cool.

Steinhardt says he has the feeling that the market may be neutralized by different factors, such as the rise of inflation and the shift from a liquidity-pushed market to one based on earnings. He wonders if the different influences might not cancel each other out, blunting the bull market, but not necessarily resulting in a decline.

What would be the refuge if very bad times came along?

"If things got very bad because in an economic contraction companies couldn't service some of their bonds, say, and as a result instead of their hearing endlessly about too much debt the problem really hit home to investors, with defaults and bank-ruptcies, then liquidity would be the key. *Only cash and cash equivalents would save you.*"

And gold?

Steinhardt replied that six or seven years ago, gold was at $800, FNMA was going broke, and nobody predicted disinflation. In those days gold was supposed to be the answer. But he is not confident of his own ability to predict the long-term future, and he says, "I've never been in gold, and wouldn't expect to be. Gold's more of a way to trade on a psychological conception— future inflation, the liberty of the Western world, and so forth— than an economic one. Aside from anything else, there's a lot of new production coming on stream. Still, if I had to take a position, I'd rather be long gold than short."

3

Philip Carret

The Money Mind

Phil Carret (pronounced "Carray") must be the most experienced investment man around: Having entered the field in the early 1920s, he can boast some sixty-seven years of immersion in the hurly-burly of the market. At ninety-one, he still arrives at his office early every morning. With his two sons, a granddaughter, and a small staff, he runs over $225 million in mostly private portfolios. (A CEO from outside the family was finally taken aboard in 1988.) In his tenth decade, he seems perfectly unimpaired in faculties. He has a large, generous face with deep lines. He chuckles often and radiates benevolence.

His office is in an old art-deco office building on New York's Forty-second Street, just across from the south entrance of Grand Central Station. On the front of his desk perches a sign saying "A cluttered desk is a sign of genius." "Look at this!" he says, grinning fondly. "My wife gave it to me." All investment managers' (as distinct from investment administrators') desks are covered by dunes of paper, from which they always hope to absorb still more facts, until an incoming tide of new papers washes over them.

Seventy-five Years of Harvard Football Games

Another large sign on the wall quotes Shakespeare: "The first thing we do, let's kill all the lawyers. . . ." Carret, nevertheless, is the son of a Boston real estate lawyer—what used to be called a conveyancer. "My first Harvard ancestor was the Reverend

Daniel Gookin in 1669," he announced with satisfaction. I told him that my father and grandfather had also been lawyers, both born in Boston, and that my great-grandfather, a clergyman, had been in the class of 1805. Carret manifestly felt that this was a seemly ordering of things.

"Did you go to the Harvard-Yale game this year?" he asked in his slight New England twang. I said I hadn't. "Very interesting game: fourteen to ten. I was on the thirty-yard line . . . almost froze to death. I'll bet I was the only one in the Yale Bowl who was there when it was christened, at the Harvard-Yale game of 1913. That was another very interesting game: Harvard won thirty-six to nothing."

Fifty-five Years of Compound Interest

Carret started the Pioneer Fund in May 1928. It had about twenty-five stockholders: members of his family and a few friends. He ran it for over half a century, until he retired as its manager. During that fifty-five-year period, Pioneer's compound annual total return was 13 percent. (It is 15 percent if you start at the Depression bottom.) That means that an original shareholder who had put in $10,000 and reinvested all his income would at the end have been able to withdraw over $8 million when Carret left. (He would also have been jarred by a 50-percent drop in the early 1930s.) Thirteen percent is not a remarkable performance figure today, but it meant a great deal when inflation was low. In any event, the lesson is that over long periods compound interest works miracles.

The management company of Pioneer is now itself publicly owned, and Carret holds only a small percentage of it. Originally, he had operated the fund singlehandedly; later, he incorporated the management company and sold most of it to Jack Cogan of Hale & Dorr, in Boston. At that point an investment committee was created: Cogan, Pioneer Fund's director of research, and Carret himself. The other two were in Boston, so every morning he would talk to them on the telephone about what he proposed to do that day. "That was all there was to it . . . that was how it was run," he says. One friend says that he has "no side whatsoever"—that is, he has no affectations or pompositics. The directors' meetings of the Pioneer Fund were cozy and informal.

On the board of the Pioneer Fund there were at one time three octogenarians: Carret himself, Jerome Preston, and Phil Cooley. From time to time stockholders thought to question this gerontocratic weighting. Carret always enjoyed that question: He is confident that age brings wisdom.

Trouble Ahead

"So you think we're going to have a depression?" I asked Carret.

"Yes, I'm afraid so. I have an associate who lives in Bethlehem, Pennsylvania. The other night he went to a cocktail party. He made a point of talking to everybody about the stock market and the economic outlook. One guy was very smug: 'I haven't any stocks at all, so the decline had no effect on me.' So my associate asked him, 'But what about your job?' Bethlehem is full of very cyclical businesses . . . Beth Steel, Mack Truck, and so forth. The smug young man was astounded. He couldn't conceive of losing his job, and yet that could easily happen to him in a depression. This is the first time in my life that I've ever been really bearish. The present situation is so much like 1929 that it's likely to have the same outcome." Carret has always been optimistic. It has been a shock to some of his friends to realize that he now anticipates a serious break, indeed a depression, in the early 1990s.

But what did he think was the right currency to keep reserves in? Short-term German bonds? "I suppose that's all right. Still, I prefer to invest in America. I'm a great traveler: I've been in a hundred countries for at least a little time, and around the world eleven times, but every time I come home, I think, how nice to be back in the greatest country in the world. The Japanese may be smarter than we are, but I'm still happier being right here."

A Depression Always Takes You by Surprise

"Nobody can be expected to pinpoint a depression," said Carret. "When I was in my first job at Blyth & Company, Dr. Wesley C. Mitchell, a professor of economics at Columbia, who invented the term 'business cycle,' came to lunch. Two partners asked him about his opinion of the outlook for the economy. Dr. Mitchell may have been annoyed at being asked for free advice, which he would have been glad to receive a fee for giving, but anyway he answered that he had been working on a book and hadn't had time to think about the economy overall. That was exactly one month before the Crash!"

I mentioned that the Harvard Economic Society announced in 1929 that there was no chance of a repetition of the economic downturn of 1920–21. "The Harvard Economic Society never should have been started," said Carret. "It was an embarrassment to the university. In 1929, just after Thanksgiving, it held a meeting in Boston. A friend of mine had a cup of coffee with Colonel Leonard P. Ayres of the Cleveland Trust, who was regarded as the number-one business economist in the country, and Jimmy Hughes, one of the great students of the stock market. Everybody agreed that the Crash had only 'blown the froth off the boom,' and wouldn't affect their or anybody's life-style. Here were some very brilliant individuals, as well informed as anybody could be, who, all the same, were absolutely wrong."* "So instinct is the best guide?" I asked. "Instinct—the subconscious— is much more reliable than statistics. One should follow one's own convictions," he adds, ruefully.

"But getting back to the inevitability of a downturn . . . ," I continued.

"I don't see how we can wring the debt out of the economy without a depression. There's just much too much of it. Think about someone who's in debt: Sometime he has to stop adding more, and sometime he'll have to pay it back. I was flabbergasted when a friend of mine—a Mormon!—got into serious financial trouble, thanks to a margin account. Mormons are very conservative people. One doesn't expect a Mormon to have a margin account. Another individual I know, who was a major stockholder of a company I follow closely, got himself in trouble. His stock went from 60 to 24. Thanks to a margin account, he

*In 1929, the society announced, *after* the Crash, that "a severe depression like that of 1920–21 is outside the range of possibility. We are not facing protracted liquidation of inventories, worldwide demoralization in commodity markets, and rising money rates." Later that year, the society proclaimed that "the easing of money is itself evidence of the soundness of the present business situation."

went from several million dollars in assets to zero, owing the government $300,000 in tax.

"In a business, debt is quite reasonable. *But margin debt— stock-market debt—is terribly dangerous, because it's so easy to get.* You can just pick up the telephone and generate debt in the stock market. A businessman has to go to his banker and explain everything: What his assets are, where his cash flow comes from, how the business works, what he wants the money for, and how the loan he wants will generate the cash to repay the bank.

"Mayor Koch is curtailing the New York City budget by $500 million. That will mean cutting a lot of people. I was given in confidence an internal memo from the chairman of a sizable conglomerate—a very well managed one. It was astonishing. Cut down all travel in general; no more first-class travel at all; he almost said to unscrew hundred-watt bulbs and replace them with twenty-five–watt bulbs." I mentioned that I had heard of someone who during the Great Depression took all but one bulb out of every room in his house. Carret chuckled.

Preferences

I explained that, studying the careers and methods of extremely successful investors, I had come increasingly to the conclusion that they often actually invented a way of investing—or at least revived one: thus T. Rowe Price, who exploited the idea of stocks with perennially rising earnings; thus Benjamin Graham, who reduced the investment art to a quasi-science with a series of formulas that worked for fifty years, until they became too popular (at least temporarily) in the 1980s; and thus Templeton, who made the whole world his investment backyard. Could Carret identify his own contribution?

Over the Counter

"*I like over-the-counter stocks.* And yet I'm more conservative than most people. Most people think that 'conservative' means General Electric, IBM, et cetera. But I've always been in offbeat stuff. They're less subject to manipulation than New York Stock Exchange companies, and are less affected by crowd psychology.

For instance, I remember Winnebago, Coachman Industries, and all the other 'rec vehicle' outfits. To justify their peak prices you would have needed to have half the population abandon their houses and ride around continuously. I avoid fads like the plague.

"Ralph Coleman had a fund called the 'Over-the-Counter Securities Fund.' It had about three hundred stocks in it. When one of them got listed, he would sell it. The fund did extremely well. In my own managed portfolios, I have about half of the equity money in over-the-counter stocks." (For a long-term chart of over-the-counter stocks, see Figure 1, page 56.)

I asked Carret if he could prove that over-the-counter stocks were an inherently better value than listed stocks. "No," said Carret. "All sorts of junk is sold over-the-counter, but also some crown jewels. Berkshire Hathaway, for instance." (It later applied for—and got—a New York Stock Exchange listing.) He said he knew Warren Buffett, who runs it.* "He's a friend of mine. He's smarter than I am. He proved that in General Foods. It was a stodgy company, mostly coffee. When Berkshire Hathaway bought the stock, I said to myself, 'Well, Warren's made a mistake this time.' It was about $60 when I noticed the transaction. In a matter of months it went to $120 . . . ha, ha!" (Carret has a deep, throaty chuckle when he tells stories of this sort. He particularly enjoys tales describing common opinions that are completely mistaken.)

For that matter, Carret is in a way an older version of Warren Buffett. Indeed, they are quite similar in appearance: round-headed men with wide grins. Both have a completely contrarian mentality: They seek what nobody wants. Both like dull stocks, such as waterworks or bridge companies, and do not mind if these sit dead in the water for long periods. Especially, both have the patient temperament of the successful value investor. They have been exchanging ideas regularly for many years.

Carret likes to see growth of earnings but adds that "if a company has increased earnings for fifteen years, it is probably just about to have a bad year.

---

*Buffett has said of Carret: "Phil has by far the best long-term record on Wall Street. . . . He should be studied by every investor." He has also called Carret "a man who knows an extraordinary amount about business itself as well as the markets. If there ever was a hall of fame for investment advisers, he'd be among the first ten in it."

Figure 1

OVER–THE–COUNTER STOCKS COMPARED WITH THE GENERAL MARKET

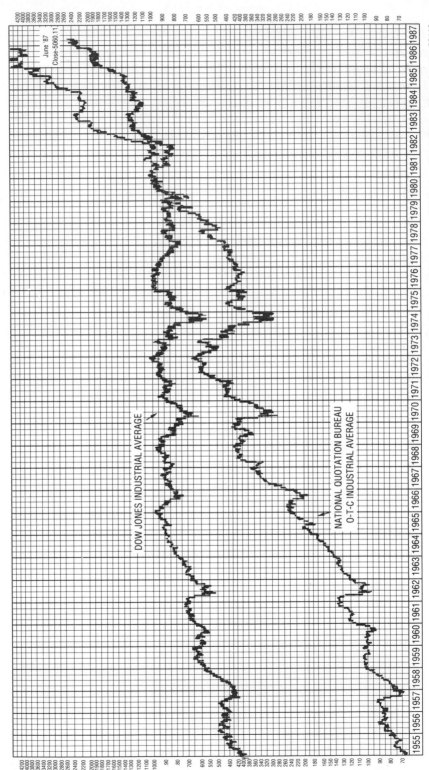

DOW JONES INDUSTRIAL AVERAGE

NATIONAL QUOTATION BUREAU
O-T-C INDUSTRIAL AVERAGE

June '87
Close-5060.11

Chart courtesy of Securities Research, a division of Babson-United Investment Advisors, Inc., 208 Newbury Street, Boston, Massachusetts, 02116.

"I do like very good balance sheets. I get floods of annual reports. I look at them all, at least briefly. *If I see that the equity ratio is low, or the current ratio is low, I don't go any further. I want no term debt, and a better than two-to-one current ratio.* If it's a utility, I want reasonable financial ratios, a good territory, and a favorable regulatory climate.

"For instance, one of my favorite stocks is Magma Power. I've had it in the family for years. In fact, I bought the old Magma at about $4, sold it at $45 when the company sold a major property and partially liquidated, and then reinvested the proceeds in the remainder. Magma has a great advantage, which is that under California law a neighboring utility is obliged to buy any power Magma generates at the highest 'avoided cost.' So it has an absolutely guaranteed market. That's a pretty good thing to have in a depression. It's not what everybody would call a conservative holding. They might never have heard of it. But to me it's very conservative."

Since one of my own rules is that we should examine the actual physical facilities of a company we are interested in, I asked Carret if he had been to see Magma. He said he had. "The original property was north of San Francisco—'The Geysers.' It's fascinating to approach it. You can see the steam coming out of the ground."

I asked him how small a company he still felt comfortable with, in terms of market capitalization or sales. "I have no fixed rules. But I usually prefer several hundred or several thousand stockholders, and a market capitalization of at least $50 million.

"I'm a collector of odd little outfits. I have a few shares of something called Natural Bridge Company of Virginia. The highway goes right over the Natural Bridge, so if you want to see the bridge itself you have to go down into the valley, from where you can look up at it. The company owns the land under the bridge. They have a restaurant and a motel. People go and stay for a day or two. Someday the state of Virginia will have a profligate administration that will buy the company for more than its market price. In the meantime, I don't mind waiting."

Owner Management

"Another important criterion for me is that *I always want to see management own a significant amount of stock*. Once I had some correspondence with the chairman of National Gypsum. He had 20,000 shares, which were selling for about $20. That meant $400,000 of stock at the time, which of course is worth a lot more today. I noticed that the president only had 500 shares, so I wrote the chairman. I was flabbergasted by his reply: 'How much stock Mr. Brown owns is his business and nobody else's.' I don't agree with that at all. It may have been true before the SEC required making the officers' and directors' shareholdings available to everybody, but it certainly isn't true today. An officer should have at least a year's salary invested in the business. If he doesn't have that much faith in the company, he shouldn't be a key executive of it. If they don't own a lot of stock, why should I own any?" asks Carret, adding that he always looks for large insider shareholdings in proxy statements.

That, I observed, seemed like a perennial principle of good business. Had Carret found that business principles had changed during his life?

"No: Business principles are just that, principles. One deviates from sound principles at his peril. Some people are smart enough to do it—to dart in and out, for instance—but they are few and far between. I saw a study that set forth the average life of a margin-account trader. It turned out to be two to three years. One customer had lasted for thirteen years before he lost all his money, but he'd started with several million."

On the subject of principles, here are Carret's twelve investment precepts:*

1. Never hold fewer than ten different securities covering five different fields of business.

2. At least once in six months reappraise every security held.

3. Keep at least half the total fund in income-producing securities.

4. Consider yield the least important factor in analyzing any stock.

*From *The Art of Speculation* (New York: *Barron's* Revised Edition, 1930; Burlington, Vermont: Fraser Publishing Company, 1979).

5. Be quick to take losses, reluctant to take profits.

6. Never put more than 25 percent of a given fund into securities about which detailed information is not readily and regularly available.

7. Avoid "inside information" as you would the plague.

8. Seek facts diligently; advice never.

9. Ignore mechanical formulas for valuing securities.

10. When stocks are high, money rates rising, business prosperous, at least half a given fund should be placed in short-term bonds.

11. Borrow money sparingly and only when stocks are low, money rates low or falling, and business depressed.

12. Set aside a moderate proportion of available funds for the purchase of long-term options on stocks of promising companies whenever available.

Knowing Management

Did he always get to know management personally? "It's desirable. But there are only so many hours in the day and so many days in the year. I have too many stocks to know everybody concerned. I might say that *I'm always turned off by an overly optimistic letter from the president in the annual report.* If his letter is mildly pessimistic, to me that's a good sign. I like a point I once heard made by a corporate chief executive, that he was less interested in hearing good news from subordinates than bad news. The good news takes care of itself. 'If I get the bad news early,' he said, 'I can do something about it.' Norman Vincent Peale once met a man who said that he was tormented by problems: problems, problems, problems. Peale replied that he had just come from a place where there were sixty thousand people with no problems. The man was excited: 'I'd like to be there!' 'I don't think you would,' Peale answered. 'It's called Woodlawn Cemetery.' "

Doctors as Investors

"I have a friend who is an eminent doctor, but about investments he constantly changes his mind. One time he said to me, 'Stocks are the pits. I'm never going to buy stocks again.' He decided he wanted to put his money into houses up in Westchester and then just collect the rents. So I asked him what he would do when he was called up at midnight about a frozen pipe. He thought about that and decided he didn't want to own houses. So he went to Merrill Lynch. He saw this huge floor full of young men at desks. He came back to me and said, 'I don't want to have my money managed by those jerks. Will you manage my money?' I told him that I didn't want to. 'Doc,' I said, 'you change your mind too much.' Doctors usually make poor investors."

I asked him what he thought was the reason. "A doctor has to be as close as possible to infallible with his patients. He can't be right two-thirds of the time. If he were only right that often, he ought to be thrown out of the profession. But in investing, it's fine to be right two-thirds of the time. So when doctors start to invest and discover how things really are, they get nervous and bothered." When *his* stocks go down, on the contrary, Carret remains completely unruffled.

"More Unique than Most"

Carret has viewed every total eclipse in recent years—eleven of them—and goes to any lengths, including one trip up the Amazon, to see one. But other than this distraction, which does not take much time, he admits to no outside interests or hobbies.

"Every individual human being is unique," says Carret, continuing, "I guess I'm more unique than most."

A person of evident frankness and honesty, Carret does not hesitate to express and act on his opinions, which are often strongly held. Some people do not care for this traditional New England downright manner; others find it praiseworthy. A friend described him as being at peace with himself: a strong, solid character, with no inner misgivings.

He was born in Lynn, Massachusetts, ten miles north of Boston. His family then moved to Wellesley, then to Lexington, where he attended high school, and later to Cambridge. He completed Harvard College (Class of '17) and a year of business school in the four years between 1914–17. This being World War I, he joined the Aviation Section of the Army Signal Corps. He completed his training overseas by September. He was ready for combat at the time of the 1918 St.-Mihiel offensive, but was offered a chance to go into air ferrying. Deciding it was better to "be a live coward than a dead hero," he took the job. Even ferrying was not without its risks: One pilot of his group of thirteen died when his plane cracked up.

On being discharged in 1919 he went to work for a little firm in Boston, long since defunct. He started at $15 a week. After five months he got a raise to $20. Feeling that so small an advance was insulting, he quit. He then decided to wander around the United States and by November of 1920 found a job selling bonds in Seattle, where he met his wife. Elisabeth Osgood had done social work in New York but, suffering like Carret himself from a certain wanderlust, had gone to Seattle and continued in social work.

A Peaceful Woman

Elisabeth, who died several years ago, was a perfect wife, according to her husband. "I used to tell her that she was 99.99-percent perfect, but actually I think she was 100-percent perfect," he says. A graduate of Wellesley, she became president of her alumnae class. She was also active in their church in Scarsdale. When the Carrets' daughter was eight years old, she was asked in school what she would like to be when she grew up. "A peaceful woman, like my mother," she replied. She was devoted and obedient, Carret says.

They returned together to Boston, and he rejoined his old firm—in sales. He quit all over again after four or five months, since he didn't like selling, and joined *Barron's*. He really had two jobs: as a feature writer for *Barron's* and a reporter on the staff of the Boston News Bureau—both being owned by the famous Clarence W. Barron. This lasted until 1927, when he decided to come to New York "to make my fortune." He joined Blyth & Company, and he and Elisabeth rented a house in Scarsdale. In due course they bought it, and lived there for the next forty-nine years. In 1975, their children being grown, they moved into a cooperative apartment in Scarsdale.

Carret and his wife had two sons and a daughter. One son

has three children and the other, two. Both sons worked in the firm, of which until recently they owned a quarter each and Carret owned half. A granddaughter is also an analyst in the firm. The Carrets' daughter married a doctor and has seven children. She first lived in Scarsdale, near her parents, but now lives in Pawling, New York.

After Charles Blyth and Dean Witter split up, Blyth, by then independent, hired Carret from *Barron's* as the house economist. Blyth, together with several foreign banks, also formed an early investment trust called American, British & Continental Investment Company. Carret ran the portfolio on a day-to-day basis and sat in on the directors' meetings. Some of the Germans got edgy about the U.S. market, and indeed questioned the safety of U.S. Steel's dividend. The Blyth partners assured the Germans that the dividend was perfectly safe. In the end, of course, it was cut, when U.S. Steel, together with the rest of the U.S. market, collapsed. Carret tells this story with his usual chuckle.

The Best Thing that Ever Happened to Me

Blyth let Carret go in 1932, during the Depression. So Carret hung up his own shingle—the best thing that ever happened to him, he now thinks . . . although he didn't like it then. At the outset he had two partners: one his own former assistant at Blyth and the other a salesman. Like everybody who started out in the Depression, they operated with extreme frugality—much too extreme, he now thinks—for their first ten years. But they made a good living and accumulated capital, both personally and in the firm. His salesman-partner brought along a clientele, but, as Carret says, "the rest of us rang doorbells, literally." Carret obtained the stockholders' list of Amerada, which he considered the best of the oil companies. He reasoned that the shareholders of Amerada would be persons of good judgment, who would understand what he had to say. He started down the list of shareholders, beginning with *a*, and called on those within a few blocks of his office at 120 Broadway. He came fairly soon to a shareholder whose name started with *b*, with whom he struck up a cordial relationship. He became a customer, and they remained friends for many years. In the course of trying to collect a bad debt, Mr. "B" had received a few shares of an obscure over-the-counter stock that printed railroad timetables. It was quoted in the pink sheets at $5 bid, $10 offered. When Carret looked up this stock, he decided that it seemed very cheap at $10, and so bought all that was offered at that price. In due course a representative of the SEC appeared to find out why he had bought it. "Do you know the management?" asked the SEC man. Carret replied that he did not and inquired, "Why do you ask?" The SEC man reported that his office kept charts on all stocks, had noticed the sudden jump from $5 to $10, and decided to make inquiries. "This didn't improve my low opinion of bureaucrats in general, and the SEC in particular," says Carret.

In 1938 he noticed that a little utility company called Dakota Power had some 6-percent bonds outstanding, due the following year. One day Carret was able to buy some bonds at $89, which he then sold to one of his customers at $93, giving himself a satisfactory profit. He soon received a call from a regional securities dealer, who had spotted the same bargain. "Did you buy those Dakota Power bonds that were offered a while back?" asked the dealer. Carret admitted that he had. "You still got them?" "No," said Carret. "What did you sell them for?" Carret replied, "It's not your business, but the answer is I sold them for $93." "That's too cheap for a 6-percent bond due to be paid off in six months," the dealer expostulated indignantly.

He has been to East and West Africa a number of times, as well as South Africa, partly for pleasure and partly for business. (He is a director of International Investors, a fund that primarily holds gold stocks.) His wife and he once rented a car and drove 1,500 miles from Durban to Cape Town, taking several days to do it. "It's a beautiful country; I have friends there." Did it make sense for American institutional investors to sell stocks of companies that operated in South Africa? "None whatever. Apartheid is morally wrong and self-defeating over the long run. But American companies are good employers, a mediating influence. The blacks don't want us to leave, either. I remember when I was on the board of a missionary organization I had a visit from a delegation of students from the Union Theological Seminary, who were agitating for the sale of stocks of companies doing business in South Africa. I told them it was silly, and then asked them, 'Why don't you do something really useful? We've dealt very badly with our American Indians. In fact, we stole the whole country from them. Why don't you do something for the Indians? Maybe you really could achieve something.' They just looked at me. There was nothing glamorous or romantic about that idea. I could see they couldn't care less about the American Indians."

The Money Mind

Carret has a name for what he says is the particular mentality of the good investor: the money mind. To illustrate it, he cites a story. "Years ago, New York went through one of its periodic droughts. You had to ask for a glass of water in a restaurant." Then one day, Carret remembered an area in Queens he had learned about, where the city collected its water charges on the basis not of consumption but of the front footage of each residence. He reflected that the city would eventually have to install water meters there, so that a distinction could be made between households that consumed a lot of water—doubtless wasting a good deal of it—and those that consumed less. He studied the subject and found that the likely candidate for the business would be Neptune Meter. He looked up the company and saw that one of the directors, an officer of Bankers Trust, held 2,000 shares—an encouraging sign. The company's figures were favorable. So Carret bought the stock for his clients and over the years was well rewarded.

"The money mind," he says, "is just a quirk, like the mathematical mind." Apropos of that, he described a friend of his who at church, instead of listening to the sermons, would let his thoughts wander over the numbers of the hymns that were posted where the congregation could see them. He could not prevent himself from playing arithmetical games with these numbers and eventually had to plead with the minister to take them down, so that he could concentrate on the sermon.

I mentioned a story in G. H. Hardy's book on the Indian mathematical genius, Srinivasa Ramanujan. Hardy was visiting Ramanujan in the hospital and mentioned that he had arrived in a cab numbered 1729. A dull number, he added. Ramanujan instantly expostulated, "No, Hardy, it is a very interesting number! It is the smallest number expressible as the sum of two cubes in two different ways."* It's hard for the layman to conceive of a brilliant mathematical—or investment—mind.

Carret Investments

In 1939, raw sugar sold for less than one cent a pound. Then came war. Carret knew that in wartime the price of sugar always rises. He sought out a Cuban sugar company with 20,000 shares outstanding, of which 13,000 were controlled by the Royal Bank of Canada. In the course of being reorganized the company had acquired a whole spectrum of different securities: mortgages, income debentures, preferred and the rest, with the common stock the tail end of the dog. So when sugar prices rose, the common stock skyrocketed. He bought a little at $1.75, and a lot more at $7–$8. He sold most of it at $60, and the last little bit at $200.

He once noticed Hearst $25 7-percent preferred, which was sold by the Hearst company through its newspapers. The preferred could vote only after four consecutive quarterly dividends had been paid. The company for years paid just one dividend a year, to retain all the voting power for the common. Carret bought some Hearst preferred for the Pioneer Fund. A number of the dealers who placed the fund attended Pioneer shareholders' meetings. Some of them used to sit up late the night before the meeting searching for lemons in the portfolio. So to be ready, Carret called on Hearst's treasurer. It had just sold one of its papers, so Carret told the treasurer that it ought to be able to sell a paper a year. The treasurer observed that on that basis the whole company would only last fourteen years. This would not be at all bad for the preferred shareholders, Carret replied. Still, to avoid embarrassing questions he sold the stock. In a subsequent meeting one of the dealers asked him, "How are you doing with your Hearst preferred?" "I sold it," Carret replied. The dealer seemed disappointed. A year later the preferred was indeed called, at double the price he'd sold it for. If he hadn't expected

*12^3 plus 1^3, and 10^3 plus 9^3.

to be needled by the dealers, he probably would have sat with it until it paid off.

"When I invest, I gamble with a certain amount of my capital, buying dogs," he says. "The usual way I lose is by buying concept stocks. They rarely work. Still, one interests me just now: Flow Systems. They use a jet of water under very high pressure to cut solid objects . . . steel, or even stacks of paper. It's a neglected stock, mostly, I suppose, because it hasn't made much money yet."

Looking at his desk, which had three or four inches of annual reports, letters, and papers on it, I said it certainly conveyed an impression of industry.

"I'm not sure that desk has ever actually been bare," said Carret. "When I was back at Blyth, the department I was in was called Economic Research. They discontinued Economic Research when they fired me. They didn't need the equipment, so I was able to buy it for a dollar. It's served me very well for sixty years."

Advice

Carret thinks the next crash could come without warning.

"I've been selling stocks and buying bonds," he says. "General Electric Credits, IBM Credits, that sort of stuff. I still have lots of stocks, though: water companies, that kind of thing. Conservative, well-financed companies that will see you through hard times."

4

George Soros

Global Speculator

George Soros probably has the top long-term record in percentage terms of any manager of a publicly held portfolio investment pool: about 34 percent per annum compounded for some nineteen years. Like Steinhardt, he makes heavy use of borrowed-money leverage; so his results are not comparable to those of a conventional fund manager. Ten thousand dollars invested in his fund when it began in 1969 was worth over $2.8 million in 1988. The Quantum Fund, his Curaçao-based vehicle, is now some $2 billion. Since he is believed to own about 25 percent of it, he is very well off personally. Like almost all great investors he began poor. Unlike the runner-up for the performance title, Warren Buffett (who also benefits from the leverage in his insurance company portfolios), he has had some bad dips. In 1981, for instance, the shares of his fund dropped 23 percent. Many of his investors were flighty European performance-chasers, and a number, fearing he might have lost his grip, withdrew—enough to reduce his fund by exactly half. However, the next year, 1982, was one of his best, up 57 percent, and by the end of 1983 the fund was bigger than ever. Within 1987 there was another horrible down draft, with the fund off $840 million, or 28 percent, in a matter of days, although it ended the year up 14 percent.

In the weeks before the 1987 crash Soros had been saying in interviews that the Japanese market was wildly overpriced, and had shorted Japanese stocks. But it was Wall Street that caved in first, catastrophically, on October 17. Two days later Soros is reported to have doubled his exposure to U.S. equities by plunging into over a billion dollars of index futures. After a brief bounce, Wall Street crashed again, and a panicky Soros had to throw in his hand. But as his broker, Shearson, dumped his S&P futures contracts, the traders, circling like vultures, refused to bid as the price plummeted from 230 to 200, a discount of 20 percent below the value of the underlying stocks. After the Soros block was out of the way, the S&P futures recovered at once, to close at 244.50. Soros also had to make heavy sales of stocks in the cash market.

It would be understandable for the shareholders to get skittish. Soros's method is inordinately difficult for most investors to understand, let alone apply, and depends on consummately honed skill, applied every day with unremitting concentration. A typical Soros maneuver, such as going long yen and short sterling on margin both ways, while immensely profitable if it works, can also have disastrous results if it doesn't.

In addition, Soros has reached the stage that all intelligent money managers—and, indeed, human beings—come to in time, of wanting to do something useful for mankind with the rest of his life. Many assemble art collections and look for someone to give them to, or go on museum or charitable boards, or enter public service, and consort with big shots. Soros himself has started and now guides a private foundation . . . a very interesting one indeed, as we shall see.

He and his pretty and intelligent second wife live on the Upper East Side in Manhattan, with a splendid beach complex in Southampton, another house in Washington, Connecticut, and a flat in London. He travels widely. He enjoys a game of tennis and is an excellent skier.

There are other individual investors who use methods like Soros's—who follow a variety of speculative ideas in different markets simultaneously, using leverage. I know one, for instance, an Italian industrial financier who lives in Lausanne, who became convinced some years ago that gold was due for a rise and put a substantial part of his very large fortune into the metal, using bank loans to magnify his buying power. He ended up buying *tons* of bullion at a clip. When the payoff came it was titanic . . . and tax free. He had no hesitation at the time about telling others what he was doing, but few of his acquaintances copied him. Another one of these prodigies, an Egyptian, at all times keeps hundreds of millions of dollars whirling around in the options market, and from time to time makes tens of millions. In his case, only his brokers know his moves. And then we have the Hunt family. Having marched up the hill, they succumbed to high-altitude rapture and rolled straight down again into bankruptcy, dropping a billion dollars attempting, with their Arab allies, to corner the world silver market. *Sic transit:* The Hunts aren't missed.

In none of these cases could an outsider have bought a piece of the action. All these global speculators are—or were—richer than Soros, but Soros is the only one who lets outside investors on board his roller coaster. Those who were bold enough to do so early have been very well rewarded indeed.

But, as I say, Soros both follows a method that permits no distractions and has, in fact, started to become distracted. So perhaps it is understandable that his investors should get wary from time to time. And indeed, Soros seems to be hesitant himself: He has always had partners on the management side, such as Jim Rogers and Victor Niederhoffer, and in 1981 started looking around for a stable of sub-managers to whom he can farm out *tranches* of his fund. Of late he has been hiring these managers and installing them in his own office, in the more usual manner of hedge funds.

George Soros (originally pronounced Dieu-de Shorosh) is an intense, squarely built man with a wrinkled brow, an angular chin, and a thin mouth. His hair is cut *en brosse*. He has a flat, slightly harsh voice and retains his Hungarian accent. (He also speaks French and German.) He is authentically cultured. His father was captured by the Russians in World War I and escaped, thus experiencing the Bolshevik revolution at first hand. George received his own lesson in survival as a boy in World War II: As Jews in German-occupied Hungary, the family was often in flight, hiding out in friends' houses. Two years after the war, at the age of seventeen, George moved to England. After attending the London School of Economics, he became an international stock arbitrageur at Singer & Friedlander. He carried out "internal arbitrage," calculating against one another the relative values of shares or bonds carrying warrants, and trading the separate elements.

Soros came to the United States in 1956, and worked at F. M. Mayer & Co. and Wertheim & Co., living in a small Greenwich Village apartment with his musically inclined German first wife, Annalise. He sold European securities, but the introduction of the Interest Equalization Tax brusquely halted American purchases of foreign issues. He spent three years on a philosophical book but gave it up, although some of its ideas are embodied in his recent *The Alchemy of Finance.** In 1963 he joined Arnhold and S. Bleichroeder as a securities analyst. The firm started an offshore fund called Double Eagle, which Soros was assigned to run in 1969. That year he wrote a research memorandum describing the attractions of a new vehicle, the Real Estate Investment Trust, or REIT. He correctly predicted that they were a good enough idea so that they would boom, go much too far, and eventually collapse. He did buy them, and when they had become over-blown in 1974 went short, making a tidy profit. He put a quarter of the fund's portfolio in Japanese securities in 1971.

In 1969, aged thirty-nine, he finally decided to hang up his own shingle and joined with Jim Rogers to found Quantum Fund—probably the most successful large fund in history. It is not registered with the SEC and thus cannot be sold in America, so the shareholders are foreigners, mostly European. It engages in multidirectional international speculation in commodities, currencies, stocks, and bonds, using massive amounts of margin. Soros says that the capital of the fund is kept basically in stocks, while its bets on commodities and currencies are done using futures and/or borrowed money. It went short the major insti-tutional favorites, such as Disney, Polaroid, and Tropicana, and thus made money in both 1973 and 1974, which for most inves-tors were horrible years. He went short Avon, the archetypal "one-decision" stock, at 120—a brilliant move.

Thanks to Rogers, the fund was one of the first to recognize the investment merits of defense stocks. It was also well ahead of the pack in high-tech, and in 1979 owned 8 percent of M/A Com,

*New York: Simon & Schuster, 1987.

and in 1980, 23 percent of Bolt Beranek & Newman; also 5.3 percent of Chem Nuclear Enterprises and 3.4 percent of Planning Research.

Insiders believe that Rogers, who had a 20-percent interest in Soros Management, was essential to the early success of Quantum Fund. Soros had the large and general ideas and was the trader, while Rogers did a lot of the country selection and was the stock analyst.

After being accused by the SEC of manipulating the price of Computer Sciences in 1979, Soros signed a consent decree; in 1986, accused of exceeding trading limits, he signed another. Neither is too significant: It is almost impossible to obey every regulation when running so complicated an operation.

In 1987 Soros set about bringing into his office a new set of sub-managers. He installed one team for risk arbitrage, one for options arbitrage, one man to work with him on macroeconomics, a team for U.S. investments, another for European investments, and, he expects, another in Japan. Also a short-side group: one internal manager, and several others on a semi-independent basis. Each subsidiary manager can run his own "book" (in Soros's terminology a "mini-account") independently; Soros himself increases the volume of any transaction if he likes the look of it. His objective, he says, is to have someone else in the office on the line or "pulling the trigger" for every transaction, with himself as coach, behind the lines, as it were, trying to observe how the rules of the game are changing.*

I have a certain feeling for Soros, since my first employer (and indeed the only one, except for the Army) was also a London-trained Hungarian émigré economist, Imrie de Vegh, who turned to investing and became a master of that craft. The Hungarians are a hard, proud people, used to defending themselves against invasion from every quarter. Their language, Magyar, can be understood by no one else. They approach the world as strangers and contemplate life without illusions. Like Soros, de Vegh sought to apply his economic savvy to a wider purpose; in addition to his investment firm he started a consultancy with Professor Wassily Leontief, the Nobel Prize–winning father of

*Both for the year 1988 and for the first half of 1989, the Soros Fund did worse than the Dow.

input-output economics, to offer macro input-output analysis to very large companies, industries, and governments. (Leontief is also, as it happens, on the board of Soros's foundation.) Anyway, Soros, who likewise does not want to be a one-sided man, has branched off in other directions, including writing a book (which, to his chagrin, almost nobody understands, not even reviewers) and starting his own foundations. He has virtually no other charitable interests, nor does he belong to clubs or associations.

I mentioned to Soros that de Vegh, who was not a good leader, had failed in his great ambition, which was to found an enduring institution. "We'll see if I do any better," said Soros. "It's not my forte, either. Still, it's fun bringing in younger people."

The Soros Foundation

Soros has started five foundations intended to encourage the liberalization of thinking in several Eastern Bloc countries. The Open Society Fund, a New York foundation, began in 1979 and operates worldwide. The Soros Foundation–Hungary, established in 1984, has as directors Wassily Leontief, Philip Kaiser, William D. Zabel, and Soros himself. Its objectives are "to support the evolution of Hungarian society . . . to enlarge the possibilities for creative activity and to support new initiatives in culture and education." It gives grants and scholarships, supports libraries and other institutions, and backs research into social change, economics, and psychology. It also supports education, the arts, and other areas. Soros says that it has become known in Hungary as "an alternate Ministry of Culture."

One of the foundation's interesting projects is a three-legged joint venture with an Italian bank and the Milan Chamber of Commerce, and a Hungarian bank and the Hungarian Chamber of Commerce. They are creating a management-training center in an old castle outside Budapest. Mark Palmer, U.S. Ambassador to Hungary, originally suggested the idea. Academician Abel G. Aganbegyan, a leading Russian theoretician of *perestroika*, attended and spoke at the inauguration, saying that some Moscow authorities had opposed Soviet participation but that he expected to start sending Soviet students to the institute in due course. The faculty will consist of five Western professors—two Americans, two Canadians, and one Briton—together with five Hungarians. Two to three hundred full-time students are expected initially.

The Fund for the Opening and Reform of China supports research, the distribution of foreign books and periodicals, study groups, and visits by artists and intellectuals abroad.

The Soros Foundation–Soviet Union supports Gorbachev's "new thinking" in the cultural and economic areas. It made a joint-venture agreement with Gorbachev's Cultural Foundation but now is becoming an independent Soviet foundation in its own right, called Cultural Initiative. Its initial objectives include enabling Soviet cultural and scientific figures and students to travel and study abroad. However, the foundation concept is unfamiliar in the Soviet Union, and has been hard to get under way. (An article in the *Washington Post* on March 7, 1988, mentioned that after a year the foundation had been unable to open a bank account in Moscow.) Now, however, it is beginning to have an impact on Russian intellectual life.

I have run into Soros's traces in philanthropy in southern Africa, where he has been skillful in identifying groups to support that not only are having a useful and original impact but also will probably survive—two criteria of creative philanthropy. I suspect that Soros will turn out to be one of the most imaginative and original philanthropists of our era, and that his importance in that role will eclipse his considerable input on the investment scene.

The Trader

Soros's book *The Alchemy of Finance* describes his transactions from August 18, 1985, to November 7, 1986.

As we will see as we go along, Soros likes exotic terms for things: He calls this trading period "The Real Time Experiment." The diary covers one of Soros's most successful periods, during which his fund's net asset value per share doubled.

The trading diary starts in August 1985. It will be recalled that the Reagan election of 1984, followed by tax cuts and a defense buildup, had set off a boom in both the dollar and the stock market. Foreign investors liked what they saw, an America resolved to stand firm against Soviet pressure, and an expanding economy that welcomed foreign participation. Seen from abroad, America's situation is indeed unique: Almost every other country in the world is either menaced by Soviet power, or else is unappetizing to investors for internal reasons. So, America, when it is feeling confident, attracts much of the world's excess capital, whether directly or through such intermediaries as Switzerland, Luxembourg, or Nassau.

The influx of foreign money during the early Reagan period lifted both the dollar and the capital markets, and helped fuel a round of economic expansion that attracted even more money, putting the dollar up further. Soros names this syndrome "Reagan's Imperial Circle." (See Figure 2, page 75, for his wondrously complicated diagram of this effect.) The usual metaphor would be a bubble, which by its nature must collapse eventually, at the latest when mounting debt-service costs exceed our ability to find new money. Even before that, however, many factors can prick the bubble, which should then burst, perhaps with a fall in the dollar and a rush of speculative capital out of the U.S. markets. That, in turn, could produce a decline in the economy, resulting in a general downward spiral.

The Start

This, then, is the background when Soros's trading diary opens on August 18, 1985. The fund is worth $647 million. Some readers will remember that at this period investors were worried that a rise in the money supply meant a boom, with higher interest rates, and subsequent bust; the economy was feared to be in eventually for a "hard landing." Cyclical stocks, beneficiaries of the boom, were strong, and stocks whose fortunes depended on low interest rates were weak.

In his diary Soros declares that he doubts this conventional wisdom *in toto*. He thinks the "imperial circle" is faltering, and thus expects the dollar to weaken and interest rates to rise, provoking a recession. So instead of buying cyclical stocks that would benefit from a continued boom, he buys takeover candidates, together with shares of property-insurance companies, then

THE IMPERIAL CIRCLE

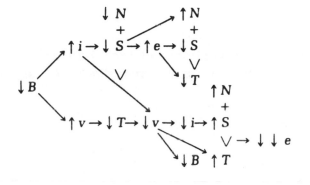

e   nominal exchange rate (number of foreign currency units for one domestic currency unit; ↑ e = strengthening)

i   nominal interest rate

p   domestic versus foreign price level (↑ p = increase in domestic prices faster than in foreign prices and vice versa)

v   level of economic activity

N   nonspeculative capital flow } ↑ = increased outflow
S   speculative capital flow   } ↓ = increased inflow
T   trade balance   } ↑ = surplus
B   government budget   } ↓ = deficit

Figure 2

enjoying one of their best years on record. As to currencies, Soros
is playing the thesis of a weaker dollar by buying D-Marks and
yen. In addition he thinks OPEC is breaking up, and so goes
short oil.

So the opening position on the board looks as shown in the
first column, August 16, 1985, of the Quantum Fund table (see
pages 77–78).

Three weeks later, on September 6, 1985, nothing has worked.
The mark and yen have both declined, and since Soros had been
long some $700 million in those two currencies—more than the
value of the whole fund—he has lost money. By September 6 he
has built up his D-Mark and yen positions to just under $800
million, almost $200 million more than the value of the fund.

Betting on the Yen

Now comes the so-called Plaza meeting of a group of five finance
ministers with their central bankers, called on a Sunday by the
U.S. Treasury. That night, Sunday in New York but already
Monday morning in Hong Kong, Soros plunges in and buys yen
heavily. The yen rises strongly, and Soros makes 10 percent on
his yen position, which he has built up to $458 million.

In his September 28 entry Soros describes the Plaza accord
coup as "the killing of a lifetime . . . the profits of the last week
more than made up for the accumulated losses on currency
trading in the last four years. . . ." Four years is a long time to
be under water! This statement certainly illustrates the difficulties
of currency trading. If the reader looks at the entries for
September 6, 1985, in the Quantum Fund table he will see that
the exposure in D-Marks is $491 million, and in yen, $308
million, or a total of $799 million, somewhat more than the value
of the fund. By September 27 D-Marks have risen from 2.92 to
the dollar to 2.68, or 9 percent, and the yen from 242 to 217, or
11.5 percent. The combination of profits and increasing the bet
have pushed the combined holdings in these two currencies from
$791 million up to $1 billion by September 27, but because of
adverse movements in the stock market and oils the whole fund
has advanced only—if that's the word—7.6 percent a share. In

Quantum Fund ($ millions)

	1985						
	Aug. 16	Sept. 6	Sept. 27	Oct. 18	Nov. 8	Nov. 22	Dec. 6
Currency Exposure							
$U.S.*	−73	−182	−289	−433	−592	−567	−569
D-Marks	+467	+491	+550	+680	+654	+668	+729
Yen	+244	+303	+458	+546	+806	+827	+826
£	+9	+10	−44	−72	−86	−87	−119
Other	+50	+45	+16	+34	+42	+40	+33
Holdings							
U.S. Stocks & Index Futures	+604	+538	+445	+253	+442	+707	+1020
Foreign Stocks	+183	+163	+142	+152	+206	+251	+271
U.S. Bonds	−113	0	−77	0	+580	+1074	+751
Japanese Bonds						+354	+300
Oil	−121	−145	−176	−37	−187	−214	−150
Size of Fund	647	627	675	721	782	841	867
Share Price ($)	4379	4238	4561	4868	5267	5669	5841

*A short position in dollars indicates the amount by which exposure in the major currencies (which are as shown) exceeds the capital of the fund.

Quantum Fund ($ millions)

1986

	Jan. 10	Feb. 21	Mar. 26	Apr. 4	Apr. 8	May 20	Jul. 21	Aug. 8	Sep. 12	Oct. 31	Nov. 7
Currency Exposure											
$U.S.*	−1	+39	+81	+63	+153	+744	+159	+1192	+221	+1141	+1076
D-Marks	+609	+783	+1108	+1094	+816	+485	+795	+164	+905	+1280	+1334
Yen	+612	+726	+492	+474	+504	+159	+549	+141	+335	−955	−956
£	−278	−343	−389	−380	+177	−21	−25	−25	+3	+3	+7
Other	+21	+81	+63	+50	+57	+148	+202	+177	+221	+201	+201
Holdings											
U.S. Stocks & Index Futures	+1663	+787	+1226	+432	+1062	+380	+53	+955	+1122	+589	+407
Foreign Stocks	+318	+426	+536	+499	+578	+573	+604	+563	+629	+460	+436
U.S. Bonds	+958	+215	+326	+652	+656	+313	−541	−503		+1073	+427
Japanese Bonds	+259						+1334	+2385	+2348	+1232	+983
Oil	−224	−55	−28	−29	−12	−75	−43	+85	+97	−127	+28
Size of Fund	942	1205	1292	1251	1290	1367	1478	1472	1484	1469	1461
Share Price ($)	6350	8122	8703	8421	8684	9202	9885	9628	9610	9296	9320

*A short position in dollars indicates the amount by which exposure in the major currencies (which are as shown) exceeds the capital of the fund.

other words, the 8–10-percent currency profit has been diluted by other holdings.

The stock market has declined, which Soros regards as reinforcing his bear position on the dollar: A poor stock market will discourage both consumer and business outlays. Also, a decline in the value of stocks reduces their value as collateral, a further depressant.

Pyramiding Against the Dollar

By the first week in November 1985, Soros has reached the peak of his speculation against the dollar: D-Mark and yen positions total $1.46 billion, almost double the value of the fund. This means increasing his commitment to a trend as the trend continues . . . also known as pyramiding. Pyramiding is a good way to sustain serious damage in margin speculation, since when the trend reverses, even temporarily, you risk being caught overexposed.

"The reason I am nevertheless willing to increase my exposure is that I believe the scope for a reversal has diminished. One of the generalizations I established about freely floating exchange rates is that *short-term volatility is greatest at turning points and diminishes as a trend becomes established*"—an important hint for the currency speculator.

Changing Rules

Soros continues by observing that other speculators have not realized this new principle, which follows from floating rates, and indeed previously he hadn't himself, or he would have been able to build up to his full position sooner, and make even bigger profits on the fall of the dollar. He further reflects that "*by the time all the participants have adjusted, the rules of the game will change again*. If the authorities handle the situation well, the reward for speculating in currencies will become commensurate with the risks. Eventually, speculation will be discouraged by the lack of rewards, the authorities will have attained their goal, and it will be time for me to stop speculating."

I urge the reader to note this passage. This is the right way to approach market movements. The fatal weakness of almost all "systems" of speculation is that they are simplistic formulas, using partial data describing a particular slice of previous experience. If the slice does not entirely resemble what comes up next, or if different data are more applicable, then the approach won't work.

You can always come up with formulas covering past events that have little use in predicting future events, because they are fragmentary simplifications. Such formulas indicate what you should do to optimize your situation on the assumption that you are playing a game with fixed rules, but the essence of understanding markets is to understand how the rules are evolving.

Returning to Soros's trading diary, in the first week of November 1985 he notes that the collapse of the International Tin Council, a cartel, foreshadows the collapse of OPEC. He is now short in the oil market to the tune of over $180 million, and in addition buys shares of oil-refining companies, reasoning that if the price of oil, their raw material, drops, then their profits will improve.

During November Soros decides that the Gramm-Rudman amendment, which is intended to reduce government expenditures, together with the Reagan-Gorbachev Summit meeting, which could force defense-expenditure cuts, may presage a strong market, so he buys stock market index futures.

In addition, the Japanese bond market has fallen, because of higher domestic interest rates. Soros thinks that since the Group of Five has agreed to stimulate worldwide economic activity, Japanese interest rates should be cut. Furthermore, he notes that *the best time to buy long-term bonds is when short-term rates are higher than long-term rates . . . when the yield curve is inverted*, as one says. He therefore buys $300 million in Japanese bond futures. (In December 1988 he commented that the inversion in the U.S. bond market between the ten- and thirty-year maturities was probably an anomaly arising from year-end adjustments, but that the inversion in England was probably a precursor of a recession.)

Fully Committed

So now Soros, with a fund of about $850 million, holds a billion and a half in yen and D-Marks, and is short $87 million in pounds; he is betting against the dollar by some $600 million more than the funds he is managing.

Also, he is long about a billion in stocks and futures plus almost a billion and a half in bonds, and is short over $200 million worth of oil.

It's hard to add all this up, because of duplication, but, roughly speaking, in November 1985 Soros has almost $4 billion of action, long and short and in various markets, on the strength of his underlying capital of around $800 million, or about five to one.

On December 8 he says, "I have about as firm a conviction about the shape of things to come as I shall ever have, as witnessed by the level of exposure I am willing to assume." It certainly seems so! That conviction is, however, quite different from what he started with back in August. Then, he considered the "imperial circle" as a final round of credit expansion to stimulate the economy and finance the military buildup; when the waterspout collapsed, everything would collapse with it. By November, he realizes what has actually happened, and is somewhat reassured: The government has organized an international campaign to control the fall of the dollar, which may thus be reasonably gentle. And the rise in the stock and bond markets helps, since stronger bond prices help the Fed to lower interest rates.

The "Bull Market of a Lifetime"

Thus, notes Soros, "We may be on the verge of a great stock market boom." Many companies have been taken over, reducing excess capacity. The companies that have not been taken over have cut costs. And the lower dollar has eased pricing pressures on American companies. Taking all this together with the emergence of a concerted international economic policy, he feels that conditions are good enough so that stocks may once again sell at a premium over their underlying assets. Still, it is not clear how the U.S. budget deficit can be reduced, or how the economies of the debtor countries can be stimulated. But the attempt to do all these things should itself be enough to improve the market's feelings.

As for OPEC, most producing countries operate with what Soros calls a perverse supply curve: that is, the lower prices fall, the more they produce, in order to attain a target level of income, forcing prices down more than ever. So he stays short in oil.

By early January 1986 Soros has made some large changes in the makeup of his portfolio. Reflecting his more bullish stance, he has increased the portion in U.S. stocks and stock-index futures by $643 million, plus an increase in the foreign stock position of $47 million to $318 million, or a total of about $2 billion. He has also added $207 billion to his U.S. bond holdings. He has shrunk his bet against the dollar from half a billion dollars to zero; that is, his net position in dollars is down to just the amount of the fund. He has also expanded his short position in oil to $224 million. Quite a month!

He notes that *the usual bull market successfully weathers a number of tests until it is considered invulnerable, whereupon it is ripe for a bust*; this will happen in due course, but that point is still a long way ahead.

Back and Forth

In February he reduces his stock position to about $1.2 billion, but by March 26 he decides that his bullish thesis for stocks is right, after all, and is reinforced by the fall in oil; so he rebuilds his position in U.S. and foreign stocks to about $1.8 billion. His fund has increased since early January from $942 million to $1.3 billion.

By April 4 he has backed off again from his stock commitments by $831 million, but in the following week he has repurchased $709 million—very nice for the brokers! By May 20 he has once more sold $687 million. These maneuvers are conducted largely in index futures.

Some Stock Conceptions

Forty percent of his stock positions, and two-thirds of his foreign stock positions, are in three conceptions: the Finnish market,

Japanese railroad and real estate stocks, and Hong Kong real estate stocks. Finland is a little-known and underpriced market, but it contains some outstanding companies. The last two conceptions are really variations of the same idea: Excessive liquidity has created a land boom in both Japan and Hong Kong. As to the Japanese railroads specifically, they have not moved in the market for over a decade and are selling at a small fraction of their underlying value. Furthermore, they have discovered that they can invest in commercial real estate with borrowed money and make a profit, since the interest on the money they borrow is lower than the return on the real estate they buy. So the Japanese railroads have become a leveraged real estate play, selling at a steep discount.

Living with Contradiction

By July, Soros is tempted by two contradictory theses: 1) We are still in a major bull market; 2) The fall of oil prices may after all engender a deflationary spiral, which will abort the boom.

To the reader it must seem odd that a speculator would operate on the basis of two opposed theories, but in fact it makes good sense in many situations involving human reactions. In military negotiations between countries it has come to be called a "two-track" position: If you don't take out your missiles I will install my own missiles; if you do take them out, I won't install mine. And, until matters clarify, I will proceed on the premise that I will be installing them, but I will try not to prejudice the opposite premise.

I have often noticed that when there are two main pressures, one favorable and one unfavorable, the stock market, instead of neatly assuming a balanced middle position, will usually at different times discount each alternative. So you have to keep both in mind and be prepared for both. For instance, war may ruin a country, and so is bad for the market. On the other hand, war means overspending, which is inflationary, so in wartime investors flee depreciating currencies and buy things, including things represented by stocks. A war threat thus often produces a violent fluctuation down, and thereafter up, as first one possibility is discounted and then the other. So to navigate through such a situation the speculator should keep in mind the likelihood of both movements taking place in due course, and make his dispositions accordingly.

Anyway, in late July Soros is once again tempted by the bear argument. The fall in oil prices, he observes, has bad economic effects as well as good ones. It is inhibiting U.S. oil exploration and oil-related expenditures generally, with the result that Texas and other oil-producing states are hard hit. Then, the new tax-reform bill, by knocking out real estate tax shelters, undercuts the commercial real estate market. Agriculture is sick and defense spending is tapering off. Indeed, the consumer remains the last strong element in the economy.

Furthermore, the fall in the dollar means that it is harder for the government to cut interest rates in order to stimulate business, since high interest rates are needed to hold volatile foreign money in the country.

So now within the "bull market of a lifetime" hypothesis Soros sees a case for the opposite. What to do? His answer is interesting: "As a general principle, I do not dismantle positions that are built on a thesis that remains valid; rather, I take additional positions in the opposite direction on the basis of the new thesis." This is also what happens if within a single fund two or more managers, pursuing different even if usually successful strategies, happen for a moment to find themselves going in opposite directions.

He gives an example, which to most investors would be puzzling. "If I start with a fully invested position and then sell short an equal amount, a 20-percent decline, even if it affects the longs and the shorts equally, leaves me only 80 percent invested on the long side. If I cover my shorts at the right time, I come out way ahead, but even if I cover my shorts with a loss I am better off than if I had sold my longs at the wrong time."

He adds that all this would be much more complicated in practice than this example, because he would be operating simultaneously in several markets. For instance, here are his moves in mid-July: "On Monday, July 14, I actually bought some S&P futures on the argument that, if we are dealing with a technical reaction, the market ought to close higher. The Dow had dropped sixty-three points the previous Monday, July 7, and the bears would expect another drop on the subsequent Monday to establish a cascadelike bear market. When the market did in fact close lower, I reversed myself on the following day, and by the end of the week I built up a short position that probably outweighs my long position. I also shorted some long bonds and went long some T-bill futures. Then I piled into the Japanese bond future market, and doubled up on my short position in U.S. Government bonds. The idea behind these maneuvers is that eventually I expect concerted action to reduce interest rates but, with the dollar declining, U.S. bonds may react negatively while Japanese bonds would move up."

How many of us would have figured that out?

These extracts from Soros's trading diary should give the reader a fair impression of his method. The book itself, of course, provides considerably more.

Recent Moves

On the international plane, in 1988 he undertook a mistaken—and expensive—move against the dollar and a successful flutter in the Thai stock market.

Of late, having accumulated a considerable pile personally and presiding no longer over a $15 million speedboat but a $2 billion ocean liner, Soros has become more conventional. A large part of his U.S. equity positions are now in blue-chip Dow stocks.

Basically he is looking for companies selling in the market below their breakup value. To this extent he has become a "value" investor, after all. His staff does the analysis, while he worries about the larger questions. His fund became the largest holder of the bonds of Sharon Steel Corporation, centerpiece of the Victor Posner fiefdom. Posner is a corporate vulture, who gets control of one company after another, installs himself and his relatives on high salaries with elaborate perks, and waits for the inevitable lawsuits. He has been tried and convicted in Florida. Sharon went bankrupt, and Soros is trying to get value for his bonds. He bought into Boeing at $45, having previously shorted it at $52, on the news that T. Boone Pickens might buy the company. Soros has also gone into a huge list of smaller positions, such as Danaker and Envirodyne. An inventory of this grab bag is found as Appendix II.

As a guide, Soros's methods are chiefly of value to other highly aggressive short-term speculators. He does have a number of specific ideas that are well worth understanding, however.

Public and Private

Montaigne drew a noteworthy distinction between his position as Mayor of Bordeaux and himself as a thinker. The mayor is supposed to set an example and make uplifting pronouncements; the thinker may—indeed must—have his own ideas: "You can put powder on your face, but not on your heart also." Similarly, Soros preaches regulation of currencies and denounces green-mailers, but while things continue as they are, speculates both in currencies and takeovers since that is what the rules permit.

Investment Techniques

Here are some of Soros's principles of speculation:

1. Start small. If things work out, build up a larger position. This ties in with his view that in a world of floating currencies trends get steadier and more determinable as they develop.

2. The market is dumb, so don't try to be omniscient. "Investors operate with limited funds and limited intelligence: They do not need to know everything. *As long as they understand something better than others, they have an edge.*" For example, when he was a European securities salesman for Wertheim, Soros discovered that the securities portfolios of the major German banks exceeded the banks' market value, so that if you bought stock in the banks you were in essence being paid to accept the operating businesses of these excellent institutions for nothing. That was all one needed to know to justify acting, and he acted. This thesis was powerful enough so that detailed information would just have been clutter. By the same token, however, Soros finds it difficult to invest in technology stocks, because there you do have to possess specialized knowledge. He thus missed the 1980s technology boom.

3. A speculator has to define from the first the level of risk that he dares assume. This is one of his most difficult judgments.

Keep It Simple

Soros says that he does not spend a great deal of time on economic study, does not read Wall Street research, and develops his opinions essentially by reading the newspapers. He also talks constantly to well-placed sources around the world.

In 1981, he had eighteen employees, mostly doing administration. "I never see them and I don't know their names," Soros said then. By 1988 he said he "had no idea . . . maybe nearly fifty."

Market Theories

There are three main theories of stock-market behavior, Soros observes: the fundamental; the technical; and the "efficient market" theory.

1. He and many others have demonstrated the falsity of the efficient market theory through consistent superior performance—which, according to the theory, is virtually impossible. Determined professors have written that the Soros phenomenon can be explained by luck; but if so, Mozart can be explained by luck. No one in the business believes it. Soros notes sardonically, "The more the theory of efficient markets is believed, the less efficient the markets become."

2. Technical analysis has a feeble theoretical foundation and does not in fact work consistently.

3. Fundamental analysis holds that value, defined in terms of earning power, assets, and the like, determines stock prices. But stock prices also change fundamental values, by permitting the sale or repurchase of shares, or mergers and acquisitions, and the like.

My own comment is that value determines stock prices— eventually. The investor, unlike the speculator, does not have to worry too much about the short term. However, Soros concludes that reflexivity is a better approach than any of these.

Reflexivity

The essence of Soros's "theory of reflexivity" is that *perceptions change events, which in turn change perception.* The usual name for this effect is "feedback." In my own language, if when the princess kisses the frog the frog turns into a prince, she will kiss him some more, he will kiss her back, and . . . I know not what. If, on the other hand, you chain a good dog and kick it, saying "bad dog," the dog will indeed become vicious and bite, provoking more kicks, and more bites.

Switching to money, if speculators are convinced the dollar should rise, their purchases may well push it up. That, in turn, will produce lower interest rates and stimulate the economy, justifying a still-higher dollar. Similarly, if many speculators become convinced that ITT or Gulf + Western or whatever is going to rise, then they will bid up the stock, and management can use it as a trading token to buy other companies on advantageous terms, thus justifying a still higher stock price.

Soros calls this reciprocal sequence of facts to perceptions to facts to perceptions, and so on, a "shoelace" pattern.

A crucial aspect of reflexivity is the imperfect understanding of the participants. (As I observe from time to time this is the essence of the military decision-making problem: The "fog of war" prevents you from having all the information you would like; indeed, by the time you have it, the situation has changed.)

Soros had hoped to develop a broad theory of reflexivity that would explain the coming great bust of the 1980s just as Keynes's *General Theory of Employment, Interest and Money* explained the Great Depression of the 1930s. He now admits that he does not have a properly formed economic theory, although he considers the idea valid and interesting, as indeed it is. Speculators have always understood it, but not necessarily the public.

Soros is particularly interested in two financial areas where reflexivity operates: the relationships between lending and collateral, and between the regulators and the economy.

The Impact of Lending on Collateral

The act of lending increases the value of the collateral the loan is based on. If, like the Japanese railroads, a company or a country can borrow money cheaply to buy productive assets at bargain prices, it can prosper. Bringing in loan money usually stimulates economic activity in general, and a strong economy enhances the asset values and income streams that build credit-worthiness.

Eventually, however, when debt rises beyond the point where it can be serviced, the collateral has to be sold, which depresses its value, throwing the process into reverse.

Most international bankers don't realize that the debt ratios of borrowing countries are favorably influenced by their own lending. Neither do they realize that the erosion of collateral values by debt repayment can in turn depress the economy.

Regulation

The least regulation usually coincides with the strongest credit expansion. This interaction has an *ad hoc* path: It is neither regular nor repetitive. Soros says that until 1982 it was a fairly straightforward succession of boom and bust. The present boom, however, has been artificially extended by keeping alive the huge clot of international bad debt through what Soros calls a "collective" system of lending, notably the different lending bank "clubs" and through the parallel emergence of the U.S. government as the "borrower of last resort," giving rise to the "imperial circle."

Soros concludes that to maintain stability, financial markets require regulation. He also points out a tendency to move between extremes: Having once suffered from excessive regulation, the United States has since been moving toward excessive deregulation.

Specifically, Soros urges the creation of an international central bank, which will maintain stable currencies, reorganize existing debt, and provide an adequate flow of new credit. "We cannot have a smoothly functioning international economy without a stable international currency," he declares. This objective may come about by having three main trading blocs—the EMS, including England to some extent; the dollar; and the yen—with coordination among the three.

Oil

Soros once proposed an international buffer stock for oil, not only to improve stability in the oil market, but also to create some of the capital needed for his international bank; he also suggested an international oil-backed currency. Today, he thinks the moment for that idea may have passed. There were three eras of ordered oil prices—excess capacity restrained by a cartel—the Standard Oil, the Texas Railroad Commission, and the OPEC periods. Now the first two are gone and OPEC is on its last legs, so eventually a new agency will be needed through which consumers and producers can stabilize prices.

He accepts that any proposed solutions to the currency and oil problems will not be perfect or permanent, but nothing is.

Equilibrium

The bandwagon effect of speculation is not explained by the equilibrium theory of classical economics, which holds that there is a natural price for most things at which transactions will occur and the market should clear. But this theory does not apply to markets with wide public participation, which fluctuate with the ebb and flow of group passions.

It would have been quite a stunt if Soros had been able to squeeze speculative market behavior into classical economics, and it's not surprising that he couldn't. Speculative markets and other conflict situations, such as war and poker, are analyzed by sociologists—and in mathematical terms by newer disciplines, such as game theory and general systems theory. Soros admits to being unfamiliar with them.

Soros argues that the concept of equilibrium in classical economics is a myth, along with a number of the other assumptions of economic theory, such as perfect competition, perfect knowledge, homogenous and divisible products, and supply-and-demand curves. In reality, he says, decisions to buy and sell are based on expectations. If a producer expects the price of his product to decline, then like a commodity speculator he will sell more rather than less as it begins to fall. In reverse, if prices rise, one would expect supply to mount and demand to fall, tending to put a brake on the upward movement. However, in some cases the reverse occurs: A currency rises, and because of the dampening impact on inflation and for other reasons the rise can become self-validating. Thus, since the supply-and-demand curves are in considerable measure determined by market influences, instead of equilibrium, you have trends.

Self-reinforcing Cycles

Soros sees the prime mover of stock prices as a combination of the underlying trend and the prevailing "bias"—usually called the standard forecast—both of which are influenced by stock prices, which influence may be either self-reinforcing or self-correcting.

Every cycle is special, but one can make a few generalizations:

1. The importance of speculative transactions increases as the trend continues.

2. Bias (i.e., the standard forecast) follows the trend; the longer the trend persists, the stronger the bias.

3. Once a trend is fixed it will run its course.

Currencies, particularly, tend to move in great waves. So adding the three generalizations together, he finds that speculation progressively destabilizes currencies. This is part of the reason for Soros's opposition to freely fluctuating exchange rates.

Boom and Bust

For Soros, the main features of a typical boom/bust sequence are:

1. The existence of an as-yet-unrecognized trend;
2. The beginning of the self-reinforcing process just described;
3. A successful test of the market's direction;
4. A growing conviction;
5. A resulting divergence between reality and perception;
6. The climax;
7. Then, the start of a mirror-image self-reinforcing sequence in the opposite direction.

The first time Soros used the boom/bust–sequence concept was in the conglomerate boom; another was his play in Real Estate Interest Trusts (REITs). In both instances, their attraction lay in the companies' reflexive ability to generate capital gains by selling additional shares at a premium over book value.

Reversal Points: "The Trend Is Your Friend."

Further, he says, things can go wrong even if foreseen: Events can only reverse prevailing opinions at reversal points, which are hard to spot. In other words, you can know that something will happen, but unless you also know when, it may not do you much good. Particularly when you are on the short side, it's essential to catch the moment of the reversal quite exactly.

Now, this is Soros, a trader, speaking. Suppose you are sure the yen will rise and you have a billion dollars of borrowed money riding on it. Next quarter or next year it may decline again, but you may have been wiped out at any point in the meantime. So for today and tomorrow what governs will be the immediate supply-demand factors, influenced by current news, moves by the authorities, and, above all, momentum. That's what is meant by the old trader's axiom, "the trend is your friend." To buck it, particularly on margin, is terribly risky, since you probably won't catch the exact moment of the turn.

For the patient long-term investor, on the other hand, who really understands the underlying values and is working with only part of his assets, the important thing is value. If you can buy a dollar of value for fifty cents, or if you can pay fifty cents today for what will grow to a dollar of value in a couple of years, you needn't worry about pinpointed timing. And one of the ways you know you're probably getting a good value is that there are almost no other buyers.

So contrarianism is the hallmark of the investor, although it can be very dangerous indeed for the margin trader.

A Flexible Theoretical Framework

By having a flexible theoretical framework, Soros hopes to be able to cope with whatever comes up. For instance, at the time his trading diary or "real time experiment" begins, he considers the "imperial circle" vulnerable: The weakness of both the dollar and the U.S. economy will, he feels, lead to high interest rates, which in turn will provoke a decline in the economy. But then the U.S. monetary authorities changed to a "dirty float," cushioning the dollar's fall. This kept interest rates down. The resulting boom in the financial markets prevented the economy from slipping into recession, and led to a prolongation of the boom.

As we see from his trading, one of Soros's most important traits—as with every successful trader—is his willingness to reverse field instantly when he realizes he has made a mistake. For example, he went short Resorts International in the midst of the vast enthusiasm for gambling stocks in 1978 and 1979. So, as described in *The Money Masters*, did Robert Wilson, in the most widely discussed short-side transaction in modern Wall Street history. But Wilson, having announced his position to all and sundry, then went off on an extensive vacation to the Orient. Resorts shares went from 5 to over 60, where he was forced to cover, costing him a fortune. Soros, on the contrary, seeing that things were going the wrong way, simply changed sides: He closed out his shorts, bought the stock (thus helping squeeze Wilson), and ended up modestly ahead.

Currency—the Existential Choice

Soros rightly observes that you can't avoid having your assets in some currency. To put it differently, if you own something, it ultimately has to *be* somewhere, just the way you have to live somewhere yourself. Most investors, and indeed most money managers, never consciously decide where they want to be; they stay put. That's fine if you're in Zurich, and less so if you're in Port au Prince.* Consciously choosing between countries other than your own comes hard to the patriot, and particularly to an American, for whom Morgan's dictum never to be a bear on the United States has been good advice. But short term, neither the

---

*I once had a charming friend who was the Ambassador from Dahomey (now Benin) to both the U.N. and to Haiti, which regarded Dahomey as its mother country—the way Mexico regards Spain. He used to go to Haiti once a year to participate in celebrating its national day. His family fortune consisted of some rental houses in Dahomey. He used to ask me wistfully whether, in the interest of diversification, in case there was trouble at home, he should not buy a rental property or two in Haiti.

dollar nor dollar stocks have always been the best choice. So, says Soros, you have to take a stand: Not to decide is itself a decision. "Sometimes I envy my more ignorant fund-managing colleagues," he modestly reveals, "who do not know that they face an existential choice.

"The historic significance of the crash of 1987 [is that] . . . it marks the transfer of economic and financial power from the United States to Japan," says Soros. He adds that "the dollar is unsound at any price. Holders of financial assets seek the best source of value, and the dollar no longer qualifies. However, the post-crash depression of the 1930s is unlikely to be repeated after the 1987 crash, precisely because it is so well remembered." The D-Mark he considered attractive early in 1989, since the Bundesbank did not want it any weaker, but he did not believe in gold, because new technology is bringing in more supplies at current prices.

Self-denying Prophecies

"My approach works not by making valid predictions but by allowing me to correct false ones," says Soros.

On October 14, 1987, he published an article in London's *Financial Times* in which he predicted a collapse in the Japanese market. He was right: It declined by 10 percent or so. Then the Japanese government intervened and it steadied and advanced higher than ever. "I think that the bubble will continue to be deflated, but the government will be able to arrange a soft landing," he has said. But, the U.S. market really did collapse, which Soros did not expect. As a result, his fund lost $800 million in a matter of days.

He also observes that "the outstanding feature of my predictions is that I keep on expecting developments that do not materialize. . . . In part because markets can influence the events that they anticipate. . . . Reflexive processes do not have a predetermined outcome: The outcome is determined in the course of the process."

Soros is a contrarian in the sense that he thinks that most institutional money managers are usually wrong: "The more influential their position, the less I considered them capable of making the right decisions."

Also, however, markets shape events; looking out from the bow, so to speak, they may give off loud warning cries when the ship seems to be going on the rocks. "So we live in an age of self-defeating prophecies," he says. Perhaps, he adds, this explains the old saw that the stock market predicted seven of the last two business collapses: *The market did indeed anticipate them, and frightened the authorities into taking action to prevent them.* That is what Soros means by the "alchemy" of the market, since unlike science, which seeks to understand,* alchemy tries to change.

New Names for Old

One of Soros's idiosyncrasies is his fondness for grandiose names for his ideas, some of which are quite familiar under their usual designations. This eventually becomes quite good fun. I have mentioned "reflexivity" for feedback, "bias" for standard forecast, the "imperial circle" for bubble, a "cooperative" for a club of lending banks, and "real time experiment" for trading diary. In his trading diary entry of December 8, 1985, he decides that perhaps the world is not coming to an end right away, and that instead things may be all right for a while. This he describes not as a reprieve but as the "Golden Age of Capitalism," which occurs four times in six paragraphs; he also announces "the bull market of a lifetime." At this point the S&P 500 stock average is about 2,000. Nine months later, on September 28, 1986, he writes, "It is better to declare the phase I have called the 'Golden Age of Capitalism' as complete and try to identify the next phase." This is the last we hear of the "Golden Age of Capitalism." The S&P is now about 2,300, so the Golden Age of Capitalism is "declared" to be at an end after nine months and a 15-percent move in the averages—probably the shortest golden age on record!

---

*To this I reply that science is regularly harnessed to politics, e.g., the Marxists' "scientific" view of history and the Nazis' "scientific" racial theories. In our own days, "political science" and indeed "concerned scientists" have often been much more political than scientific. "By calling politics science," Soros observes cynically, "you can influence events more."

Advice

We are now in yet another self-reinforcing and ultimately self-destroying cycle, the merger mania of the 1980s.

Market players cannot stop a boom from developing, even if they realize that it is bound to lead to a bust. Staying entirely out of the market is neither possible nor advisable: Since modern economies are linked, there is no place to hide. So the correct strategy for a speculator is to stay aboard for the ride, and then try to step off the bandwagon before it breaks down, to suffer as little damage as possible. Soros did this successfully during the REIT bubble, it will be recalled.

As to the boom-bust sequence, those who believe in the trend are perforce going to be right until the trend changes—the reversal point. The problem, therefore, is to catch that moment as exactly as possible.

The byproducts of an economic contraction, including unemployment and a falling standard of living, are so painful that the monetary authorities always move to prevent the contraction from developing—which is possible when credit is expanding. But *the recession we may be facing now will occur when borrowing capacity is contracting, an unprecedented and dangerous situation.*

Soros believes that the RJR Nabisco takeover and the fall of Michael Milken represent a climax, like the time Saul Steinberg tried to take over the Chemical Bank during the conglomerate epidemic. (He thinks that the Bush administration should attack the tax deductibility of the interest payments on debt incurred to finance takeovers.) The current vogue of splitting up stocks into different kinds of components is part of the same syndrome.

Will this boom-bust sequence develop as they usually do? Today's trends, allowed to carry on to their logical conclusion, would indeed result in the breakdown of the system. But the duty of the authorities is to prevent that, and so far, except for a slipup in October 1987, which produced that market crash, he feels they are doing a skillful job.

5

Old Money

*New Money that Has
Learned How to Survive*

To turn new money into old—that is, preserve your savings and
make them grow—a family must somehow grasp three truths.
First, the problem is extremely difficult: The rest of society yearns
to erase the claim on it represented by your capital, and pursues
that objective unremittingly, through tax, inflation, regulation,
labor demands, and other weapons. In the unending duel between the saver and society, society almost always wins in
time: Most family fortunes are eventually undermined.

The second truth to grasp is that the task of managing capital
well can only be achieved by someone who is able and experienced, and gives it the closest attention. So usually a family's best
strategy is to hire and carefully supervise a superior specialist, the
way one hires a surgeon or a lawyer.

The third truth is that finding that superior specialist is itself
a difficult job. The best investors rarely deal with individual
clients. And the best probably won't stay the best: They get too
big, and there's always a succession problem. So the family must
understand this subject well enough to be able to preside over the
process. How have some famous families gone about doing it?

A while back the Rockefeller family office announced that it
was forming the Rockefeller Trust Company to administer some
170 trusts for individual family members. "In time," said a
spokesman, Rockefeller Trust "may accept trusts from outside
clients." Despite a five-generation Rockefeller tradition of keeping
financial doings hidden inside the family, and indeed hidden *from*

much of the family, I would bet that Rockefeller Trust will in time share its investment savvy with outsiders as a full-fledged investment counsel firm.

In much the same way, the Phipps family in-house investment office, Bessemer Trust, decided in 1974 to look for outside accounts. One prize nonfamily client was the then White House Chief of Staff, Donald Regan, who placed his blind trust with Bessemer when he became Treasury Secretary in 1981.

President Reagan took advantage of the evolution of yet another family office, Starwood, which looked after the Sears, Roebuck fortune of the Rosenwald and Stern heirs. (Starwood comes from German Stern—"star"—and Wald—"wood.") Starwood was sold in 1983 to Associated Financial Services, but President Reagan's manager split off to go into business for himself.

Is this a trend? And when the family office, that silent steward of dynastic wealth, opens its doors to hoi polloi, does that create an opportunity for families of lesser means that need financial advice but can't afford an agency of their own?

Or does it make more sense to go to an investment advisor who has always been an investment advisor, never dominated by a single family?

Let us consider in more detail these two standard solutions to family financial management—noting, incidentally, how they tend to grow together. I'll start with some generalities and then examine a few specific examples.

The Family Office

A family office often begins when the original patriarch, perhaps a highly successful businessman, assigns to a trusted administrator, frequently an accountant, the job of keeping track of his personal affairs: monitoring dividends and income, verifying and paying bills, updating insurance, handling chores to do with his house, and the like. Eventually, the tycoon's wife and children may use the apparatus. Then, in response to demands from the family, the Office adds clever ways of getting things done: it has a favorite travel agency and limo-rental company, favored treatment in particular restaurants, and ties with Claridge's and the

Plaza Athénée. It will know a reliable theater-ticket broker, party caterer, and orchestra, a moving company, handymen, and have a good relationship with an employment agency for domestics.

If the husband orders Broadway tickets through his club, his wife will want to do so, too, with the Office keeping track. Some offices have been known to walk clients' dogs; now they may hire professionals and bill the client. At the upper end of the scale, one of our own client families was displaced from the throne of a small country. We helped organize a campaign to try to restore it, in the course of which thousands of letters were written, meetings held, *démarches* made to Congress and the U.N., and the like—without success, alas. Daughters of the rich often become fascinated by horses. If required, the Office may keep an eye on the construction of barns and training facilities, maintain expense records and depreciation schedules. The Office will also count the members' days of residence in each state or country so that they don't tumble by mistake into a high-tax jurisdiction.

In time, the patriarch's accountant hires a secretary and takes on his own assistant. It's easy for the family to get addicted to not having to pay bills and balance checkbooks, so the Office becomes progressively more indispensable. Indeed, thanks to its convenience, the second generation may never learn how to write a check, read a bank statement, or follow a budget.

Eventually, the patriarch starts to worry about what will happen when he is no longer there to guide the family. Having noted the unworldliness of his children (which, indeed, he has helped to bring about) he will probably put their inheritance into trusts. He then adds a family lawyer and an investment specialist to the team.

When he dies, the manager of the Office finds himself in charge of things. If the Office has developed strong investment skills, everything should carry on well enough. If, on the contrary, it has evolved into essentially an accounting and hand-holding operation of the obsequious sort, it may well lose the toughness of mind required to make money with money.

Infantilization

Perhaps at this point we start to see some weakening of the moral fiber of the family—"infantilization," as a younger Rockefeller has called it—and a corresponding increase in the muscle of the Office. In one case I know of, two sons of the original account- ant, now formed into a company of their own that still manages the family's affairs, have a yearly meeting with the descendants of the patriarch. The two sons—themselves in middle age—sit on one side of a table facing the assembled posterity. They deliver a report on the family's affairs, answer questions, and, after a break for lunch, engage in some hesitant futurology (they're not inves- tors). In this particular instance only one member of the third generation, now eighteen strong, is pursuing a conventional business career. None, therefore, could presume to displace from control of their affairs the two sons of the original assistant. This phenomenon is familiar to students of history: the Shoguns dominating the imperial family in Japan, the mayors of the palace elbowing aside the Merovingians. It is likely to have a debilitating effect on the original dynasty, unless in the third or fourth generation a palace revolution puts the hired managers back in their place.

Here's a tale from my own experience, disguised slightly. A pair of Cleveland businessmen founded a tube-manufacturing company. They were highly successful. The second generation continued to build the company. The third generation lost interest in business and sold the company over the heads of management to a German group for $30 million. (*Their* children, the fourth generation, have little inclination to do anything at all.)

The Germans then discovered that they couldn't run the company from a distance and sold it back, via a leveraged buyout, to six key executives, at about the price they had bought it for three years earlier. These executives made several moves that they had been restrained from performing before they were owners. After barely eighteen months they resold the improved company to a New York Stock Exchange corporation for approx- imately $100 million, making themselves a profit of about $70 million! The executives all became wealthy . . . and clients of ours, as it happened. The third- and fourth-generation children of the original founders are fit to be tied.

Now we are helping the families of the six executives to set up trusts and charitable foundations in such a manner that their children will escape the enfeebling result of too much money that befell the founding family—they hope. Since right before their eyes is the depressing example of that dynasty, whose loss of vigor created the opportunity for our clients, and since they are highly intelligent and able, they should succeed in this delicate problem if anybody can—for a generation or two, anyway.

The hard-bitten and realistic ways in which they avoid such degeneration in Boston, whose tradition of money management is older and at least as good as New York's, is illustrated by the story of a friend of mine from an eminent family there. He was asked to step into his father's study a few days before starting as a freshman at college. His father showed him how much the tuition and expenses came to, then handed him a stack of note forms calling for repayment of the entire amount over a period of years after graduation. My friend was startled, but signed. He got into the habit of hard work, which, indeed, he came to enjoy. He's kept it ever since.

Metamorphosis

In any event, if by degrees the family loses its spunk, the Office will usually also begin to stagnate. The personnel become older and less imaginative; providing prompt and accurate accounts becomes a higher virtue than foreseeing dangers and seizing opportunities.

Some of the more alert family members will start wanting to make their own arrangements. If trust provisions lock them into the Office, they may become irritable, like a chained dog. Otherwise, many family offices discover the same solution: Admit clients, and let any family members leave who want to. The service will thus be kept competitive both in price and in performance. I am all for this solution, which seems to me to produce only benefits without any significant disadvantages, as long as the new clients get exactly the same treatment as the old family ones. A risk is that if the Office is mediocre or worse in its investment skills, then in the loosened-up structure it may be deserted by a number of the family members. Too bad! In any event, such a family office has now emerged from its chrysalis and metamorphosed into an investment-counsel firm.

Investment Advisors

In the early years of the investment counsel business the services offered were crude by today's standards. I like the tale of the New York clubman in the terrible 1930s who glanced at his watch, sprang up, and announced to the crowd at the bar that he had to run: He was going to see an investment counselor. The others were impressed. Not many had enough cash to pay their dues, and scarcely required help investing the surplus.

After an hour the member came back, thoughtful. "Well, how did it go?" asked the others. "First, he asked me how much money I had," answered the member, taking a big swallow of his drink. "I told him, $200,000." "What did he say to do?" asked another member. "He told me to put $190,000 into U.S. Treasury bonds." The circle nodded wisely. Can't be too careful! "And what about the other $10,000?" "He said to give it to him!"

Originally, many investment counselors limited their advice to suggesting whether you should be in stocks or bonds or mortgages. They have come quite a way since those days. Now a full-service firm tells you *which* stocks or bonds to buy, and handles taxes, real estate, oil and gas, venture capital—dozens of things. This type of firm came into existence in the early 1930s to provide individuals with the sorts of investment services offered by a family office.

There seems to be some inverse relationship between the investment acumen of a firm and its skill in trusts, taxes, and other aspects of personal finance. When a law firm, skilled in trust and estate administration, or a team of accountants that has looked after a family's affairs evolves into a full-service office for a number of families, often it will be perfect at handling executorships, paying bills, and doing taxes—but will not have the investment skill of a money-management firm that has depended on performance to build its name. Sometimes, indeed, like Charles Pratt & Co., it will farm out the investment function altogether. Similarly, if a money-management firm moves into estate planning and the like, it will usually not be as capable in those fields as an accounting or legal-based firm. Other than that, there is no one mode that governs. Styles in firms range from opulent to shabby, old-fashioned to trendy, aggressive to passive, investment driven to personal-service driven.

Less and less, however, are the big investment counsel firms or bank trust departments really interested in providing the hand-holding kind of family office service. One reason is the explosive growth of corporate pension-fund management, which has drawn off many of the abler practitioners. (Karl Marx's dream has come true, although not in the way he expected it to: Our workers' pension funds are now the largest owners of corporate America.) It's hard to give equal weight to the problems of a family whose accounts total $400,000 and to a $50-million pension fund you're also looking after. To give absolutely equal attention to the smaller account you must be motivated, like a craftsman, by professional satisfaction, not by wanting to make a lot of money. And personal service is expensive to provide. So most investment firms, which do want to make a lot of money, are moving toward the pension area as fast as they can. I was startled to realize while researching this subject that our own company is apparently the largest pure family-oriented investment-counsel firm in New York. Curiously, investment-counsel firms that only advise the institutional customer whether to buy stocks or bonds have now reappeared. The service is called "asset allocation strategy" and commands substantial fees.*

It's hard for banks to provide truly "personal banking services," just because of their size and their rapid personnel turnover. Here's an episode I would have given a lot to have seen. I heard about it from a client, a member of a substantial New York family ("Mr. Oldname") who had asked for a meeting with the head of his bank's personal-banking division ("Mr. Biggo") to complain about inattention to his affairs. Lunch was proposed. From the bank's side, there was Mr. Biggo, a couple of investment people, and the man in charge of the relationship, whom I'll call Mr. Contact, together with the latter's assistant.

Mr. Oldname arrived promptly, with the courtesy of the aristocrat, and was chatting with Mr. Contact and the assistant.

---

*Although it doesn't necessarily work. A *Wall Street Journal* article of May 16, 1989, showed that at the start of the powerful 1989 market rise the most fully invested of the ten large services was only 55 percent in stocks; three had no stocks at all, and three had only 10 to 30 percent.

Then arrived the two investment men, and finally Mr. Biggo. That dignitary strode firmly up to Mr. Contact, pumped his hand vigorously, and said heartily, "Hello, Mr. Oldname! It's great to see you again. You're looking wonderful!" The real Mr. Oldname stared in stupefaction, while poor Mr. Contact turned green.

The Older Person

Elderly people with no relatives living nearby can become quite dependent on their family office or investment counselor or law firm. This follows simply from the flagging business energy of the client. Tasks that would have been handled with enthusiasm at forty may be boring and difficult at sixty, and quite out of the question for a seventy-year-old widow. In all such cases, a team that has been continuously surveying the family's affairs for fifteen or twenty years and understands the interplay between the generations can be extremely useful. For instance, we once had the case of the dishonest companion of an elderly woman client who had moved to Miami. After a while we noticed some odd withdrawals of capital. An accountant went down to investigate and soon realized that our client's companion had been helping herself with both hands. She had even forged her employer's signature on a check to buy herself a Cadillac! We sent another woman from the office down to stay with the client while we went through the painful but necessary ritual of notifying the police, packing off the companion, persuading the dealer to take back the Cadillac, and so forth.

Who Pays the Tab?

Investment-counsel firms have a sliding scale of fees: They may charge, for example, 1 percent on the first million of capital, ¾ percent on the next million, and so on down. When there are a number of portfolios—children's trusts and the like—the manager always aggregates the whole collection for billing purposes. The family then faces the following puzzle: If the overall fortune is $5 million, and the fee starts at 1 percent per annum on the first million and is down to ¼ percent by the last, how should the cost be divided? Should the total fee be applied evenly pro rata over the entire capital? Or should the older and richer generation pay the fee at the higher rate, considering that it's tax deductible? This would give the later generation—in, presumably, a more modest bracket—the benefit of the lower rate. Usually the second solution is adopted. The senior generation assumes more than its share of the burden, as a form of intergenerational tax planning.

The SEC, incidentally, now permits registered investment advisors to receive performance incentives in the form of a participation in capital gains, heretofore generally limited to hedge-fund operators and the like. This arrangement, which encourages taking excessive risks with the client's money, probably won't (and shouldn't) appeal too much to the old-money world.

To Hell with the Cheese, Let Me Out of the Trap

Investment counselors regularly have to extract their clients from failing venture-capital deals. I'm sure that all of my peers in this profession have had such cases. A rich older man (now, alas, called in Wall Street jargon a "high net worth senior citizen"), attracted by the idea of a prestigious retirement occupation, puts up some capital to back a company promoter and becomes chairman of the new enterprise. However, through overoptimism, bad management, dishonesty, or all three, things go wrong. If the backer, hypnotized, is unwise enough to put up more and more money as things degenerate, or if he has endorsed the company's paper, he can end up in a serious pickle. Often one has to hire a lawyer and technical consultant, pull everything apart, and then force a sale—or at least make the promoter develop proposals to raise additional money from outside sources—instead of following the lazy solution of getting it all from the client. (It's also healthy to bring in outside money because the investors may well be tougher or more resourceful than the client feels he can be, given the history of his relationship with the promoter.)

Lawrence Coolidge, a Boston investment counselor, describes another variation of the detoxification problem. A client came to his office accompanied by the leader of a cult he was on the point of joining, to pick up his stocks and bonds; he wanted to turn them over to the cult, which required a vow of poverty. Coolidge invited the client into his office and closed the door. While the swami cooled his heels outside with the briefcase he had brought to carry off the bundle of securities, the client, at Coolidge's insistence, executed a deed of gift then and there: achieving his objective of poverty, to be sure, but for the benefit of his family, not the cult.

Trusts

Coolidge's firm, by the way, along with others, encourages clients to form revocable trusts, a handy means of hanging on to capital. There are two main kinds of trust: irrevocable and revocable. In the former, one permanently turns property over to independent trustees who manage it in the interest of the beneficiaries. A husband often leaves the income from his estate to his wife for life, for instance, with the principal to his children or grandchildren thereafter. Such trusts frequently produce considerable tax savings.

Revocable (also called *inter vivos* or living) trusts, on the other hand, are a way for an individual to package himself financially for management purposes. They do not ordinarily have any tax effect. As the name implies, the settlor or grantor can undo the whole business with a stroke of the pen. Many family offices (particularly, I observe, in Boston) are fond of revocable trusts, and have each family member create one, which is then managed by the trustees. This permits a relatively carefree existence, if that's what you want. If you feel like embarking on a world cruise, off you go: The trustees pay the bills and take care of everything while you're away. If you need more traveler's checks, you just send a cable.

Of course, this costs money, and requires an extra tax return. So why bother? One of the best reasons is that it interposes a level of control, a brake, between the individual and the fortune. "HAVE FOUND ENCHANTING CHALET IN BARILOCHE" cables the excited beneficiary, "ONLY $200,000, REDUCED FROM $400,000." "UNWISE," cables back the trustee, gloomily. The grantor *could* just dissolve the trust and buy the chalet, but somehow rarely does. An even better example is the imprudent girl beneficiary who becomes enamored of a Greek playboy on the Riviera. He

wants her to put $800,000 into a marina on Corfu or a game
lodge in Kenya. "I'd love to, Iannis," breathes the infatuated
damsel, "but I've got to ask the Office." "Why?" demands her
admirer. "Can't you just do what you want? It's your money,
isn't it?" "Oh, but I have to," she replies. "We always ask the
Office." Rightly! By the time the trustees' squad of glassy-eyed
deal-killers have brought realism to the cash-flow projections and
redone the legal arrangements, our young lady should discover
whether Iannis is really interested in her or just her bank account.

This example suggests the quasi-sacerdotal function with
which the family office sometimes becomes invested. The Office,
like a Shinto shrine, acts as the bridge between the present generation and its ancestors, the curator of its *lares* and *penates*. Thus
the New York office of one old family maintains its register of
births and deaths, keeps up the family cemetery on Long Island,
and records who's buried where—the family itself having long
ago abandoned the estates they once built out there, either for
Florida or the cemetery itself.

Today, in any event, as I mentioned at the outset, this priestly
role is being made available to outside clients, as many a family
office opens to the public. And of course, when you reach the fifth
generation of family, with, say, 150 cousins, including many with
different names, you essentially have multiple-client families
anyway. Here are some examples.

Room 5600

This modest title covers a staff of 200 that manages the affairs of
some 80 members of the Rockefeller family from a suite at the
top of Rockefeller Center. It has been an extraordinarily secretive
operation, which talks little to the press or anyone else. The
rapacious original John D., who founded Standard Oil, made
about $900 million—equivalent to perhaps ten billion today. Late
in life he began to contribute substantial amounts to charity. In
1934 his son John D., Jr., set up five trusts for his children of
about $50 million each. These trusts today control 90 percent of
Rockefeller Group, Inc. (formerly, Rockefeller Center, Inc.).

The Group, in turn, has four principal holdings: Rockefeller
Center Properties, Inc., which owns Rockefeller Center's twelve

art-deco buildings in the heart of Manhattan appraised at $1.6 billion; four other buildings in the same complex worth perhaps $1 billion; and Cushman & Wakefield, Inc., the real estate company bought from RCA in 1976 for about $25 million and probably now worth over $125 million. Also, there are Rockefeller Center Development Corporation, which holds properties outside Rockefeller Center itself; Rockefeller Center Telecommunications Corporation, set up to provide "state-of-the-art" telecommunications services, initially to Center tenants, and now to the public; and Radio City Music Hall Productions, Inc. Outlet Company, which operates seven TV and four radio stations, was bought in 1984 for $332 million, and sold again in 1986 for over $600 million.

The fourth main holding, Venrock Associates, a family venture-capital limited partnership, runs about $150 million and has invested in both public and private companies, including Apollo Computer, Apple Computer—of which it was the largest initial backer—Businessland, Centocor, Convergent Technologies, Evans & Sutherland, Intel, and Mentor Graphics. In the early years the key decisions were made by Laurance S. Rockefeller, a highly experienced venture capitalist. Today, none of the general partners are Rockefellers.

Every Rockefeller generation has tended to keep control for as long as possible. The third generation, for instance—"the Brothers"—yearned to escape the authority of their father, John D., Jr. Lindsley Kimball recounts in *The Rockefellers: An American Dynasty** how "Winthrop came to me with tears streaming down his face and said, 'Oh, how I wish I could do *something* on my own.' " And sister Abby describes a curious meeting with Don O'Brien, Richardson Dilworth, seven or eight assorted people from the Office and an accountant named Joe Lee:

> They handed out a little red portfolio with all "my" investments in it. Everything was so altogether done that I could hardly feel like a participant. Dilworth suggested to Lee that he run through my investments. He did, giving me a little synopsis of what each was doing. He got to Exxon and said, "Well, here's an old friend." Then

*By Peter Collier and David Horowitz (New York: Holt Rinehart & Winston, 1976).

came Mobil, and he says, "Now, Mobil is a kind of little sister to Exxon." That kind of stuff. Good-humored, but clearly meant to put distance between me and the money and leave in question the degree to which it is *mine*. It worked. I felt like I had a mask over my face and was being laid out ready for an operation. Room 5600 is an institutional replica of my father's manner; it prevents one from asking questions that might explain its inner logic.

Some of the fourth-generation Rockefellers have kicked up their heels in recent years, including backing philanthropies that the original John D. would have deplored. Laura, daughter of Laurance S. Rockefeller, declaims, "It's very hard to get rid of the money in a way that does more good than harm. One of the ways is to subsidize people who are trying to change the system and get rid of people like us." This desire to atone visibly for the sins of a patriarch, which in its extreme form might be called the Patty Hearst syndrome, is found in many rich families. The descendants often enter liberal politics, in the fashion of the Kennedys or Averell Harriman.

The fourth-generation Rockefellers have generally been kept on a tight leash, receiving only a fraction of the full income earned by their trusts, but there are now twenty-two of them, together with fifty or so in the fifth generation. A number of the fourth are deeply involved with philanthropic concerns for which they need money, while the fifth generation, not surprisingly, often feel they should have cash to live on and to finance business interests. All concerned were startled to find from a study done in 1983 that the income on total assets of the Rockefeller Group amounted to only about 1 percent a year. One reason is that Rockefeller Center, the centerpiece of the family's wealth, traditionally has not been run to maximize profit. The Center is said to spend more money on maintenance per square foot than any other such office block in New York. Also, a number of long-term Rockefeller Center leases were signed in the early 1970s at roughly $26.50 per square foot, compared to twice that for recent leases in the area; only as the old leases expire can they be renewed at higher rates. And Radio City Music Hall has lost money for decades, if full taxes and overhead are charged to it. Every now and again the family decides to close it, whereupon a vast neighborhood hubbub arises and they relent.

About the time that all this was sinking in, David Rockefeller, chairman of Rockefeller Group, Inc., hired Richard Voell as president to try to turn things around. Voell was a logical choice, since he had been active in the salvage of Penn Central, rationalizing its extensive real estate assets and helping it diversify into other businesses, as well as doing a similar job for Beatrice Companies.

Voell found that the Rockefeller Group was well along in making $2 billion of real estate commitments in areas that included a serious risk of oversupply, including Houston and Dallas, so he pulled back from those projects. While he was at it he jettisoned an oil and gas venture and a container company.

The 1984 purchase of Outlet Company for $332 million was financed largely through debt, as was a payment of $400 million to Columbia University for the land under Rockefeller Center, so for a while the debt service on these massive obligations largely devoured the Group's cash income. To create some liquidity, both to oblige family members needing cash and to create a fund for new opportunities, Mr. Voell turned to Rockefeller Center. An outright sale would have incurred estimated taxes of $400 million. Instead, he came up with one of the largest property-financing transactions in history, a real estate investment trust called Rockefeller Center Properties, Inc.

The trust, which holds the original twelve Rockefeller Center buildings, sold $750 million in common stock, plus $550 million in Eurobonds, mostly convertible into stock in the year 2000, representing a total value of $1.3 billion. The idea of becoming a partner with the Rockefellers has given the deal a certain attraction. But as analysts studied this transaction, it was increasingly perceived as a better deal for the Rockefellers than for the new investors. Optimistic assumptions about New York City commercial real estate occupancy rates have been necessary to justify the value of the common stock. It took all the drum beating and hype that the selling group could command to move the shares, which indeed were selling at or below the offering price long after, despite a huge advance in the general market. The Rockefellers are only one of many groups of New York real estate magnates that, while professing confidence in the future of

Manhattan office buildings, have chosen this moment to admit the public as "partners."

Then in 1986 Voell sold Outlet Company—only bought in 1984—for $625 million. What do you do with almost $2 billion? First, pay down the Group's debts. After that, Voell would doubtless be glad to apply his entrepreneurial talents to building up a multi-industry holding company, which perhaps could be taken public on the New York Stock Exchange. To create further liquidity for family members who wanted to sell, some outside investors have been brought into Rockefeller Group itself: the family of Italian auto tycoon Gianni Agnelli, along with Texas centimillionaire Belton Kleberg Johnson.

As I mentioned, Room 5600 has also formed a small internal trust company. And it is reasonable to expect that Rockefeller Trust will eventually seek outside clients. If it does, it will be imitating the family office of a rival clan, the Phippses.

Bessemer Trust

Henry Phipps grew up next to Andrew Carnegie (properly pronounced Car-NAY-gie) in Allegheny City, Pennsylvania. His father was a shoemaker who used to employ Carnegie's mother as a "binder." Henry Phipps himself was good at figures. He became an accountant for Andrew Carnegie, who was then building up his huge steel company, and later Carnegie's partner. When J. P. Morgan conceived of United States Steel, he realized that the wily Carnegie's holdings were an indispensable component. In a famous meeting between the two, Morgan is said to have asked, "What's your price?" Carnegie pushed a piece of paper with figures on it across the table. Morgan glared at it (his usual expression) and nodded. It worked out to about $226 million for Carnegie, more than double what he had sought a short time before, and $43 million for Phipps—roughly a billion in today's money. Receiving the news, Phipps burbled, "Ain't Andy wonderful!" Afterward, Carnegie, encountering Morgan, said wistfully, "I should have asked for $100 million more." "I should have paid it," Morgan responded crisply. This revelation did not make Carnegie's day.

Henry Phipps turned to philanthropy on an immense scale:

clinics, public baths, playgrounds, libraries. The next generation, however, had different concerns. Henry's children, Amy (Guest), John, Helen (Martin), Henry C., and Howard, felt strongly that charity should begin and, if necessary, end at home. They built palaces, notably John's at Old Westbury, which had three polo fields, just in case. The Phipps children at one point owned a third of Palm Beach. When John moved between these two social centers he (or the family office) convoked a nine-car special train: three cars for the family and its retainers, three for the trunks, and another three for the polo ponies and their tack.

All this was organized financially under an extraordinary structure called the Family Plan. Henry Phipps placed nearly all the assets that he did not give away in a series of trusts. To manage each trust, he appointed a family instrument, Bessemer Trust Company of New Jersey, jointly with a family member. But Bessemer is in turn owned by the trusts it manages, and is controlled by family members under a formula giving much greater authority to the older generations.

Even more singular, the trusts themselves generally contain one main holding: Bessemer Securities, a Phipps family investing company, which buys stocks and bonds, real estate, oil and gas, venture-capital deals, and so forth. Its shares can only be sold to other members of the family. Thus, there is no way a low-ranking member can have a direct say in the management of his own assets. Funded with $75 million in 1911, Bessemer Securities had by 1987 grown to $1.5 billion. Although that's an impressive figure, it actually works out to a bit over 3.7 percent per annum compounded, after taxes and distributions, of course. Bessemer Securities buys the same stocks for its Phipps clients as Bessemer Trust does, but also goes into private deals that are not necessarily shared with Bessemer Trust.

The personal services then offered by Bessemer were the most extensive of any family office, with John Phipps's nine-car special trains at the high end, but practically anything one could desire going down from there. The Office would open and close the house in Palm Beach, rush around the staff plumber if the toilet got stuck, mow the lawn and fix the roof, hire servants, bring the boat down from Newport, and of course walk the dog if the family sailed off to Eleuthera. Major chores, such as a repainting, were rebilled. The rest of these services, which chiefly benefited the second and third generations, constituted, in effect, a large unreported—and thus untaxed—dividend. Very nice, although not exactly in the spirit of the tax laws.

By the time the Family Plan reached the fourth and fifth generations down from the original Henry Phipps, however, restlessness emerged here and there among the troops.

A 1957 study by auditors Lybrand, Ross Brothers & Montgomery found a pattern of insider transactions among certain Bessemer trustees and executives and held that Bessemer had done much less well for its beneficiaries than an outside investment company might have. With that, third-generation family member Esmond B. Martin began a legal struggle to extract his trust from the Bessemer structure. Some investments in real estate that lost the family $87 million in the early 1970s didn't help morale. (Old Henry Phipps believed in real estate instead of bonds, but he never used borrowed money to buy it—only cash.) After the land debacle Esmond Martin was joined by his first cousin, polo-playing Winston Guest, whose extravagant existence had obliged him to sell off his Palm Beach estate and many of his antiques and art works. Their legal efforts produced only modest results until 1974. In that year Bessemer, to pay for its own modernization, sought to levy retroactive commissions on the trusts it managed. The ensuing brouhaha saw Martin and Guest joined by Guest's sister, Diana Manning, and another cousin, Margaret Boegner. This time the result was a victory for the dissidents: A New Jersey court cut the commissions by almost half.

During all this time the family was paying millions of dollars a year more in taxes than it needed to, because Bessemer's earnings were subject to corporate tax, followed by personal taxes when the money was distributed to the trusts. So after a while Winston's son, Frederick Guest, II, joined the group seeking to wriggle out from the Family Plan.

Then, in the early 1970s, Bessemer made a wise decision: to bring in outside accounts, in addition to looking after the affairs of its 200 Phippses. To see outsiders paying the same fees blunted the criticism of the less happy family members. "Going public" means subjecting your performance to analysis by outside clients who can leave if they aren't happy, and so keeps you on your toes. Having a larger mass to work with both spreads the overhead and makes it possible to hire better people.

In recent years, thanks to superior performance, good management, and a gilt-edged image, accounts under management have risen to some $5 billion. Fees from the Phipps trusts are only a third of the total. Bessemer looks for large accounts only: Its minimum annual fee is $45,000, based on an exceptionally stiff 1 percent on capital all the way to $3 million before scaling down, and 1.25 percent a year on "emerging growth" and foreign securities. (The foreign investments have, in fact, done poorly.) In recent years Bessemer's best performers have been its balanced portfolios, which have fared outstandingly well, followed by its equity accounts.

Still, one piece of advice Bessemer—or, for that matter, Room 5600—will probably never give its clients is to model their trust arrangements on the Phipps Family Plan!

The Fall and Rise of U.S. Trust

We have considered family offices; now let us look at the oldest American investment management firm, U.S. Trust Company of New York, which opened in 1853, with the advanced notion, for that day, of not only acting as trustee for its clients but also giving them advice on their investments.

In those days common stocks were a curiosity. There were only twenty-four issues traded on the New York Stock Exchange, compared with thousands today. So the idea of diversifying one's holdings through stocks and bonds—and even less through mutual funds and real estate investment trusts—practically didn't exist. Trust assets were likely to be in real estate or other tangible property that the trustee or owner could manage personally.

But as industry proliferated at the beginning of this century, the wealth of a typical prosperous family usually fragmented into holdings of a number of companies, so that the rich needed professional help in looking after their fortunes. U.S. Trust came into its own. The other well-known trust companies that grew up with this century have mostly turned into commercial banks, leaving their trust work as a sideline. U.S. Trust, while it did build up its commercial side somewhat, always emphasized trusts.

Now it is one of the handful of trust purists within the banking field. Also, its customers need cash from time to time: Even six-figure executives sometimes need a loan. So for a modest eighth of a percentage point, say, *over* the rate they would pay at other banks, U.S. Trust customers are whisked through the application process to collect their funds. They don't seem to mind the extra cost, as the price of the hand-holding.

At one time, U.S. Trust was the blue chip of bank trustees: staffed by wise, experienced trust officers, who knew about life, money, and families. My own maternal grandfather, a Morgan partner, put his trusts for his children and grandchildren there as a matter of course.

But so often success prepares the way for complacency and thus for trouble. "The Trust Company," as for a while it grandly called itself, became almost a club, and lost the tough-minded originality required for survival in a difficult, competitive world containing such puzzles as inflation, high-tech, social change, and the Japanese. Everything got too graceful.

The quick road to investment disaster is losing one's sense of the perils of trendiness. In the stock market you can only make money by doing what everybody else is not doing. If you join in some collective euphoria or panic, you can lose a bundle. One way to avoid that is to have a wise, experienced czar in charge, like Morgan's Longstreet Hinton in the old days: one who understands the investment game through and through, and has the authority to force changes when necessary. He can select and control the young tigers, and the clients can see he really knows the whole world as it is, not just in the sterile form of computer printouts. (Plato's parable of the cave applies marvelously to the flat, shadowy knowledge one derives from numerical data.) But when the old czar passes from the scene he may be replaced by one of the narrow-minded tigers, who will probably mess things up. After that, the directors may bring in a new manager from the commercial side of the bank, with a mandate to impose order and restore profitability. However, not being an investment man he will have trouble bringing sound investment practice and farsighted strategy to a confused situation.

U.S. Trust relearned all this the hard way. It was whipsawed by the growth-stock mania of the early 1970s—the "one-decision stock" heresy. The idea then was that a few companies—the "nifty fifty" or "vestal virgins"—were vastly more desirable holdings than the rest because once you bought them you could hold them forever. You needed to think no more about the subject. That was going to make for ease of management, and splendid profits for all concerned.

Alas, in 1974 and thereafter this religion, as all Wall Street religions eventually must, collapsed. From 50, 60, or even 70 times earnings many of the nifty fifty—Avon Products, Polaroid, Xerox—declined to 10 or less times earnings, and often lower earnings at that. Once again, the trees failed to grow up to the sky. Portfolios that had loaded up on such stocks at high prices sustained fearful losses. Worse, when the market started to recover, it wasn't the growth stocks but the "smokestack" stocks that led the way—U.S. Steel, General Motors, and so forth.

U.S. Trust fired the "favorite fifty" managers and hired new ones who often threw out the "one-decision" growth stocks near their lows, just as they were starting to recover, and bought into the "smokestack" stocks near their interim highs.

So there was yet another round of firings, accompanied by many spontaneous departures. At the bottom, U.S. Trust's research department had shrunk from twenty to four! The bank is over a century old and likes to talk of continuity. But to the customer, continuity means people, not the date on the certificate of incorporation. A client had little sense of continuity after being introduced to five successive heads of the pension department between 1976 and 1979.

All this didn't help performance, which was subnormal through the mid-seventies. In fact, a former drawing card, the pooled pension and profit-sharing account, ranked in last place out of 172 such funds nationwide in 1978, as reported in the *American Banker*.

The turmoil on the investment side was matched by confusion in policy. The bank had started offering personal financial services and tax shelters to its customers. Tax-shelter investment is inherently risky: The tax break wouldn't be there otherwise. But some of the trust company's choices were disastrous, including Home-Stake Oil and Western Properties, which led to a class-action suit against U.S. Trust by its own customers. As a result of all this,

U.S. Trust became one of the handful of old-line money-management firms that was running less capital in the mid-eighties than a decade before.

Finally, in 1979, the directors turned to Daniel P. Davison, a Groton-Harvard Morgan Guaranty veteran, and a commercial banker rather than an investment man. Davison didn't shrink from brutal steps. After he had studied the situation he simply closed down the tax-shelter activity and much of the personal financial-planning business. He also gave up international banking and deemphasized both pension management and lending to big corporations, where the bank's relatively small size meant that it could only get the crumbs from the table.

A few years later he made the ultimate hard decision and took the bank out of commercial banking entirely! Here is a pruned version of his explanation of this move.

> The problem in a nutshell is that the commercial banking market has greatly diminished and the numbers of players in the market have vastly increased.
>
> The diminishment of the commercial banking market started when a relatively dormant financial instrument known as commercial paper forgot its place in the financial establishment, where it had been financing international trade, and crept into the financing of business inventories and temporary corporate needs, traditionally the fiefdom of commercial banks.
>
> One illustration should suffice: When I made my first banking call in 1962, there was about $2 billion in commercial paper outstanding. When I, along with my bank, finally abandoned the business in 1987, there was $79 billion outstanding in nonfinancial corporate paper.
>
> There are *no* commercial banking prospects with large corporations. A more efficient financing method has evolved. The business is dead and beyond recall.
>
> At this point, enter also Mr. Michael Milken and 'junk' bonds. It seems to me history is beginning to repeat itself as another financial instrument starts to disintermediate [i.e., leapfrog] the banks in one of the key remaining commercial banking markets. It is estimated that the high-yield market grew from $8 billion in 1977 to a current total outstanding of $150 billion.
>
> Foreign banks have long had a foothold in the U.S. banking scene, but it is relatively recently that they have become active

domestic lenders. Ten years ago, the foreign-bank share of domestic commercial and industrial lending was 8 percent of the market. This has grown, according to the latest figures (1987), to 16 percent. The equivalent dollar volume is up from $17 billion in 1977 to $91 billion in 1987.

Congress and the state legislatures decided one of the solutions to the thrift problem was to give them broader banking powers, permitting them to make commercial and industrial loans. This poured gasoline on not one but two fires. The commercial banking market had a new set of credit suppliers, which the commercial banks needed like a hole in the head. The thrifts were presented with the opportunity of losing large sums of money rapidly instead of slowly through negative interest margins. Not surprisingly, as a group these inexperienced lenders jumped at the opportunity to immolate themselves. What had been a bad situation became a national disaster, which if it doesn't precipitate a financial panic will in all likelihood smolder into the twenty-first century.

Having drastically slimmed down the organization, Davison concentrated on the bank's traditional business of managing trusts and private portfolios for substantial individuals. "I think it's best to concentrate on basic blocking and tackling," he says, and (in a pleasantly scrambled metaphor) "stay close to home base." So far, his efforts, after a painful initial period, have been successful. The bank's return on its own capital has risen, portfolio performance is keeping up with the averages, and the bank has updated (or backdated) its image by opening a small midtown branch in the handsome old James Goodwin house (built by McKim, Mead & White) at 11 West 54th Street, closer to its carriage-trade customers. There's also a tile-roofed subsidiary in Palm Beach. Talk of sale of the whole bank, current some years ago, is heard no more.

For the Fifty-fourth Street branch, Edwina Sandys was commissioned to do a suitable sculpture for the foyer. It turned out to be a man—bearing a distinct resemblance to the CEO himself—walking a dog. Davison denies that staff members walk dogs—although it is imaginable that they might hire dog walkers, not to mention cooks, maids, and other help, to spare clients undue stress. Other attentions include helping clients arrange to stay in nursing homes, forwarding allowance checks to children in boarding schools, and even typing their term papers. The company has also made wedding and funeral arrangements. On the other hand, where such services used to be included in the hefty fees, they cost extra these days.

Some amenities have disappeared under Davison. Tea carts and huge vases of flowers used to be routine, but no more. Three of the eight Williamsburg-style dining rooms, where clients lunched cozily with their trust officers, have been turned into offices.

To avoid a repetition of the fatal period during which the trust company took strong—and wrong—positions on the investment outlook, and thus ruined overall performance, the stock-picking authority has in essence been given back to the portfolio managers, rather than dictated from on high. This is a safer position from the standpoint of the institution, although not necessarily better for long-term results than finding a really able man to set general policy.

"There are multitudes of people who claim to be champions of the poor, the disadvantaged, and the helpless," Davison likes to say, "but as far as I know, we are the only self-advertised reverse Robin Hood."

Family Office or Investment Counsel Firm?

With the Phippses and other wealthy families now offering to share their savvy with the needy rich, should one rush, funds permitting, to take advantage of this opportunity? Or should one look for a traditional investment counselor? I don't think there's a general answer. It requires individual analysis. The personal-service aspect is easy to assess, like a hotel: If they have what you want, good. But the investment side is much harder to evaluate. Almost every firm can produce a good performance record, *if* it can choose the starting date and define the categories being measured: A dull "equity" account can become a good "balanced" account, for example. And anyway, the unsuccessful practitioners join up with good ones, and acquire their history and performance record, just the way when several banks merge over a period of years, the date of the oldest one becomes the date of the surviving entity. So you have to look deeper than that. To evaluate investment success, you have to analyze how performance is achieved and then be knowledgeable enough to draw the conclusions. Not easy!

Here are some general comments. As I said at the outset, to preserve capital a family needs to give its best attention to how the problem is being handled, like a monarch supervising his government. Many a well-known family office has failed to do its job, and the family, *déclassée*, has dropped off the map. Indeed, it almost always happens sooner or later. So a famous old name on a firm is not necessarily a guarantee of quality, only of price. If, soothed by its bland atmosphere, your family stops paying close attention, you may well be worse off than before.

Then, investing is ultimately an individual affair, like hunting, not a collective one, like choral singing. You therefore need to get to know the individual investment decision-maker, and to possess enough familiarity with his craft to assess his decisions. Always make notes on his explanations. Most skillful investors lose their superiority because they get too busy and become distracted. They join boards of directors, take frequent trips, give lectures, write lots of letters (even, heaven forfend, books), and talk at length to clients. If permitted, the clientele will eventually swamp the outstanding investor. So the client needs to keep an eye on the key investment man, but not to the point of interfering with his work.

Finally, an experienced person can usually tell when he's in the presence of a dedicated, keen, and able group, and when he's being skillfully soft-soaped. One day or another, almost all human enterprises reach the latter stage. The same is true of size. In the golden words of Professor C. Northcote Parkinson, growth means complexity, and complexity, decay. It's unlikely that anything very large will remain outstanding. To use Wall Street jargon, a structure tends to regress to the mean, to become bland and bureaucratic. It's time then to consider moving on. So if you're qualified to judge and can take the trouble, you may well be better off finding a group that's still in its dynamic phase. Still, most people seeking exceptional investment advice don't succeed in their quest, any more than most people can find excellent, cheap, undiscovered restaurants.

As we have seen, for the outsider, clubbing together with a

rich family in a family office turned investment counsel firm
should ensure that someone with clout is there following what's
happening and, one hopes, making management changes when
necessary. But don't take that for granted!

6

George Michaelis

Apostle of Return on
Equity

George Michaelis's mother was born in Russia. In 1920 she left
to be raised by an aunt in Germany, leaving again for Brussels
after Hitler came to power. There she met Michaelis's father, a
patent attorney involved in a color photo chemical business. The
Michaelis family, being Jewish, fled Brussels for Marseilles in late
1940. George's father was interned by the Vichy government in
a camp in the Pyrenees for six months. Upon his release, the
family went on to Martinique, and thence to California, where
his partner had moved to be close to the movie industry. Mr.
Michaelis, however, died within two weeks of arriving in
America, leaving his widow and George himself, then aged four.

When Michaelis was growing up, it was assumed that he was
going to become a painter. Then at school he discovered an
aptitude for mathematics. Realizing that he would never be able
to live on his earnings as a painter, he concentrated on
engineering while at UCLA from 1954 to 1957. After a semester
at Berkeley in 1958, he went to the Harvard Business School,
graduating in 1960. He feels now that he received a poor education overall, because of its narrow emphasis on mathematics and
engineering. He is all too aware of the subjects he has missed,
such as history and philosophy. He likes to buy books on such
matters but can't find time to read them, so they have a way of
piling up. As a result, when he bought a new house some years
ago, book space turned out to be a major problem. (I suggested
that one solution is to get books from a lending library: The

return date on the slip provides an incentive to get through the book in the two or three weeks available.)

Michaelis is well built, of medium height, with a dark complexion. He has a neat, dark black mustache and black hair thinning on top. Some deep wrinkles furrow his lower forehead. He speaks in a melodious baritone. He met his attractive blond second wife, Mimi, on a trip to Sun Valley in 1982. A son by his first marriage is studying at Berkeley.

After leaving business school he had a series of operating and financial jobs with Norton Simon and with Whitaker Corporation, and from 1969 to 1971 was with Hohenberg & Associates, a Memphis cotton-broking family business that wanted to go into venture capital. Then Graham Henderson, a friend who had joined Source Capital, a closed-end fund listed on the New York Stock Exchange, called on Michaelis for help. Source had been started in 1968 by Fred Carr, one of the hot "gunslinger" operators of that period. In the fashion of the times, Carr sought to force superior performance by speculating in unseasoned issues, private placements, and illiquid "letter stock" on which the fund, for its appraisal purposes, could put almost any value it wanted. Alas, when the market declined in 1969–70, the fund collapsed. So George Michaelis, with an investment philosophy that could scarcely be more different from Carr's, was brought over in 1971. He became head of the fund and its parent company, First Pacific Advisors, in 1977.

He was exceedingly successful. A calculation in the summer of 1988 showed that over the previous fifteen years the total return of Source Capital was exactly three times that of the S&P 500: The gross gain was 1200 percent, compared with 400 percent for the general market, a record exceeded by only sixteen other funds, putting it in the top 5 percent of all equity funds. From 1977, when Michaelis became president, through 1987, the compound annual total return was 19 percent. Among closed-end funds, Source Capital has often ranked first in performance.

Source Capital sold at a sharp discount from its asset value for a number of years. (Warren Buffett bought in when it was selling for only half its net asset value.) So, in 1976 the management decided to start paying out a 10-percent annual return based on net asset value. The plan worked: The discount was largely closed. Of course, had the fund not earned the 10 percent, they would have had to dip into capital, but in fact this has only happened once, in 1987. The dividend has been increased fourteen times over twelve years for a total increase of 150 percent.

Michaelis confesses he is not primarily motivated to maximize the return on his investments, because of his low tolerance for risk. He maintains excess liquidity: A 10-percent cash position is the lowest he ever gets. He was 20 percent in cash before the Crash of 1987, and in mid-1988 his cash level was 18 percent. "You must invest with the one hundred-year storm in mind," he says. "It is most unlikely to occur, but one has to survive if it ever does." And 1974, he adds, was not as bad as markets can get.

Michaelis tries very hard to avoid significant losses and does not mind lagging the averages if the market breaks away in the upside. As a result, however, his fund only had one quarter from 1973 to 1988 in which it declined more than the S&P 500. In the dreadful fourth quarter of 1987 it fell only 13.5 percent, compared to the S&P's 22.5 percent.

"One must understand the interaction between intelligence and emotion as they in turn respond to the market. As Robert Kirby, head of Capital Guardian Trust, has observed, 'Stocks are much more volatile than the businesses they represent.' Thus, a successful investment man must be able to control his emotions. There are many ways to succeed in this business, but you must learn what you are good at in order to play to those strengths. I have a low tolerance for risk, so I like it best when I am at no disadvantage because of that characteristic." In my own language, if you have a weak serve, there's no use coming in to the net behind it.

He describes himself as not very flexible. "I know that," he says, "but I like to do things my own way so that I can't be frightened off by the inevitable setbacks." Michaelis doesn't try to buy into the dynamic phase of a growth company. Had he been lucky enough to buy H&R Block stock when the company had 1 percent of the national tax-preparation business, he would probably have sold it when it got to 2 percent of the national total, he says; thus, he rarely gets the ten to one upside play.

Benjamin Graham's investment credo was to buy assets at a discount. Michaelis suggests a variation: *Earning power is as valuable as assets, therefore try to buy earning power at a discount.* If appropriate, Michaelis is prepared to pay up for the assets in a business if the earning power is exceptional.

What he does is quite easy to explain in a mechanistic way, says Michaelis. The companies he buys tend to have several specific features; here are a few:

1. They are high-profit enterprises: Normally they would have a high return on equity and a high return on total assets. And the high return on equity should be sustainable.

2. Their earning power is not hostage to the business cycle.

3. They are successful for identifiable reasons. There is usually a good reason for a 25-to-30-percent return on capital. If he finds such a return, he tries to figure out where it's coming from. Having worked that out, he tries to evaluate the sustainability of those high returns. Then he can have ample confidence in the whole investment.

Michaelis is also debt-averse. The debt level of companies that he holds tends to be about 15 percent of total assets, compared to 25 percent for the average company in the S&P 500. High-profitability companies generally do not have lots of debt, and what debt there is tends to get worked off by the operations of the business. Such companies thus have an additional margin of safety. And if a wonderful opportunity comes along, the cash-rich company can take advantage of it.

By insisting on high returns on equity and a low debt ratio, Michaelis is kept out of new ventures and companies whose fortunes may (but also may not) be going to change for the better in the future. He invariably holds well-established businesses with long histories of stable operations.

"Kellogg, for example, is an extraordinarily successful company," he says. "When I tried to work out the explanation, I eventually perceived that it was a matter of economy of scale. By controlling 40 percent of their principal market and being two and a half times as large as their next competitor, they can advertise and manufacture more efficiently, and their consumption pattern is not as volatile as it would be if they just had a modest market position. As a result, even if Kellogg did a bad job for four or five years—not that this has ever happened—it would only suffer some loss of market share. Its basic profitability would not be eroded.

"*Cash generation is an excellent test of high profitability.* Take Melville, which we've held since 1970. Can you imagine a business worth $350 million that would generate $2 billion worth of cash in a decade? And yet that's what Melville was able to do. Actually, Kellogg is much the same: The only question is what they will do with the cash. Melville is extraordinary in that it has operated very successfully in a business without obvious barriers to entry by other competitors.

"Its management is outstanding in the operation of stores in shopping centers, and has extended its skill from its start in footwear retailing to clothing, drugs, toys, and home furnishings. But of course the big question is, will the future be like the past?

"The return on Melville's equity has averaged 24 percent for the last decade and 23 percent for the last five years. Earnings have increased in each of the past fourteen years, and in twenty-three of the last twenty-four years. Sales, earnings, dividends and book value have all grown at approximately 15 percent per year for the past decade.

"Ten years ago, Melville had $354 million of equity capital, $74 million of long-term debt, and $129 million of cash and equivalents. This last decade Melville has internally financed over $1 billion in net capital investments and acquisitions, and paid about $600 million in dividends, while reducing debt by $20 million and adding over $200 million to cash. This extraordinary cash generation is the result of Melville's high return on capital.

"We foresaw the growth in earnings and dividends which Melville's profitability would create. Over the past four years, this investment has given us a 21-percent compound annual return, not achieved through market revaluation of an initially under-valued stock. There's been some revaluation—from 10.5 to 12.0 times earnings—but even without that the investment would have earned us 18 percent over the period. In other words our 21-percent return derived from the successful operation of the business over this period rather than from any ability to predict stock price movements.

"Another company I like a lot, and where you can understand the underlying business, is Bandag. It dominates the business of precured tread rubber for tire retreading. Roy Carver developed the business and patented many aspects of his discoveries. Now his son, Marty Carver, has taken over. The essence is its dealer structure, and the secret of that is that Bandag has tied up the key truck-service outlets almost everywhere in the United States. They do everything possible to make their dealers profitable, and not only in tires. They give them all sorts of services and advice, which they can identify by looking around their dealer network. For instance, if they find that one dealer has an outstanding computer system for that business, they pass it on to the others. In this way they hone the business to generate high returns and enormous cash flow. The cash flow is used to buy back stock of the company. They've retired 40 percent of the stock over the past ten years.

"Marsh & McLennan is another company I think very well of. Together with Johnson & Higgins, which is private, Marsh-Mac is the biggest insurance-service company in the world. It handles the Fortune 500 companies, and now that it has bought Bowring in London, world corporate business in general as well. *As a result, they have become a tollgate for the largest companies: There are only so many places a giant company can go to get its insurance handled, and if a customer leaves one of them he will have to go to one of the others.* Within the same industry Marsh-Mac's business is inherently better than American International Group's business, for while AIG is well run, Marsh-Mac earns a much higher return on its capital and with much less inherent risk. And Proposition 103 in California, putting a ceiling on automobile insurance premiums, is a horrible portent. The old-line companies in California must have done a dreadful PR job. Marsh-Mac should be largely immune, though.

"Again in the insurance world, Crawford Company is most interesting. It's one of the largest insurance adjustors in the country: Claims adjustment is about half of their total business. They have offices everywhere—over 700 locations in the U.S. and Canada. So it's the service company of choice when a prime carrier doesn't have an office in a territory where an adjustment is required. It's illogical for a larger company to go into competition with Crawford in a territory where it can only reasonably hope to get the second or third call from a potential customer. As they grew from about a quarter to over a third of the adjustment market, they gained enormous economies of scale. Of course, compared to the big recent earnings gains of some other consumer companies, their growth doesn't seem so remarkable, but it's extremely steady.

"The property and casualty insurance cycle is now deteriorating, and the market is failing to discriminate: When underwriters are unpopular, Marsh-Mac and Crawford are unpopular, too, quite illogically. Marsh-Mac should earn $4 to $5 a share for the next few years or so, and then move up to $7 to $9. One of these days the stock will jump. When it does, it could happen so fast that you wouldn't be able to move in time to take advantage of it. In other words, it's best to own it now and just wait patiently for the move.

"Bristol-Myers is another wonderful outfit we own a lot of. It has enjoyed thirty-five years of consecutive earnings growth, has a 25-percent return on equity, substantial excess cash, and virtually no debt. It, too, is under a cloud, because the company is believed to have head-on competition coming from Nestlé in the infant-formula business. Also, a significant part of that business—and this is even true of Abbott Labs—is funded by government and is going on a competitive-bid basis, meaning increased competition. But that's essentially a one-year problem: After you've moved to the lower level of profitability the growth should resume at the same rate. Abbott and Bristol-Myers have both been weak in the marketplace for the same reason: competition in infant formula, which, however, affects Abbott more." Should one own both? Michaelis does. "They are slightly different companies. Bristol is more the typical company I like; with Abbott, you get better growth but a lower dividend."

At a price, Michaelis is enthusiastic about IBM. It earns 20 to 25 percent on its equity even in a poor year, has more cash than debt, and by being so much larger than its competitors can spend money on research and development far more effectively than its rivals. "IBM is a company that in the early eighties began planning for considerably more rapid growth—15 percent to 18 percent in their mainframe corporate business—than developed.

The big customers didn't bite, partly because of the dollar, partly because of the fallout from lower oil prices. And the rapid advance of computing power meant that many big mainframes weren't needed. Given IBM's no-layoff policy, this meant several years of profit squeeze. But now with the mid-sized product line available and capacity in both personnel, through attrition, and manufacturing in line with sales, things have come back in balance. The AS400—IBM's new mid-range computer—has an excellent backlog. So earnings should grow at a mid-teen rate for a few years. At around ten times earnings, you have a bargain. They're repurchasing stock aggressively and can afford to raise the dividend for the first time in five years."

Rohr is one investment that didn't work out as expected. Although Michaelis spotted several of the operating and financial characteristics he likes, he missed some hazards. Rohr has a very strong position in a particular specialty, aircraft engine nacelles and landing gear. It has essentially no competitors except those plane manufacturers who make these parts for themselves, which few do. Thus, it has about 90 percent of its market. It sells its parts whether the prime manufacturer is McDonnell Douglas or Airbus or Boeing. The company wisely refuses to diversify out of the business it dominates. When Michaelis made the investment it was virtually debt-free and had a large cash hoard. What he missed was that Rohr was in the late stages of many of its programs, with resulting high cash flow. The business changed as the company was forced to take on a lot more risk in developing a series of longer-term programs. Its negotiating position was not strong, as Boeing, for example, could undertake some of these programs itself. Rohr's cash hoard disappeared when the company developed a negative cash flow of $150 million. Michaelis sold out in September 1987 with a small profit.

Price Consciousness

Michaelis follows about 300 companies but will only consider purchase when the stock seems extremely cheap. Michaelis usually has a target price for his stock. When it falls below the target, he starts buying; the lower it gets, the more he buys. So, he says, he never expects to buy all or even most of his stock near its bottom. There's a risk that he may start to buy too soon, but he hopes still to be a buyer when the bottom does come along.

Michaelis is likely to sell when a stock gets moderately overpriced. He suspects he tends to sell too soon. He describes himself as a "singles hitter," one who is not looking for doubles and triples. Thus, as mentioned, he sold H&R Block at the end of 1986 at 25½. He had held it for a long time, but it seemed expensive. "H&R Block has a wonderful tax-preparation business: no inventories, no receivables, and no fixed assets. But there's no way to make it grow. So the question is what the company will do with its cash besides paying a high dividend. The key, therefore, is not to pay too much for the stock, which is another way of saying not to hold it after it gets too overpriced."

Michaelis likes to build his position in a stock over a period of time. "There's nothing like owning a stock for giving you a feeling for it," he says.

He rarely invests in themes. He says he has never been successful in the type of reasoning that says, for instance, "Americans are getting older, so let's invest in . . . in. . . . " "The crutches business," I suggested. Michaelis grinned.

Finance Company Bonds

When it comes to bonds, Michaelis either accepts no credit risk at all or else wants to be significantly compensated. So he never buys AA corporate bonds, as against AAA. For an advantage of thirty basis points, it isn't worth it. When the bond market does become interesting, he will buy governments. On the other hand, at a price Michaelis is prepared to "play around" in suspect bonds. As a shareholder he feels a compulsion to stick to top quality, but in the bond business is prepared to go into potential bankruptcies. For instance, he made a lot of money in Texaco bonds after the company declared bankruptcy, and similarly bought Chrysler Financial bonds some years ago when Chrysler itself got into desperate financial trouble.

He professes to a good understanding of finance companies. In bankruptcy their senior bonds make quite safe investments unless there is actual fraud involved. *In every recent bankruptcy or potential bankruptcy that he knows of, the underlying finance company presented an investment opportunity with considerably less risk than the bonds of the parent company.* He did splendidly, for example, in the bonds of International Harvester (now Navistar) Financial, which he still owns and expects to hold to maturity.

"If one buys the senior obligations of a finance company at a big discount from face value because there is a general fear of bankruptcy, it is almost impossible to lose money," Michaelis says, "assuming there's meaningful equity underneath." If the finance company actually goes into bankruptcy, interest payments stop and cash builds up, the creditors claim acceleration, and get paid off sooner. If it doesn't, you earn the return implied by the distressed price. He cites Montgomery Ward and International Harvester, where one earned a high return on one's money even though no actual bankruptcy developed.

When LTV went into bankruptcy, a subsidiary had two bond issues outstanding secured by the Indiana plant that was one of the best installations in the LTV Steel complex. The very day LTV went into Chapter 11, Michaelis bought all the bonds in sight at substantial discounts from face value. They recovered to par. Similarly, when Wickes went into bankruptcy, he was ready and waiting, since he had been eyeing its subsidiary, Gamble Credit.

A number of investors are now interested in this maneuver, such as Randy Smith of R. D. Smith & Co., Mutual Shares, whose assets increased from about $150 million in 1982 to over $2 billion six years later, and Martin J. Whitman. Whitman, who teaches part time at Yale, has employees who haunt the courtrooms, ferreting out the opportunities. As a result of new competition the returns have become less spectacular. Still, Michaelis likes this specialized arena, because it is not correlated to the stock market. In 1987, for example, he made 40 percent on his Texaco bonds, even though the market was down 30 percent. Michaelis sticks to the simpler side of the business, generally the senior securities, because he doesn't want to spend an enormous amount of his time on the intricacies of subordinate paper valuation.

Specialized Bonds

Leveraged recapitalization companies, such as Multimedia and Harte-Hanks, sometimes create junior bonds. Both of these are zero coupon for five years, and then turn into 16-percent bonds. The underlying businesses are completely solid. The Harte-Hanks zeros have risen because the company is buying them in. Michaelis has sold them and switched to Multimedia, where he has a "big, big" position. The question now is what to do with that money when he gets it back.

In searching for defensive holdings, Michaelis has said that he generally finds convertible debentures issued in the European market (Euro converts) more attractive than U.S. issues. Euro converts are available on a wide range of U.S. and foreign issuers. Virtually all are issued with fifteen-year maturities, against twenty-five years for their domestic equivalents. Furthermore, many Euro converts provide for redemption at the holder's option, generally five years after issuance, often at prices substantially above the offering price. And, some Euro converts are not subordinated, as is universal in the U.S. market. Such senior issues have substantially less credit risk, making them considerably more attractive.

For example, Ford Motor Company had a number of senior convertible issues available in the Euro market, with maturities from 1983 to 1988. Michaelis bought them in the late 1970s and early 1980s as a low-risk way of capitalizing on a resurgence of Ford's profitability. As senior obligations with relatively short maturities, these bonds represented a far safer way to invest in Ford than owning the underlying common stock. All these bonds have been converted.

Although he focuses primarily on U.S. companies, Michaelis occasionally responds to attractive opportunities in foreign bonds. Lonrho is a major international company with interests in natural resources, publishing, and resort hotels. Based in England and run by existing management for the past twenty-five years, Lonrho has been highly successful. Noting that Michael Price of Mutual Shares was buying a major position in early 1987 in Lonrho common, Michaelis realized that the Lonrho convertible bonds were highly attractive, at a slight discount to their equity conversion value of 115, and providing a redemption put at 118 in April of 1991. The bonds provided a full equity participation, and even if that never happened the redemption put guaranteed a modest profit. Similar opportunities have existed from time to time in outstanding British companies, such as Pearson and Fisons, as well as such U.S. issuers as American Brands, American General, CBS, Eastman Kodak, St. Paul Companies, and Texaco, among others.

Derivative Instruments

Michaelis distrusts futures, options, hedges, "insurance," and the other devices that are now flooding the marketplace as fast as they can be dreamed up by ingenious promoters.

He says that he sees as many people failing in the investment world because they are too smart as because they are too stupid. Intellectually active persons are attracted to intellectually elegant conceptions, such as complicated derivative instruments, which are likely to distract them from the more fundamental truths, which are often simple and obvious. For instance, he says, "Take CMOs—collateralized mortgage obligations. You cut up a package of mortgages into separate streams: short, medium, and long-term bits. An investor who wants to get his money back in a hurry can buy into a five-year pool, and a long-term investor can go into a twenty-year pool. That's very fine and clever. However, in a market collapse you would have chaos and horrible mispricing. How can you translate each stream of earnings back to its present value, factoring in the different prepayment rights and the like, which most people in the market wouldn't even know about? Right now, Salomon and Merrill Lynch make a nominal market in these instruments, but if there were ever a real market collapse they couldn't handle it. There would be a mess. For instance, look at the plain vanilla Ginnie Mae market: we've put out a Ginnie Mae jumbo for bids, and gotten spreads of two to three points in what is supposed to be a perfectly orderly market!

"In the bull market in bonds that began in 1985, during which rates dropped from 14 percent to 7 percent, the mortgage bankers stopped bothering to hedge. The bankers who didn't hedge made a killing, whereas those who matched the maturity of their mortgages with their borrowings in the market didn't do nearly as well. Then in March 1987 the bear market in bonds suddenly began, and the bankers who hadn't hedged rushed into the forward market to cover themselves. That created incredible inefficiencies. We were prepared to buy their bonds, but by going out two or three months into the futures market we could get the equivalent of 15 percent on our money. So the bankers, by relying on the existence of what turned out to be a weak support, actually took greater risks than they normally would have."

Asset-rich Companies

Michaelis points out that thanks to the LBO mania, there are very few companies that are still cheap on an asset basis. There are probably almost none of any size that would satisfy the Benjamin Graham criteria.

If there are any, they are likely to be in the technology sector, which as we spoke was still severely beaten down; many of the companies had cash hoards that amounted to a significant part of their market price.

"Fine," I replied, "but the problem is that you know that a high-technology company is actually going to spend that cash to achieve its objectives. So sooner or later it will cease to be an asset play and once again be a high-tech prospect."

Michaelis, amused, told the story of Daisy Systems. "When I first noticed Daisy, before the 1987 crash, it was selling for 7½, had no debt, and held 4 in cash. After the crash it got down to 5. My wife and I bought some at 5½. It doubled, and I sold some at 10½. Then it drifted back down to 8. All of a sudden it was the object of a contested takeover. It got rid of all its liquidity in order to make itself less attractive and went heavily into debt. Now the stock is down to 4¼!"

Honesty

Michaelis comments sardonically that it is interesting to see the judgment of the market on the honesty of management as reflected in the premium or discount of voting versus nonvoting stock. "For instance, there was a high premium in the voting stock of Resorts International, which implied that the market expected Donald Trump to abuse his inside position . . . as he did. Brown Foreman's voting stock, on the contrary, sells at a discount. The investing public is confident that management will act honestly and fairly."

Michaelis adds that he prefers a company run with the old-fashioned Protestant work ethic, whose management has been in place for a long time and has a large ownership share. The compensation of the top executives is often outrageous in a company where management thinks in terms of exploiting its position rather than acting as stewards of the shareholders' interest.

Investment Management

Michaelis remarked that Warren Buffett often asks someone he is talking to on the telephone, "What are you buying?" Once, walking with Michaelis, he demanded, "Give me your three best investment ideas." But Buffett never says anything about his own transactions. To be sure, he might be copied by other investors. When he started buying stock in Twentieth Century Industries, for example, the shares started to rise as the word got out, from 16 to over 20, in a declining market. Three or four years earlier, on the contrary, Buffett's transactions had made little difference: Nobody seemed interested at the time in his purchase of General Foods.

Michaelis does not think that the business of managing funds for corporate pension funds will be as satisfactory in the future as it has been in the past. In the first place, most plans are overfunded, so the growth of incoming capital shouldn't be as strong in the future. Another problem is mergers and acquisitions, as illustrated by Michaelis's experience with PSA, once a client. Guided by Rick Guerin, PSA had a value-oriented investment approach, with four or five managers and heavy over-funding in its pension plan. USAir bought it and decided that there were too many value managers. Michaelis lost the account.

Performance Monitoring

And what about performance monitoring?

"A necessary evil. It has further shortened the time horizon of corporate investors, which works to their disadvantage. That business got a boost back in the latter 1970s, when, after the debacle of 1974 and the passage of ERISA,* a number of corporate investors decided that they needed protection against what they perceived as the inadequacies of the big banks' trust departments. Those trust departments had been urging their corporate clients to invest their pensions in grossly overvalued 'one-decision' stocks, the rage at that time. The corporate treasurers realized that their own stocks were vastly more attractive than the high-multiple issues that their advisors were putting them into, so after the collapse they lost confidence in those advisors. Thus, the performance monitors seemed to offer a ready-made solution. But in fact they don't help much. They tell you how you would do if the future were the same as the past—but it won't be.

"The latest notion, put forward by Barr Rosenberg's old firm, BARRA, is developing the 'normal portfolio.' They have ten or so categories: big caps, small caps, beta, high-tech, growth, and so on. Then they rate the managers, not against the S&P but against the category standard. This is a consultant's dream, since they change the 'normal portfolio' all the time, and thus wed the client to the consultant."

"The consultant has essentially taken over," I suggested: "You've gone onto autopilot."

"Exactly," said Michaelis.

Advice

As mentioned, Michaelis likes Kellogg, Melville, Bandag, Marsh & McLennan, Crawford, Bristol-Myers, and IBM. He would shun investment of new capital today in any company with significant economic exposure to a recession. With Bristol-Myers and Melville he feels reasonably comfortable. But an economic environment where plant utilization has reached an eight-year high and unemployment is at a fourteen-year low can't be considered

*The 1974 Employee Retirement Income Security Act.

promising. There's no slack in the system. In the summer of 1988 he considered stocks much cheaper than in the summer of 1987, but interest rates were higher, and heading the wrong way. (Right afterwards short rates shot up.) So the 12 to 13 times earnings that many stocks sell at is acceptable, but still, a long way from the price-earnings ratios of 8 or 9 that were available a few years ago.

In the 1970s, Michaelis observes, one could buy shares of many outstanding businesses at reasonable prices. If a stock then got too high there was enough opportunity in the market so that one could sell it to buy another that was still undervalued. For instance, when H&R Block became overpriced the market was broad enough to permit him to sell it and buy Deluxe Check Printers instead. Today that is much harder. He never foresaw that there would be too much competition for really good stocks to permit that flexibility. So Michaelis thinks that selling too soon is a bigger sin today than it was.

At a time when the market is selling for twice book value and yielding little over 3 percent, valuations can erode as well as expand, he observes. Indeed, in the last five years, valuation expansion has been the overwhelming source of equity returns, even when good bargains were available. So now there is a particular premium on finding very, very good businesses: "coffee can" stocks, to quote an expression of Robert Kirby—stocks you can leave alone for five years with confidence that they will grow steadily in value over that time.

7

John Neff

Discipline, Patience . . . and Income

Which money manager would financial professionals choose to manage their own money?

A good answer is one whose name most nonprofessionals wouldn't recognize: John Neff, of Berwyn, Pennsylvania. He is little known outside the investment community because he is modest, gray, and unspectacular. He looks and acts not at all the Wall Street hotshot, but the midwestern executive: nice house a little way out of town; wife of over thirty years; modest, unfashionable, and slightly messy clothes; no magnificent paneled office, just the disorderly, paper-strewn den one expects of a college department head. He doesn't get into the newspapers, least of all the gossip columns. Main Line society has never heard of him. And yet, he is one of the most eminent financial figures in the country. Indeed, in several polls he has, as I say, been the choice of money managers to manage their own money.

Neff has run the Windsor Fund for twenty-four years. Through 1988 it had a compound annual return of 14.3 percent versus the S&P's 9.4 percent over the same period. For the last twenty years he has also run Gemini Fund, a closed-end dual-purpose investment company. It, too, has grown at about twice the rate of the market. Finally, over the more than ten-year period he has run Qualified Dividend Portfolio One it has yet again approximately doubled the performance of the market. Year in, year out he is likely to be among the top 5 percent in performance of all funds. So it's no accident. Even more surprising, he keeps up this performance even though he now runs a huge amount of capital. Windsor Fund by itself has for a number of years been in the multi-billion-dollar class, and at $5.9 billion at year-end 1988 has become one of the largest equity-and-income funds in the country.

Neff is a "value" man: He only buys when a stock is too cheap and acting badly at that moment in the market; and he infallibly sells when, by his criteria, it is too expensive, again always when it is acting strongly in the market. He buys stocks that are dull, or to use his own terms, "misunderstood and woebegone," and sells when the market has gotten the point and has bid them up to fair value, or over fair value. In this he is a classic contrarian.

Where Neff differs from his peers is in his *insistence on income. Neff claims that the market usually overpays for the prospect of growth*, but growth stocks have two drawbacks: First, they suffer from high mortality—that is, often the growth doesn't continue long enough after it has been recognized—and second, *you can often get a better total return from a slower-growth company that is paying a high dividend right now.*

He argues the case this way: Suppose you begin on January 1 with a stock whose earnings and thus, eventually, stock price will grow 15 percent a year, but which has to reinvest essentially all its free cash to finance that growth. So you get almost no income. On December 31 you hope to be 15 percent richer through capital gain. Now suppose on the contrary you have a stock with a much more modest growth rate, such as 10 percent, but which, because it does not have to finance high growth, can afford to pay a comfortable dividend—5 percent, say. Here again, at the end of the year you are 15 percent richer: partly because the stock is 10 percent more valuable through earnings growth, and partly because you have put 5 percent in your pocket from dividends.

But which of these strategies is the best? Neff is utterly convinced that it's the latter, because it's more certain.

Most of the time, of course, dividends have been taxed much more heavily than capital gains, so after-tax growth has been much more attractive. At the moment, however, the two tax rates are similar. And in any event, a large part of Neff's constituency consists of tax-free pools of capital, such as pension funds.

Part of the reason for the weight given by managers to growth, in addition to the tax considerations, may be that until recently individuals measured their progress by capital appreciation only. Only after the domination of the market by institutional investors did total return become the standard measurement. Also, in looking at his own portfolio appraisal, an investor enjoys the sight of huge capital gains, and is less aware of the amount of income that he has (or has not) collected. An institution is intensely conscious of that past income.

The future dean of the "growth and income" school was born in Wauseon, Ohio, outside Toledo, in the Depression year 1931. His parents were divorced in 1934. His mother then remarried, to an oil entrepreneur who moved the family all over Michigan and eventually to Texas. Neff attended high school in Corpus Christi. He held outside jobs all the way through school and, having little interest in his classes, received indifferent grades. He was not popular with his fellow students. After graduating he took a variety of factory jobs, including one in a company that made jukeboxes. Meanwhile his own father had prospered in the automobile- and industrial-equipment–supply business, and persuaded Neff to join him. Neff found that experience extremely instructive. His father, he says, taught him the importance of paying great attention to the price you pay. "Merchandise well bought is well sold," his father liked to say.

Neff then spent two years in the Navy, where he learned to be an aviation electronics technician. On receiving his discharge, he resolved to finish his education, and so enrolled in the University of Toledo, studying industrial marketing. His interest was fully aroused, and he graduated summa cum laude. Two of his courses were corporate finance and investment, and he realized that he had found his métier, having previously thought that finance was a world reserved for Ivy Leaguers. While still at the University of Toledo he married his wife, Lilli Tulac, a native Toledoan. The head of Toledo's Department of Finance at that time was Sidney Robbins, an extremely able student of investments, who in fact was given the important job of updating Graham and Dodd's famous *Security Analysis*. So from the first Neff was exposed to the value theory of investment, which is much easier to quantify, and thus to teach, than the growth, or qualitative, approach. Later he attended night school at Case

Western Reserve to earn a master's degree in banking and finance.

Neff hitchhiked to New York during his Christmas vacation of 1954 to see if he could get a job as a stockbroker. He was told by Bache that his voice didn't carry enough authority, and that until it did, they would only take him as a securities analyst. Lilli didn't like New York in any event, so Neff did indeed become a securities analyst, but with Cleveland's National City Bank, where he stayed for eight and a half years.

In time he became head of research for the bank's Trust Department. However, as a Graham and Dodd disciple he believed that the best investments were the least understood, and thus often found himself at odds with the Trust Committee, which preferred big-name stocks that would reassure the customers, even if they didn't make them money. His mentor, Art Boanas, was a dyed-in-the-wool fundamentalist, who insisted that the key to investment success was simply digging deeper than the next fellow, and constantly testing your figures. When you make up your mind, he said, stick to your conclusion; and above all, be patient. This style of investing became Neff's own, and has served him well.

After Cleveland, in 1963, Neff joined Wellington Management in Philadelphia. (That name was chosen because the founders thought that the Iron Duke's title sounded solid.) A year later, in 1964, he was offered the job of portfolio manager for Wellington's Windsor Fund, which had been founded six years earlier.

At Windsor Neff has a staff of four, led by Chuck Freeman, who has been with him for twenty years. Of course, he has access to the parent company's analytical staff of eighteen, located in Boston. He does not discuss his compensation, but he admits to being very comfortably off—"in the good seven figures." Part of his employment package is an incentive fee, so that he and his group get paid more if Windsor performs well. Still, in his private life he operates with the same philosophy that he applies to buying stocks. His house has few frills except for a tennis court, on which he plays a ferocious game on Saturdays. He likes to describe how cheaply he has bought equipment or clothing, shopping for his footgear at Lou's Shoe Bazaar and his jackets at Sym's, a discounter. When his daughter bought a car he studied the deal and sent her back to demand a $500 rebate. In his office he sits in a rocking chair and often ends a phone conversation with a homespun "Okey-doke!" He says that he loves to read history, particularly European, and to travel.

Neff has an earnest, broad, humorous face, with a large chin and a wide, up-curling mouth that reveals a sequence of expressions. His high forehead is surmounted by silver hair, and he wears metal eyeglasses perched on a small nose. He speaks with a gravelly Midwestern voice. A pen is stuck in the pocket of his white shirt. He wears argyle socks.

Sometimes his frugal ways lead to investment opportunities. He was analyzing a company called Burlington Coat Factory Warehouse Corp., and by way of field work sent his wife and daughter to sample the wares of one of the chain's discount stores. They came back with three coats and a strong buy recommendation, which Neff accepted, acquiring half a million shares.

In a somewhat similar way, when Ford brought out its Taurus model Neff became enthusiastic about both the car and the company. Explaining the investment interest of Ford, Neff pointed out that the company had little debt and $9 billion in cash. The difference between Ford's management and GM's, he says, is night and day. GM is arrogant, while the men who run Ford are "home folks," who know how to hold down costs and avoid delusions of grandeur. The president eats with the men from the assembly line, so he knows what they are thinking. A Ford assembly-line worker makes several thousand dollars a year in bonuses, while a GM worker gets next to none. Neff began buying Ford heavily in early 1984, when popular disillusionment with the automobile manufacturers had driven the stock down to $12 a share, two and a half times earnings! Within a year he had accumulated 12.3 million shares at an average price of under $14. Three years later the stock had reached $50 a share and had brought Windsor a profit of almost $500 million.

Neff points out that securities analysts discussing the automobile industry begin by guessing the number of automobiles that will be sold in the following year. Every few months they alter their forecasts to reflect current thinking. They almost never talk about trucks. And yet both Ford and Chrysler derive more of their profit from trucks than they do from cars! Neff believes that two-thirds of Ford trucks are sold to individuals, not businesses. Young people, particularly in the Southwest, buy pickup trucks, and mini-vans are becoming increasingly popular at the expense of station wagons. The U.S. manufacturers have about 85 percent of the domestic market in trucks; the Japanese have trouble competing, since in Japan itself trucks are not nearly as popular as here, so they do not have a big home market on which to develop their export lines. Also, there is a 25 percent tariff on trucks that enter the United States.

In 1980 the University of Pennsylvania asked Neff to run its endowment. Its performance over the previous decade had been the very worst of ninety-four college endowments. Neff reconstructed the portfolio along his usual lines of gray, uninspiring, unpopular but cheap companies. A few of the trustees objected to this approach, urging him to buy the stocks that were exciting investors at the time. This predilection was, of course, a reason why the performance had been poor previously. Neff, however, resisted these urgings, and over the next decade the University of Pennsylvania endowment advanced to the top 5 percent of all such funds.

We discussed Harvard Management and the complicated way it manages the university's capital. "The one I run for Penn couldn't be more different," Neff said. "I keep it simple!" He mentioned, chuckling, that he had asked Walter Cabot, when Cabot took over as manager of Harvard's endowment, "Why don't you just put it all into Windsor?" . . . and added, somewhat unkindly, that in November 1980 he noticed in the *New York Times* that Harvard Management had proudly announced that it was 32 percent in energy stocks, exactly at the top, just before the collapse of OPEC. He himself went 25 percent into oils in 1986, *after* the collapse, when investors were filled with gloom about the prospects for oil. He put 5 percent of his fund—the limit for one stock—in Royal Dutch and 5 percent in Shell T&T—actually different sides of the same enterprise. His lawyers, however, said that for legal purposes they qualified as two different holdings.

Neff shares two characteristics with many other great investors: He was poor as a boy, and he is a compulsive worker now. His stepfather could never seem to do well, and so the family always had to struggle. He says that he resolved early that he would handle money astutely when the time came. He works sixty to seventy hours a week, including fifteen hours each weekend. In the office he concentrates virtually without interruption and drives his staff extremely hard. He is tough and harsh when he feels that a job has not been properly done. On the other hand, he invites staff participation in his decisions, which they like.

Techniques

Neff is quite realistic about his own performance, and in some of Windsor's annual reports, particularly when the news is good, issues a "Report Card" on his transactions. They are often remarkably candid and interesting. (See Appendix VI.) One wishes that other managers would assess their own performance in the same spirit. Of course, not many managers are as fortunately situated as Neff when it comes to reviewing what they have done.

Not surprisingly, given his conservative techniques, Neff's performance tends to rise more slowly than the market in good times, but it also usually declines less when the market is weak.

He points out the importance of skillful executive work in running large portfolios: *The good manager moves faster, particularly in selling on adverse news.* In a bank, when something goes sour in a holding, the managers responsible hate to crawl back before the trust committee and say that they were wrong. (Also, you risk trouble with the beneficiaries if you sell a stock at a loss.) Neff has no such committees to deal with, and also, since he is rarely looking for the same developments as other investors, the change in his opinion is unlikely to coincide with a wholesale exit from a stock. He can slip out of a stock almost as inconspicuously as he entered it.

He tolerates a very high concentration in a few industry groups. For instance, in the 1988 annual report the automotive group reached 22.2 percent of the entire portfolio, banks were 16 percent, and insurance had risen to 13.8 percent in the teeth of gloomy predictions for the underwriting outlook. Including savings and loans, the lending area represented 20.8 percent of Neff's portfolio. Adding insurance, the whole financial sector came to 37 percent. Airlines reached 7.2 percent of the portfolio in 1987, during a period of grim industry news.

In other words, while he has relatively few ideas, he backs them heavily. Indeed, in his 1988 report the ten largest positions represented over half the assets of the $5.9-billion fund. Thus, we see a third of a billion dollars in Citicorp, which many investors shunned for fear it was going broke, over half a billion in Ford, and about three-quarters of a billion in just three insurance companies. That's real self-confidence!

One justification for these high concentrations is that he isn't taking far-out gambles: Since he buys only the very cheapest merchandise, should something go wrong, it hasn't too far to fall.

Bargain Hunting

Neff is considered an outstanding securities analyst. Although in recent years he has not himself ordinarily made company visits, he talks to companies at length. He has a team of analysts working for him, but when a new stock comes into view, he is likely to lead the charge, or, in his own language, to "gang tackle" the problem. By the time he and the team are finished, they should have accumulated the information they require. After almost thirty-five years' experience in his profession, Neff has already bought or studied a high proportion of the companies that he is considering for purchase at any time. In other words, it is often a question of updating his knowledge, rather than starting from scratch.

He is constantly looking at industry groups that are unpopular in the market. He confines his research to stocks with particularly low price-earnings ratios, and, ordinarily, unusually high yields. And, in fact, over the many years that Neff has run Windsor Fund, the average price-earnings ratio of his portfolio has been around a third below that of the general market, while it has on average yielded 2 percent more.

He has described himself as a "low-P/E shooter." However, unlike Benjamin Graham, he is concerned with the underlying nature of the company. He wants a *good* company at a low price. Some of the criteria he insists on are:

1. A sound balance sheet;

2. Satisfactory cash flow;
3. An above average return on equity;
4. Able management;
5. A satisfactory outlook for continued growth;
6. An attractive product or an attractive service;
7. A strong market in which to operate.

This last is a most interesting point. Neff claims that investors tend to pay too much for companies with high growth rates, so they aren't the answer, while no growth means that there is something wrong with the company itself. So the bargains where he does most of his buying often run at about an 8-percent growth rate.

What You Get for What You Pay

Neff has an interesting way of comparing stocks, or groups of stocks, with other stocks and with the overall market. Windsor's portfolio overall has an estimated 9.5-percent growth rate together with a 4.9-percent yield, or a 14.4-percent total return. The average price-earnings ratio of the stocks in the fund is 6. So he divides the 14.4-percent total return by 6, giving 2.3 as what he calls the "what you get for what you pay for it" or "terminal relationship" figure.

In early 1989 the overall market had a growth rate of 8.5 percent and a yield of 3.7 percent, for a total return of 12.2 percent. Dividing this by the market's price-earnings ratio of 11 gives 1.15 as the comparable "what you get for what you pay for it" result. So, by this reckoning Neff's whole portfolio is almost exactly twice as attractive as the market as a whole.

Neff lays out or "arrays" these figures for specific stocks to compare their relative attractiveness. He does find that his earnings estimates for the stocks he buys are usually more optimistic than those of Wall Street in general, or in his term, more "aggressive."

Income in Windsor Fund has grown 17 percent compounded, probably because of Neff's practice of selling stocks that have gone up, and whose yields have therefore fallen, to buy lower-priced stocks with high yields.

How to Buy

In determining the price he is prepared to pay for a stock, Neff projects earnings over a number of years.

Then, he determines a reasonable price-earnings ratio that a normal market should put on those future earnings. This, in turn, gives him a target price several years out. He then calculates the current market's percentage discount from that price, from which he derives the indicated percentage-appreciation potential.

Of course, subjective factors have to enter in to some extent. For instance, if Neff has unusual confidence in the stability of the growth rate, or if he considers management to be exceptionally skillful, then all the figures are adjusted. In reverse, unfavorable factors may reduce the target price.

He calculates the similar consolidated figure for his existing portfolio, which he designates its "hurdle rate."

If the indicated compound growth rate of a stock he wants to buy is not at least as high as the "hurdle rate" of the existing portfolio, then he defers purchase until the stock falls to where it does equal the hurdle rate.

There are, of course, times when he somewhat deforms this method. For instance, if he has raised cash in his portfolio and the market starts up, then he will buy stocks below the hurdle rate in order to get the cash invested. (This is another way of saying that he expects the hurdle rate to rise soon.)

Within the portfolio, Neff weights the holdings according to their calculated appreciation percentage. With seventy to eighty stocks in the portfolio, implying an average size of slightly over 1 percent, he will in practice put 5 percent into one stock if he develops a real conviction; indeed, he will buy several positions of that size within a single group. In other words, if he is confident, he will act with force. And he usually is confident. Regarding the future, for example, Neff's opinion in early 1989 was that the market should hold in the 1900–2200 range on the Dow until investors become convinced that inflation is going to be contained. At that point, long bonds would come down in price, and the stock market would rise.

Neff's method should, one would think, be highly susceptible to the use of computers, to filter through the stocks of target companies and make value comparisons. In fact, however, Windsor does not use computers. Nor does it use the dividend-discount models and other mechanical devices that are favored by some institutional investors. In that way, Neff is surprisingly old-fashioned.

When it comes to actually executing a purchase, Neff is again extremely disciplined. He has his target price, and he waits for the market to come down to that level. He waits and waits, and if the stock doesn't get there, he simply won't buy it. Neff is ordinarily able to buy stocks below their opening prices of the day. That is, in spite of the size in which he deals, he succeeds in buying on intra-day weakness.

How to Sell

Neff's selling discipline has two parts: the market price at which he is willing to sell a stock and the tactics of executing that trade.

As to the target selling price, again it is based on the "hurdle rate" of the whole portfolio. When the market thinks well enough of the prospects of one of his companies so that it rises, in due course the company's further appreciation potential will fall below that of the rest of the portfolio. When it gets down to only 65 percent to 70 percent of the whole portfolio's appreciation potential, Neff starts to sell. He likes to make a substantial sale initially, and then let the rest of the stock go as it moves on up. If it falls back he will stop selling. If it falls enough, he becomes a buyer again.

When the time comes to execute an actual sale on an exchange, Neff is extremely careful. He almost always wants to sell into market strength that day, and avoids accounting for more than a quarter of the trading in a given issue. Of course, if a stock starts running up, it makes less difference to him what proportion of the trading he is responsible for. Here again, Neff can usually sell a stock higher than its opening price on the day of the trade.

The largest element in trading costs is the impact that the transaction has on the market. So the skill of his traders means that Neff's operations have little impact on the price movements of stocks he is dealing in.

Patience

One of Neff's theories is that one should sell a stock before it has achieved its full potential gain. One must leave a sufficient incentive for the next buyer to take the merchandise off your hands.

Still, a feature of Neff's method is that he does not mind waiting almost forever if a stock he owns does not realize its potential. Here he differs from some other "value" buyers, who like to see something happen within a year or two; if it doesn't, they move on. Neff will hold a company for years, as long as its outlook remains satisfactory and it remains cheap relative to the rest of the portfolio.

Dull and Woebegone

Since the stock groups that Neff considers to be good value will virtually always be out of favor in the market and viewed with suspicion by investors, they generally partake of a common characteristic: *A stockbroker would have trouble selling them to a customer.*

For instance, when he made his huge bet in Ford, which I have described, the industry was in deep disfavor among investors. Chrysler's virtual bankruptcy had shaken them, and the news of rising Japanese penetration sounded alarming. So the car companies got down to extremely low prices, and Neff moved in massively. This was true of his commitments in oil, the financial group, and indeed most of his other big conceptions.

Advice

1. *Citicorp.* Investors have been shunning banks. They are all supposed to be insolvent. Having gagged on Third-World debt, the big banks have now in many cases sunk half their equity into wormy leveraged buyouts. But for Neff, these dismal tidings represent much more opportunity than risk. Within the industry, one must discriminate between the sound regional banks, which often have no significant exposure either to LBOs or Third-World loans, and the money-center banks, which do. But within the money-center banks, if you can find one that is underpriced, but

in fact sound, you can do well, since that group is viewed with particular suspicion. Neff cites Citicorp as having the characteristics he wants. He considers its management to be the smartest in the business, and says that the heavy reserves it has set up against developing-country loan losses more than cover the actual risk. If you could extract all Citicorp's LDC loans at a "haircut" of 50 percent and invest the rest in Treasury bills, it would only reduce earnings by about $1 a share, he notes. But Citicorp has achieved a prodigiously successful buildup in its consumer activities. That business, with an extremely solid growth rate, is now worth more than the whole bank is selling for in the market. And Neff points out that Citicorp is now half a consumer bank, with only part of that activity in and around New York City. It has a solid franchise all over America particularly in credit cards, but also in mortgages and small loans. The consumer-banking business should grow at 15 percent a year.

Institutional banking has faltered, ever since the strongest companies learned how to place their own paper in the market, rather than borrowing from their bankers, but Citicorp has shrunk its institutional business to match that loss of opportunity. Citicorp has already raised its common equity to 4 percent of assets, as banks are being required to do. It will continue to strengthen its balance sheet rapidly, as its dividend is only a third of what it earns and it has tax-loss carryforwards from its 1987 writeoff.

What about the big banks' exposure to the hazards of the leveraged-buyout business? Neff wouldn't touch junk bonds, but the banks' loans to the companies are senior to all bonds, are paid down quickly, and should be safe enough.

2. *Delta Airlines*. In much the same way, Neff likes Delta Airlines. "An airline!" one asks. "Aren't they all bust? Don't they all have horrible labor troubles?" "Yes and no," Neff says. That Eastern is in trouble doesn't mean that they all are. Delta has very few labor problems, since it's basically nonunion; the employees are hardworking, it's a reasonably low-cost operation, the company is very well financed, and "it has a predictable earnings stream. So the group is depressed and Delta with it, but Delta is different from the group." Neff holds a lot of Delta stock.

3. *The Thrifts*. An even more alarming industry is the savings-

and-loan associations. Many analysts claim that it will take $100 billion to bring them back to solvency. So the whole group is in deep disfavor. Ahmanson, a California-based thrift, however, appeals to Neff. The company has implanted representative offices in Eastern states. It does not share the troubles of the industry, and yet the stock has been selling for six times eventual earnings.

Neff notes that, like the thrifts, a great many of his holdings are either regulated or semiregulated. Again, this gives rise to investor suspicion, and yet things may not be as bad as all that. So you find bargains.

4. *Restructured Companies.* As to the "stub" stocks, companies that have been recapitalized with only minimal equity, Neff finds them similar to venture-capital deals, except that in ventures you expect to fail in six out of ten tries, whereas with the LBO "stubs" you should probably only lose three out of ten.

5. *Growth Stocks.* In early 1989, Neff felt that the values in growth stocks had improved so markedly against the standard industrials that "even a hard-core value shooter like myself has drifted into that environment," as he puts it. Coming from him, the recommendation carries conviction.

8

Ralph Wanger

Small Metaphors

I hope I will not offend too many of my biographees by saying that the one with writing talent is Ralph Wanger.* Most of them have a lot to say, but only Wanger frames general ideas in picturesque similes that can both delight and amuse a reader. "Most mutual-fund writers write an economic forecast of some sort which is both boring and wrong," Wanger says. "I'd rather be lively and wrong." His Acorn Fund reports, a selection of which follows as Appendix VIII, dispense lessons in history, psychology, and philosophy, as well as investing. Here is a sample:

Zebras have the same problem as institutional portfolio managers. First, both seek profits. For portfolio managers, above-average performance; for zebras, fresh grass.

Secondly, both dislike risk. Portfolio managers can get fired; zebras can get eaten by lions.

Third, both move in herds. They look alike, think alike and stick close together.

If you are a zebra, and live in a herd, the key decision you have to make is where to stand in relation to the rest of the herd. When you think that conditions are safe, the outside of the herd is the best, for there the grass is fresh, while those in the middle see only grass which is half-eaten or trampled down. The aggressive zebras, on the outside of the herd, eat much better.

On the other hand—or other hoof—there comes a time when lions approach. The outside zebras end up as lion lunch, and the

*It's a compulsion to write, more than talent, that makes a writer, though.

skinny zebras in the middle of the pack may eat less well but they are still alive.

A portfolio manager for an institution such as a bank trust department cannot afford to be an Outside Zebra. For him, the optimal strategy is simple: stay in the center of the herd at all times. As long as he continues to buy the popular stocks . . . he cannot be faulted. To quote one portfolio manager, "It really doesn't matter a lot to me what happens to Johnson & Johnson as long as everyone has it and we all go down together." But on the other hand, he cannot afford to try for large gains on unfamiliar stocks which would leave him open to criticism if the idea fails.

Needless to say, this Inside Zebra philosophy doesn't appeal to us as long-term investors.

We have tried to be Outside Zebras most of the time, and there are plenty of claw marks on us.

So much for stock selection. Here is Wanger on market timing:

This time, the zebras are in a canyon, with the lions asleep at the far wall. Every zebra is going to munch grass right up to the lion's nose, then bolt down the trail just before the lion pounces. Unfortunately, it is a narrow trail, and in fact, the zebras will pile up into a helpless clot at the first narrow point and become instant steak tartar. Many large institutions claim that they can do a "market timing" quick switch from stocks to cash, or cash to stocks, for billion-dollar portfolios in a very illiquid market. No way. Any such strategy can only generate a highly volatile market, featuring lots of short but sizable swings as the chartists whipsaw themselves with bad guesses and high transaction costs.

Wanger even hypothesized a "Metaphor Committee," whose "ruthless and unsleeping members . . . can pounce at any time, crushing an overworked simile, dismembering a mixed metaphor, or deflating an unintelligible aphorism." The committee also weighs economic forecasts and mathematical models:

It has become popular in recent years to put one's metaphor into a series of equations which can then be run on a computer, adding a veneer of infallibility implied by the neatly typed-out rows of numbers. . . .

All models have an inherent limitation on their validity, the Cricket Limit. There is a nearly perfect mathematical fit between air temperature and the pitch at which crickets chirp. As the temperature drops, crickets chirp more slowly, down to about 50 degrees Fahrenheit; one might expect the song of the cricket to decline some more in pitch as the night cools from 50 degrees to 45 degrees. This doesn't happen; under 50 degrees, the cricket packs it in, and stops chirping altogether. No matter how reliable the relationship of two variables has been (such as interest rates versus inflation) there is no reason to think the relationship will hold for previously unknown levels, as happens when inflation rates soar.

The late "windfall profits" tax on oil suggested an arresting image:

> This is a good example for the Metaphor Committee: the largest tax increase in history, an excise tax on petroleum, by being deceptively named, has lulled the American people into acceptance.* However, the zeal with which our elected representatives are burrowing into this enormous pile of money (roughly $140 billion)— it was certainly a windfall for them—reminded me of something I had read recently . . . , the cover story of the November 1979 *Scientific American:* "Ecology of the Dung Beetle." This fascinating article described in detail what happens when an elephant dumps its load on the African plain. Three different kinds of beetles show up in minutes. The little ones burrow into the pile, others bury little pieces on the spot, and the third kind, the big ones, scoop out big balls and roll them away. Once you read this fine article, the Senate Finance Committee will never look the same.

Wanger looks for metaphors in investing, he says, in order to grasp the sources of profit and growth in a company, the aims and thinking of the management, the competition and the dangers. "As long as the metaphor remains apt, the stock is a hold; if the reason to own a stock is no longer valid, the stock should be sold."

Starting Out

Wanger is a short man with a round face, which, since he loves little jokes, often bears a quizzical, humorous expression, although in repose it can be dour. He is balding on top, and wears large

---

*The Chinese enjoy unique skills in this domain. The old government, fining farmers who didn't produce their quota of opium, called it a "Laziness Tax." When, fleeing the Japanese, the government vanished into the hinterland, this was styled "Long-Term Defense."

glasses with thin, dark frames. The first time I met him, many years ago, he sat down in my office wearing a black Greek sailor's cap of the type worn by New Yorkers visiting Maine, which he kept on throughout our talk. He has a very quiet voice, approaching a whisper.

Born in Chicago, Wanger received a B.S. and M.S. in Industrial Management from the Massachusetts Institute of Technology. Management is not a science, says Wanger; instead, it is based on a knowledge of psychology, common sense, and a good disposition. "The principles of management don't change. You try to get other people to work in the same direction that you are, and you make sure that your direction is a sensible one. And you try to get someone else blamed if you fail!"

After a dismal job with Continental Casualty, now Continental Group, Wanger entered the investment business in 1960 at Chicago-based Harris Associates, which had begun two years earlier. He says he liked investing because the pay was good and "there's no heavy lifting." He worked as a securities analyst and portfolio manager until Michael B. Harris formed the Acorn Fund. Wanger became portfolio manager, and in February 1977, president. When Harris founded the fund, he did not think it would ever become very large, so only ten million shares were authorized. By 1986 the fund had exhausted this quota and had to seek shareholder permission to issue additional shares.

Wanger married his second wife, Leah Zell, a Harris security analyst, in June 1985. He has three children—Wanger calls them his "old children, i.e., with paychecks"—by his first marriage and two by his second.

Performance

Wanger confesses that to some extent his outstanding record is a function of bureaucratic stalling. He filed for SEC approval of the Acorn Fund in 1969. The okay was only granted six months later. From that exact inception date through year-end 1988 the compound growth rate, ignoring taxes, was about 17 percent. If, however, you begin at the end of calendar 1970 (by which time the fund had advanced 30 percent from inception), the compound growth rate over the period drops to 15 percent, an example of how deceptive statistics can be if not fully analyzed. In any event, for the decade from 1978 through 1988 Acorn grew at 18.8 percent a year compounded, compared with 16.1 percent for the S&P 500.

According to Wanger, Fidelity and some other fund-management groups have incubated infant funds, starting with modest capital. Hot stocks were fed in to generate an outstanding initial record. If the start-up is good enough, they launch the fund publicly. If not, they put it in the deep freeze or merge it. So the records of existing funds sometimes bury less successful components, just as dozens of failed car companies went into General Motors. A compound rate of return in the 12-to-15-percent area, he feels, should be a reasonable objective for a good investor. Indeed, to my mind it's not worth it for most people to try hard to beat that figure, since even 12 percent compounded doubles in six years and will eventually make you rich, if you can avoid breaking the flow. (There's an example later, in "Conclusions.")

One piece of good luck for Acorn, and thus for Wanger, was Houston Oil. In the terrible stock market of 1973–74, Houston's discoveries maintained its stock price, and, Wanger says, "kept Acorn from collapsing during that period. Indeed, without that one stock, there probably wouldn't be an Acorn Fund today."

This was in line with a trend he spotted at the time and articulated in a 1976 report: Since the price of energy was rising, and would rise further, "one should invest in energy producers, and move out of investments in energy users." Similarly, one should invest in companies that make things for energy producers, such as Cameron Iron Works and Mine Safety Appliances.

Philosophy

Wanger's investing philosophy has two essential components:

1. Look for *good small companies*, which are more attractive investments than big ones.

2. Identify the major trends and, unlike T. Rowe Price, who looked for the *leaders* of the trend, buy companies that will *derive benefit* from the trend.

THE "SMALL COMPANY EFFECT"

Growth of a dollar from 1926 to 1988

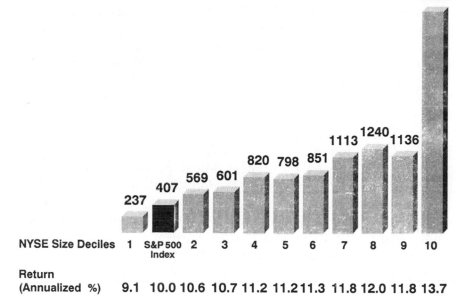

1926-1988 NYSE size decile portfolios with annual rebalancing.

Source: Dimensional Fund Advisors, Inc.

Figure 3

Small Companies

In aggressively seeking smaller companies with superior potential, Wanger capitalizes on the "small firm" phenomenon that University of Chicago professor Rolf Banz documented in 1978. Professor Banz found that companies with low market capitalizations had above-average returns, even after adjusting for their higher risk. (The "small company effect" is shown in Figure 3, above.)

Wanger "wants to buy the stocks of small companies below their economic value, let the companies grow, and resell them as proven successes at full economic value. Individuals often sell small companies below their economic value and buy mature companies at full value, thus providing the other side for our trades."

Even the armies of analysts employed by the large institutions neglect small companies. In 1973 Wanger wrote that his fund "had $14.4 million invested in thirty-nine companies, for an average investment of $369,000 per company. This number of investments gives us diversification without our owning so many stocks that we cannot follow each individual company. Acorn can accumulate an adequate position (let us say $200,000) in any but the smallest class of company. A fund of $100 million or more cannot invest in small companies and still keep its number of holdings to a manageable level, so large institutions, as a rule, put most of their money into large companies." Now, however, his fund has grown to over $500 million. He says, "as the portfolio has grown, the mathematical process controlling the portfolio turns out to be Long Division. Small-company investing turns out to produce average dollar holdings in stock of about three million dollars. So, if we have $500 million to invest, Acorn will end up with 166⅔ names in the portfolio."

To provide this large inventory of potential holdings Wanger collects ideas from a whole farm team of regional and smaller brokerage houses. He gives out annual awards, called the "Scarlet A" awards, to his best sources. "Most institutional money managers like to say that Wall Street research is useless," he says, "but then they take thirty calls a day from Wall Street."

Trends

"I see real change in people's life-styles," says Wanger. "Twenty years ago at parties almost everybody had a cigarette in one hand and a martini in the other. The idea of getting up early and jogging would have seemed absurd. Middle age in those days was a safe harbor against such behavior. But we didn't know what was coming next. Had doctors known what the future held, they should have switched from cardiology to sports medicine. Look at me: Here I am, fifty-three years old and training for a ski race: Nutso!" (He is an avid skier.)

"This profoundly affects how people spend their time and their money. For instance, there are now lots more old people around with bad backs and bad knees—which require treatment and create an economic opportunity for someone."

"For Hillenbrand," I observed. Hillenbrand is a leading American manufacturer of hospital beds and of caskets.

"Hillenbrand gets you sooner or later," said Wanger, wistfully. "Really, though, it's just a well-run company. It's like Worthington Industries. If the two of them swapped managements, there'd be grumbling, but after six months they'd be doing about the same. Both are below-average businesses run by above-average people. *Often you have businesses that are run by geniuses and don't do very well. The competitors are also geniuses, so nobody gains an advantage.* Take the semiconductor companies: Mostek or Fairchild. The semiconductor transformed the world, but until recently the whole industry had probably lost money on balance. Only a tiny handful of companies did well. A far larger number didn't. It's like the oil business: It transformed the world, but many of the companies haven't done too well themselves. Or, indeed, the railroads in the nineteenth century.

"If you had bought all the stocks and all the bonds issues put out by all the railroad companies, you would probably have lost money. The capitalization of the American railroads was an international wealth transfer—a Marshall Plan in reverse. It took the savings represented by the English and Scottish trusts and moved the wealth over here. It couldn't have been done more neatly if it had been planned. The net return to all those investors was probably close to zero."

I grumbled a bit at this, pointing out that the theory of the railroads' rights of way had been to bind the country together, losing money on the carrying business if necessary, but offsetting the loss with the land grants that went with the concession.

"The land rights, of course, were where the money was," said Wanger, "not the carrying business. If you had put $1 million into railroads in 1880, you probably broke even. If you had put it into Chicago real estate, however, you would have made an infinite fortune in the next forty years. By 1910 Chicago, stimulated by rail transport, was the fastest-growing city in the world.

"*In a transforming industry, the big money is made outside the core business.* Going back to transistors, even though the transistor companies as a class didn't do very well, TV broadcasting, cable TV, computers, and data processing have been tremendous businesses. IMS International, for example, bought computers and used them to generate services that were not previously available. Computation has had a constantly declining cost structure: Every year you can do more for less. When I was at CNA Insurance, we installed a $3-million IBM 705 computer system. There were three full-time IBM people on hand just to change tubes. It had a six microsecond cycle time, and a 40K memory. Today, a $2,000 machine could eclipse our $3 million setup. In fact, just three years later CNA couldn't sell its 705 system. For that matter, they couldn't even give it away. It wasn't worth enough to get anybody just to cart it off."

I suggested that the investment business itself was experiencing a huge transformation because of the computer.

"It certainly is," agreed Wanger. "Index funds, data bases: It's scary. Someday you'll be able to go to a computer store and pay $80 for a 'portfolio manager' program. You'll put in everything that's known, and I'll be out of business myself. We're in the middle of a revolution that hasn't stopped revolving. Take computer chess, a good way to track the software industry. An early chess program, Sargon I, could play chess according to the rules, but was slow and crude. A sensible player could beat the machine. Sargon II could play what really looked like a chess game. It was faster, and at my level I was happy to beat it. Sargon III is out now, and if you can beat that one, you're damn lucky. And Sargon IV and V are already coming down the pike. People are refusing to play against computers! It's like this in field after field.

"There's a program now to automate supervisory processes— running a utility company, for instance. The hands-on manager of a utility plant needs to reset the dials constantly to optimize his results according to conditions, such as changes in the grade of coal the plant is using. Today, an 'expert system' can probably do it better. Aviation's another example: The autopilot can already land the plane in conditions where the pilot can't. Soon the human pilot will be a backup in case the autopilot breaks down." This is of course the central point of Tom Wolfe's *The Right Stuff:* For the scientists, a spacecraft is a computer-run machine, in which the "pilot" is just a passenger, like a lab animal; on that occasion, though, the "lab-animal" pilots revolted successfully, since the human-interest side of the project attracted the funding.

"The Chicago banks," Wanger continued, "used to have substantial security-analysis staffs, and ended up performing consistently worse than the averages. Now they've laid off the big staffs and use computers instead. So they've moved up to achieve average results, and at much lower cost. This is disconcerting to those of us who believe that the application of human intelligence to the investment process should provide an added value. I notice, though, that the Vanguard index fund is well up in the top 100 funds."

The Dow Bubble

I raised the question of what I call the bubble in the Dow created by indexing. Every time a pension fund—which would normally have quite strong growth-stock representation—sells a couple of hundred million dollars of stocks and buys the S&P Index, its growth-stock representation is cut somewhat and the standard industrials—the equivalent of the Dow—increased. This self-perpetuating trend has helped produce a superior performance by the standard industrials over the broader averages, which is particularly noticeable if one compares the Dow to the Value Line Average. "That's one of the longest cycles in the financial area," said Wanger: "About ten years from valley to valley. We've now had five years of underperformance of the smaller stocks—since 1983. *So there should be a big kick when the cycle turns. The last time, in 1974, the result was extraordinary.*"

Rising in the East

A big Wanger investment bet is the future prosperity of the Pacific rim. The populations of some of those countries seem to work harder and to have more business sense than anyone else.

So how should the investor take advantage of this development? One way is to focus on what Wanger calls the embourgeoisement of, for instance, Singapore. Some years ago he took a cruise starting from there. On the boat was a Chinese family of nine. The grandmother had come to Singapore as a slave . . .

yes, a slave! Her children, though, were already working in the government. Thanks to entrepreneurship, there is an explosive growth of the middle class in the Pacific. As Wanger noticed, the newly rich go on trips. He has capitalized on this tendency by having three related vehicles in his fund: Cathay Pacific Airlines, based in Hong Kong, and thought by many to be the best airline in the world; Singapore Air; and Malaysian Airline Systems. "Cathay and Singapore Air hire teenage girls, very selectively," he notes. "Not being constrained by government regulations, they then lay them off again in their twenties and hire new ones." Aren't mature women more competent flight attendants than girls? "Yes, but they're not as interesting to look at on a six-hour trip," he answered.

If one wanted to invest in an airline, one would seek a line with a very large route structure, short feeders, little discounting, and traffic growing at a high rate. Both Cathay's airport in Hong Kong and Singapore's in Singapore represent a substantial part of the country. In other words, there's no feeder problem. The areas they serve include countries with real GNP growth of 8 to 10 percent, which is all the more extraordinary considering the large agricultural component of their economies.

"The Japanese have come to America *en masse*, the Taiwanese will be close behind, and after them will come the overseas Chinese in the Far East. Hotels in Hong Kong fill up as fast as they can be built, and the same will be true in Hawaii and then on our West Coast. Today's low dollar also means that Americans will take their vacations in the dollar zone." This implies prosperity for Carnival Cruise Lines, which dominates the low-priced segment of the cruise business, and in which Wanger said he had bought a lot of stock.

A logical vacation play is Disney, although Wanger says it is too big a company for him. He bought stock in the Japanese Disney World. When it quadrupled, he sold it again. "It may be the best single piece of property on earth," he says. "Every day there are 30,000 people lined up at 8 A.M. waiting to come in, and this would probably be true whatever the entrance price was.

"The Taiwanese, incidentally, announced they were going to try to help redress the dollar imbalance: They would buy a fleet of Boeing 747s at $500 million each, which would boost American exports. What they didn't also announce was that these planes would soon be bursting with merchandise being shipped from Taiwan to America!

"Waterford-Wedgwood is another way to play the wealth of the Pacific countries: There's no better brand name in the world. It's 200 years old! The Japanese and the overseas Chinese love those products. The ex-colonies remember the imperial connection and buy the top U.K. products when they can. Also, people now live in small, anonymous apartments. So the ability to set a nice dinner table is a prime luxury for the Asian wife. Today, the luxury end of the world is a good end to be in. I'd buy Tiffany and short Crazy Eddie. On the same reasoning, Neiman-Marcus is an extremely interesting business franchise."

Cracks in the Crystal Ball

It isn't easy to spot the real trends. In his March 31, 1984, report Wanger analyzed some predictions made by futurologists in 1972. Twenty developments were foreseen, including several to do with cheap energy by 1985: drilling oil wells offshore in deep water, continued growth of nuclear power, the development of such low-grade fossil fuels as lignite, synthetic fuels, and solar power in a quarter of new homes.

However, only deep-water drilling has come to pass to any significant degree. The moral that Wanger derives from this is simply that *technology is extremely hard to forecast*. The predictions were presented by wise and knowledgeable experts, but were wrong; even more important, they missed the important changes that have come about since 1972.

He goes further: "In any environment, you're going to have some creatures that are better adapted than others, and those are the ones that will prosper and grow. We're in a world where the environment changes at an increasingly rapid rate. In a rapidly changing world, twenty or thirty years of solid corporate growth could even be a warning sign: Chances are, things have changed enough so that whatever the hell made you a success thirty years ago doesn't work anymore. I think that by concentrating on smaller companies you improve your chances of catching the next wave. You could be one of the guys riding the crest instead of one of those just trying to hang on."

No News

In watching trends you should be on the alert for negative as well as positive investment ideas, like the Sherlock Holmes story of the dog that *didn't* bark. For instance, in the winter of 1987–88 there were no stories about shortages of gas: relatively few oldsters shivering in their Bronx apartments, and so forth. This meant that fuel was in plentiful supply. That's not front-page stuff: The news that's fit to print is the bad news. But cheap fuel is good for the airlines, for instance. "And for the motels, and for Disney," I added.

"Exactly," said Wanger. "Similarly, once a year or so one encounters the 'catastrophe in India' paradigm: The monsoon comes every year, and the resulting floods temporarily render thousands of people homeless. However, all this usually means is that the monsoon has indeed arrived. The people return to their homes later. The real news would be if the monsoon didn't arrive."

In other words, Wanger suggests that when one *doesn't* read about "Catastrophe in India—Thousands Homeless," it may well mean that the rains *haven't* come on schedule, and one should consider soybean futures.

Skylab Is Falling!

Hyper-exaggerated news can also create an opportunity. The threat of a nuclear-plant meltdown or a tornado fascinates reporters and the public far out of proportion to the actual danger involved. Thus, in 1979 when Skylab was breaking up, airline flights were canceled all over the country. But had Skylab fallen and 500 pieces of scrap metal rained down, the odds of one hitting any American would have been 1 in 20,000. Since NASA had some ability to control the landing area, the odds must have been 100,000 to one. Since about 130 Americans are killed in car accidents every day, the chance of being killed in a car was several million times greater than by Skylab.

Wanger asks the sensible question: "Why don't people consider risk in proportion to its true statistical probability?" One answer, he says, may be that people don't like to do mathematical calculations to figure out the real odds. And of course the unusual makes a better media story than the commonplace. But, he says, "the 'Skylab Effect' tells us that there are sound companies with a small risk of trouble that are good buys because *the market is too fearful of unlikely disasters.* When something bad happens, a stock may go down much more than the news warrants. This has its own Wall Street name: 'overdiscounting the bad news.' " So, as he points out, if you can find a good company when the market is cowering at inflated horror stories, there are profits to be made.

Some companies even do better as things get worse. H&R Block, for instance, makes money on tax complications, Commerce Clearing House from government regulations, and insurance brokers from difficult times. Wanger calls this category misery stocks.

Good Companies

Wanger has three tests of a good company—what he calls the "tripod" of growth potential, financial strength, and fundamental value.

1. Growth potential lies in five areas: a growing market for the company's product, good design, efficient manufacturing, sound marketing, and healthy profit margins. High profitability is always the result of enjoying a special niche, such as technological skill: He cited Scitex, which designs computer systems for graphic arts. He likes companies with a dominant market share, such as Mine Safety Appliances, which makes safety equipment. "It's better to be the best company in the lily-bulb industry than the third-best company in the tractor industry," says Wanger. A television station, or a regional shopping mall, or a newspaper can exploit a local monopoly. The Rouse Company is a dominant company in the shopping center business, having developed Faneuil Hall in Boston and the Harbor Project in Baltimore. Among media companies, he likes the *New York Times*—which,

he points out, "no one is going to start importing from Taiwan," and A. H. Belo, which owns broadcast properties and the *Dallas Morning News*. Their official earnings are meaningless: One must look at the cash flow and the underlying asset value.

Then, Wanger looks for outstanding management, which understands its business, is skilled in marketing, and is dedicated to its customers. He prefers companies where managers own a large enough stake in the company for their interests to coincide with those of the other shareholders.

2. Wanger wants to be sure that the company enjoys a strong financial position: low debt, adequate working capital, and conservative accounting. A strong balance sheet will allow growth without the need to dilute the existing shareholders' equity capital.

3. Finally, the price must be attractive. Wanger points out that institutional investors go through periods when they confuse a company with its stock; you can have a good company and a bad stock.

To verify value in the marketplace, Wanger has devised an infallible touchstone—*the Quit Test*. "What you do is play a game in which you assume that one of your eccentric friends who runs a large bank has just offered to lend you a great deal of money at about 10 percent interest, with which you may tender for all the stock of the company you are studying at the current market price. If you study the company and say 'Boy, this is terrific! Give me the loan and I'll do it. I'll quit my job and go run that company. It's a tremendous bargain,' then you probably have a good stock. And if you say, 'Gee, I think I'd rather stay where I am,' then there's not enough in that stock and perhaps you'd better look somewhere else."

Investment and Speculation

To value a stock, Wanger has his analysts estimate a company's future earnings or, for an asset play, its breakup potential, both about two years ahead. The computer then calculates what the price-earnings ratio should be at that time, based on a conventional dividend discount model, and thus produces a target price.

It calculates the expected rate of return if the stock advances to that level from its current market price. He then screens for those rates of return to determine where his analysts' expectations are different from those of the market.

Speculative rights are the privilege of guessing whether the market's going up or down. Through options, hybrid securities, and other derivative instruments, a speculator can buy speculative rights without owning the underlying investment. But for the true investor, pure investor's rights may suffice. The "Prudent Man Rule" almost requires that you buy a stock in order to keep it, the way you buy a house, rather than to trade it, like commodities. "Not for speculation," says the Rule, which represents a lot of ripe wisdom. Most fiduciaries who depart from it—a widespread situation today—cost their beneficiaries money. Of course, a very good investor will not only be satisfied with the earnings and dividends, but will also outguess the market, so that he will in fact achieve a speculative enhancement. On the other hand, he may achieve less speculative enhancement than somebody else will pay him for it. Indeed, people generally pay too much for the right to speculate. So perhaps one should sell them what they desire so earnestly.

The Rubenstein Rule

Wanger takes a "top-down" approach. He starts by determining the areas of the market that look particularly attractive. He limits his analytical problems by confining his portfolio to a few good stocks from those areas. He calls this the Rubenstein Rule: *Either a stock group is worth playing heavily or not at all*. This comes, he explains, from a story of Artur Rubinstein judging a piano competition in London. Rubenstein was asked to score contestants on a scale between one and twenty. When the competition ended, the sponsors were dismayed to find that the maestro had graded most contestants zero, a few twenty, and none in between. They asked why he had scored in such an extreme manner. "Simple," replied Rubenstein. "Either they can play the piano or they cannot."

An attractive investment area must have favorable characteristics that should last five years or longer. Wanger's portfolio turnover is very low—historically, around 25 percent per annum. That is, he sells an eighth of the portfolio a year to buy other things. If the central reason or "metaphor" for having bought the stock in the first place remains applicable, it is held. As a result of this low turnover Acorn has historically had one of the lowest expense ratios among equity funds.

Recently the big groups in the Acorn portfolio were information (28.9 percent), consumer goods and services (17.1 percent), industrial goods and services (10.6 percent), finance (10 percent), real estate (8 percent), energy (3.8 percent) and foreign stocks (16.5 percent). Foreign stocks have replaced energy as a major group.

Advice

Wanger likes firms that sell access to software or data bases. The constant decline in computer prices means that these suppliers, such as the IMS International division of Dun & Bradstreet and Information Resources, enjoy constantly improving business. IMS tracks the sales of drugs worldwide and reports on them to pharmaceutical manufacturing bases. Information Resources' systems collect and analyze information on sales of consumer packaged goods to test and evaluate marketing plans. Acorn's largest holding in computer software is Systematics. The company's software services perform virtually all the data-processing requirements of banks. Pansophic systems offers software to increase the efficiency of data communications information management and retrieval on a wide range of computer systems.

Side beneficiaries of the speeded-up computerized processing of insurance claims are Colonial Life & Accident, which specializes in small claims, and United Fire & Casualty Company.

Real Estate

In the 1970s a friend told Wanger that no institution ever invested in real estate. Another told him that his bank had no real estate stocks on its approved list. He thanked them for the tip and went out and bought Koger Properties and Continental Illinois Properties. "After all," he explained, "my helpful friends had just explained why real estate stocks were cheap, and told me who would be willing to buy them from Acorn in a few years at higher prices." Wanger now says that, first, most dwellings have at least doubled in the the last ten years, as investors are well aware; second, American and foreign investors are bidding for good-quality real estate at 10–14 times cash flow, while real estate stocks can be bought at 5–10 times cash flow. And third, institutions will eventually come back into real estate after the shakeout among the REITs.

"Rockefeller Center Properties," said Wanger, "was a short at its issue price of $20. Now, it is essentially an indexed bond. Its income should rise to offset rising consumer prices. Indeed, it should be the last survivor if New York goes to the devil."

"What about rent control?" I asked. "They're now talking about introducing commercial rent control in New York, having polished off the cheap rental housing market with residential rent control." "Exactly," said Wanger. "My college roommate's mother, a widow, had most of her assets in an apartment house in the Bronx. It provided decent housing to a number of middle-income tenants. Thanks to rent control, her income from the apartment fell below her maintenance cost, so she had to give up, and lost the property. The building became worthless, was demolished, and is now a vacant lot. I don't know who gained from that! In fact, the politicians, through rent control, turned a good middle-class district into a vast urban desert. But that shouldn't extend to Rockefeller Center."

Wanger sees commercial real estate as a fine hedge against inflation, but insists on companies that are well financed and well run, such as Greif Bros., which is in lumber and construction.

Shopping centers straddle three Wanger investing ideas: real estate, energy conservation, and the pleasure trend. "For instance," he has written, "shopping centers are good investments because the big, covered-mall regional shopping center saves time and store-to-store driving energy by bringing dozens of stores into the same place. The most successful stores have been users of information, in most cases televised advertising, which builds national-brand identification and chain-store images." Examples of shopping center companies he holds include Sizeler Property Investors, with centers in Louisiana, Florida, and Alabama; and

Weingarten Realty Investors, whose holdings are primarily in Texas.

Banking

Wanger likes to describe a situation in *Sylvie and Bruno* by Lewis Carroll, the author of *Alice's Adventures in Wonderland.* In this story a professor runs up a modest bill with his tailor. When the tailor presses him for payment the professor offers to pay twice as much if he can have a year's grace. So a few years later the professor owes the tailor £2,000, but knows that since the tailor will always accept another year's delay in return for another double, the tailor will never get paid. The book was published in 1889, and Wanger has calculated that if the two characters were still around, the professor would owe the tailor about £1,000,000,000,000,000,000,000,000,000,000,000,000.

"When the borrower is an almost-real country like Argentina or Poland, and that country has no collateral and no intention of paying off its loan, when do banks figure that they have a deadbeat professor on their hands?" Wanger asks. "Every rollover of a weak bank credit just pushes the principal amount up a little higher into fantasyland." Precisely because of these fears, some banks are undervalued. Wanger especially likes small regional ones, such as First Hawaiian or Wilmington Trust Co. "But we'll try to find the ones run by bankers, not by tailors," he says, adding that the term "aggressive banker" should be recognized as contradictory on its face, like "aggressive mistress."

The Pacific

As mentioned, Wanger is highly optimistic about such Pacific areas as Taiwan, Hong Kong, and Singapore. One can play this concept via the airlines, notably Cathay and Singapore; tourist companies, such as Carnival Cruise Lines and Disney; and luxury products, such as Waterford glass. One can look at the Acorn portfolio to track Wanger's choices.

9

Managing Harvard's Money

As treasurer of Harvard, Paul Cabot ran the university's endowment, which grew from $200 million to $1 billion in the fifteen years under his management, as an account at his firm, State Street Management & Investment, for which he charged a nominal $20,000 annual fee. Later, the size of the endowment warranted creating a separate structure under Harvard's own control to do the job. In 1974, therefore, Harvard Management Company came into existence.

That year I remember visiting the infant company's neat, modern offices on the sixth floor of a small building at the corner of Federal and Franklin streets in Boston, only a few hundred yards from Paul Cabot's State Street Management. I met the new head, Walter Cabot, and his chief of equity investments, John Chase. In 1986, I visited again. The amount being managed had tripled and the space quadrupled, to four floors of the same building. Today, Harvard Management employs about 120 people to run an endowment of more than $4.6 billion and has an annual budget (for more work) of about $10 million—quite a way up from Paul Cabot's $20,000! Even so, it runs a tight ship: Harvard spends less than a quarter of a percent of its portfolio on management, comfortably below many other universities.

After more than a decade, however, the office no longer seemed quite as modern. The furniture in the entrance area was mismatched and a bit tacky, that favorite Boston effect of looking up-to-date as of a few years back. In the anteroom, one encountered salesmen from the big New York brokers, for whom the

Harvard endowment is an important port of call. A New York institutional broker may sport a snappy black pin-striped suit, a pale blue shirt with white collar and cuffs, a Hermès tie, and black Gucci moccasins. The managers walking about the office have the somewhat rumpled look of deans. (Has any proper Bostonian in history ever worn new shoes or a new hat?) I liked the contrast between the spiffy visitors and the slightly shabby curators of the endowment . . . who, nonetheless, have the money.

By my third visit, in 1988, Harvard Management had moved to the Federal Reserve Building in downtown Boston, a few blocks from the waterfront. It is an exceedingly modern affair, though not yet in Boston's new typical "postmodern" style.*

Harvard Management remains, fittingly perhaps, one step behind the *dernier cri*. There is no name on the glass entrance doors to the Harvard Management offices on the fifteenth floor. Within, cool gray-beige walls match beige wall-to-wall carpeting. The furniture is motel-contemporary, halfheartedly "distressed" to look a bit older. The flavor of things had changed since my last visit: fewer New York stockbrokers about and more secretarial chatter.

The genesis of Harvard Management Company occurred about the time George Putnam, '49, a hard-bitten Bostonian with bright blue eyes, became treasurer of the University in 1973. Putnam also headed a family company that had sold out to Marsh & McLennan, and found it harder to make time available; he was working half time for a modest compensation, and Harvard Management Company was only one of his many jobs as treasurer. The Corporation, Harvard's governing body, determined that Harvard needed its own management structure exclusively for the endowment. First, Putnam hired Walter Cabot to run it. This Cabot, a nephew of Harvard's former treasurer, the small, peppery, profane Paul Cabot, had spent seven years working in Putnam Management, and became a principal of Wellington Management.

---

*Boston's traditional drab brick was slow to yield to the modern glass palaces of so many American urban areas, but downtown Boston has now rushed past that phase. Postmodern buildings are sprouting everywhere: vivid colors, odd decorative accents, heavy stonework.

Then Putnam took on George Siguler (pronounced SIG-uler), barely twenty-six and working at Investor's Diversified Services in Minneapolis. Siguler had telephoned Putnam one day seeking a job. Putnam invited him to come to Boston and found him familiar with the new technical devices used in endowment management: securities lending, futures, bond immunization, and the like. Siguler talks in rapid, high-pitched tones and is usually bursting with ideas. Putnam offered him a position running the trading desk, together with a number of the exotica, notably venture capital.

Conventional appearance notwithstanding, Harvard Management was from the first a distinctly jazzy outfit. One remarkable innovation that Walter Cabot and Siguler made was an options-trading desk. Options trading is hard to reconcile with the "Prudent Man Rule." It is a gambling game that you participate in only if you think you are more skillful, after costs and taking account of risk, than the pack. You are not a casino, with a percentage advantage over the outsiders; rather, you hope that by being a more skillful player you have an advantage over the other players. An active options-trading desk can best be compared to an airport control tower handling more planes than it is programmed for, with a tornado tearing up the runway. Perhaps, to make the analogy complete, the whole business should also be under enemy attack, à la Pearl Harbor. Anyway, it is an exhausting effort involving hour after hour of hair-trigger, computer-guided decisions, to outguess some of the smartest brains around.

Originally, the options-trading manager, Bing Sung, and his group bought and sold options based on the underlying holdings in the Harvard portfolio. Later, this constraint was removed so the traders became free to buy and sell naked options, which are unrelated to the holdings of the endowment. They might as well be trading currencies or commodities. It's just a game without an investment component. It's also a type of activity that incurs the risk of very heavy losses. The action is so fast that the operation can be extremely hard to control. An individual may go berserk before you catch him. So you set strict guidelines, you supervise things as closely as possible with computers, and you hold your hat. (Banks occasionally sustain currency-trading losses in the hundreds of millions of dollars.) Siguler and Bing have now both left. Cabot says the use of derivative instruments has become much more conservative.

Harvard University's general financial goal is a long-term "total return"—income plus capital gains—of 8 percent. Of this, half, or 4 percent, is distributed to the university for operating expenses. (Harvard's budget, about $800 million a year, includes a payroll for 3,000 teachers and 9,000 other employees.) The 4 percent that is not distributed is added back to capital to allow for inflation and some growth. In addition, the university expects to collect the equivalent of 2 percent from outside gifts, and thus be able to spend the annual equivalent of 6 percent of its portfolio.

Harvard Management has three main "accounts." The first is "The President and Fellows"—by far the largest. Essentially a large mutual fund, it handles the endowments of the university in general plus those of the various schools. The "Central Harvard" component of "President and Fellows" is actually very small. Most of President and Fellows is off in one or another separate pocket: the Divinity School, the Fogg Museum, the endowed professorships, and so forth.

There are also a couple of hundred million dollars divided among about 250 nonpooled accounts that are Harvard controlled, or headed Harvard's way: the Harvard-Yenching Institute, a large series of charitable lead trusts, and the like. (Commingling them would make for easier management but would only be possible if Harvard Management had a trust company charter, which it doesn't, although that idea is always under consideration.)

Then, Harvard receives frequent gifts in kind, ranging from I Tatti (Bernard Berenson's villa outside Florence) to a boat, a farm, or whatever. Harvard Management copes with these assets, holding them or developing them if appropriate, disposing of them if not. A building by itself without means of support is usually a far-from-welcome gift. These days, before Harvard will accept your great-grandfather's château in Newport as a permanent asset you must also provide a dowry sufficient to maintain it. Harvard, not being in the National Trust business and wary of becoming "land-poor," will reject a gift that could create an endless drain and insist on an escape hatch if it is accepted. It made an exception for I Tatti, whose overhead became a serious bother and eventually required a separate capital campaign of its own. Visiting alumni complain of dowdiness, but the university feels that its own income should go for teaching.

A fourth function of Harvard Management is to look after the university's loose cash; that is, it acts as a huge money fund. Every day the excess cash of all the schools and endowments is drained off into the pool, where it is managed collectively.

Going Outside

From the first, Walter Cabot's team resolved to engage a number of subsidiary managers for parts of the investment portfolio, in the hope of improving performance and learning something from an exchange of views with other thinkers. The number of different pools within the endowment runs between twelve and fifteen. A committee of senior management allocates money among them.

Beginning in 1974 Harvard spent a lot of time with Cambridge Associates, a performance-monitoring firm, trying to find outside managers who did much the same things as Harvard did in-house, but might do them better. After interviews with 250 firms, 5 were chosen: for equities, Eberstadt & Company, Fiduciary Trust and MacKay-Shields, all of New York; and for bonds, Brown Brothers, Harriman, also of New York, and Scudder, Stevens & Clark, of Boston. Each was given $25 million, or $125 million in all, representing somewhat over 10 percent of the then Harvard portfolio.

Funds managed by external advisors now account for about 5 percent or 6 percent of Harvard's total portfolio. Including limited partnerships, leveraged-buyout pools, and the like, which amount to another 5 percent, perhaps a total of 11 percent of the whole is managed outside the office. (At one point, as much as 15 percent was managed outside.)

Today, none of the original group of external advisors is still in place. I commented wryly on this phenomenon, and Walter Cabot observed that all too frequently decisions based on the performance-monitoring approach get you on board a trend just as it's ending. I replied that I had often written that tying on to the manager or mutual fund that has done best in the last few years is one step short of the best solution: better to find an investment strategy that is out of vogue, and then hire an excellent manager or fund in that category.

> The correct approach is to analyze a successful manager's technique for the last ten years or so. If the results have been achieved in a first-class way, then you should ask whether the kind of stocks he specializes in have had a big play recently or whether on the contrary they are in the discard and represent outstanding value.
>
> If the latter, then perhaps you have something. You make sure the manager in question is still employing his perennially successful but recently unpopular method, and then hire him. You should participate strongly in the recovery that will be along sooner or later. The same manager will probably just have been fired by an overly performance-conscious institution because of two bad years—the same bad years that have coiled the spring for his type of issues to rebound.*

For that, of course, you must know a lot about the investment market and must exercise originality, so it's a less comfortable technique than the performance-monitoring approach. However, it should also be more profitable.

Cabot finds the way pension funds are run today to be exceedingly conservative: "They're using the same methods and products they were when I was there ten years ago." Harvard, on the contrary, is constantly trying new things. "If you've got to find ten different ways to skin a cat, you do it," he says, "because if you don't, you are going to be left behind." I greet this conception with a certain skepticism: The essence of investment has changed little for at least a century, and many new things are distractions that don't actually improve matters significantly. Even if they do for a while, soon others are using the same devices, so you lose your advantage without shedding the distraction. Still, handsome is as handsome does.

Anyway, having found out that the performance-monitoring technique did not work very well, Harvard switched to a different

*John Train, *Preserving Capital and Making It Grow* (New York: Clarkson N. Potter, Inc., 1983).

(and in my opinion more effective) approach: Identify managers who can do things that you can't. There are now eight of these in place:

1. Two foreign-equity managers: Oxley & Co. and Grantham, Mayo, Van Otterloo, both in Boston.
2. Two foreign-bond managers: the Worldinvest division of Bank of America, London, and S. G. Warburg, London.
3. Two hedge funds: Charter Oak, run by Jerry Fine in Westport, Connecticut, and Calluffo Associates of Portsmouth, New Hampshire, run by Tony Calluffo.
4. A specialty insurance fund: PSCO Partners, run by Philo Smith Co., in Stamford, Connecticut.
5. A price-to-book value ratio fund run by Donald B. Smith, in Paramus, New Jersey.

Cabot says that he finds it very hard to identify consistently superior managers. It is indeed!

Even the best outside managers can have little effect on Harvard's overall performance. So, says Cabot, "the relationship with the manager—discovering his best ideas—is probably even more important to us than any performance advantage." He likes to have able people come in from outside on whom his staff can test their concepts. The staff also derives useful investment insights from members of the Harvard faculty, thanks to their familiarity with a number of economic and scientific areas.

A technique used by one manager of foreign equities is interesting. Grantham, Mayo, Van Otterloo, whose principals split off from Batterymarch Management in Boston, runs $85 million in foreign stocks for Harvard. They developed an approach based on the thesis that the best-known European stocks—the equivalents of our "nifty fifty" of the early 1970s—were overpriced compared to their less well-known counterparts in the same countries. The firm therefore bought secondary foreign stocks instead of the best-known ones. This is a correct strategy in a bull market, but in bear markets the secondaries sometimes just fade away.

The pricing anomaly arises in the first place because of an investment technique favored by Swiss banks, which in general are not well informed on specific stocks in, say, Spain—certainly less so than Spanish institutional investors—but do consider themselves knowledgeable on various countries' overall situations. So if a Swiss banker concludes that Spain is turning the corner, he will tell his customers, *"On va jouer la carte de l'Espagne,"* and buy three or four of the biggest and best-known Spanish stocks—always, however, ones enjoying high market liquidity. That way he can get out quickly. So the stock market capitalization of the biggest stocks tends to be disproportionately greater than the next category down. In time this distortion tends to smooth out, so you buy the secondary stocks and wait.

Indexing

Some years ago Harvard Management decided that since the return of most investment managers did not equal the S&P 500, it would "index" a substantial part of the entire portfolio, so that it should do no better and no worse than the S&P. An indexed portfolio is in essence frozen into a basket corresponding to whatever it is indexed to—the Dow Jones, the S&P, or whatever. This has the advantage of reducing the size of the portfolio that actually has to be consciously managed. With 20 percent, say, of your stocks indexed, you are only worrying about actively managing the remaining 80 percent. As Cabot said, "If we have $470 million indexed, or 25 percent, out of our $1.9 billion in marketable securities, it means we have that much less money from a liquidity standpoint to have to think about." To me that idea may be true, but the conclusion seems a *non sequitur.* If, after costs, you can beat the averages, you should manage as much of your own capital as possible. If you can't, then you should manage very little.

Sometimes an index future sells at a significant premium or discount to the underlying basket of stocks. At such times, Harvard trades back and forth between the futures and the underlying basket. In Cabot's words, "We have an active—not passive—index fund. It uses derivative products for the main body of the fund. It gives us an anchor. Most managers underperform the index, so we figure if you can't beat 'em, join 'em. It's very liquid. We can add or reduce risk easily." Today, the volume of trading in financial futures vastly exceeds the volume of trading in the actual stocks on the stock exchange, so financial futures have become quite an "efficient market," and it seems unlikely that significant profits will be generated from this maneuver in the future.

I asked how the index fund had performed relative to the managed holdings in the Harvard portfolio over five or ten years. Cabot wasn't sure.

Product Lines

At the outset, the internally managed equities were divided into three "product lines":

1. A large capital growth stock "fund," whose manager looked hard at the underlying strength of each company owned.

2. A "value product," whose manager tried to buy cheap stocks, whether or not they were interesting as businesses. Cabot observes that it is hard to avoid buying such stocks when it is already late in the cycle and other things seem overpriced. The analytical technique involves studying such ratios as price to earnings, price to book value, price to sales and cost, looking for depressed earnings that will rebound, comparing yields, and the like.

3. "Niche" stocks: intermediate or small companies, preferably those that are expected to grow vigorously for some time.

When it is considered appropriate, assets are shifted from one "product line" to another. Also, if a manager of one "product line" wanted to buy a stock that really belonged to another, he was supposed to check with the manager of the other "product line" so as to avoid duplication of basic research.

"By last year," Cabot told me in 1987, "Harvard had given up the 'product' conception it once had—the value product, the growth product, and so forth. Now it holds a single 'select equity portfolio.' Twenty percent of it is in smaller-growth stocks today. We believe they are cheaper and will do better. We have very few investments in 'industrial America.'

"We look a lot at the relative values within the whole portfolio. For instance, should one buy Dow, a fine company, or should one buy Bankers Trust? Dow is at fifteen times earnings and Bankers Trust is at four times. We try to be value conscious. To do that, you have to be early, so the exact timing will probably be off. You have to have patience and perseverance, and hope that the value will be recognized eventually. We have a basic understanding of business, how businesses will prosper, and what businesses are worth.

"One change in the last couple of years is that we have tried to wean the organization away from the Wall Street brokers. In the early days we spoke to them a lot. Now we find them a distraction. They are investors of the moment, not for the long term. In order to generate commissions, they have to sell. So we call on more and more companies ourselves. We find that brokers generally don't have a perspective for the valuation process— whether one group is more interesting than another group. Within a single group, of course, such as drugs, sometimes a broker will have lots of useful knowledge."

Building a Team

Cabot feels that most investment managers consider themselves to be engaged in an internal competition—rightly, of course, in brokerage houses, since they are fighting for commissions. At Harvard Management, since everybody is working on one portfolio, Cabot encourages a noncompetitive, generalist attitude. He finds that it is easier to attract an able manager if he can take part in the whole process, rather than working as a stock analyst, for instance, in one particular industry. Cabot says that he is trying to build up a team with good *collective* judgment, rather than an assemblage of specialists. He points out, for example, that "if you don't understand bonds and interest rates, it's hard to understand economic cycles and therefore bonds versus industrial stocks. Similarly, if you don't understand stocks, you will have an imperfect understanding of the bond market." So from the newest to the oldest, all the principals at Harvard Management are involved in the entire investment process. To that end, Cabot likes to hire people who seem able to think, and then move them around.

Base salaries at Harvard Management are competitive within the investment business. Speculation has it that Walter Cabot makes about half a million dollars a year. Harvard does not like to reveal the exact figure, since financial salaries are so much higher than academic salaries. A type of performance bonus has been cautiously introduced, although an employee cannot, of course, gain an ownership position, since essentially the enterprise is a co-op. Performance bonuses do tend to create internal competition, and thus are hard to reconcile with collegial thinking.

The company hasn't had too much employee turnover. Three of the early key staff members have departed: John Chase, George Siguler, and Bing Sung, the options wizard; also, an exceptionally able chemical analyst went to Morgan Stanley, and a couple of others have hung up their own shingles. Still, not too bad.

In *Great Good Fortune*,* a book on Harvard's endowment, author Carl A. Vigeland attributes much of Harvard Management's early organization and emphasis on novel investment techniques to George Siguler, who, he says, was Putnam's vicar for Harvard Management matters. He did indeed put Harvard into stock lending and the use of derivative instruments, but the opinion around the company is that he was stronger on such devices than on overall judgment. He was not really a leader or administrator, they say, and thus was less important than the Vigeland book implies. Furthermore, Putnam did not create Harvard Management with Siguler as his general delegate; rather, Siguler was basically under Cabot, and both were told what to do by the directors.

So does *Great Good Fortune* give a misleading impression? I asked. "It's a terrible book," said Cabot, shaking his head. Others familiar with the topic agree. Still, it does bring a measure of *glasnost* to a subject hitherto held as something of a holy mystery.

Going Private

"I would like to deliver superior results for this account," says Cabot. "How can I get them? I don't believe we can pick stocks and bonds in a fashion demonstrably to our benefit. There is too

*Carl A. Vigeland, *Great Good Fortune: How Harvard Makes Its Money* (Boston: Houghton Mifflin, 1986).

much flow of information out there. I don't think we can achieve our objective through conventional methodologies of picking stocks and bonds. So how will we get to our goal? The pension-fund business has traditionally been extremely conservative and tradition bound. Pension-fund managers are usually concerned with their relative performance compared to other such managers, not their absolute performance. The endowment business, on the contrary, seeks a real return, not a relative return. So endowments are often early in new investment ideas: real estate, venture capital, private deals, and the like. They act like owners, not like hired guns, who are more likely to fight for relative performance and thus more likely to get into trouble sooner or later. Thus, the universe of endowments has had superior performance over a long time to the universe of pensions. We have acquired the owner's mentality as against the hired gun's mentality," said Cabot.

"With this thesis in mind, we look for areas of investment mispricing. We got a notch up through securities lending,* which we did very early. The problem with securities lending today is that there are too many people doing it, so they have driven down the margins and taken away most of the profit. Then we were early in the use of derivative products. We noticed that they were being used by the brokerage community in managing its own assets, but not by pensions or endowments.

"We've now moved into private investing, in equities that are unquoted in the marketplace, such as new ventures, leveraged buyouts, oil and gas assets and explorations, and real estate. We've found the pricing less competitive there. We can structure a deal favorably, so the returns are better. Obviously, there is a give-up in liquidity.

"We have a very active trading desk. We do day trading and arbitrage of futures versus the basket. A lot of small trades at the margin should give some improvement in overall performance. There are lots of little divisions that can add up to a better result.

"One can also, of course, look for the big strategic conception. We don't think we have that particular skill.

"We started putting cash in the private market area about ten

---

*Making securities available to stockbrokers for a fee so that they in turn can accommodate short sellers.

years ago," Cabot observes. "We carry each investment at cost
for two or three years, until we can see how it is developing. We
now have $700 million in this category, including real estate and
ventures. The time-weighted return on those investments, penal-
ized by idle cash, seems to be about 25 percent, so it's a highly
satisfactory result. In the late 1970s parts of the area were more
interesting than now, because there was less money available for
that market. Today, oil and gas are more attractive and real
estate is less attractive.

"Our lawyers felt that we ought to have a corporation to
insulate us from the possible risks of litigation in this type of
investment, so we created one, Aeneas Group. We called it that
because Aeneas went through all sorts of trials and tribulations
before coming out all right. We have three partners and five
employees looking after this whole category. They cover the entire
waterfront: oil, real estate, high-tech, and everything else. I tell
these guys: Take an opportunistic approach to what you see in
the market—don't try jamming capital into categories. If a
manager is told to invest $200 million in some particular
category—real estate, or whatever—he will do that, and will
make some bad moves. There is no pressure on these guys to put
money into any category, just to make good investments."

In the summer of 1988 Aeneas held the following (in millions
of dollars):

		Future Commitments
Venture capital (mostly high-tech):		
Partnerships	191	100
Direct investments	117	0
Real estate	142	150
Leveraged buyouts	163	90
Public, but illiquid	101	15
Oil and gas	74	3
Total	788	358

"We seem to have a number of Greek names around here.
Beside Aeneas and Phoenix, another one is Femus, which we use
to hold companies where there is a risk of unrelated business
income."

And who was Femus?

"I can't quite remember," said Cabot. (It turned out to be Polyphemus, the Cyclops who imprisoned Odysseus and his companions in a cave, eating one of them from time to time, until Odysseus blinded him and he and the survivors escaped.) "We also have Lavinia,* a partnership that Allen & Company in New York runs for us that engages in risk arbitrage. It has had a 15-to-16 percent return over an eight or nine year period. We have about $20 million in it.

"If Harvard is to do exceptionally well, it will probably be in the private-deal area rather than in the portfolio area. We probably have thirty venture-capital partnerships.

"We're always trying out some smaller new ideas. For instance, we have an in-house computer-driven fund, and an in-house risk arbitrage fund."

I asked Cabot about Warren Buffett's observation that it was somewhat irrational to buy into new ventures, since the outside investors in a start-up usually put up all the money for perhaps half the company. The rest goes to the earliest seed-money backers, the inventor, the inside management, and so on. Better to wait two or three years for the next bear market and buy into the company, or one like it, for less than the cash in the bank, with the operating business free.

Cabot did not rise to this idea. "There are only occasional windows in the life of a company, between when it is just an idea and when it turns into an IBM. The greatest mispricing is at the very beginning, when of course you have a substantial corporate risk but little pricing risk. But after the initial public offering, it's principally pricing risk." As an example, Cabot cited the difficulty of coping with high-tech investing. "The answer is that we do it through our private investments. We have $800 million in that category, with commitments for another $400 million. Of that $800 million, close to $300 million is in venture-capital partnerships or venture-capital direct investments, of which a large part is in high-tech companies.

"It's very difficult for us to buy exotic holdings in the public marketplace. We fool around with genetic-engineering companies and so on, but we're not much good at it and we don't really

*Daughter of Latinus and betrothed of Aeneas.

understand it. In private investing, people still invest as they did twenty years ago: They check the company out fully, they talk to the competition, they talk to academics. You know you're going to be stuck with a holding for three or four or five years, so you get to understand it very carefully. In large-scale institutional investing, that's no longer done today.*

"As to venture capital, we're participants in about sixty limited partnerships. We also make direct investments in venture-capital deals, but only from among those already bought for us by the managers of our limited partnerships, so the list has been filtered before we start. Of a hundred or so in all, only five or six are in deep trouble, which is much less than what you would ordinarily expect."

"And buying directly from the company is cheaper than paying the management fee?" I asked.

"Of course," said Cabot. "And we probably avoid quite a few big losers using this technique."

I asked about real estate.

"We think the values are just not there today," said Cabot. He considers real estate near a top, and finds the properties that are being offered to him unattractive, although Harvard Management has a substantial position in one, Property Capital Trust, on the American Exchange, of which Cabot is a trustee.

Oil and Gas

Oil and gas, on the other hand, he considers cheap. Harvard Management has put together a team to explore a variety of solutions to the problem of how to take advantage of this opportunity. One way to participate in an improvement in oil and gas prices might be for Harvard Management to buy participations in oil and gas loans from banks in the oil patch. Cabot's scenario is that lower prices will drive the high-cost producers—the U.S. strippers, the North Sea, and Alaska—out of business. Imported oil will then rise to 50 percent of total U.S. consumption. In 1987 he felt that one could get a total return on energy investment in the high-teen to the low-20-percent area on reasonable assumptions and with no undue risk.

*It is by most of the investors studied in this book, however.

"We're kind of excited about the oil and gas business," he said. "We began two or three years ago with zero knowledge. We were aware, however, that there was no new money going into the oil and gas world, and that drilling costs were way down. We felt that over some period the world and/or the United States should be short of energy. We felt that if we could find good reserves and qualified partners, and hung on to our holdings over a considerable period of time, we would probably do quite well. We looked at several hundred deals. A lot of them involved lousy partners or lousy deals—the reserves were inadequate.

"Finally, we settled on three or four areas. We have made a major investment in Harken Oil, which is quoted over-the-counter, but is in fact not liquid. We bought it at $1 or $2 a share. It got to $7 before last October, and then dropped to $4 and change. We hope that it will become a very major independent oil and gas company. It owns E-Z Service, which operates gas pumps outside convenience stores. Harken is a major leg of our strategy, in that it is constantly buying proven reserves.

"Then, we wanted to be in the exploration business, both offshore and onshore. In April 1987 a group of educational institutions put up $290 million, of which Harvard's share was $50 million, to create Smith Offshore Exploration, formed by Lester Smith of Houston and George Baker of New York, by coincidence a descendant of the Baker who gave his name to Harvard's Baker School of Business Administration. Smith's drilling program in the Gulf of Mexico will consist largely of a joint venture with a subsidiary of Brooklyn Union. The project hopes to drill ten to twelve offshore wells a year over the next three years. We're banking on a very skillful team drilling off the Gulf Coast. We've already made some big finds.

"For the onshore part, we formed a company with the Cullen family in Texas. We're looking in Oklahoma, Texas, and to some extent in Louisiana. Those are our two exploration plays. We have also made some smaller investments in proven resources.

"We also made a major investment in a large private drilling-equipment company. The deal came to us and we brought it to Warburg Pinkus, who formed a group. They are in the jack-up rig business. They have sixteen or eighteen rigs. The company was in or near Chapter 11 when we first saw it. It's like buying rigs at 10 cents or 15 cents on the dollar.

"Overall, we hope to be able to create and find returns of 9 percent or 10 percent at today's oil prices, and more if the price of oil rises."

Wouldn't it be easier to buy a major oil-field service company, such as Schlumberger or Halliburton?

"Schlumberger does not meet our South African policy,"* said Cabot, "so let's consider Halliburton. It should have a good move if oil prices strengthen, but not any 30 percent a year. We hope for an entrepreneurial return from an entrepreneurial risk; in other words, 30 percent continued over a period of years. For instance, in Smith Offshore, there was to be a takedown in tranches. But so far the early hits will pay for the later commitments, so we're getting a free ride. For the long term, we know we're giving up current income for future income and that these holdings are illiquid, but that's perfectly appropriate for Harvard."

Within the bond portfolio, Harvard makes extensive use of foreign currencies. Its guidelines permit $500 million in foreign bonds, of which 30 percent can be denominated in foreign currencies. Cabot says that the recent superior performance of the fixed-income portfolio derives largely from holding foreign bonds.

How does one decide which currencies to hold? "Through extensive travel and consultation with outside advisors for the international portfolio." In early 1988 Cabot believed the dollar "could remain soft. . . . The portfolio has held Deutsche Marks, pounds, and Swiss francs—but for the moment, at least, no yen."

The Crash

In the Crash of 1987, Harvard dropped 13 percent, compared to 21.6 percent for the S&P. How did it get off so lightly?

"In the spring the equity ratio was about 73 percent. Between spring and October, in a series of moves, the equity exposure was reduced to the high 40-percent area. This was a painful transaction in terms of performance, since the market went on rising

*The company, which is incorporated in the Netherlands Antilles, has not actually signed the Sullivan Principles.

into late August. The push for superior performance, however, kept many money managers fully invested right up to the crash in October. They were afraid they'd miss something.

"In October 1987 I don't believe we sold many stocks in the cash market. We did, however, make use of our expertise in the futures market. We think that this helped our performance in the downturn. One advantage of having a lot of the assets in-house is that you can make substantial moves across the board, which isn't possible if you're dealing mostly with outside managers. During that period, anyway, we bought long-term bonds, we shorted the Japanese stock market out of the foreign manager's portfolio—a mistake, as it turned out—and we shorted against our private portfolios. In other words, by having control of the situation we were in a better position to manage risk than someone who worked through intermediaries. Every morning we knew where we stood. We could orchestrate the whole *schmear*."

To this another insider adds, "That's the other side of the George Siguler question: Thanks to him, Harvard was ahead of the pack in developing an in-house capability in the management of options trading. So when massive and quick moves were necessary, Harvard was able to act. That saved the company in October 1987; there's no doubt about it."

Summing Up

How well have all these different approaches and maneuvers actually worked out in practice?

The answer is about what an experienced investor would probably expect: well enough, but not outstandingly. The way a good investor does really well is by understanding the subject perfectly, and then making large bets on neglected values; or, alternatively, by engaging in successful futurology. The Harvard approach is based on making a very large number of small transactions, and going into all sorts of exotica in much the same way and at much the same time as other people in Wall Street.

A second problem is that the duty of the people overseeing a large pool of capital is to identify, judge, and change the hands-on managers; this Harvard Management Company cannot reasonably be asked to do of itself. As to this point, there was an excellent discussion of college endowments, including Harvard, in the October 26, 1987 *Fortune*. It compared the three-year results of the seven largest. Two were outstanding: Yale, with a 19.7-percent average annual return, and Princeton, with 17.7 percent. The remaining five were quite closely grouped between 16.4 percent and 16.9 percent, with Harvard almost exactly in the middle, at 16.7 percent—significantly behind the leaders.

A performance calculation for twenty-three of the very largest U.S. pension and endowment funds—perforce a sluggish group—shows that for the five years ending June 30, 1988, Harvard had a compound annual rate of return of 15.3 percent, compared with 18.9 percent for the top fund, and a median of 12.1 percent, placing Harvard fourth among the twenty-three. This improvement in relative standing derives from Harvard's aggressive lightening of its equity exposure in 1987.

A number of the specialists *Fortune* consulted for the article commented on Harvard Management's approach. A point generally made concerns diversification of management. For instance, *Fortune* cites George Keane, who runs the Common Fund: "With Harvard's method in mind, he adds, 'we wouldn't think of having a single manager for a billion dollars.' " The problem is that one person has trouble being both referee and player. If a board of trustees has an outstanding investment committee that can monitor outside managers, they can keep active managers on their toes. One specialist told *Fortune* that he "prefers small money-management firms where the partners have a stake in the business." They'll probably try hardest. But if the in-house managers run almost all the endowment, and the trustees are not really tough enough about performance, then the operation may seek a comfortable existence at the expense of achievement.

Here is a point *Fortune* makes several times:

> Once upon a time, late in the dizzy bull-market party of the Roaring Twenties, the chairman of Princeton University's investment committee, a banker named Dean Mathey, decided that the level of stock market prices was unsustainable. He quietly moved the university's endowment out of stocks and into bonds. For one full year his decision proved dead wrong. The market waltzed to new highs. Then the Crash hit, and the Depression. Mathey's switch to bonds, a shrewd deflation hedge, was vindicated.

Fourteen years after the Crash, with the stock market languishing midway in World War II, Mathey acted again, selling 80 percent of the university's bonds and replacing them with common stocks. The chairman of the trustees' finance committee denounced Mathey as reckless and irresponsible, pointing out that the great lesson of the Depression was that bonds were the only prudent and conservative investment for a college endowment fund. Forced to defend what would again prove to be an exquisitely timed maneuver, Mathey wrote in reply: "The only true test of conservatism is to be right in the future."

Fortune quoted the manager of the Princeton endowment: "The secret is for institutions to have the guts, courage, wisdom, and luck to find a Dean Mathey or a Ted Cross, then to have people on the investment committee who are wise enough to understand these men and to judge them—and to cut them off at the knees and roll them into the closet if they mess up."

The ultimate in this approach is exemplified by Warren Buffett's excursion into college-endowment management. In 1968 he became a trustee of Grinnell College, in the hope that he would help with their investments. The sequel is described in my own recent book on him, *The Midas Touch:*

In 1976, attending a conference in New Orleans on the economics of newspapers, Buffett discovered that Avco Corporation had decided to sell its television stations. Under FCC rules Buffett couldn't buy the stations for Berkshire Hathaway, because of the TV holdings of the *Washington Post.* So he proposed . . . that Grinnell College try to buy one of them, if it could be gotten at a bargain price. His first choice was the station in Cincinnati. Unfortunately, the Grinnell board spent so much time discussing how to finance the transaction that Multimedia, not Grinnell, bought the station, for $16 million. (Grinnell responded by buying $315,000 worth of Multimedia stock, which subsequently soared.)

Buffett's second try was Avco's TV station in Dayton. This time he decided simply to make a bid and only later to arrange financing. He offered $12.9 million in 1976, representing two and a half times the gross revenues of the station. He won. Late in 1984 Grinnell sold the station again, to Hearst Corporation for $50 million. This transaction doubled Grinnell's endowment, which now represents $127,000 per student, compared to $180,000 per student for Harvard and $121,000 for Yale.

Harvard Management's approach to managing the endowment is up-to-date, even perhaps a bit trendy, and has produced respectable results. By developing a team with a solid understanding of values it should avoid such catastrophic losses as befell the Ford Foundation in the 1970s. By staying well diversified among types of investments and among different investment techniques Harvard should avoid unpleasant surprises. But as things stand now it will be hard for it to produce outstanding results, because it is not geared to making big long-term moves—the successful scramble to reduce equity exposure in 1987 being an interesting departure. Oil is an authentic bet, but not a big one. Big, successful moves need bold, masterful managers—who are rarely collegial.

Cabot's observation that if Harvard does exceptionally well it will probably be in private deals rather than in its main portfolio may well be true; however, the main portfolio represents 85 percent of the endowment.

10

Peter Lynch

Relentless Pursuit

How can it be that a single individual, virtually without a staff, and managing an enormous mass of capital—the $10-billion Magellan Fund—greatly outperforms a large, able organization—the best that the governing body of an old and famous institution can assemble—handling only a fraction as much money? That is, how does Peter Lynch do so much better than his neighbors at Harvard Management?

The chief reason is that a supremely capable individual—and Peter Lynch is one—easily outmaneuvers a large committee, which essentially describes Harvard Management. Wellington, who never lost a battle, also never held councils of war; Napoleon liked to say that one general was enough for an army. In other words, the trick in those two competitive games, investment and war, is to find the ablest chief available and, under philosophical guidance, give him his head. If he is not the ablest chief available, change him. But don't expect an assemblage of less able men to outmaneuver him. One sees this principle in chess. A grand master will often play simultaneous games against twenty or thirty members of a chess club. He walks to each board, pauses briefly, makes his move, then passes to the next. Usually, he will settle for a draw with one or two of the strongest players and trounce all the rest. The point is that in most games concentration of decision-making is precisely how you achieve the best results. Peter Lynch has two research assistants—one to collect Wall Street news and attend company presentations, and the other to call companies and go to research meetings. When asked

if he mightn't like another, he responds vaguely: Perhaps . . .
someday . . . you spend so much time talking to them. . . .

It also helps to be rather free with the emoluments. Peter
Lynch is a hired hand, but he knows what he is worth, and his
employer, Fidelity Management, pays him several million dollars
a year, probably about ten times what the top stock picker is
getting at Harvard Management. Peter Lynch is one of the
highest-paid portfolio investment employees in the world. But he
is worth it many times over.

How so? Well, Peter Lynch essentially created the Magellan
Fund. Since he took charge in 1977, it has become the largest
mutual fund in history, $12 billion in assets at its peak in August
1987, and $8.4 billion at March 31, 1988. It has over a million
shareholders, and incidentally pays Fidelity, its managers, $60
million a year in management fees and as much as several
hundred million in sales commissions. (The 3-percent sales
commission goes straight into the pocket of management; there
are no salesmen.) For that matter, Magellan's annual performance bonus, which it invariably earns, comes to 0.2 percent of
its $9 billion capital, and thus alone amounts to almost $20
million a year. Lynch has well earned his share of this bonanza:
As the Biblical injunction goes, do not muzzle the ox as he
treadeth out the corn. All that growth is based on his performance: $10,000 put in Magellan when Lynch took command in
1977 was worth over $200,000 by 1988.

This investment prodigy is the son of a professor of mathematics at Boston College, who later moved to the John Hancock
Company. He got cancer when Peter was seven and died when
he was ten, leaving the family in straitened circumstances. His
mother went to work for a manufacturing company, and Peter
went from a private school in second grade to a local public
school—a good one, to be sure. He attended high school in
Newton, Massachusetts. Summers he worked as a caddy, which
is where he began hearing about the stock market. Businessmen
out golfing exchange investment ideas, and some businessmen are
very well informed.

Young Peter sank $1,250 of his savings in one of the stocks he
heard about, Flying Tiger Line, a way of riding the explosive
growth of the Pacific countries as well as the development of air

freight. He bought in at $10. Flying Tiger went up and up. Peter sold some to get his money back, and then sold more in dribbles all the way up. The last went in 1989 when the company was taken over by Federal Express. By the time he had cashed in most of his stock he had made enough money to pay for his graduate study at the Wharton School of Finance in Philadelphia.

First, however, came college. Here a second golf-derived bonanza came his way: Boston College had a $300 partial scholarship intended precisely for caddies, which Peter won. Later the Goddess of Golf smiled upon him yet again: In 1966, waiting to start in at Wharton, he got a summer job at Fidelity. There were seventy-five applicants, but Peter was the one who had caddied for D. George Sullivan, the president of the company. He joined the ROTC at college, and on emerging from Wharton spent the required two years in the Army. He was sent not to Vietnam but ("lucky even then," he says) to South Korea. In 1969, after being discharged, he was offered a permanent job at Fidelity, starting as a metals analyst, and has worked there ever since. He has now become so successful that he can no longer squeeze in time for golf.

In 1974, after a few years in analytical jobs, Lynch became Fidelity's director of research, while continuing to cover the chemical, packaging, steel, aluminum, and textile industries. Such a job provides a marvelous chance to learn deeply about securities. One is essentially running an active think tank that maintains constant, systematic coverage of all of industry, endlessly visiting companies, then concentrating intensively on the most promising fish that turn up in the net. One's task is to develop opinions that, over and over again, are checked against actual results. Finally, one is constantly comparing one's ideas with those of one's peers in the same department, honing information and judgment.

In analyst meetings, he urges his colleagues not to tear down each other's ideas—"Don't rip up my Volvo idea," as he says— but rather to explain why their own ideas are good ones. He also finds that such meetings are 90 percent heat and 10 percent light. "They're so emotional!" . . . And, often, he adds, too theoretical.

For those who have never actually been in the securities business but are nevertheless interested in the process, perhaps from managing their own portfolios, a useful comparison might be what happens when, after having only played weekend club tennis, you enroll at a really tough tennis camp intended for future professionals. And not just for a few weeks, but for a number of years. You are constantly learning new strokes, new tactics, and day after day, week after week, year after year perfecting your skills, playing with top instructors and opponents in an environment of constant pressure. There is no comparison between the knowledge and skill of such a player, either in tennis or securities, and the ordinary casual participant. What is more, the most successful ones have a ferocious, competitive drive that can scarcely be imagined by their part-time counterparts. The rewards, both in prestige—mostly among one's peers, to be sure— and in cash can be intensely gratifying.

In 1977, after eight years as a permanent employee at Fidelity, Lynch, now thirty-three, was put in charge of a little fund that Fidelity had around, Magellan. Originally intended for foreign securities—whence the nod to the eponymous Portugese navigator—Magellan had been started in 1963; two years later it was hit by the Interest Equalization Tax, intended to support the dollar by discouraging U.S. investment abroad, and was forced to reorient itself toward domestic securities. In 1976 it absorbed Essex Fund, with $14 million. When Lynch took over it had only $22 million in it, concentrated in relatively few holdings, and was an almost invisible part of the Fidelity empire. In 1981 Magellan, then about $50 million, absorbed Fidelity's Salem Fund, which was of similar size.

Lynch's Techniques

Lynch's cardinal advantage over the legion of his competitors, besides his basic talent, is simply the enormous dedication he brings to the task. Lynch tries harder. Indeed, one finds it rather exhausting just to think about his routine. In twenty years of marriage he has taken two proper vacations. "I went to Japan and just saw companies for five days and met Carolyn in Hong Kong. So we had Friday, Saturday, and Sunday in Hong Kong. Then I saw companies Monday, Tuesday, and Wednesday in Hong Kong. Then we went up into China for two or three days. Then, I saw companies in Bangkok. Then, we saw a little bit of

Bangkok. Then, I flew to England and I saw companies for three, four days there. It was a fabulous time." Not every wife's conception of "a fabulous time"! A stockbroker who accompanied him for some days mentions that in a country where things barely get going at ten o'clock in the morning Lynch insisted on starting to see companies at eight, and was quite grumpy that none could be found to talk to him at six! When at the end of the day the idea of dinner was raised, Lynch begged off: "I gotta read four annual reports by tomorrow." This broker said he had never seen someone so well prepared for company visits. Lynch estimates his mileage as 100,000 a year, implying 400 miles a working day, which would be impressive for someone who was on the road full time, quite aside from someone based mainly in an office.

He is off to the office by car pool at 6:15 in the morning— reading all the way in—and back by 7:15 at night in a Fidelity car (after eighteen years in the bus), still reading.* He gets two or three feet of reports and recommendations every day, which are neatly piled on a table at one side of his office until he gets to them. Every lunch he is talking to a company. He also comes in on Saturdays to look through his stack of reports, but only reads in detail about 5 percent of what is there. He may also read for a few hours on Sunday mornings before attending mass with his family.

Lynch finds that *there is no relationship between the length of a recommendation and its value.* Very often the most convincing idea will be encapsulated in a paragraph. That being so, the short, meaty reports are those he likes best. He is an indefatigable note-taker, and I have described his unending cycle of company contacts. Knute Rockne had a pleasantly lame description of success: "If every man does his duty perfectly on every play, a touchdown will result." In a similar vein, Lynch: "If you see enough companies and do enough work, you'll either

---

*A few years ago, in his mid-forties, he suddenly discovered that reading in the car on the way to and from his office was beginning to make him carsick. This is a widely noticed effect. However, he also found the cure. He asked an ophthalmologist friend of his who is a fellow trustee of the Massachusetts Eye and Ear Infirmary (which Lynch calls "Massaineer") what could be done, and his doctor friend offered a solution. If one reads using ambient light, the pupil of the eye expands, and in that state one is susceptible to motion sickness while reading. If, on the contrary, you reduce ambient light and focus a spotlight on the page, then you do not get carsick. So that's what Lynch does now.

be there when a company is doing poorly and is turning around, or you'll call them up a little later and they'll say things are better." This is a reminder that Lynch's basic objective is to *catch the turn in a company's fortunes*, which might be described as the time-efficient technique of deploying capital. Often, there is a one- to twelve-month interval between a material change in a company and the corresponding movement in its stock. That's what Lynch wants to capitalize on.

The Baleen Whale

Although a whale is a very large affair, many of them subsist not by eating big fish but rather by acting as huge strainers. A baleen whale, for instance, cruises rapidly through the ocean with its mouth open, taking in thousands and millions of minuscule sea creatures. The tiny proportion of good stuff is sifted out by the baleen and goes on into its stomach; the junk is expelled. One can think of Peter Lynch as a dark-suited mobile strainer, processing hundreds and hundreds of bits of information a day. Some of it arrives passively, like the krill scooped up by the whale; a lot, though, is deliberately hunted out. Brokers fall in the first category: Lynch hears from some two hundred of them. He might receive several dozen brokers' telephone calls on an average day.

Ordinarily, Lynch doesn't accept calls directly. Callers have learned to leave concise messages with his secretary or one of his two traders. He may return one call for every ten he receives, but he will initiate calls on subjects of concern to him. Either way, he exhorts the person at the end of the line to compress his message to a minute and a half and actually starts a kitchen timer when the conversation begins. After ninety seconds, *brrringg!* Or he will just end the conversation: "Sorry, I got another call comin' in." Pretty soon the callers get the point about brevity. Even in that short time he will quite often ask some key questions several times, perhaps in different ways, like a cross-examiner.

Shoe Leather

Lynch's most solid investment information comes from company visits. After so many years in a big investing institution, he has

gotten to know hundreds upon hundreds of well-placed executives in the business world who desire nothing more than to be
obliging to institutional stockholders, their most important
owners. What's more, you learn how to interpret what you hear.
Some company presidents promise more than they can deliver,
some are always overcautious, some are honest and reliable.
Knowing which is which gives the professional an inestimable
advantage. And visit them he does, forty or fifty a month, five
or six hundred a year. He groups them, of course. If he goes to
see one company in Minneapolis, he wants to see several. One
efficient method is to attend regional company conferences
arranged by local brokerage houses. Montgomery Securities has
them for West Coast companies, Robinson-Humphrey has a
famous one in Atlanta, and Prescott, Ball & Turben for the
Midwest. At these occasions, several dozen companies will field
their best men to present their cases in the most concise and
informative way possible, and there is time for questions—an
excellent way to stay up-to-date. And if Lynch is intrigued by
what he hears he might visit the plants afterwards. Similarly,
there are conferences on particular topics, of which the best
known are those staged by San Francisco's Hambrecht and Quist
on high-technology companies—not that Lynch feels comfortable
in high technology.

In reverse, Lynch himself is a first port of call for companies
that want to tell their stories to the Boston investment community. At any time a score or so companies will be in town to
deliver their pitch. Lynch could schedule four an hour if he
wanted to. To give an idea, here is his schedule of possible
meetings one day in December 1988:

    7:45 James Rosenberg/Katherine Hensel
    8:00 Continental Illinois
          Scotty's
          Chuck Clough—Chief Investment Strategist
          Jim Dougherty—Business Services, Advertising
          Doug Augenthaler—Pollution Control
          Interest Rate Market Sector Review
          LSI Logic
    9:15 Motorola
    9:30 Cigna

9:30	Michael's Stores
10:00	Ron Morrow—Tobacco
10:00	Convex Computer
10:30	Quaker State
10:30	Jerrico
11:00	Louisiana Pacific
11:00	Teradata
12:00	Freddie Mac
	Optrotech
	TransTechnology
	Scotty's
	Quaker State Corp.
	Sonex Research
	Fay's Drug Store
	Peter Anker—Metals
	Dave Lippman—Drugs
	Dan Benton—Microcomputers/Mainframes
	Ann Knight—Autos
	J. Rosenberg/K. Hensel—Regional Banks
	Ken Gassman—Retail
	Les Ravitz—Chemicals
	Bill Becklean—Telecomm Equip
	Suzanne Cook—Oil Services
	Marc Cohen—Tobacco
	Les Pugh—Euro Food Mfg.
2:00	Continental Illinois
2:30	Envirodyne
3:30	Optrotech
4:00	Ann Knight—Autos
4:30	Wells Fargo
5:00	Raychem
5:00	Steve Eisenberg—Leisure

A key element of Lynch's technique is his *insistence on first-hand contact with his sources*. Fidelity has about thirty in-house analysts, plus their assistants, and many other portfolio managers besides himself. He used to see them at the biweekly meetings of all the fund managers and analysts, which have since given way to analysts' daily notes. Twice a month, there are meetings of the growth-stock managers. Lynch could just rely on the information ingested and processed by this system. But he wants direct, regular contact with each company. *Investment managers who don't do this basic spadework, are, in Lynch's opinion, shirking their job.*

Lynch hates it when a broker recommends a stock without providing good reasons: "Peter, I have a deal for you."

"You say, 'John, you're a hot spook, but I want to see her picture,' " Lynch comments. He ignores the broker's record of previous successes and treats such a recommendation as though it had been slipped anonymously under the door. He wants the background. So he visits the company's plant. When he likes what he sees, his reaction, he says, is " 'Aha, this thing is really good.' You have to know that, you can't do it secondhand. Otherwise, one day you wake up and say, 'What the heck am I doin' here?' "

Many nonprofessional investors would like to be Mycroft Holmes, Sherlock's brother, who sat in his club, where no one was allowed to talk to a member, and solved crimes by reading and thinking. These investors hope that they can sit at their desks with their computer screens and brokerage write-ups and do an adequate job: "Big Bucks in the Comfort of Your Own Home!" Alas, it's not that simple. The real pro *begins* from that level of knowledge, and these days he's probably the one whom the nonprofessional is buying from or selling to. To compete you have to make use of every instrument available, the key one being firsthand knowledge.

But can anyone really master the facts on so many industries, so many countries? Sure, says Lynch. Take insurance: "When I took over the management of the fund in May of 1977, I had never been interested in the insurance industry. But within a year, 20 percent of the fund was in insurance stocks. I've owned Kemper for eight years. I visited them once and spent several hours there. I wanted to know the business. But I haven't actually been there again since. I talk to them, though."

Networking

All highly successful investors have loose or formal alliances running from one or two to dozens of members, with whom they have learned they can profitably swap thoughts. As one of them said to me, "If I have a dollar and give it to you, between us we still have only one dollar. But if I give you an idea, we *both* have an idea." Lynch says that these "buy side" peers, not stockbrokers, are his best source of useful ideas. Obviously, you don't tell them what you are buying at that very second, but you swap your general insights for theirs. It certainly stands to reason that a select few fellow buyers, each of whom is serviced by hundreds of stockbrokers, would be a better source than the brokers, since the buyers stand far higher up the intellectual food chain.

Here are some outside professionals whose opinion he particularly respects. All the ones from Boston, along with Lynch himself, frequent the Down Town Discussion Group, which meets for dinner six times a year.

> George Boltres of Tiedman, Kerlin, Boltres, New York
> William Burt of Endowment Management & Research
>   Corp., Boston
> Ken Cassidy of Cassidy Investments, New York
> Anthony Cope of Wellington Management Co., Boston
> Peter DeRoetth of Account Management, Boston
> Thomas Duncan of Frontier Capital, Boston
> Charles Flather of Middlegreen Associates, Boston
> Richard Goldstein of Richard Goldstein Investments, Denver
> John Gruber of Gruber Capital Management, San Francisco
> Kenneth Heebner of Loomis, Sayles & Co., Boston
> Philip Hempleman of Ardsley Partners, New York
> Edward Huebner of Hellman, Jordan Management Co.,
>   Boston
> Donald Keller of Keystone Custodian Funds, Boston
> David Knight of Knight, Bain, Seath & Holbrook, Toronto
> J. David Macey of One Federal Asset Management, Boston
> Joseph McNay of Essex Investment Management Co., Boston
> Ernst von Metzsch of Wellington Management Co., Boston
> Michael Price of Mutual Shares, New York
> Oscar Schafer of Cumberland Associates, New York
> Albert Stern of Citibank, New York
> Matthew Weatherbie of Putnam Management, Boston

In a recent book he also listed some of his favorite brokers:

John Adams, Adams, Harkness & Hill

Mike Armellino, Goldman, Sachs
Steve Berman, County Securities
Allan Bortel, Shearson Lehman
Jon Burke, Robinson Humphrey
Norm Caris, Morgan, Olmstead, Kennedy & Gardner
Tom Clephane, Morgan Stanley
Art Davis, Prescott Ball & Turben
Don DeScenza, Nomura Securities
David Eisenberg, Sanford Bernstein
Jerry Epperson, Wheat First Securities
Joe Frazzano, Oppenheimer
Dick Fredericks, Montgomery Securities
Jonathan Gelles, Wertheim Schroder
Jane Gilday, McKinley Allsopp
Maggie Gilliam, First Boston
Tom Hanley, Salomon Bros.
Herb Hardt, Monness, Crespi, Hardt & Co.
Brian Harra, Brean Murray, Foster Securities
Ira Hirsch, Fourteen Research Corp.
Ed Hyman, Cyrus J. Lawrence
Sam Isaly, S. G. Warburg
Lee Isgur, Paine Webber
Robert Johnson, First Boston
Joe Jolson, Montgomery Securities
Paul Keleher, W. H. Newbold's Son & Co.
John Kellenyi, Drexel Burnham Lambert
Dan Lee, Drexel Burnham Lambert
Bob Maloney, Wood Gundy
Peter Marcus, Paine Webber
Jay Meltzer, Goldman Sachs
Bill Miller, Legg Mason
Tom Petrie, First Boston
Larry Rader, Merrill Lynch
Tom Richter, Robinson Humphrey
Bill Ritger, Dillon Reed
Elliot Schlang, Prescott Ball & Turben
Elliot Schneider, Gruntal
Rick Schneider, Cyrus J. Lawrence
Don Sinsabaugh, Swergold, Chefitz & Sinsabaugh

Stein Soelberg, Baird, Patrick
Oakes Spalding, Adams, Harkness & Hill
Stewart Spector, Furman Selz Mager Dietz & Birney
Joseph Stechler, Stechler
Jack Sullivan, Van Kasper
David Walsh, Bear Stearns
Skip Wells, Adams, Harkness & Hill

Lynch, who spends most of his day talking to companies on the telephone or personally, once said that either he or his research assistant checks with most of the companies he holds once a month. This implies almost 2,000 completed calls, and more attempts, or, assuming five minutes each, about forty hours a week just for that operation.

"When I actually see a company, I try to dig in: 'The capital spending was $420 million last year; what is it this year? The depreciation was $288 million last year; what is it this year?' Management is much more on your side when you've done your homework."

What to Look For

Lynch's endless quest, his endless searching among companies, is directed above all toward the *obvious winner, based on changes in the key variable.* As he goes back repeatedly to a given company or industry he spots changes. Business has been dreadful for a year. Then it's not quite so bad. "Even when a company just moves up from doing mediocre business to doing fair business, you can make money," he says. Perhaps inventories are coming down. He learns of something afoot that will change things—a better regulatory climate, a new product or service. So he starts to buy, not just the top company in the group, as T. Rowe Price would, or what seems like the most attractive bargain, as Warren Buffett would, but, like James Rogers, the entire group, *in toto:* quite possibly dozens of companies. Then, as they start to move, he may winnow the list down to a favorite few.

I underline Lynch's emphasis on the *obvious* winner. Lynch claims that if other investors made as many calls as he did, they, too, would spot the changes in company fortunes that he does, and would almost always recognize the same buying opportunities. "You have to stay tuned," he often says.

There are, of course, a couple of differences between Lynch and most investors, or they would do as well at his game as he does. First, he has a sure enough grasp of the material to be able to act swiftly and smoothly, without troubling to get more facts than necessary . . . just enough to be right most of the time.

A second advantage Lynch has is that since he can evaluate and develop buying and selling targets all across the range of his huge repertoire of actual and possible holdings, he is exposed to far more opportunities than most investors. Most fund managers reason that since knowing more than the competition is the key to superiority, they will focus on a limited area: "value" stocks, growth stocks, Japanese stocks, resources companies, insurance companies, banks, or whatever, and rarely be outtraded in their chosen sector. But when that sector gets overpriced, as from time to time it surely will, what then? One is always tempted to carry on anyway, exposing the portfolio to the risk of a terrific header, or else branch out into some apparently different underpriced sector, where, however, one can easily make mistakes out of ignorance.

Lynch's technique of being prepared to deal in practically any stock whatever places the same sort of demands on a manager that a secondhand jewelry dealer would experience if he branched out into paintings, rare books, antique rugs, coins, furniture, manuscripts, etchings, and then commercial and residential real estate and wholesale vegetables. Auction galleries have a wide range of expertise, but they have considerable staffs to which specialized authority is delegated: a paintings department, a furniture department, and so on. Lynch has access to Fidelity's research, yet makes all his own decisions.

Lynch is a bit over six feet tall, slim and athletic-looking, with silver hair over a pale, finely modeled, almost spiritual face that is faintly suggestive of a much handsomer Andy Warhol. He is pleasantly rather than elegantly turned out. A brown tweed suit rises from black wing-tipped shoes. A white button-down shirt is topped by a red knitted tie whose ends are a foot apart.

He speaks rapidly and profusely, using a colloquial, even somewhat adolescent, choice of words: "So I say to myself, gee, what'm I do'n?" In talking, he waves one or both of his hands, sometimes with his glasses in them, smiling faintly. His high tenor voice has a mild Massachusetts (not necessarily Boston) accent.

Lynch describes himself as typically Irish and gabby—when not working, of course. In response to questions he will start to answer, launch into a digression, and then babble on about what is in his mind, realizing eventually that he has gone off the point. Asked about an eventual career evolution, he says he might like to teach someday, and one can readily believe it. He has a lot to say, and, I would guess, would be glad to talk forever—particularly about stocks, although he is fond of chatting about Marblehead and the rebuilding of his house there.

Lynch likes to describe his own performance: five years, ten years, year by year. He points out that although under his management each share of the fund has gained twentyfold, during the period there have been eight declines of between 10 percent and 30 percent. Each year he has beat the average fund and admits to no *calendar* down years in the past eleven. He took a hard knock in October 1987, though, and finished his fund's *fiscal* year to March 31, 1988, down 9.6 percent, compared to a fall in the Dow of 10.9 percent.

Quite surprising, in my experience of notable investors, is Lynch's balanced, calm, modest, and unassuming approach to his profession and to life—except, of course, for his phenomenally intense preoccupation with his work. Geniuses and obsessives usually have some burr under the saddle: poverty or family trouble in youth, or physical or social burdens, or some blow of fate later on that pushes them to pass their rivals. Lynch was presumably affected by the early death of his father and his family's resulting sudden change in circumstances, which would have made him feel alone and responsible for his own destiny. Who knows? And one forgets today what it once was to be an Irish Catholic in establishment Boston. The inordinate drive of the Kennedys is a familiar example. Lynch mentions that when he joined Fidelity there were only one or two other employees who were not Ivy League graduates! He showed them. The same stimuli often lead hyperperformers to become self-centered, subjective, and tyrannical. Lynch shows no trace of that. Those around him all praise his relaxed and unassuming manner. Most have never heard him raise his voice or express irritation.

At Home

Lynch and his wife, Carolyn, who is from Delaware and whom he met at Wharton, have three children, all girls. I mentioned to him that I, too, have three girls and found that situation highly satisfactory. He nodded fondly: "I wouldn't trade any of them for two boys and a hundred thousand shares of IBM," he said.

The Lynches have lived in various places around Boston during their marriage. Since 1982 they have occupied a large house with a noble prospect of the harbor in Marblehead, a town they love. It has a modern exterior, and when bought, was almost unfinished inside. They have been remodeling both the inside and the outside without interruption ever since, adding extra space, putting old woodwork into the austere rooms they found, chipping, painting, drilling, and hammering.

Lynch's doctor has told him that it is a good plan to go for a stiff walk—defined as four miles an hour—every day. So after supper, he and Carolyn embark on a forty-minute hike around Marblehead. He finds this gets the blood racing and makes him feel revved up.

At Work

He has a large, cluttered corner office in the Fidelity Building at the end of a corridor populated by other fund managers, who manage less money and have offices somewhat smaller and somewhat less cluttered than his.

Lynch's office approaches the ultimate in clutter. Against a window run two yards of reports in a horizontal parade, and in front of them vertical stacks of the reports that have come in during the week, arranged by categories. Manila files litter the floor. Inches of paper blanket his desk, and I counted some sixty yellow legal pads peeking out here and there from the debris. The writing on the top sheet of each pad covers a concern of the moment: companies that fill some particular criterion, such as interesting insider buying; questions to ask the officer of a company when he calls back; notes that need to be expanded . . . whatever requires attention. I asked him if placing the yellow pads in a series of vertical racks across one wall above his desk would make it easier for him to put his hand on them instantly. He seemed puzzled. He scooped up a file off the floor, glanced at it, and said, "If this guy calls me back—he's the CEO of a company—I want to be able to talk to him right away about what I'm interested in, so I need to have it right here." I suppose the point is that he can put his finger on what he wants quickly enough, and he knows roughly where in the jumble everything is lurking. Perhaps we have here the difference between artificial order—the garden of a French château, for example—and working order, such as a jungle, which looks chaotic to the passerby, but makes sense to God or a naturalist.

Even the walls of the office are a muddle: giant pictures of his children (slightly askew), prints, posters, framed share certificates. Almost hidden among the papers is a single beige telephone, flanked by a row of framed family photographs, and, like an alp rising behind foothills, a computer terminal on a side table.

In his office his conversations with colleagues are terse in the extreme. From time to time a head appears around the door and emits a squirt transmission of a few dozen syllables. Lynch will reply with a grunt or two; the head vanishes. The conversations are like the soundtracks of old speeded-up movies of the 1920s.

Invest Before You Investigate

The essence of Lynch's technique is *fluency*, letting his portfolio flow easily from one idea to another. He notices some apparent opportunity in the market and moves on it forthwith, without delaying for extensive analysis. Of course, this requires both flair and a sure judgment based on a long experience of the subject. One is reminded of superb generalship: At Salamanca, Wellington watches Marmont marching parallel to him across a valley. Suddenly he spots an advantage. "By God! That'll do," he announces, snapping shut his telescope and crisply issuing the orders that will destroy his adversary. Or Nelson at the Battle of the Nile: After months of chase, he sweeps around a headland to find the French fleet anchored against the shore in a defensive position. It is close to nightfall. Another commander would have reconnoitered, devised a plan, and instructed his captains. Nelson does not hesitate an instant . . . In the failing light he daringly slices in between the land and the enemy vessels on their unprepared side, anchors his ships so two can pound each hapless Frenchman, and has battered the French fleet to bits before it can even recover its foraging parties from shore.

Similarly, Lynch, detecting a market inefficiency, will act immediately. The domestic car companies seem cheap: He buys Ford, Chrysler, and GM. They go up; he adds a collection of foreign ones—Volvo, Subaru, Honda, Peugeot, and Fiat. The relative positions change again; he calmly reverses field. Dreyfus, the mutual-fund management company, falls from 35 to 17 in the crash of October 1987. The market fears that the fund business may be in trouble. But there is $15 a share in cash, and Dreyfus has such a strong money-fund department that it should gain business on balance. So Lynch buys Dreyfus. He also usually takes small positions in stocks that *may* be interesting—what he calls his farm team—so that he will be reminded to follow them.

Since, like a racing skipper, he is constantly changing course to take advantage of small shifts in the wind, there is unending movement in Lynch's portfolio. Many holdings only last a month or two, and the entire list turns over at least once a year on average. Lynch feels that if he were doing his job perfectly the turnover would be even greater.

Mechanically, this creates interesting problems. Lynch has about 1,400 holdings; the largest 100 represent half the total capital, and 200 represent two-thirds of it. On a typical working day he transacts some $50 million of purchases and $50 million of sales. To conduct this huge volume of business he has only three traders. Barry Lyden does the buying and Robert Burns the selling. Anita Stuart understudies both. Ordinarily there would be a hundred or so issues in each trader's book; that is, a hundred that Lynch wants to buy, if he can get them cheaply enough, and a hundred that he wants to sell, if they reach his price targets. His traders are extremely price-sensitive. Rather than bashing in and trading a block all at once, like many big traders, they will withhold their bids or offers if the stock moves away from them and wait until it comes back. He will typically drop out of the market altogether if he learns of a large competitive order, reasoning that he is better off waiting for the other fellow to get out of the way and buy when the stock falls back again, if it ever does. Less than 5 percent of Lynch's trades are bigger than 10,000 shares. (Many institutional managers usually deal in 100,000-share blocks.)

Lynch's policy is to seek to profit from what many investors would consider minor price anomalies. In such a huge list of holdings and prospective holdings there will at any moment be dozens that he thinks have gotten ahead of themselves, in which he will be doing some selling, and dozens of others experiencing some price weakness that he will take advantage of to do some buying. Here his technique differs radically from most other investors and resembles that of a market maker, who, handling a dozen or two issues, has become so attuned to the rhythm of his stable of stocks and the factors that move them that he trades them back and forth, back and forth, year after year, making endless small profits over and over, getting slowly richer in the process. The big difference, though, is that most specialists work twenty or thirty stocks at the most, while Lynch is operating with a couple of thousand, and constantly changing ones at that.

Lynch believes in an old trader's rule: *If you buy a stock because you hope something will happen, and it doesn't happen, sell the stock.* Wall Street has a sardonic expression for this idea: "An investment is a speculation that didn't work out." You had an idea, based on an expectation; you were wrong. So now you really have no reason to own the stock and should sell it cleanly and quickly. Lynch says he often sells too soon. "But *you don't get hurt by things that you don't own that go up*. It's what you *do* own that kills you.

"Of the stocks that I buy, three months later I am happy with less than a quarter of them. So if I like to look at ten stocks, it's better for me to buy all ten, and then go on studying and researching. Perhaps I won't like a number of them later on, but I can keep the ones that I do like, and increase those positions. And companies keep changing as you look: Competition may intensify; a problem plant may be sold off or closed; a competitive plant may burn down. So if you stay tuned, you can find that the fundamentals are changing.

"Or even if they don't change, the stock may go from $20 to $16. Perhaps I bought 10,000 at $20, and then I'll buy 100,000 at $16. If I look at ten companies, I may find one company that is interesting. If I look at twenty companies then I may find two. If I look at forty, I may find four. If I look at one hundred, I may find ten. If other people saw as many companies as I do, I think that nine out of ten of them, when they heard the same story, would say, 'Wow,' just the way I do, and be able to make the same buyin' decision. You have to be a good listener in this business. And of course you may not be able to decide on the first visit. It may happen a year later or two years later."

The Private Investor's Advantage Over the Professional

When a consumer contemplates buying a major appliance, such as a stove, says Lynch, he researches it carefully. He asks his friends who own one and looks it up in *Consumer Reports*. Similarly, when he buys a house he will bring in a builder to look at the plumbing and wiring and will check whether the local school system is deteriorating. But when this same man buys a stock, he will often do it on the basis of a tip, without any research at all.

And yet the individual buyer *should* have "an unbelievable advantage" over the professional. He can take his time, and concentrate, and can just stay put, the way he holds on to his house. If he had to buy and sell every month or every week he would go crazy.

Similarly, Lynch suggests that individual investors take careful note of retail products, services, and purveyors that they find outstanding. He gives examples from his own experience: Taco Bell, Volvo, Apple Computer, Dunkin' Donuts, Pier 1 Imports, and (thanks to L'eggs) Hanes.

Surprises

Successes in real estate often come as a surprise to the buyer. You make a good purchase, the value improves, you do nothing, it improves further. Lynch says that his experiences with stocks resembles most people's with real estate: *The best results flow from a progression of surprises.* He buys with no particular long-term objective. The stock goes up; it still looks good, so he holds on to it; then it goes up some more. For instance, when Ford eliminated its dividend in 1981, Lynch bought it, and still holds it. He bought Unisys ten years ago and Chrysler more than seven years ago. He bought Chrysler, and nine months later he realized that the situation was much better than he had first supposed. He bought Stop-n-Shop; after a while there was good news, then more, then more, and bit by bit the stock advanced twentyfold. The stocks in which Lynch has made large amounts of money have often been surprises. When, on the contrary, his initial reaction to a story was "Wow," he has often lost money. Rarely do things turn out as favorably as hoped.

Asking the Competition

One of Lynch's preferred devices is favored by most good investors. It is to *ask the man you are interviewing about his rivals across the street. It isn't too significant when the competitors pan a company, but it is important when they say something nice about it.* For instance, the other steel companies praised Nucor: a new formula, new people, doing the right things. Lynch looked into it and bought the stock. Nobody knows a company like the competitor who has to battle with it day after day in creating new products and struggling for market share. John Templeton has a standard formula: "If you weren't working for your present company, who would you most like to join instead?" Once when Lynch was visiting United Inns he was struck by the respect with which its management spoke of one of their competitors, LaQuinta Motor Inns. The very next day he telephoned LaQuinta. After a while he called in person, and in a matter of weeks had sunk 3 percent of Magellan's capital in the company.

There is another byproduct from asking executives about matters outside their own company: investment ideas about its suppliers or customers. News from a construction outfit that sales are much stronger than generally realized could start Lynch thinking about forest products, cement, gypsum, or roofing materials.

Visiting Sears, he may find that carpet sales are improving. While calling on a retailer, he may find that shoes are selling badly, but that sneakers are going very well. What then? Stride-Rite, which makes leather shoes for children, bought the Sperry Division of Uniroyal, and thus got Topsiders. But what really worked for it was Keds, which it was almost forced to take as part of the deal, and which now constitutes over half of Stride-Rite's earnings. Lynch says that he was feeling sick that he hadn't caught Reebok, but "then I said, 'Hey, I've got a person over here that's participating in all this.' Funny things happen along the way. You really have to keep your eyes open." So he bought Stride-Rite and cleaned up.

Lynch points out that *it makes a great deal of difference how much the person who tells you a story actually knows.* If the head of a steel company reports sharply improved industry conditions, that's real news. But if he tells you that great things are stirring in the fiber-optics business, then perhaps you'd better look for confirmation from someone with better credentials. And yet it is odd how easily investors are seduced by tips from well-placed people in a different industry from the one that the tip is about.

Insider Buying

Lynch carefully watches when corporate insiders buy their own stocks. An insider, he notes, may *sell* his company's stock for many reasons. He may be buying a house or raising cash to exercise stock options. *But the insider only has one reason to buy: to make money.* It is safe to suppose that an insider will only buy if what he sees gives him good reason to be confident. *A company, Lynch observes, will rarely go bust in the face of heavy insider buying.* He particularly looks for a *depressed stock being scooped up by middle-level insiders*, even more than by CEOs.

Fidelity now has a little team following insider trading. They receive and condense reports from the New York Stock Exchange and the SEC and put out charts showing where the insiders have bought in the past. There are about eighty-five companies shown on the buying side of the insider transactions report, and about fifty on the selling side, which is only significant if a number of executives are selling a large part of their position. If an officer has 10,000 shares and sells 1,000 to finance a house, that is not significant. If, however, he has 45,000 shares and sells 40,000 of them, and several other officers are making sales of comparable size, that is of the greatest significance, and merits careful study and, probably, action.

Growth

Growth for Lynch is of course a cardinal virtue in a company, and growth stocks are the largest single category in his portfolio. Nevertheless, growth companies are for him by no means the only attractive category to hold. Anything may be underpriced or overpriced at some time, and thus a buy or a sale. However, in talking of growth, *Lynch looks particularly at unit growth*, even more than earnings growth. T. Rowe Price, the original apostle of growth-stock investing, looked for companies that reported higher earnings in each successive business cycle. However, higher earnings may derive from raising prices or from skillful acquisitions. Lynch looks for rising numbers of physical units sold, quarter by quarter and year by year.*

"The very best way to make money in a market is in *a small growth company that has been profitable for a couple of years and simply goes on growing*," says Lynch.

Hitting It Big

Lynch makes a point well understood by speculators. While the key objective of the investor should be to avoid a major loss, the occasional huge winner will offset a number of small losses. Managed account holders often get this wrong. Here is the psychology: A trust beneficiary with $1 million looks at his state-

---

*Annual reports may or may not state a company's unit sales. If not, securities analysts in the old days would sometimes go to the factory and count the number of tractors or whatever coming out the back door. Today this is generally impractical. My own firm, which is growth-oriented, tracks the approximate growth in unit sales from the reported figures by multiplying two ratios: the retained operating margin on sales and the turnover rate of gross operating assets . . . the latter being a measure of the capital required to produce a dollar of sales.

ment of account. He sees that quite a few stocks bought several years back for $30,000 and $40,000 are now selling for $100,000 or $130,000. Good: That's what he's paying the bank to do for him. He scans the report further. Then he comes upon a most distressing spectacle: The holding of U.S. Bumf has declined from $60,000 to $35,000! Horrors! That $25,000 loss would pay for the Cadillac he had just told his wife she couldn't buy! Why should anyone pay the Flatulent Trust Company a fee to buy junk like that? Sue!

The Flatulent's response to this prospect is, understandably, to shrink from taking any risks at all. However, Lynch points out, that's a self-defeating reaction. "If you have five stocks, and three go down 75 percent, one goes up tenfold, and one goes up 20 percent, you still have good performance for those five. . . . Just do the exercise; you make so much on the one that goes up tenfold it just overwhelms the ones you lose 50 percent, 75 percent, or 90 percent on." The actual math would go like this, assuming five stocks bought for $100 each:

Losers	Winners	Overall Result
$100 − 75% = $25	$100 + 20% = $ 120	
$100 − 75% = $25	$100 + 900% = $1,000	
$100 − 75% = $25		
$300 becomes $75	$200 becomes $1,120	$500 becomes $1,195

Lynch further observes that it is easier to make big percentage gains in stocks of small companies than of big ones. It is much harder for a stock in the Dow Jones Industrial Average to triple than it is for a little company on the American Exchange.

High Growth, High Multiple

Lynch points out that a company selling at a high price-earnings ratio may have farther to fall than one selling at a low price-earnings ratio. However, if you get the facts right, you make more in a company selling at a high price-earnings ratio, assuming that the earnings justify the price. He cites as an example a company selling for twenty times $1 earnings per share, or $20, and growing 20 percent a year, and a company selling for ten times $1 earnings per share, or $10, and growing 10 percent a year. After a year, the first company will be earning $1.20 and the second company $1.10. In the tenth year, the first company will be earning $6.19, and if it is still selling at twenty times earnings, the market price will be $123.80. If, as often happens, the price-earnings ratio has declined, to fifteen, say, then the market price will be $92.85.

In the meantime, however, the company whose earnings growth is 10 percent will be earning $2.59, implying a market price of $25.90, a quarter or so of the high-growth company.

Whisper Stocks

Lynch finds one of the worst traps to be buying exciting companies that do not have earnings. He can remember buying dozens of companies where—had the story come true—he would have made 1,000 percent on his money, and losing every time. And yet, and yet . . . ! Wonderful new stories appear—"the sizzle, not the steak," as he says—and again he will bite, and again he will lose.

A useful investment concept that Peter Lynch has coined a name for is the "whisper stock." By this he means a company that his source—otherwise reliable—lowers his voice somewhat to describe, saying, "I have a great company that's a bit too small for a fund, but that you might want to consider for a personal account."

The reliable source then describes some irresistible idea, which will be a huge winner if it succeeds: Bioresponse, which extracts antibodies from cow lymph; Smith Labs, which has a remedy derived from papaya for slipped-disc troubles, and the like. He cites Alhambra Mines, American Solar King, American Surgery Centers, Asbetec Industries, Bowmar, Comdial, Integrated Circuits, Vector Graphics Microcomputers, National Health Care, Televideo, Trion, Priam, and Sun World Airways. Lynch claims that he has invariably lost money on these conceptions.

"Diworseification"

Lynch distinguishes between companies that intelligently expand into related businesses where their knowledge and skill are appli-

cable and wild, unplanned purchases of companies that management hopes it can handle, but often can't. In general, Lynch feels
that companies with excess cash are better advised to repurchase
their own stock than to expand into business areas that may give
them lots of trouble.

Hot Stocks

The stock Lynch says *he most wants to avoid is the hottest stock
in the hottest industry*—the one that gets the most favorable
publicity, that every investor is told about by other investors
. . . and then collapses. He cites any number of formerly hot
industries: digital watches, mobile homes, health-maintenance
organizations, cheap wall-to-wall carpeting companies, disk
drives, oil services—and, indeed, Xerox. In all cases, *the high
growth is a honey pot for the competition*, which strikes the hot
company just when it has spent huge sums to expand in order to
hold on to market share. So its profit margin collapses, it gets into
a financial bind, and since it is followed by every possible security
analyst and speculator, its fall is precipitous.

Desiderata

As some simple criteria of a desirable investment, Lynch suggests
looking for a company selling at a low price-earnings ratio that
earns 15 percent to 20 percent on equity, and 10 percent or so
on revenues. Also, it should have a strong and understandable
business franchise, so that it does not need to be run by
supermen.

Unlike many investors, Lynch loves *simple businesses that
anybody could run*. Other investors often prefer what might be
called the athletes, the top businesses with wonderful managements in highly competitive areas—Procter & Gamble or 3M or
Texas Instruments or Dow Chemical or Motorola—which, tough-
ened by decades of successful struggle, have developed lean, hard
teams that make opportunities, scramble for markets, and
constantly push growth by finding new products. Sure: That's the
company you'd want your grandfather to have started. But for
Lynch the crux is that you don't need to insist on anything

wonderful, just a good-enough company that's selling too low and won't fall apart before the stock moves back up to where it belongs. In his words, he wants a company that any fairly good group of new managers could take over and run with reasonable confidence that things would hold together for a few years.

Management or the Business?

It is not in the nature of business in general to do as well as, for example, a Bristol-Myers or a Melville, with twenty years of consistently rising earnings. If one sees such a phenomenon, it is probably not management that should get the credit, but the business itself. Even if management is the essence, Lynch finds that he has little chance of finding that out. "I may eventually discover that they're pretty smart, even if they don't sound like Johnny Carson."

One characteristic a company may have that lessens worry about management is that it enjoys what securities people call a niche: something unique or at least special. He cites Fort Howard,* the dominant company in making paper from recycled paper; or Service Corporation International, a chain of funeral homes that is steadily buying the best existing homes in new locations; or Dunkin' Donuts, which seems to go on and on in its simple business; or Regis, the largest independent beauty salon chain, specializing in shopping malls; or Rockaway, which makes postage meters. His dream, he says, somewhat surprisingly, is *the growth company in a slow-growth industry*: You know something has to be profoundly right about the situation.

The same reasoning explains why Lynch is not comfortable with high-tech companies: They may be just fine, but that doesn't do him much good if he can't understand them. "How can I know if one outfit's random-access memory is better than someone else's?" he asks. In reply, one can only say that some analysts do try to know just that; but they are usually specialists.

No Inhibitions

Except for this one blind spot, Lynch has almost no inhibitions. We've seen him buying funeral homes and motels; many of his

*Later taken private in a leveraged buyout.

favorites have names that old-fashioned folk might find disconcerting.

Cracker Barrel	The Pep Boys—Manny, Moe & Jack
International Dairy Queen	Pic 'N' Save
Dunkin' Donuts	Tasty Baking
Genuine Parts	Tootsie Roll
LaQuinta	Toys 'R' Us
Luby's Cafeterias	WD40
National Sanitary	

Many of these companies are much more solid than they
sound. The Pep Boys, a Philadelphia auto-parts supplier, is in fact
seventy-five years old and still getting stronger, so it's not strange
that Lynch thinks well of it. Genuine Parts has had twenty-five
years of up earnings and a market capitalization in the billions.
International Dairy Queen has some 7,000 outlets around the
country. It uses its earnings to buy back its own stock.

Lynch says that he has an edge because *a lot of the people he
competes with are not looking for reasons to buy. They are
looking for reasons not to buy*: The company is unionized; GE
will come out with a competitive product that will kill them; or
whatever. There is a whole list of biases that scare most investors
away from studying the situation at all. *"To make money, you
must find something that nobody else knows, or do something
that others won't do because they have rigid mind-sets."*

Grim Businesses

Lynch points out that some businesses are intrinsically repulsive,
and thus can often sell at attractive prices simply because most
investors don't want to touch them. He cites Service Corporation
International, which expanded for years, ignored by the market,
until it owned 5 percent of all the funeral homes in the country.
In due course Wall Street woke up to the stock, by which time
it had advanced twentyfold. Another example is Charles River
Breeding Labs, much beloved of the Boston community, which is
in the business of breeding rats for cancer experimentation.
Another is Safety-Kleen, which washes the greasy automobile
parts that lie around gas stations.

Going Abroad

The inefficiencies of international investing can be astonishing. Lynch described visiting one of the major brokers in Sweden. No one from the firm had been to see Volvo, which was only 200 miles away in Gothenburg. In Sweden, Volvo is the equivalent of IBM, General Motors, and General Electric. In England, five or six analysts will have visited any big company within a month. But this would not be true in Germany, France, Hong Kong, or Thailand.

If you aren't inhibited, *you can sometimes find great bargains abroad because the markets are less efficient.*

His lack of inhibitions also lets him invest abroad without qualms. He just compares the foreign company with its domestic counterpart and decides which he prefers: Ford, Subaru, or Volvo (at one time his largest holding)? Procter & Gamble or Unilever? Uniroyal or Michelin (in which he hit a homer)?

AKZO or Du Pont? "You can arbitrage one against the other, depending on the price. Take depreciation. You determine what the gross plant account is, and then what AKZO's annual depreciation is as compared to Du Pont's, say. If AKZO has a 4 percent depreciation rate and Du Pont has 2 percent, you know AKZO's profits are understated."

Corporate taxes are still 50 percent in Germany, at a time when taxes elsewhere are much lower. Germany will thus have to cut its taxes, or people will build their plants in Spain or Ireland, where taxes are minimal. So one can expect that eventually German business will report better profits on unchanged business.

There are only a couple of Swedish insurance companies whose securities are listed. At a time when the combined ratios were improving in the United States, and rate increases were general, one knew that soon the industry was going to make money worldwide. Skandia, however, went on reporting poor results in the newspapers, while its competitors dropped out of the business. The stock didn't advance until it actually showed a profit in its reported results. Lynch had bought it by then, and made eight to ten times his money.

Lynch says that he has had a far higher proportion of successes in Europe than in the United States. Three months after purchase he has been happy with a good half of the companies he has bought in Europe, compared with only a quarter of his U.S. buys. "French brokers are terrible," he says. "You analyze a company division by division, and you find that it cannot possibly realize the projections made by the brokers. They've pulled the figures out of a hat."

Among countries, Lynch is likely to be most comfortable with the ones that other fund managers are uneasy about and thus don't have large holdings in. Take Italy, for instance: It has one of the highest savings rates in the world and a few years ago introduced the concept of mutual funds, which would pull lots of money into stocks. When Lynch bought IFI on the Milan exchange, it was capitalized at only 40 percent of just the value of its holdings in Fiat and some other companies. SIP, a telephone company, was selling for 1.5 times its cash flow. In other words, Italian companies have been extraordinarily cheap.

Spain? He has big positions in Telefónica and Endesa.

Mexico? Teléfonos de Mexico is a favorite.

When Lynch bought Del Haize Frères it was selling for much less than the value of just one of its holdings, an outstanding U.S. supermarket company, Food Lion.

Lynch is happiest buying stocks abroad that American institutions are just beginning to accumulate. Some of them have huge market capitalizations and can absorb a heavy investment. After this process has gone on long enough, though, the stocks get over-owned by Americans and it's time to move on.

Be Alone

The same principle applies to his purchases of American stocks. As he once said, "I don't like anybody but myself to own these things. If you're wrong, and institutions own the stocks, everyone heads out the door at once. If you're right, it doesn't make any difference—the stock will eventually go up anyway."

For that matter, it applies to the market as a whole. He likes the investing public to be anxious, noting the old saw that the market "climbs a wall of worry." "Once," he noted, "there were plenty of worries: the recession worry, the ozone worry, the new-president worry, the drought worry." This, to him, implied that the market was all right: When things were really grim in 1982, the market was at its bottom. "When the news seems terrible, that's when you make the big money in the market," he has said. Once when he was buying a spread of semiconductor companies in the teeth of poor industry conditions he observed, "If I'm right I could make 400 percent and if I'm wrong I might lose 60 percent." Good-enough odds! "As far as that goes, you can sometimes make twentyfold, while the most you can possibly lose is 100 percent. The public doesn't understand that."

Formulas and Simplifications

Lynch has a brusque, commonsense contempt for many if not most of the formulas that are peddled as shortcuts to stock-market success. He avoids the economic "overviews" and industrial-sector allocations that trust companies favor as a substitute for knowledge and flair; likewise, weighty punditry on economics and market analysis.

It follows from this that he doesn't believe in the old-fashioned approach quaintly called "modern portfolio theory," which essentially means that you don't understand the companies that you are buying, but instead fit them into categories and play with the categories.

How about trends, momentum? "No," says Lynch, "I don't care whether the stocks are going up, down, sideways." There is, however, one exception: catching the turn. That maneuver attracts Lynch strongly. He wants to make a partial investment a bit ahead of the turn in the fortunes of a company, and then build up his holding as the turn actually occurs.

Lynch gives little weight to a company's dividend policy. In his own language, "I can't say that dividends are something I feature."

A horrible fallacy, said Lynch, is buying a stock simply because it has gone down, what is called bottom fishing. If the market thought that Federated Fido was worth $50 six months ago, and it's $20 today, then it must be a bargain! But that was true when it was at $40 and then at $30, and it may well be true when the stock goes down to $10. You have to have a clear conception of the true value and work only off that, not off the stock's recent performance history.

Big Ideas

Lynch wants to be in the position of buying Company A at $20 a share rather than Company B at $30 a share, and then of selling A after it has moved to $30 in order to buy B at $20. He points out that several small gains make a very large one: "Six 30-percent moves equal a four-bagger," he says. His is a technique of relative values, not of majestic conceptions. "I never make any big decisions," he has said. "I don't even want to be in the position where I make one big decision. I'd like to make a couple of small decisions every day." In other words, a few hundred a year. You can't go massively wrong that way. On the contrary, the law of averages, if you are better than the average investor, must infallibly pull you farther and farther ahead. "But you have to know when you're wrong. Then you sell. Most stocks I buy are a mistake."

Fifteen Minutes a Year

"I spend about fifteen minutes a year on economic analysis," he says. "*The way you lose money in the stock market is to start off with an economic picture. I also spend fifteen minutes a year on where the stock market is going. All these great, heady, thinking deals kill you.*"

He finds that worries based on economic predictions are particularly useless. "We don't make economic judgments," he has said. "We don't have somebody here saying we're going to have a recession, so you can't buy electronic stocks, or we're going to have a boom, so you should buy Colgate-Palmolive. Nobody called me to tell me about the recession in 1980 and 1981," he observes dourly.

Lynch notices that people always ask him about the outlook for the economy and the stock market and other such large and general questions. But nobody can give those answers. And even if they could, companies like Procter & Gamble or Colgate should not be affected by such fluctuations. If, instead, one buys a company that has inherent problems, one can lose all one's money even in good times.

"The GNP six months out is just malarkey. How is the sneaker industry doing? That's real economics."

Options

He also avoids options, futures, and other so-called derivative instruments. There is an excessive cost to these devices, which eats up too much of the profit. Lynch deplores the absorption by the options market of the funds that once went into the shares of smaller companies. *The options market is a gigantic, useless, expensive gambling casino*, whereas the same money might have been available to finance small, new companies, which really need it. (Lynch admits, though, that he has a lamentable record in new companies. He likes to cite a small airline in which he took what must presumably be called a flyer and which went bust.)

Takeovers and LBOs

"All the tips I've gotten on takeovers have been wrong," Lynch has said. He has 0 for 200, he told me. "I've had takeovers, but they've always been surprises." *He is indignant about leveraged buyouts in general, because, he says, they prevent the investing public from participating fully in a recovery following a decline.* Here's the logic: Several companies are all selling at 20, let us say. Then in a market slide or because of bad news they all decline to 8. The bad ones never come back. But the good ones reorganize and bounce back. Along come the managements or some takeover artists who offer to buy out the shareholders at 12, which enough shareholders accept to enable the new owners to "freeze out" the remainder. The insiders sell off assets to pay themselves back. But if that hadn't happened, the stock might have gone to 40 or 50. So the public has suffered the loss and been done out of the recovery! This painful experience is more likely to befall the shareholders of secondary companies: A Gillette or Sterling Drug or Kraft has so many people interested in it that the shareholders will get a fair price.

Lynch also observes sardonically that some investment banker or other will always, for a huge fee, issue a "fairness opinion," to the effect that the bid of 10 for a stock now selling at 8 is "fair." But the buyers know it was 20 a while before and fully expect it to be 20 or more again, so looking two or three years ahead, is 10 really fair?

Desk-bound Analysis

Lynch observes that while you must of course master a company's figures, balance-sheet analysis by itself is inadequate. " 'Very cheap statistically' can be a real trap," he says. "Book value can be hopelessly misleading. There is nothing in the balance sheet of Coca-Cola for the goodwill of the name and the logo, for instance. Then, you can have a company with $200 billion in assets and $100 million in debt: Fine, except that sometimes the assets turn out only to be worth $50 million. So even figures may in reality be very subjective.

"However," he says, "if a company has a good balance sheet when I buy it, that gives me a big edge. If it doesn't turn around I can perhaps lose a third of what I invest. But if it does turn around, then I can do very well indeed."

Lynch observes that when he has lost almost all of an investment, it has often been because he should have kept in better touch with what was happening to the balance sheet.

The Computer

Lynch does not believe that the computer will ever replace a good analyst. The reason is that what counts is the discovery that a company is doing better than expected. There is no way of finding this information out faster than through a telephone call. Indeed, it is not enough just to call the same way any other caller does. If Lynch telephones a company, learns that the business is deteriorating, and decides to sell, a buyer will probably telephone the company and hear the same news. Still, whoever knows the executive better will have a better sense of the shadings of his words. "I tell you, you deal with some people, they're always upbeat. Other people, they're always so gloomy, you'd think it was a short sale. Then you get down to it, business has slipped. The computer won't tell you if it's going to last a month or a year."

Allocation

Completing his repudiation of conventional trust company practice, which, based on an economic "overview," puts a portfolio into categories—cyclicals, utilities, and the like—and massages them by computer, *Lynch entirely avoids conscious "asset allocation," either between stocks and reserves, or between industrial sectors.*

He does, however, have a framework for his portfolio that is quite original. Among stocks, he has four conceptual categories. He had been running the Magellan Fund for three or four years before some outside shareholders who studied the portfolio pointed out to him what the different categories of holdings in fact were. He had not originally bought the holdings to fit into those categories.

1. Growth companies on which he would hope to make two or three times his cost over time.

2. Underpriced asset plays, "value" stocks or smaller blue chips. He is looking for a rapid gain of a third or so, after which he is likely to move on promptly.

3. Special situations and depressed cyclicals.

4. Defensive stocks, which he holds in preference to cash. "A market player has 50 percent of his portfolio in cash at the bottom of the market. When the market moves up, he can miss most of the move."

In a way, what Lynch is really saying is that if a stock is cheap, that is a much higher degree of reality than some vague notion as to what the market will do next year. Particularly, however, if a great many stocks are cheap, or indeed most stocks are cheap, in the eyes of an experienced appraiser, then it begins to follow that the whole market is cheap, not vice versa.

Lynch never holds actual cash or cash equivalents. Rather, he holds conservative stocks with substantial yields, in stable industries. They should not be too much affected by economic downturns and should hold up well in market declines, although they lag during market rises. This category might include 100 or 200 stocks: food companies, advertising agencies, telephone and gas utilities, financial companies, and retailers. This group, since he is not looking for big gains, is also where his highest turnover occurs. "If a stock goes up, because it's had a road show or for some other reason, but the fundamentals are unchanged, then I'll sell it and add to the others in the category."

Advice

Will Lynch offer a guess as to the best prospects for stock-market happiness over the coming years? Yes. The price-earnings ratios of growth stocks range between the same as the standard industrials and twice the standard industrials. Recently the growth stocks have been selling at the same price-earnings multiple as the standard industrials, so they apparently have plenty of room to move up. In Lynch's words, "I would think you'd be better off with good-quality, medium-sized, and smaller-growth companies."

Obsession

To sum up the whole matter, Lynch is obsessed with the stock market. His wife was quoted in an article as saying that on their first date, when he was at the Wharton School, his entire conversation was about stocks and the stock market. Well, dedication right from one's youth is what it takes for greatness in any field: to win an Olympic gold medal in gymnastics, to beat the Russians at chess, to paint like Hokusai or (for better or worse) Picasso, to star in the New York City Ballet, to start a great computer company. And Lynch is in that league. Great success, alas, usually requires obsession. Differently put, you won't get there if you don't love it so much that you'd rather do it than anything else, whether or not it's worth that dedication. As an old French saying put it: "*La joie de l'esprit en fait la force*": Loosely, "the spirit's joy gives it power." Delight in his craft is Lynch's secret.

11

Conclusions

There are basically three ways to do unusually well in the stock market:

1. Buy stocks that are cheap and sell them when they are reasonably priced: value investing.
2. Buy into companies that will grow and grow and grow, and stay along for the ride. (For some examples of great growth stocks, see Figure 5, pages 241–243.)
3. Discover a whole new investment area.

Terribly cheap stocks are usually under a cloud at the time, or perhaps overlooked. The market exaggerates bad news, so if the real prospects of a company decline by a quarter because of an adverse development, the price of the share may fall by half. Thus, in value investing the attractive stock is often the one that's smashed down by bad news. False bad news is best, but true bad news is fine. The same works in reverse for good news, whence my maxim, *"Nothing exceeds like success."**

The easy buy-sell rhythm to catch in playing the value game is the basic four-year stock market cycle—which, to be sure, often lasts more or less than four years. At the bottom almost everything is ridiculously cheap, and at the top almost everything is extravagantly overpriced. Thus, the great value investors studied in my previous book, *The Money Masters*, often have a four-year buy-sell cycle. (The top growth investors in that book often hold

---

*That in turn is one reason why in life high-flyers often crash to earth: They weren't as great as they seemed.

their outstanding stocks as long as they stay outstanding—
sometimes for decades.) I did not know what to expect when I
started in on this volume, but it turns out that for some of today's
masters the cycle is much shorter: as little as a few months, or
whatever time it takes for a purchase to attain a previously
calculated price level. This is a hard discipline for an ordinary
investor to follow, and in any event will probably run up transaction costs.

The growth investment techniques described in the earlier
volume remain valid for the masters in this one, but some of the
value investment techniques are different. In general, short-term
investing is a sucker's game, enriching only the brokers; however,
the greatest of today's value investors are able to carry it off.

Relentless Pursuit

Short Kwi was famous in his own right, famous as a hunter
. . . it was his technique of hunting to be relentless in his pursuit;
therefore, if he shot an animal [with a small, weakly poisoned
Bushman arrow] and suspected others to be in the vicinity he would
let the wounded animal run where it would while he hunted on and
shot another, and another, and when all were as good as dead he
would rest, then return to pick up the trail of the one that he felt
would die the soonest. He almost never lost an animal, for his eyes
were sharp and he could follow a cold trail over hard ground and
even over stones; he could tell from fallen leaves whether the wind
or passing feet had disarranged them . . .*

A technique we find in this book is what might be called
relentless pursuit: constantly scanning the herd for new stocks to
pick off for limited moves, rather than as long-term commitments. Here, for example, are some contrasts between the traditional long-term investment style, as exemplified by Warren
Buffett, Philip Fisher, T. Rowe Price or Ralph Wanger, and that
of one of today's slalom artists, such as George Soros, Michael
Steinhardt, Peter Lynch, or, sometimes, John Neff:

*Elizabeth Marshall Thomas, *The Harmless People* (New York: Alfred A. Knopf,
1959).

LONG-TERM INVESTOR	RELENTLESS-PURSUIT TRADER
1. Stay with long-term trends	Catch changes early
2. Buy for the long term	Constant turnover
3. Ride through minor setbacks	Sell on possible adverse developments
4. If the price becomes excessive, wait for the earnings to catch up	Sell if the stock gets ahead of itself
5. Give preference to existing holdings that you are familiar with	Comparison-shop ruthlessly
6. Put your eggs in one basket	Diversify extensively
7. Develop a congenial investment philosophy and stick to it	Have no prejudices
8. Know everything about a few big things	Know a lot about many things
9. Develop helpful rules and formulas	Avoid formulas
10. Understand each company intimately	Buy batches of companies that together represent a thesis
11. Know management intimately	Don't worry much about management
12. Trust to the magic of quiet long-term compounding	Force the pace
13. Don't worry too much about the exact price you pay or receive: over a five or ten-year holding period it should be unimportant	Be very conscious of price in both buying and selling: multiplied by many transactions it is critical

In the relentless-pursuit technique, one tries to enter at a reversal point, setting a precise target for the later sale. This method can only be practiced successfully by authentic masters at the height of their powers, like Short Kwi. It also involves high turnover, meaning heavy transaction costs, unless the dealing side of the operation is conducted with great skill. So one should follow the further discipline of always buying on weakness and selling into strength. That requires either a price-sensitive broker or putting in carefully set limit orders.

George Plimpton, in one of his "professional amateur" experiments, played quarterback with a pro football team. He had a simple assignment: Snatch the ball from the center, then spin around and hand it off to the back sprinting across behind him. Over the years the team had so honed the rapidity and accuracy of its plays that Plimpton simply could not perform this move

230

A MEASURE OF GROWTH STOCK VALUATION

THE PRICE-EARNINGS RATIO OF THE NEW HORZIONS FUND,
WHICH INVESTS ONLY IN GROWTH STOCKS, COMPARED TO THAT
OF THE S & P 500

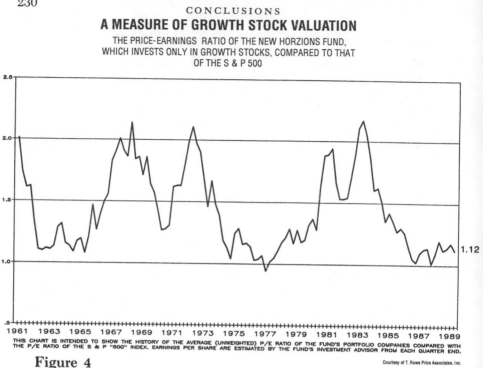

1.12

THIS CHART IS INTENDED TO SHOW THE HISTORY OF THE AVERAGE (UNWEIGHTED) P/E RATIO OF THE FUND'S PORTFOLIO COMPANIES COMPARED WITH THE P/E RATIO OF THE S & P "500" INDEX. EARNINGS PER SHARE ARE ESTIMATED BY THE FUND'S INVESTMENT ADVISOR FROM EACH QUARTER END.

Figure 4

Courtesy of T. Rowe Price Associates, Inc.

before the back had raced past beyond reach. In competition with first-class opponents, one must function at the limits of the possible. In investing, that is what Soros, Steinhardt, Lynch, and Neff are doing. The nonprofessional can scarcely aspire to that degree of skill, and supposing wrongly that he has it may be expensive.

Growth or Value?

Is the growth or the value approach more valid today?

The price-earnings ratio of growth stocks in general oscillates from the same as the Dow stocks to twice that of the Dow. This is shown in Figure 4 (above), which uses the prospective p/e of the stocks in the T. Rowe Price New Horizons Fund as a surrogate for growth stocks in general.

In mid-1989, therefore, while the Dow does not seem particularly attractive compared to either bonds or growth stocks, it also appears (as both Lynch and Neff observe) that growth stocks are good value compared to both bonds and the standard industrials. One can predict with confidence that in due course the price-earnings ratio of growth stocks as a class will advance to 1.5 times that of the Dow, and in time probably to 2.0 times that of the Dow.

It is not easy to calculate the rate of return of a growth stock. One method is to project its earnings for a reasonable number of years, and then assume that they will trail off to the level of the mass of all stocks—"regress to the mean." Then you calculate what discount rate will reduce that stream of earnings to the present market price. That gives the indicated rate of return. As I write, my own estimated rate of return on this basis for the growth stocks that I think I understand is over 20 percent, a far more attractive figure than either short Treasuries, long bonds, or the Dow stocks.

Some such calculation of the comparative indicated rates of return should be kept current by a serious investor, and his strategy should to a certain extent depend on their relative standings at the time.

Spotting Change

Many investors, such as James Rogers and Ralph Wanger, and, in the previous group, T. Rowe Price and Robert Wilson, hunt constantly for trend changes they can take advantage of—the "top-down" approach. Price called it, felicitously, seeking the "fertile fields for growth." He and the others mentioned look primarily to the world outside their door. More Japanese motorcycles? Fiber optics? Pipeline companies exhausting their gas reserves? A new regulatory environment? One then checks with industry sources and starts investigating particular companies.

The other method of catching trend changes is that of Peter Lynch, whose endless talks with the companies themselves will reveal changes at their own level—the "bottom-up" approach. (As mentioned, he also suggests getting investment ideas from products and services you encounter, although for him that's a sideshow.) Either way, though, it is change that the investor hopes to observe and take advantage of before his competitors.

New Investment Areas

A surprising number of the greatest investors develop a new approach, like an art collector who finds and exploits an overlooked category: American naive art, "floating world" prints, scrimshaw, African sculptures, silhouettes, Haitian folk paintings, or whatever.

Here are some examples. In the mid-1930s, after the Crash, common stocks became most attractive, precisely because shell-shocked fiduciaries wouldn't hear about them as investments. A few practitioners, such as Paul Cabot, founded financial empires based on that simple conception. Then, Benjamin Graham formulated and tested a series of rules for buying particular types of conventional stocks so cheaply you almost couldn't lose money. Decade after decade the Graham method worked admirably. He published his method and its results, but almost nobody followed his example, until, some time after the period when I wrote about him in *The Money Masters*, a geometrically increasing number of neo-Grahamites piled in and the field became overpopulated.

T. Rowe Price popularized the idea of "growth stocks" and devised a series of principles for buying them. By the late 1960s this approach had become excessively popular, and that category became grossly overpriced.

Phil Carret and others concentrated in the neglected over-the-counter world, with signal success.

After World War II a few hardy spirits realized that Japan was destined to be a great industrial power, and that some of its premier companies—the equivalents of our GE, Ford, and Prudential—were selling, adjusted for everything, at three or four times earnings. Fantastic killings were made by the handful of investors who knew that things really were what they seemed and dared to act on their knowledge. More recently, others noticed the Italian economic miracle, and James Rogers uncovered a series of emerging countries.

Lately the ill-famed Mr. Milken made a fortune by developing a market for lower-grade corporate ("junk") bonds.

In other words, it has always been possible in the past to notice neglected techniques or neglected areas of investment. The reader can reasonably ask if there are any today. Yes, I see several.

One that seems obvious is selling short, particularly now that there is no tax penalty as compared to capital gains. I presume that Soros is right and that the swarming of the LBO artists must eventually push that sector of the market much too high—as indeed it became in mid-1987. A similar swarming took the "one-decision" growth stocks into the stratosphere in 1972–3, followed by a horrible bust. According to Soros, an LBO blowoff will also be followed by an LBO bust.

Someone who understands the values can see clearly enough when the market capitalization of a company—or a class of companies—is wildly in excess of what an experienced private business—as distinct from a blind pool organized by a broker— would be willing to pay for the same merchandise to be held as an investment. So in due course there should be a short-side opportunity here. (It's best to wait until the collapse actually starts: As we see from Japan, what is too high can still go *much* too high.)

A mistake in judgment can cost the short-seller a fortune as a large position goes heavily against him. To this, one counter is the Grahamite technique of great diversification. Benjamin Graham maintained that to be safe one should, if possible, buy *every* stock that fulfilled his criteria. This would reduce the hazards of the few-eggs-in-one-basket approach. So in reverse, when selling short stocks that are crazily overpriced, one should again have the widest possible diversification. If a 10 percent short position goes up five times (which happens) you will be so uncomfortable that you may sell out just at the wrong moment, fearing that one more double will put you in the poorhouse. If you limit your shorts to one percent positions, you can contemplate the bubblings in the cauldron with less concern.

Even then, short-selling is an extremely disquieting activity, which should only be undertaken by professionals. Still, I would think that in the future there would be more limited partnerships conducting this specialty. The best short-sellers seem to operate exclusively on that side of the market, and I would thus expect to see more all–short-side partnerships being offered.

What else? At one time farmland ranked as a prime conservative investment. It still does today in some countries abroad. A large part of American agriculture, together with its bankers, is in desperate straits. And yet as James Rogers has observed of other industries, there can't be an America without farmers. So agriculture almost has to be made more attractive, or at least come up from under water. But again, as I can attest from experience, it is a difficult game, only for highly experienced hands-on professionals. So buying raw agricultural *land*, not operating farms, seems safest.

There are always areas that were formerly prosperous and fashionable but are now so unpopular that almost no prudent trust officer will consider them. One can take it as a general rule that what was once in fashion will again be in fashion, so with an open mind you usually can find opportunities.

There are also always things happening in art itself, "collectibles" and the like. However, that's another category, speculating, not investing. An investment should by definition have a satisfactory return from underlying earnings, so that it could be a comfortable holding in the absence of any market. If you are dependent on the changing tides of opinion to push it up (and down), it's just a speculation.

Investing Internationally

If the proportion of all American institutional money invested abroad were to correspond roughly to the market capitalization of the major foreign exchanges as compared to ours, then most of a U.S. institutional portfolio should be invested abroad. Thanks to local chauvinism, this won't happen. Still, the proportion will surely rise in coming years, so U.S. institutional portfolio money should continue flowing overseas. If you can plant yourself ahead of time in the places where it's just arriving you should do well, and a fund is the easiest way. Human qualities are more important than resources, and in economic terms some of the best countries are around the Pacific rim. The Chinese are the economic yeast of that area, so a good place to look is the countries where the Chinese are well accepted: One thinks of Thailand and Indonesia.

Also, you should have some bets in the fastest-growing countries abroad even if they're already discovered. Here again, a fund is convenient.

Investment Opportunity: $O = V - P$

All investment opportunity consists of the difference between the value and the perception (Opportunity=Value−Perception). That is, if you can find something tradable that is seriously mispriced you can make a profit.

So with any of these strategies, the cardinal rule is that *you must understand the values.* This starts, of course, with fully studying and understanding the basic figures ("numbers," in financial jargon) of any company that you invest in. All too many investors and indeed stockbrokers do not know the average age of the plants of a company they buy, or their depreciation rates, or the variations in the profit margin, or how its inventory turnover compares with its competitors'. (It seems incredible, but most do not even master the prospectuses and 10Ks of their companies.) Spread sheets along the lines of James Rogers's are an excellent way to start, assuming that one carefully contemplates what emerges. (When I entered the business, one usually spent years doing industry spread sheets.) In addition to the figures, firsthand knowledge of the companies themselves is essential. The investor who can't spare the time for that work should hire someone else to invest for him.

Market Timing

What about trying to catch the overall market's ups and downs? The masters disagree. George Soros, Michael Steinhardt, Phil Carret, John Neff, and others, including Warren Buffett and Benjamin Graham from the previous collection, can and do switch between equities and defensive holdings according to whether the market seems a bargain or overpriced. On the other hand, Peter Lynch and Ralph Wanger, together with Philip Fisher and John Templeton from the earlier group, believe that this maneuver usually doesn't pay.

So, manifestly, there is no rule.

For a *trader,* and particularly for any margin operator, who will be wiped out if he is caught for long on the wrong side of a move, there's no choice: Timing is central. However, for a qualified stock picker that need not be so. If one is convinced that a wonderful stock is going to rise twenty-fold in twenty years, although from time to time there will be drops of a third or so, one may well decide to ride through the whole business, rather than squeeze out any additional gains that periodic buying and selling might provide. Traders like Peter Lynch or Michael Steinhardt can buy and sell to advantage, but a long-term investor of the T. Rowe Price or Philip Fisher school (and these days even Warren Buffett, for his core holdings) would say that you were all too likely to outsmart yourself: You may execute a deft sale, but all too frequently you fail to get back in before the stock moves up again out of reach.

Most excellent stock analysts are poor market analysts and vice versa, like batters and pitchers, but a poor market analyst can still succeed entirely through stock analysis. Indeed, the best sign that the overall market is cheap is that there are a lot of obviously cheap stocks around.

If you are going to attempt market timing, how do you go about it? First, measure where equities stand in relation to fixed-income securities. At the beginning of 1989, for example, if you could have owned the Dow Jones Industrial Average, you would have had underlying earnings of about 8 percent on your money. But both short treasuries and top-quality bonds were yielding 9 percent or 10 percent, so the standard industrials were not particularly attractive in comparison.

However, as Soros underlines, speculative waves roll on just because they are rolling on. So you can be right on the fundamentals and still out of sync with the market for considerable periods. Try not to worry about it.

How About Mutual Funds?

One might conclude that while it is very difficult to copy the techniques of, for instance, a Peter Lynch or a John Neff, one could well buy a piece of their action by investing in the Magellan Fund or the Windsor Fund; the same for Michaelis's Source Capital, Wanger's Acorn Fund, Soros's Quantum Fund (for foreigners), and so on. In other words, aren't selected funds a satisfactory solution? They can be. Fund management is one of the few areas in life where the good often costs no more than the bad, and sometimes less. But there are now more funds available to the bewildered investor than there were stocks on the New York Stock Exchange when I entered the business! So how to go about choosing?

First, one must find an appropriate fund for the season. Don't buy a growth or high-tech fund just after there has been a big run-up in those stocks. In other words, buy a fund in an investment sector that is out of favor at the time. Very few funds indeed are superior over many successive time periods. It's likely that the front-runners of one year will lag in a later year. Second, to speak of a "fund" can be misleading: There is one individual behind it all. Make sure that the key man is still at his post and doing what he has always done best in the same way as before.

The greatest peril for the fund investor is jumping aboard a "hot" fund just before the merry-go-round collapses at the end of a bull market. Several such cases have been mentioned in this book and its predecessor, including Jerry Tsai's Manhattan Fund, the largest ever underwritten at the time it came out, during the last moment of speculative rapture just before the crash of 1973–74. Most of the holdings of the fund collapsed or even went out of business in the subsequent decline, and the fund was a disaster. The chapter on George Michaelis in this book describes the rise and fall of Source Capital, a similar pastiche assembled by Fred Carr, which cost its shareholders a bundle.*

Second, shun excessive costs. Never buy a "load" fund—one sold with a commission. Only buy a closed-end fund at or below

---

*Andrew Tobias's latest book, *Still! The Only Investment Guide You'll Ever Need,* offers this formula:

CATCH A RISING STAR

But there's more than one way to beat the market. Two highly successful mutual funds, Twentieth Century Select and Twentieth Century Growth, have long outstripped the competition by seeking companies on a roll. If reported sales and earnings from continuing operations begin to accelerate—never mind why, and never mind that others may have anticipated this before the reports were issued—these funds buy, and never mind the price. What's more, far from hoping a stock is neglected, these funds will only buy if trading volume is in an uptrend. Says *Forbes* of Twentieth Century's James Stowers, "He wants proof that other investors are interested, and he wants to see the price moving up." "If you're the only one who knows about it," *Forbes* quotes Stowers, "nothing's going to happen." Or, as *Forbes* quotes John Maynard Keynes (no mean investor himself): "When betting on the outcome of a beauty contest, don't bet on the girl you think is prettiest, bet on the girl others think is prettiest."

Of course, if you like this system, you're probably best off letting Twentieth Century execute it for you.

The book (which is in fact full of interest) appeared in October 1987. Within a month Twentieth Century Growth dropped almost a third, and Select over a quarter.

its historically usual discount. Beware of redemption and 12b-1 fees, and the costs of high turnover: 25-percent turnover a year is high enough, and yet most funds do three times that much, at your expense. This can easily consume 2 percent a year of the capital: better for the broker than the shareholder.

Third, a good small fund—$100 million, say—will ordinarily do significantly better for you than a big one. An outstanding fund will get so big it becomes mediocre. So you must keep looking for new managers. Indeed, the probability of a good fund getting too big means that, as with a good stock, the investor should discover its excellence early, in order to be aboard during the best period. That's not easy. One should develop a list of candidates, and then carefully research the ones that seem appropriate in the light of conditions at the time.

Fourth, good performance will eventually attract too much money. For instance, Peter Lynch has been outperforming the market by a smaller and smaller margin as his fund has grown to huge size. This margin was 26 percent a year for his first seven years, when the assets were in the low hundreds of millions; it has been 2.2 percent during the last five years, with the assets over $5 billion.

All this takes careful study. A number of services offer to help you with that job: special issues in such publications as *Forbes* and *Money*, monthly subscription services, and personal advisors working on a fee basis. If you rely on fund issues of magazines or subscription services, which are relatively cheap, you will still have to do a lot of work yourself to be confident. Their suggestions should be considered hints, not solutions.

I have analyzed the operations and results of the fund-selection service offered by Republic National Bank of New York, whose investment department specializes in mutual funds. This analysis, in the form of a review in the *Wall Street Journal*, appears as Appendix xii. I found that the cost of hiring Republic to find a selection of good funds roughly offset the performance benefits thus achieved, except for diversification and peace of mind, which, to be sure, are valuable.

How, beside its performance, should one size up the management of a fund? One good clue is the manager's own quarterly and annual statements. Usually they are gassy, but it would be hard to read Ralph Wanger's letters to the shareholders of the Acorn Fund, or George Michaelis's to the shareholders of Source Capital, or Warren Buffett's to the shareholders of Berkshire Hathaway without realizing that here are men who really understand what they are doing. I have made a point of printing as appendices excerpts from the shareholder reports of most of the managers described in this book. Readers can compare them with others that they may encounter.

There is, of course, one situation in which investment through funds is almost indispensable: covering sectors in which one could not otherwise as a practical matter participate. These might include the Far East and the world of high technology. No lay investor can be expected to know how to invest on a remote continent, or in a business world beyond his experience, such as at the frontier of scientific innovation. Most of the masters in this book (and its predecessor, except for Philip Fisher) profess to be mystified by high technology. This does seem to constitute an inefficiency in the market. So I would say that for most readers an interesting approach might be to conduct systematic growth and/or value investment on one's own, while using specialized funds for specialized purposes.

Company or Fund?

I find that on balance it is about as easy to find a good company as a good fund, and I think that should be true for most readers as well. And a good company doesn't depend on a single individual the way a fund does, may not get fatally oversized as easily, may keep its superiority longer, and saves that burdensome extra overhead.

The quasi-science of security analysis is of course no simple matter, but in one form it can be fairly straightforward—buying great growth stocks when they are attractively priced. Here are pictures of a few. (See Figure 5, pages 241–243.) Identifying, buying and following a few such stocks is no harder than picking outstanding funds. The wonderful company has an immense advantage: It is a whole *system*, with depth of management, assets, and an understandable business franchise. You aren't betting on the touch of one man. You must stay on top of things to be sure the company isn't getting into trouble, but that's also true of a fund.

Performance

The total performance figure of all money managers is better than that of the whole market, thus apparently verifying the old poker joke: "Let's all play carefully, boys, and perhaps we can all win a little." It's not true, of course. Most portfolios do worse than the averages: Their collective performance is that of the averages, diminished by the transactional costs, which are considerable. What happens next, however, is that unsuccessful managers merge with successful ones, so the surviving entity displays its superior record. The failures disappear from the calculation. Perhaps a comparable statistic is that although most restaurants you see appear to be doing quite well, four-fifths of all American (and New York) restaurants fail in their first year. The same location is often taken over repeatedly until someone finally succeeds. Thus, if you look at existing restaurants you may get an unrealistically favorable impression. So too with investment managers. And as I've mentioned, funds can be reclassified: A lagging stock fund may become a superior balanced fund.

In any event, bursts of superior performance are less important than *consistent* performance, which has astonishing results. Consider a young person I'll call Pennysaver. He (or she) contributes $2,000 a year for eight years to a tax-free IRA or pension plan and then stops; the money then grows at 10 percent, a modest assumption. The table on page 244 shows what happens: At retirement age Pennysaver is in good shape.

Even modest steady growth eventually makes you prosperous. Any other tactic, particularly one that incurs significant declines from time to time, may fatally interrupt the flow, particularly if it occurs just before the money is needed.

So, search for superior performance, but treasure consistent performance. There is nothing in the world like compound interest.

Figure 5(a)

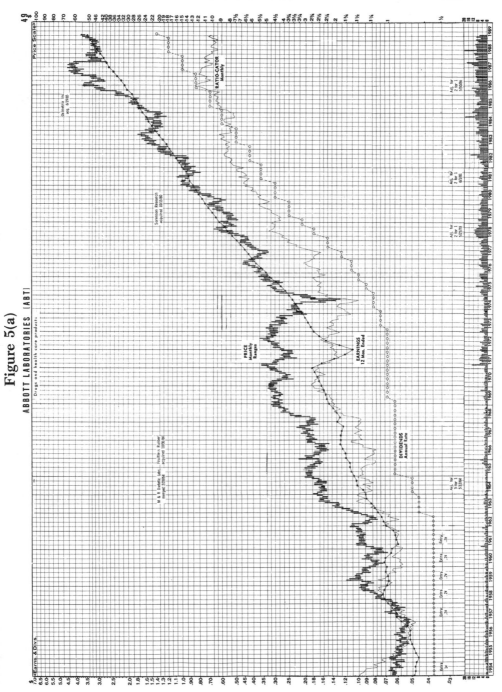

ABBOTT LABORATORIES (ABT)

Drugs and health care products

Figure 5(b)

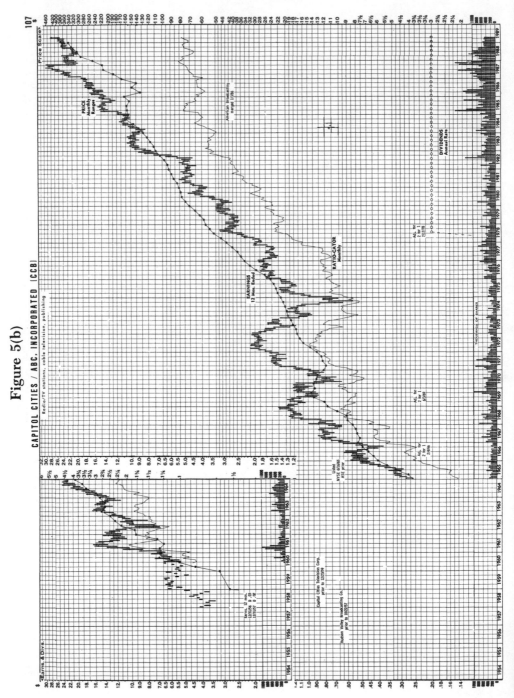

CAPITOL CITIES / ABC, INCORPORATED (CCB)

Radio/TV stations, cable television, publishing

Figure 5(c)

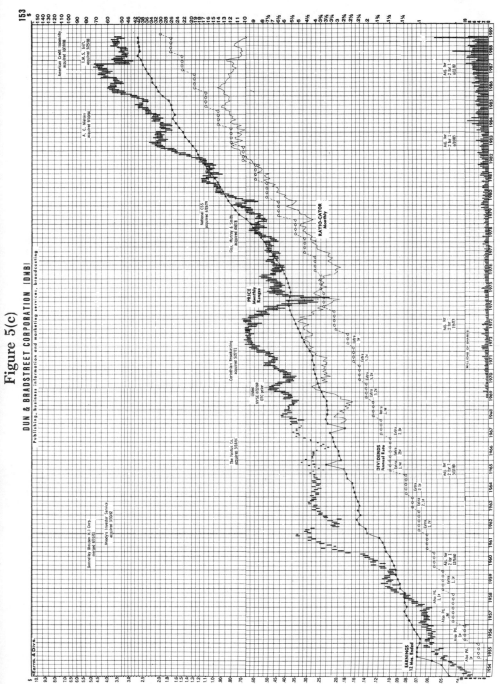

DUN & BRADSTREET CORPORATION (DNB)
Publishing, business information and marketing services, broadcasting

Pennysaver's Progress

Age	Contribution	Year-end Value
19	$2,000	$ 2,200
20	2,000	4,620
21	2,000	7,282
22	2,000	10,210
23	2,000	13,431
24	2,000	16,974
25	2,000	20,872
26	2,000	25,159
27	0	27,675
28	0	30,442
29	0	33,487
30	0	36,835
31	0	40,519
32	0	44,571
33	0	49,028
34	0	53,930
35	0	59,323
36	0	65,256
37	0	71,781
38	0	78,960
39	0	86,856
40	0	95,541
41	0	105,095
42	0	115,605
43	0	127,165
44	0	139,882
45	0	153,870
46	0	169,257
47	0	186,183
48	0	204,801
49	0	225,281
50	0	247,809
51	0	272,590
52	0	299,849
53	0	329,834
54	0	362,817
55	0	399,099
56	0	439,009
57	0	482,910
58	0	531,201
59	0	584,321
60	0	642,753
61	0	707,028
62	0	777,731
63	0	855,504
64	0	941,054
65	0	1,035,160

Reverse Engineering

One technique that a reader of this book should find congenial is to buy stocks from among those favored by outstanding fund managers: Use the masters as a filter. They constantly scan each other's portfolios, so there's no reason not to do the same. It's not somehow unsporting.

You should observe a few obvious rules:

1. *Make sure they really are outstanding managers.* Everyone in my position encounters investors who brandish a sheaf of brokerage house recommendations for some stock, or a compilation of mutual fund holdings showing that it's one of the most widely held positions. But this, for a professional, would establish a *prima facie* case against the stock. An institutional favorite has two strikes against it. Look instead for stocks held by one or possibly two or three authentic masters, not by a large number of mediocrities. There are also services that compile these holdings.* Ask a financial library or a bank or brokerage house, or look at the ads in investment publications. The information arrives later that way, though, than if you get the reports straight from the funds.

2. *Only consider such a list a screen or "universe" from which you select a few candidates for further examination.* Then study those stocks fully. Work through their reports line by line.

3. *Talk to the company,* if you know what to ask it, as well as to some of its competitors and customers, and to industry specialists.

4. *Establish that these are or could be long-term conceptions, not just trading maneuvers.* Ralph Wanger, Warren Buffett, and George Michaelis, for instance, usually buy for the long term, Peter Lynch for a trade, and John Neff operates in both categories. Look at a stock's chart of earnings and dividends for starters. A great long-term growth stock looks quite different from a depressed cyclical perhaps ready for a bounce.

5. *Make sure that the masters are adding to their holdings, or*

---

*Including: CDA Investment Technologies, Inc., Rockville, Maryland; Outstanding Investor, New York, New York; H. F. Pearson & Co., Huntington, New York; 13D Research, Inc., Brewster, New York; Vickers Stock Research Corp., Huntington, New York.

at least maintaining them. A lot of other investors beside yourself will be watching, so when a master starts to sell it may have repercussions, particularly if it's a stock he is known to have liked for a long time.

6. *It's easier, if you are a non-professional, to specialize in one or two areas:* a *type* of stock (low-multiple, long-term growth, emerging growth, niche companies, or whatever) or an *industry* (media, consumer products, specialty chemicals, natural resources). Stock selection is a competitive situation, and thus intrinsically difficult. Focusing makes the job easier, which increases the likelihood of success, as in any other form of exploration.

All in all, then, reverse engineering some choices of the masters is an excellent tool for most investors.

Investment Is the Art of the Specific

None of the masters in this book relies on the tools so beloved of pundits: regression analysis, modern portfolio theory, industry overweightings and underweightings, technical analysis,* or higher math. Except for Soros, whose method is unique and inimitable, and to a lesser extent Steinhardt, they focus on the specific, rather than on "overviews" and big ideas, which essentially attempt to render general, simple, and easy what is intrinsically specific, complicated, and hard. Those formulas and abstractions are not how superior results are achieved in the real world. Successful investing means knowing all about the companies you own. So look to the particular; let others be distracted by the generalities, the formulas, the simplifications.

Alfonso the Learned modestly observed that had he been present at the creation he would have given God some useful hints for the better ordering of the universe. My own would be

---

*Andrew Tobias offers a pleasant "technical analysis" story. There was a $600 seminar on such matters in New York's Waldorf Astoria Hotel on December 6–7, 1986. One of the most promising gurus was Norman Winski, described in the invitation as follows: "In 1975, he became a member and market maker on the floor of the Chicago Board Options Exchange. During an eighteen-month period, 1976–1977, he successfully parlayed $500 into nearly $1,000,000." (Tobias observes that one could scarcely do that *un*successfully.) The invitation forgot to mention a little problem: In September 1977—still ten years before the famous seminar—Winski went bust.

that our species is much too easily seduced by vast ideas, particularly in politics, the opiate of the people, but also in the stock
market, the encephalogram of the human race: Our hopes and
fears for the future are reflected in those wiggly lines. Most of the
time, however, vast unknowable ideas distract from the specific
and knowable.

For example, as Paul Samuelson has pointed out, the three
distinguishing economic features of the Reagan era were huge tax
and export deficits and high real interest rates. *None* was
predicted in 1980. And the crash of 1987 was universally expected
to halt U.S. economic growth—which instead boomed. So don't
spend too much time on next year's GNP. As Lynch says, "How
is the sneaker business doing? That's *real* economics."

Envoi: Midas

This book is a guide to investment success. But my last message to the reader is this: Understand the process, the way you should understand medicine and government, but don't try too hard yourself. The people who sustain the worst losses are usually those who overreach. And it's not necessary: Steady, moderate gains will get you where you want to go.

Furthermore, trying to achieve great wealth—that is, far more than you need—is in fact irrational. You have to give up too much getting there, and having done it, you're often worse off than before. Midas is ruined by the gold he craves.

Our nature, says Shakespeare, is subdued to what it works in, like the dyer's hand, and in pursuing great wealth you become a money-person. You see the world through dollar-sign binoculars.

Then, the exaggeration of any principle becomes its undoing, as the excess of a stimulant becomes a poison, and changing greed from a sin into a commandment dissolves the soul of a family. The children of excessive privilege are often purposeless and unhappy. What gain is worth that loss?

And great wealth spoils ordinary human contacts. Everybody wants something. Of the Rothschilds in their pride it was said that they had no friends, only clients. Indeed, the hurly-burly of humanity, from which great wealth insulates itself, its joys and trials is what we're made for.

Philanthropy, to be sure, is meritorious, but on a large scale becomes a political act: The tycoon who extracts large sums from the public to build a museum in one place rather than another has not created new beauty, but imposed his priorities on society.

The rational approach is to trust in a sufficiency of wealth as a by-product of useful life. Happy are those who find fulfillment in their families, their work, and their civic duties, and hope for the best.

Appendixes

I

James Rogers's
Investment Worksheet

REDMAN INDUSTRIES, INC. (RE-NYSE)

(April 1; 12/31 for '73 '74) ($000s)	4/1968	1969	1970
SALES	74798	109814	117352
DEPRECIATION	1017	1075	1083
OPERATING INCOME			
OPERATING MARGIN			
OTHER INCOME			
OTHER EXPENSES			
PRETAX INCOME	3353	10079	11536
PRETAX MARGIN	4.5%	9.2%	9.8%
TAXES	1606	5082	5500
TAX RATE	47.9%	50.4%	47.7%
EARNINGS AFTER TAX	1747	4997	6036
EQUITY	—	—	—
MINORITY INTEREST	—	—	—
NET INCOME	1747	4997	6036
EARNINGS PER SHARE	0.25	0.71	0.80
DIVIDEND	—	—	—
OUTSTANDING SHARES			
BOOK VALUE PER SHARE			
EQUITY	10364	15546	29005
NET/EQUITY, *1st*		48.2%	38.8%
DEBT/EQUITY RATIO	43.8%	21.1%	11.7%
PENSION ARREARS/EQUITY	—	—	—
LEASE COMMITMENTS/EQUITY	—	—	—
RECEIVABLES/SALES			
INVENTORIES/SALES			
ADVERTISING			
RESEARCH AND DEVELOPMENT			
CAPITAL EXPENDITURES			
C-E/DEPRECIATION			
C-E/GROSS PLANT & EQUIPMENT, *1st*			
C-E/NET P & E, *1st*			
RANGE	3–3¾	28⅝–15¾	18½–5⅛
BACKLOG			
BACKLOG/SALES			
NUMBER OF STORES			
SALES/STORE			

1971	1972	4/1973	12/1973	12/1974	3 MOS. 4/1975	1976
107065	159502	243806	276255	173249	18786	114288
946	1072	1683	1562	1742	—	1449
		23344	22804	3441	(2941)	(1045)
		9.6%	8.3%	2.0%	—	—
		—	—	—	—	—
		435	2262	4014	787	2122
8369	14246	22909	20542	(573)	(3728)	(3167)
7.8%	8.9%	9.4%	7.4%	—	—	—
3911	6532	10752	9731	(230)	0	0
46.7%	45.9%	46.9%	47.4%	—	—	—
4458	7714	12157	10811	(343)	(3728)	(3167)
—	—	—	—	—	—	—
—	—	—	—	—	—	—
4458	7714	12157	10811	(343)	(3728)	(3167)
0.59	0.99	1.54	1.37	(.04)	(.47)	(.36)
—	—	—	—	—	—	9052
						1.01
33544	39940	50797	34906	10161	—	9158
15.4%	23.0%	30.4%	15.5%	—	—	—
10.8%	13.5%	10.6%	85.1%	195.1%	—	237.2%
—	—	—	—	—	—	—
—	—	—	—	—	—	—
						9.2%
						8.1%
						531
						36.6
						—
						—
30⅞–12¾	37¾–20¼		23¼–3½	7⅞–1½		4½–1⅜

REDMAN INDUSTRIES, INC. (RE-NYSE) Continued

(April 1; 12/31 for '73 '74) ($000s)	1977	1978	1979
SALES	132835	183950	237794
DEPRECIATION	1388	1385	3042
OPERATING INCOME	(874)	9593	17198
OPERATING MARGIN	—	5.2%	7.2%
OTHER INCOME	—	—	627
OTHER EXPENSES	1475	1291	800
PRETAX INCOME	(2349)	8302	17025
PRETAX MARGIN	—	4.5%	7.2%
TAXES	0	3985	7683
TAX RATE	—	48.0%	45.1%
EARNINGS AFTER TAX	(2349)	4317	9342
EQUITY	—	—	—
MINORITY INTEREST	—	—	—
NET INCOME	(2349)	4317	9342
EARNINGS PER SHARE	(.26)	0.47	1.0
DIVIDEND	—	—	0.06
OUTSTANDING SHARES	9115	9138	9196
BOOK VALUE PER SHARE	1.55	2.46	3.85
EQUITY	14149	22488	35369
NET/EQUITY, *1st*	—	30.5%	41.5%
DEBT/EQUITY RATIO	127.0%	68.7%	21.7%
PENSION ARREARS/EQUITY	—	—	—
LEASE COMMITMENTS/EQUITY	16.5%	8.4%	15.1%
RECEIVABLES/SALES	8.1%	8.4%	6.9%
INVENTORIES/SALES	7.9%	7.2%	5.3%
ADVERTISING			
RESEARCH AND DEVELOPMENT			
CAPITAL EXPENDITURES	546	1262	1517
C-E/DEPRECIATION	39.3%	91.1%	49.9%
C-E/GROSS PLANT & EQUIPMENT, *1st*	2.0%	4.9%	4.0%
C-E/NET P & E, *1st*	2.8%	7.2%	5.9%
RANGE	5¾–2½	4⅞–2⅜	7⅝–3½
BACKLOG			
BACKLOG/SALES			
NUMBER OF STORES			
SALES/STORE			

1980	1981	1982	1983	1984	1985	1986	1987
279375	241879	248735	262782	345391	339283	341531	372727
2159	2616	3127	3602	3642	3799	3886	3904
22001	8754	7286	5488	10731	8351	6435	7124
7.9%	3.6%	2.9%	2.1%	3.1%	2.5%	1.9%	1.9%
2363	4786	6327	4432	5048	3162	4390	4077
739%	775	1042	3152	2751	2387	2124	2443
23625	12765	12571	6768	13028	9126	8701	8758
8.5%	5.3%	5.1%	2.6%	3.8%	2.7%	2.5%	2.4%
11275	5570	5364	(749)	5434	4075	3959	3937
47.7	43.6%	42.7%	—	41.7%	44.7%	45.5%	45.0%
12350	7195	7207	7517	7594	5051	4742	4821
—	—	—	—	—	—	—	—
—	—	—	—	—	—	—	—
12350	7195	7207	7517	7594	5051	4742	4821
1.3	0.76	0.74	0.77	0.78	0.52	.49	.49
0.1	0.20	0.30	0.30	0.30	0.30	.31	.32
9295	9511	9737	9743	9752	9755	9755	9755
4.80	5.49	5.86	6.32	6.81	7.05	7.22	7.39
44631	52823	57027	61735	66541	68724	70443	72142
34.9%	16.1%	13.6%	13.2%	12.3%	7.6%	6.9%	6.8%
16.2%	15.3%	24.3%	20.7%	14.6%	16.5%	13.4%	12.5%
—	—	—	—	—	(7.4)	(7.8)	(9.3%)
10.0%	9.3%	6.4%	3.9%	2.5%	3.9%	2.7%	2.2%
6.3%	7.8%	6.6%	8.9%	7.8%	8.0%	8.4%	8.6%
5.3%	5.1%	4.9%	7.3%	7.2%	5.7%	9.0%	8.0%
5631	7512	10061	4234	7652	3935	5346	6361
260.8%	287.2%	321.4%	120.9%	210.1%	103.6%	137.6%	162.9%
15.2%	17.6%	22.4%	7.8%	13.9%	6.4%	8.5%	9.7%
24.0%	27.9%	37.1%	12.6%	23.1%	10.6%	14.6%	17.0%
$9\frac{3}{8}$–$4\frac{1}{8}$	$11\frac{3}{4}$–$6\frac{1}{8}$	$14\frac{3}{4}$–9	$25\frac{1}{2}$–11	$27\frac{1}{2}$–$11\frac{1}{2}$	$12\frac{3}{8}$–8	$12\frac{5}{8}$–7	$11\frac{1}{8}$–$6\frac{7}{8}$
	4900	9600	20000	18300	11100	13200	11600
	6.2%	3.9%	7.6%	5.3%	3.3%	3.9%	3.1%

REDMAN INDUSTRIES, INC.

PERIOD	SALES	PRE-TAX	MARGIN	TAXES	T.R.	EARNINGS	INTEREST	EQUITY	NET	E.P.S.
6-76	38366	620	1.6%	298	48.1%	322	—	—	322	.04
9-76	36435	(419)	—	(201)	—	(217)	—	—	(217)	(.02)
12-76	29721	(394)	—	(97)	—	(297)	—	—	(297)	(.08)
3-77	28313	(2157)	—	—	—	(2157)	—	—	(2157)	(.24)
6-77	42037	1651	3.9%	792	50.0%	859	—	—	859	.09
9-77	46338	2249	4.9%	1080	48.0%	1169	—	—	1169	.13
12-77	47229	2375	5.0%	1140	48.0%	1235	—	—	1235	.13
3-78	48346	2027	4.2%	973	48.0%	1054	—	—	1054	.12
6-78	60908	3980	6.5%	1910	48.0%	2070	—	—	2070	.23
9-78	61557	4201	6.8%	2017	48.0%	2184	—	—	2184	.23
12-78	58710	4662	7.7%	1852	39.7%	2810	—	—	2810	.30
3-79	56619	4182	7.4%	1904	45.5%	2278	—	—	2278	.24
6-79	72504	6343	8.7%	2918	46.0%	3425	—	—	3425	.37
9-79	73868	7148	9.7%	3288	46.0%	3860	—	—	3860	.41
12-79	70070	5955	8.5%	2739	46.0%	3216	—	—	3216	.34
3-80	62933	4179	6.6%	2330	55.8%	1849	—	—	1849	.20
6-80	54752	2003	3.7%	952	47.5%	1044	—	—	1051	.11
9-80	61160	3099	5.1%	1489	48.0%	1603	—	—	1610	.17
12-80	64669	4242	6.6%	1858	43.8%	2376	—	—	2384	.25
3-81	61298	3421	5.6%	1271	37.2%	2172	—	—	2150	.23
6-81	70322	5565	7.9%	2244	40.3%	3321	—	—	3321	.34
9-81	67710	3341	4.9%	1432	42.9%	1909	—	—	1909	.20
12-81	52879	(112)	—	(29)	—	(83)	—	—	(83)	(.01)
3-82	57824	3777	6.5%	1717	45.5%	2060	—	—	2060	.21

6-82	66326	2459	3.7%	1032	42.0%	1427	—	—	1427	.15
9-82	64930	1747	2.7%	740	42.4%	1007	—	—	1007	.11
12-82	59306	1312	2.2%	561	42.8%	751	—	—	751	.08
3-83	72220	1250	1.7%	361	28.9%	889	—	—	889	.09
6-83	89050	5239	5.9%	2237	42.7%	3002	—	—	3002	.31
9-83	94562	4286	4.5%	1834	42.8%	2452	—	—	2452	.25
12-83	82128	3652	4.4%	1576	43.2%	2076	—	—	2076	.21
3-84	79651	(149)	—	(213)	—	64	—	—	64	.01
6-84	98120	4073	4.2%	1820	44.7%	2253	—	—	2253	.23
9-84	92159	4057	4.4%	1798	44.2%	2259	—	—	2259	.23
12-84	75628	686	0.9%	310	45.2%	376	—	—	376	.04
3-85	73376	310	0.4%	147	46.9%	163	—	—	163	.02
6-85	90965	4155	4.6%	1859	44.7%	2296	—	—	2296	.24
9-85	89919	4256	4.7%	1901	44.7%	2355	—	—	2355	.24
12-85	85261	1139	1.3%	513	45.0%	626	—	—	626	.06
3-86	75386	(849)	—	(314)	—	(535)	—	—	(535)	(.05)
6-86	94273	1184	1.3%	547	46.2%	637	—	—	637	.07
9-86	95776	3282	3.4%	1497	45.6%	1785	—	—	1785	.18
12-86	94066	2456	2.6%	1155	47.0%	1301	—	—	1301	.13
3-87	88672	1836	2.1%	738	40.2%	1098	—	—	1098	.11
6-87	99539	3526	3.5%	1409	40.0%	2117	—	—	2117	.22

REDMAN INDUSTRIES, INC.

DIVISION SHEET

(April 2) (000s)	1977	1978	1979	1980	1981	1982	1983	1984	1985	1986	1987
Manufactured Housing											
Sales	89442	124315	170690	209737	170673	183502	178845	234237	233516	239689	271542
Operating Income	(1833)	5351	13064	16067	7424	9183	3262	6672	5628	5733	9872
Margin	—	4.7%	7.7%	7.7%	4.3%	5.0%	1.8%	2.8%	2.4%	2.4%	3.6%
Building Products											
Sales	43393	59635	66354	68631	63605	65233	83937	111154	105767	101842	10185
Operating Income	2459	4787	5955	6720	2740	(156)	4411	5718	4518	3189	(127)
Margin	5.7%	8.0%	9.0%	9.8%	4.3%	—	5.3%	5.1%	4.36%	3.1%	—
Mobile Home Parks											
Sales			750								
Operating Income			(199)								
Margin			—								

REDMAN INDUSTRIES, INC.

Buys

Date	Name	Position	Quantity	Price
5/31/83	Weatherford, William	D	1000	23.50

Sells

Date	Name	Position	Quantity	Price
12/31/82	Redman, James	CB	1100	20.5
1/7/83	Redman, James	CB	28,900	20.5
2/3/83	Redman, James	CB	50,000	20
	Friedling, Harry	O,D	48,370	20.38

REDMAN INDUSTRIES, INC.

DEBTS MATURE IN:	1979	1980	1981	1982	1983	1984	1985	1986	1987	1988	1989	1990	1991	1992
As of 4/78	1401	3375	5190	2927	3030									
As of 4/79		155	149	108	114	121								
As of 4/80			200	200	200	200	200							
As of 4/03/81				350	350	350	350	350						
As of 4/02/82					523	925	899	921	710					
As of 4/01/83						1010	991	1023	822	863				
As of 3/30/84							1800	1400	1219	1040	993			
As of 3/29/85								1359	1301	1076	1017	942		
As of 3/28/86									1911	858	858	793	801	
As of 4/3/87											975	793	801	1236

II

Soros Fund Management
Equity Holdings

Soros Fund Management Equity Holdings (March 31, 1989, 13-F Report)

Name of Issuer	Shares or Principal Amount	Fair Market Value	Investment Discretion Sole	Investment Discretion Shared/Other
AMR Corporation	27,500	$ 1,636,250	X	
AMR Corporation	3,000	178,500		X
Addington Resources Inc.	56,700	1,729,350		X
Affiliated Publications Inc.	180,000	7,650,000	X	
Agency Rent A Car Inc.	22,500	423,450		X
Alcide Corporation	120,000	375,000		X
Alico Inc.	19,600	614,950		X
Amax Inc.	50,000	1,212,500		X
Amerada Hess Corp.	75,000	2,812,500	X	
American Cyanamid Company	545,000	27,931,250	X	
American Express Company	57,000	1,802,625		X
American Greetings Corporation	13,000	302,250		X
American Stores Company	61,800	3,568,950	X	
American Telephone & Telegraph Co.	200,000	6,300,000	X	
Anheuser Busch Companies Inc.	100,000	3,525,000	X	
Anheuser Busch Companies Inc.	10,000	352,500		X
Aristech Chemical Corporation	10,000	342,500		X
Arkla Inc.	450,000	9,337,500	X	
Augat Inc.	10,000	123,750		X
Autodesk Inc.	12,900	387,000		X
Automatic Data Processing Inc.	5,500	200,750		X
BTU International Inc.	38,900	306,338		X
Balfour Maclaine Corporation	10,000	76,250		X
Baltimore Bancorp	33,200	431,600		X
Bank of New York Co. Inc.	200,000	8,800,000	X	
BankAmerica Corporation	100,000	2,444,500	X	
Bear Stearns Companies Inc.	46,900	709,363		X
Big Bear Inc.	10,000	383,750	X	

Company	Shares	Value		
Black & Decker Corporation	419,100	3,120,063	X	
Boeing Company	403,400	27,532,050	X	
Boeing Company	1,500	102,375		X
Bowater Inc.	20,700	587,363		X
Burlington Resources Inc.	782,200	37,447,826	X	X
Burlington Resources Inc.	22,400	1,072,400		X
Burr Brown Corporation	26,900	289,175		X
CBS Inc.	13,000	2,255,500		X
C Cor Electronics Inc.	57,400	861,000		
CMS Energy Corporation	1,020,000	25,500,000	X	X
CMS Energy Corporation	11,000	275,000		X
CRS Sirrine Inc.	16,400	545,300		X
C 3 Inc.	17,800	195,800		X
Caesars World Inc.	81,000	2,430,000		X
Castle & Cooke Inc.	17,000	448,375		
Cellular Communications Inc.	374,166	11,412,063	X	X
Chase Manhattan Corporation	100,000	3,756,650	X	X
Chaus Bernard Inc.	49,700	329,263		X
Chicago Milwaukee Corporation	113,000	15,481,000	X	X
Chubb Corporation	53,900	3,665,200	X	X
Church's Fried Chicken Inc.	46,300	312,525		
Citicorp	500,000	14,875,000	X	X
Claire's Stores Inc.	103,400	827,200		
Clark Equipment Company	8,400	284,550		X
Cleveland Cliffs Inc.	21,400	583,150		X
Coastal Corporation	9,200	311,650		X
Colgate Palmolive Company	407,400	19,504,275	X	X
Collagen Corporation	56,200	779,775		
Columbia Pictures Entertainment Inc.	14,600	253,675		
Commercial Intertech Corp.	110,500	2,431,000	X	X
Commonwealth Edison Company	479,600	15,646,950	X	X
Commonwealth Edison Company	20,000	652,500		X
Consolidated Freightways Inc.	84,000	2,509,500		X

Soros Fund Management Equity Holdings (March 31, 1989, 13-F Report) (continued)

Name of Issuer	Shares or Principal Amount	Fair Market Value	Investment Discretion Sole	Shared/Other
Consolidated Stores Corp.	37,600	$ 291,400		X
Contel Corporation	25,000	1,259,375	X	
Control Data Corporation	25,700	526,850		X
Corning Glass Works	269,900	9,176,600	X	
Crystal Oil Company	6,645,143	13,290,286	X	
Cypress Semiconductor Corporation	210,000	2,231,250	X	
DCNY Inc.	153,100	2,698,388	X	
Danaher Corporation	182,800	2,970,500	X	
Daniel Industries Inc.	60,000	840,000		X
Data General Corporation	149,000	2,235,000		X
DataProducts Inc.	71,500	1,197,625		X
Datascope Corporation	5,500	200,750		X
Delta Air Lines Inc.	4,500	264,938		X
Delta Air Lines Inc.	30,000	1,766,250	X	
Diebold Inc.	21,900	938,963		X
Digicon Inc.	20,987,947	1,259,277	X	
Dime Savings Bank New York FSB	11,300	155,375	X	
Dow Chemical Company	594,100	54,508,675	X	
Dravo Corporation	83,700	1,600,763		X
Dresser Industries Inc.	100,000	3,712,500	X	
du Pont (E) I de Nemours & Co.	16,800	1,717,800	X	
Ecolab Inc.	12,900	345,075		X
Ecolab Inc.	170,000	4,547,500	X	
Elsinore Corporation	42,664	15,999	X	
Emhart Corporation	198,000	7,845,750	X	
Environmental Systems Company	22,400	190,400		X
Erbamont NV	625,800	17,835,300	X	

Company	Shares	Value					
Executone Information Systems Inc.	10,000	32,500				X	X
FHP Corporation	19,200	427,200					
Federal Express Corporation	38,500	1,737,313		X	X		
Federal National Mortgage Association	100,000	6,375,000				X	X
Federal National Mortgage Association	9,700	618,375					
Federal National Mortgage Association	44,300	1,074,275				X	
Financial Benefit Group Inc.	115,762	376,227		X		X	
Financial News Network Inc.	35,300	308,875		X			
First Chicago Corporation	200,000	7,600,100				X	X
First City Bancorp of Texas Inc.	11,000	324,500					
First Executive Corporation	121,800	1,887,900		X	X	X	
Foster Wheeler Corporation	430,400	7,316,800		X	X	X	
Freeport McMoRan Resource Partners LP	1,000,000	27,625,000					
General Dynamics Corporation	72,700	3,943,975				X	X
General Mills Inc.	5,000	296,110				X	X
Georgia Pacific Corporation	250,000	10,562,500		X			
Goodrich B F Company	1,361,600	69,952,200		X			
Grace W.R. & Company	100,000	3,037,500		X			
Halliburton Company	200,000	6,025,000		X			
Harley-Davidson Inc.	129,100	3,647,075		X			
Harley-Davidson Inc.	4,000	113,000					
Heritage Media Corporation	30,200	158,550				X	X
Hogan Systems Inc.	45,000	236,250		X		X	
Holly Corporation	10,000	375,000		X			
Home Depot Inc.	134,900	4,890,125				X	
Honeywell Inc.	24,300	1,612,913		X			
Houghton Mifflin Company	23,400	1,055,925				X	
Huffy Corporation	69,900	1,153,350					
IDB Communications Group Inc.	377,500	3,114,375		X		X	
IMO Delaval Industries Inc.	15,500	300,313					
Immunomedics Inc.	240,000	1,170,000		X			
India Growth Fund Inc.	20,000	192,500		X			
Infotechnology Inc.	59,800	500,825		X		X	

Soros Fund Management Equity Holdings (March 31, 1989, 13-F Report) (continued)

Name of Issuer	Shares or Principal Amount	Fair Market Value	Investment Discretion Sole	Investment Discretion Shared/Other
Inspiration Resources Corporation	45,100	$ 360,800		X
Interco Inc.	760,000	2,280,000	X	
Interco Inc.	86,800	260,400		X
International Minerals & Chemicals Corp.	1,379,200	56,030,000	X	
Intervoice Inc.	54,100	669,488		X
Itel Corporation	10,000	210,000		X
Ivax Corporation	279,400	3,841,750	X	
J P Industries Inc.	12,000	211,500		X
Kansas City Southern Industries Inc.	713,000	26,291,875	X	
Kansas Gas & Electric Company	196,700	3,909,413	X	
Kansas Gas & Electric Company	22,000	437,250		X
Karcher Carl Enterprises Inc.	9,480	239,700		X
Kay Jewelers Inc.	65,875	798,734		X
Kenai Corporation	16,920,188	169,202	X	
Kentucky Central Life Insurance Company	10,000	133,000		X
King World Productions Inc.	998,100	24,952,500	X	
Korea Fund Inc.	50,000	1,762,500		X
Leslie Fay Companies Inc. (The)	21,700	287,525		X
Lexington Savings Bank	31,000	313,875	X	
Lilly Eli & Company	50,000	5,143,750	X	
Lilly Eli & Company (Wts Exp. 03/31/91)	1,000,000	34,625,000	X	
LIN Broadcasting Corporation	360,000	31,770,000	X	
Litton Industries Inc.	20,200	1,532,675		X
Lockheed Corporation	75,000	3,506,250	X	
Lockheed Corporation	3,800	177,650		X
Longview Fibre Company	13,500	872,438		X
Lukens Steel Incorporated	16,200	463,725		X

Company	Shares	Value		
Lyondell Petrochemical Company	56,000	1,610,000	X	
MCI Communications Corporation	1,100,000	31,487,500	X	
MGM UA Communications Company	18,500	309,875	X	X
Manufacturers Hanover Corporation	100,000	3,600,000		
Mapco Inc.	43,200	2,700,000		X
Mattel Inc.	30,000	356,250		X
Maxicare Health Plans Inc.	10,000	2,810		X
Maxxam Inc.	30,000	825,000	X	
McDonald's Corporation	4,000	205,500		X
Medical Care International Inc.	99,800	1,334,825		X
Mentor Graphics Corporation	13,100	422,475		X
Merck & Company Inc.	469,900	30,426,025	X	X
Merck & Company Inc.	2,000	129,500		X
Mercury Entertainment Corporation	179,000	67,125		
Mesa Ltd Partnership (Depositary Unit)	155,400	1,903,650	X	
Methode Electronics Inc.	117,500	514,063	X	
Metro Mobil CTS Inc.	12,750	788,906	X	
Metro Mobil CTS Inc.	38,250	2,304,563	X	
Mexico Fund Inc.	295,000	2,175,625	X	
Milton Roy Company	23,400	312,975	X	
Minnetonka Corporation	97,500	2,595,938	X	X
Mitchell Energy & Development Corp.	123,200	1,694,000	X	
Mobile Communications Corp.	19,000	684,000	X	
Mobile Communications Corp.	24,900	896,400	X	
Monsanto Company	205,000	19,244,375	X	
Monsanto Company	2,500	234,688		X
Nipsco Industries Inc.	350,300	4,729,050	X	
Nipsco Industries Inc.	33,000	445,500		X
N W A Inc.	5,000	424,375	X	
N W A Inc.	56,400	4,786,950		
Nashua Corporation	163,700	6,466,150	X	
National Intergroup Inc.	19,200	331,200		X
National Semiconductor Corporation	177,700	1,310,538		X

Soros Fund Management Equity Holdings (March 31, 1989, 13-F Report) (continued)

Name of Issuer	Shares or Principal Amount	Fair Market Value	Investment Discretion Sole	Investment Discretion Shared/Other
Neorx Corporation	62,300	$ 404,950		X
Newmont Mining Corporation	22,000	874,500		X
Northeast Bancorp Inc.	85,000	5,652,500	X	
Nu-West Industries Inc.	1,333,592	21,004,074	X	
Office Depot Inc.	58,500	1,447,875		X
Ohio Mattress Company (The)	34,800	856,950		X
Pacificare Health Systems Inc.	18,500	416,250		X
Panteras Corporation	58,800	367,500		X
Parker Drilling Company	371,000	2,179,625	X	
Pennwalt Corporation	35,500	4,628,313		X
Pennzoil Company	100,000	8,362,500	X	
Pep Boys (The) Manny Moe & Jack	17,000	223,125		X
PepsiCo Inc.	6,000	267,000		X
Petrolane Partners L.P. (Depositary Unit)	9,200	234,600		X
Phicorp Inc. Pa.	112,600	1,660,850		X
Pitney Bowes Inc.	150,000	6,393,750	X	
Pitney Bowes Inc.	1,400	59,675		X
Pop Radio Corporation	11,600	152,250		X
Provident Life & Accident Ins. Co. Amer.	58,625	1,172,500	X	
Provident Life & Accident Ins. Co. Am	331,500	7,293,000	X	
Quick & Reilly Group Inc.	39,000	516,750		X
RJR Nabisco Inc.	1,229,783	106,837,398	X	
RJR Nabisco Inc.	17,056	1,481,740		X
Reebok International Ltd.	46,200	658,350		X
Reynolds & Reynolds Company (The)	15,600	421,200		X
Robins A. H. Co., Inc.	1,823,900	48,561,338	X	
Rollins Environmental Services Inc.	22,500	241,875		X

Company	Shares	Value		
Safeguard Scientific Inc.	33,000	528,000	X	
Sahlen & Associates Inc.	326,424	449,429		X
Sara Lee Corporation	5,000	243,750	X	
Scherer Healthcare Inc.	9,400	324,300	X	
Sea Containers Ltd.	45,000	2,070,000	X	
Seeburg Corporation	32,600	12,225	X	
Shaklee Corporation Delaware	11,800	327,450	X	
Sizzler Restaurants International Inc.	16,100	293,825	X	
SmithKline Beckman Corporation	15,000	913,125		X
Squibb Corporation	3,000	204,750	X	
Standard Register Company	17,900	337,863	X	
Student Loan Marketing Association (Non-voting)	78,000	7,429,500		X
Sun Electric Corporation	39,100	806,438	X	
Sun Microsystems Inc.	45,000	725,625	X	
Super Valu Stores Inc.	18,500	448,625	X	
TIE Communications Inc.	280,000	420,000	X	
TW Services Inc.	1,571,700	49,705,013		X
TW Services Inc.	12,600	398,475	X	
Talman Home Fed. Svgs. & Ln Assn Ill.	15,000	151,875	X	
Tambrands Inc.	100,000	6,062,500		X
Tekelec	12,600	176,400	X	
Tesoro Petroleum Corporation	45,000	556,875	X	
Texas Eastern Corporation	13,300	674,975	X	
Texas Eastern Corporation	231,900	11,768,925		X
Time Inc.	4,200	486,675	X	
Time Inc.	19,900	2,305,913		X
Trimedyne Inc.	44,900	617,375	X	
Trion Inc.	15,200	172,900	X	
Tyco Laboratories Inc.	394,800	13,966,050		X
UAL Corporation	146,200	17,105,400		X
Union Carbide Corporation	50,000	1,456,250		X
Union Corporation	79,200	1,019,700	X	

Soros Fund Management Equity Holdings (March 31, 1989, 13-F Report) (continued)

Name of Issuer	Shares or Principal Amount	Fair Market Value	Investment Discretion Sole	Investment Discretion Shared/Other
U S Healthcare Inc.	112,500	$ 1,139,063		X
United Telecommunications Inc. Kansas	342,500	18,923,125	X	
United Telecommunications Inc. Kansas	3,000	165,750		X
Universal Foods Corporation	45,000	1,625,625		X
Unocal Corporation	75,000	3,187,500	X	
VSB Bancorp Inc.	15,000	157,500		
Varian Associates Inc.	41,500	1,079,000		X
Wang Laboratories Inc.	120,000	1,020,000		X
Warner Communications Inc.	275,000	12,890,625	X	
Webb Del E. Corporation	10,600	160,325		X
West Point Pepperell Inc.	307,308	17,708,163	X	
West Point Pepperell Inc.	18,400	1,060,300		X
Willcox & Gibbs Inc.	459,354	8,096,114	X	
Windmere Corporation	23,000	600,875		X
Wolverine Exploration Company	372,089	1,882,770	X	
Wolverine Exploration Company (Wts Exp 12/31/93)	186,788	396,925	X	
Woolworth FW Company	160,000	8,020,000		X
Xerox Corporation	11,500	679,938		X
AGGREGATE TOTAL		$1,338,431,992		

III

Extracts from Source Capital
Commentaries

September 30, 1978

Source Capital came into existence at a time of excessive optimism in the securities markets. In retrospect, both stocks and bonds were significantly overpriced and the broad market averages are still below their levels of a decade ago, despite the 70 to 100 percent increases in earnings, dividends and book values. Even the stock of as exceptional a company as IBM, which has more than tripled its earnings and raised its dividend over sixfold while remaining debt-free and accumulating excess cash, is approximately unchanged over the period. We strongly believe that this inability of stock prices to make any headway in the face of such continuing growth is clear evidence of the significant overvaluation which prevailed over a decade ago.

Far from being an indication of the long-term future, we find in this erosion of multiples the source of our fundamental optimism. Despite the overwhelming breadth and rapidity of the recent decline, we know that price/earnings ratios will not shrink forever, nor will dividend yields increase unendingly; rising earnings and dividend payments and the increase in underlying asset values through the reinvestment of retained earnings and the inflationary increase in existing real assets must ultimately be reflected in higher stock prices.

December 31, 1978

Most major investors seem to have become preoccupied with a variety of investment techniques and approaches which would have, in retrospect, provided better returns than those actually achieved.

Thus, a widespread preoccupation with market timing has developed in an attempt to capitalize on the sharp, volatile advances and avoid the painful periods of decline. In addition, there has been a significant and continuing move away from the equities, particularly growth equities, and an increasing attention to income securities. This trend is in response to the superior performance of such securities in recent years. Similarly, there is now a tendency for major investors to consider alternative approaches, such as investment in foreign securities, real estate, options, etc., based upon the perceived past performance of these markets. We believe that all of these trends are largely based on an extrapolation of past experience, rather than in response to a carefully reasoned analysis of current values and opportunities.

In the past year, stock prices have managed to withstand an incredible series of adverse economic, financial and political developments. Inflation has increased from 6.8% to 9%, short-term interest rates from 6½% to over 10%, and long-term rates from 8% to 9%. The prospects for a peace treaty between Egypt and Israel which were so promising a year ago are now highly questionable, and oil production in Iran is virtually halted in the wake of the overthrow of our country's major ally and the strongest military force in the Middle East. Despite this litany of woe, stock prices are actually higher today than they were in early 1978. We believe the reason for this paradox lies in the extraordinary undervaluation of U.S. common stocks relative to virtually all historic bench marks of value, relative to the current and reasonably foreseeable level of interest rates, relative to stock prices in other countries, and certainly relative to potential gains which are possible in a better investment climate.

March 31, 1979

Developments in the equity markets thus far in 1979 have justified the positive stance we took in our Letter to Shareholders in the December report. We argued that equity values in the public market were compellingly attractive despite widely recognized problems of accelerated inflation, high interest rates, oil shortages, a weak dollar and political instability in many critical parts of the world. The pervasiveness and recognition of these problems is reflected in the following editorial from *Harper's* magazine.

> It is a gloomy moment in the history of our country. Not in the lifetime of most men has there been so much grave and deep apprehension; never has the future seemed so incalculable as at this time. The domestic economic situation is in chaos. Our dollar is weak throughout the world. Prices are so high as to be utterly impossible. The political cauldron seethes and bubbles with uncertainty. Russia hangs, as usual, like a cloud, dark and silent, upon the horizon. It is a solemn moment. Of our troubles no man can see the end.

That this incisive description of today's problems was actually written in *1847* only serves to reinforce our conviction that investors should base their decisions upon reasonable judgments of investment values rather than becoming preoccupied with elaborate hypotheses of possible future events and their possible impact on market prices.*

---

*Michaelis should have mentioned that stocks rose by a third in the subsequent four years. (J.T.)

June 30, 1979

An astute investor whose abilities we highly respect has observed that stock prices are much more volatile than the businesses whose ownership they represent. Thus, well established profitable businesses tend to be stable, consistent, even surprisingly predictable, and are capable of withstanding periods of adversity without lasting damage. In contrast, stock prices are uncertain, variable, capricious, unpredictable and highly responsive to short term transient influences. It is ironic that so many investors devote so much effort to the exceptionally demanding challenge of predicting these volatile short term price movements. We prefer to direct our energies toward accumulating the basic knowledge necessary to identify and value the essentially stable, profitable, superior business enterprises in which we have an investment interest.

H & R Block has been an excellent investment for Source, providing a total return of over 20% annually since its initial purchase in August, 1973, at less than $10 per share. At that time, with the company earning 33% on its unleveraged equity, we felt the stock was undervalued at 9.9 times earnings, 3.1 times book value and yielding 3.2%. Currently, still debt free and earning 32% on equity, the stock remains undervalued at 9.2 times earnings, 2.5 times book value and yielding 6.7%. In retrospect, it is clear that the success of this investment stemmed from a correct assessment of the potential earning power and dividend growth inherent in Block's business rather than from any ability to predict stock price movements during the intervening years.

June 30, 1980

Profits are the discretionary funds available to the owners of a business after providing for all costs required to maintain the ability of the enterprise to operate at current levels. Such real profits must ultimately be reflected in spendable cash. As expressed by George A. Roberts, President of Teledyne, Inc., "Net income without cash is not necessarily net income." Viewed from this perspective, it appears that most U.S. corporations have become harnessed to an inflationary treadmill in which the operating demands to expand assets constantly exceed the net cash generated from operations. The resulting deficit has been funded by increasing debt without generating sufficient subsequent cash flow to maintain balance sheet and income ratios.

September 30, 1980

Stock prices have increased substantially and are currently at record levels. Our equity oriented investment portfolio has clearly benefited from this bull market environment. However, this rapid appreciation in the face of higher interest rates has significantly narrowed the range of attractive investment opportunities. Higher prices have led us to sell part or, in some cases, all of our holdings in companies in which we have maintained an investment for many years. We have also been forced to look further into the future to justify many of the positions we continue to hold.

The almost inevitable corollary of rapidly rising prices is an increasing level of risk. Yet, it is just such a pattern of rapidly rising prices that feeds the desire for gain and dissipates the fear of loss as a healthy countervailing force in the market. The indicators of excessive speculation are beginning to reappear in the high volume on the American Stock Exchange and the over-the-counter markets, a hot new issue market and large percentage gains in low price stocks. As economist Peter Bernstein has recently pointed out, "markets have rhythms of their own that have more to do with their past history and the collective memories of their participants than with the underlying economic fundamentals." Thus the stock market has been out of favor with both individual and institutional investors for so many years that the momentum of investors rediscovering the equity market is an extremely powerful force. Furthermore, the extreme segmentation of the market which has concentrated current interest into a limited arena leaves wide areas of the equity market still relatively undervalued on a long-term basis as evidenced by the continuing interest in corporate takeovers.

The foregoing comments lead us to conclude that there is too much long-term opportunity still implied in the current level of the market to allow our uneasiness to lead to excessive selling.

June 30, 1981

Virtually no one would disagree with the characterization of recent bond market experience as "the worst of times." It has become virtually axiomatic that debtors benefit and lenders lose from inflation. However, this oversimplification completely ignores the rate of interest and its relationship to the rate of inflation. Lenders can clearly come out ahead if the interest they earn more than offsets the decline in purchasing power of the capital they have lent. Except for a few short intervals, this has never happened during the past forty years. However, an extraordinary change has taken place in the past eighteen months which appears to have redressed the balance of risk and reward *from* borrowers *to* lenders. Long-term interest rates have risen 1,000 basis points in the past twenty years but fully half of this increase has taken place during the explosion of the last eighteen months.

In stark contrast to interest rates which run from 20% to 14% —short to long—recent price behavior in the economy, where it is not deflationary, is at least distinctly disinflationary. Broad measures of price inflation have receded to single digits and are continuing to moderate cyclically. Clearly, the current level of short- to intermediate-term interest rates provides an enormous real return. The 17% interest returns on one-year certificates of deposit are probably close to 1,000 basis points in excess of the 7–8% inflation which appears likely over the next year. *Never have lenders been so liberally compensated for the use of their capital.*

December 31, 1981

One astute observer of the financial scene who recognized the potential returns inherent in Source Capital's investment portfolio early last year was John Train. Writing in the March 2, 1981, issue of *Forbes* magazine after reviewing the 1980 Annual Report, Mr. Train assessed Source's outlook as follows:

Source looks for undervalued issues, which are often found in unpopular industries. It can thus get left behind when the market tears off after a specialized enthusiasm, as it did, for example, last year after the energy and technology stocks . . . As a general rule, though, the time to buy a good fund is when its particular technique has been out of favor for a year or two. Underperformance in the recent past sets the stage for a catchup in the future.

September 30, 1982

We have commented for some time upon our perceptions of the increasing relative attraction of fixed income securities and the general scarcity of high quality companies at below average valuations. The advance in stock prices was triggered by a sharp decline in interest rates. Lost amid the ballyhoo of the new bull market of the 1980's is the fact that the bond market has substantially outperformed the stock market even in the most recent quarter, not to mention the past year. The total return on bonds as measured by the Salomon Brothers High Grade Bond Index was 21.5% in the quarter just ended versus 11.5% for stock prices as measured by the Standard & Poor's 500 Stock Average. Even more startling is the fact that over the past year bonds as measured by the Salomon Brothers Index provided a total return of 45.5% versus 9.8% for the Standard & Poor's 500 Stock Average. The foregoing comparisons illustrate quite clearly that while recent action in the stock market has captured the headlines, truly spectacular returns have been available in fixed income securities.

Stock prices have advanced sharply since the end of the quarter breaching once again the historical 1000 level on the Dow Jones Industrial Average. The current level of stock prices seems to have gone well beyond simply reflecting the higher capitalization rates that are implicit in the current lower interest rate structure. Stock prices appear to be anticipating and already discounting a meaningful gain in profits produced by economic recovery in 1983. While the economy is in many ways well positioned to experience an economic recovery, the early indications of such a recovery are either very weak or not yet visible. While it is sometimes advisable to pay for profits in advance of their realization, the current level of stock prices provides relatively little inducement to do so.

March 31, 1983

Writing in late October, we expressed our views as follows: "Returns on government bonds of 11% . . . are still well in excess of the currently falling

rate of inflation . . . Major investment gains are made when things turn
out better than expected. Our thoughts are simply that the expectations
implied in the current level of stock prices seem to leave less room for such
pleasant surprises than is the case in bonds."

Even the most casual of financial market observers will recognize that events
of the past half year have shown those judgments to have been at odds with
subsequent market behavior. The economic recovery which was only a poten-
tiality in October is now a weak reality with reductions in earnings estimates
still far more prevalent than increases. Nevertheless, the equity market has
forged ahead to record levels ignoring stubbornly high interest rates, an illusive
and weak recovery, and disappointing profits.

The 60% gain in stock prices since last summer in the face of persistently
high interest rates has produced an environment in which stocks can hardly be
characterized as being deeply undervalued. The Standard & Poor's Industrial
Stock Average is currently selling at a 40% premium to underlying stockholders
equity. Even a sharp 20–25% profit gain this year followed by a further 15%
gain in 1984 would only bring the return on equity to 13% this year and 14%
next year. Such returns, if achieved, barely justify the current premium in the
market which, given the current level of interest rates, leaves little room for
disappointment.

June 30, 1983

Hard as it seems today, only a few years ago investments in "obscure"
companies such as Weis Markets or Hillenbrand Industries were viewed as sterile
investments unlikely to produce significantly above average returns and they
were valued accordingly at a discount to the market. A similar degree of skepticism is now attached to investments such as Eastman Kodak, Philip Morris, and
Marsh & McLennan. These companies' virtues are ignored or discounted, while
their problems seem endless. Their stocks are "overowned" and are being liquidated to move into more aggressive investments. Consequently, they now sell at
discount prices.

While Eastman Kodak, Philip Morris, and Marsh & McLennan are much
larger and better known companies than Weis Markets and Hillenbrand Industries, we believe they currently possess the same key ingredients of quality and
value which made the latter stocks such successful investments over the past five
years.

December 31, 1983

Most market participants, amateur and professional alike, are inherently
speculators rather than investors. To quote Lord Keynes, an eminent economist
who was also an experienced and able investor, "Most investors are, in fact,
largely concerned, not with making superior long-term forecasts of the probable
yield of an investment over its whole life, but with foreseeing changes in the

conventional basis of valuation a short time ahead of the general public. They are concerned, not with what an investment is really worth to a man who buys it 'for keeps,' but with what the market will value it at, under the influence of mass psychology, three months or a year hence . . ." Even 48 years after the foregoing was written, the fact that such efforts to anticipate short-term trends produced by "mass psychology" have repeatedly proven self-defeating for all but the most nimble few, seems insufficient to prevent widespread employment of such speculative techniques.

Keynes himself learned this lesson the hard way—from his own personal experience. Keynes is best known for his *General Theory of Employment, Interest, and Money* from which the foregoing quote is selected. However, Keynes had a long history as an investor, both personally and professionally, acting as investment advisor to college endowments and as a director of public investment companies and insurance companies. There are many paths to heaven, and while Benjamin Graham is undoubtedly the founder of modern security analysis and of the investment philosophy founded on value-based individual security selection, Keynes arrived at the same conclusions at much the same time following a very different route.

Ironically, Keynes started out convinced that he could utilize his economic understanding of what he called "the credit cycle" to profitably time the market by switching between stocks, bonds and cash. In 1924, Keynes was a founding director of The Independent Investment Company, an investment trust, whose prospectus informed potential investors that "fluctuations in the relative values of long-dated and short-dated fixed-interest securities and of ordinary shares are all affected by a periodic credit cycle . . . with the result that considerable profits can be made by changing from one class to another at the appropriate phases of the credit cycle." By 1938, Keynes had learned better. In a letter to R.F. Kahn, burser of King's College, Cambridge, Keynes wrote, "I can only say that I was the principal inventor of credit cycle investment and have seen it tried by five different parties acting in detail on distinctly different lines over a period of twenty years which has been full of ups and downs; and I have not seen a single case of success having been made of it . . . most of those who attempt it sell too late and buy too late, and do both too often, incurring heavy expenses and developing too unsettled and speculative a state of mind."

Keynes ultimately came to embrace a value-oriented investment approach based upon "a careful selection of a few investments having regard to their cheapness in relation to their probable, actual and potential *intrinsic* value over a period of years ahead and in relation to alternative investments at the time." A few years later, Keynes wrote, "I am generally trying to look a long way ahead and am prepared to ignore immediate fluctuations if I am satisfied that the assets and earning power are there. My purpose is to buy securities where I am satisfied as to assets and ultimate earning power and where the market price seems cheap in relation to these." Commenting on market fluctuations, Keynes points out, "Advantage can be taken of them more because individual securities fall out of their reasonable parity with other securities on such occasions than by attempts at wholesale shifts into and out of equities as a whole."

Today's economists, preoccupied with their computer models, have spawned a "modern portfolio theory" of financial market behavior which it is impossible to describe without extensive use of the Greek alphabet and mathematical formulae, and which is just as impossible to apply in practice as was Keynes' original "credit cycle" concept. The major conclusion of "modern portfolio theory" is that it is largely futile to attempt to "beat the market" by superior security selection because markets are simply too efficient. Keynes knew better, and Keynes did better, because he learned from his own experience that markets are recurringly emotional, irrational and inefficient. The difficulty lies in marshaling the intellectual skill and the emotional discipline to capitalize on this inherent inefficiency in some organized manner.

The inventor of the infamous "credit cycle" concept of market timing also said the following: "The management of stock exchange investments of any kind is a low pursuit, having very little social value and partaking (at its best) of the nature of a game of skill, from which it is a good thing for most members of our Society to be free."

March 31, 1985

The willingness of would-be acquirers to pay substantial premiums to recent market prices for controlling interests of major public companies warrants commentary. This phenomenon is cited as evidence of undervaluation in the current equity market. While there is an element of truth to this, it is important to understand that the acquisition of an entire business will justifiably warrant a significantly higher price than what small fractional interests of that business are worth in the auction market. There are a number of sound reasons for this phenomenon:

◆ The tangible assets of a mature, profitable business which have been substantially depreciated for tax purposes by the existing owners can be written up to current value and depreciated again by a new owner who acquires the entire business. Thus, the new owner may have a significant portion of the pre-tax earnings previously paid in taxes to Uncle Sam available as a return on his capital investment. In this way the government becomes a partner in helping the new owner acquire the business.

◆ If the business being acquired is encumbered with little or no debt, then the acquirer who finances a major portion of the purchase price with debt again has Uncle Sam as a partner since the interest cost on his acquisition borrowings is deductible against the pre-tax earnings of the business. In this way, cash flow previously paid out in income taxes is available to pay interest on money borrowed to acquire the business.

◆ While the amounts may vary, the acquisition of one corporation by another will generally result in the elimination of most of the corporate administrative overhead of the acquired company. The elimination of such expense can represent a meaningful increase in profitability and the sale of related corporate assets (headquarters office buildings, planes, cars, real estate, etc.) can quickly reduce the effective purchase price.

December 31, 1985

Stock market total returns result from the interaction of three variables: corporate profitability, dividend payout ratio, and equity valuation. To illustrate, imagine a stock called "The S&P 400" which will earn a 14% return on its equity and pay out 45% in dividends. If such a stock could be purchased at book value and continues to be valued at book, it will generate stock market returns equal to its 14% return on equity. However, if it is purchased and continues to sell at 1.8 times its book value (the current market valuation), it can only produce an 11.2% stock market return.

Yield	$=$	$\dfrac{\text{Return on Equity} \times \text{Payout Ratio}}{\text{Price/Book Value}}$	$=$ 3.5%
Growth	$=$	Return on Equity $\times$ Reinvestment Rate	$=$ 7.7%
Total Return	$=$	Yield + Growth	$=$ 11.2%

Only a paltry 11.2%! How is that possible? That is actually less than the portfolio return achieved on Source Capital's net asset value in any of the past eleven years! The answer lies in recognizing that past returns, both in Source's portfolio and the overall market, have received an enormous nonrecurring contribution from the expansion of equity valuations in recent years. In less than four years, the market valuation of corporate equity has expanded from a 10% premium to approximately an 80% premium over the book value. This extraordinary expansion of equity valuations, fueled by the decline in interest rates, has permitted the stock market to produce shareholder returns of 20% annually during a four year period when return on equity averaged less than 13%! Once this process of multiple expansion runs its course, its benefits to stock market investors lie in the past and future returns will again be harnessed to the limitations imposed by corporate profitability as discussed above.

We have no doubt that the pendulum of valuation can swing still further. The fact that price to book value multiples reached highs between 1.9 and 2.3 each year during the entire period 1955–1973 would seemingly indicate that valuations still have some room to expand. However, interest rates and debt levels were far lower during that earlier period of elevated valuations and the rapid multiple expansion of recent years would seem to indicate that the rise in equity valuations has reached a range of diminishing potential.*

June 30, 1986

The full magnitude of the valuation explosion of recent years can best be appreciated by reviewing the relevant data in the table below. It is clearly evident that while we generally have been able to maintain a portfolio of

---

*In the event, stocks rose by three-quarters, where they were grossly overvalued, within two years. (J.T.)

superior businesses at a valuation advantage to the market, the sharp expansion
in market valuations has also been reflected in Source's equity portfolio. While
there is some comfort in the fact that our stocks are "cheaper than the market,"
we find the market as a whole fully valued by standards of long-term market
history.

This judgment is reinforced in the short-term by distinct warning signs of
excessive optimism in both the volume, quality, and trading activity in new
public stock offerings. The total dollar volume of new stock issues in the second
quarter of 1986 expanded sharply to a record $14.6 billion vs. the previous
record of $11.7 billion during the second quarter of 1983. There have been 92
initial public offerings in the first half of 1986 vs. 99 for all of 1983. Finally,
over-the-counter trading volume relative to trading on the New York Stock
Exchange set records in May and June of this year of 90% and 97%, respectively, breaking the previous record of 89% set in June, 1983. These short-term
warning signals currently serve to reinforce our cautious assessment of the
valuation data presented.

	S&P 400	
	P/E Ratio	Price/Book
1978	8.2	1.2
1979	7.5	1.2
1980	9.6	1.4
1981	8.2	1.2
1982	11.9	1.3
1983	12.6	1.5
1984	10.5	1.5
1985	14.9	1.8
1986	18.4	2.1

Sources: Source Capital Annual Report, Standard & Poor's
Corporation, as of June 30, 1986.

December 31, 1986

The current market environment seems best characterized by Sir Isaac
Newton's first law of physics—the law of momentum which posits that "bodies
in motion tend to remain in motion." This market is very much "in motion"
marching to the drumbeat of easy money, competitive takeovers and program
trading. By established standards of equity valuation, stock prices have reached
levels which have served to mark the upper boundary of market valuation for
the past 40 years. This judgment is clearly illustrated in the accompanying chart
utilizing dividend yield as perhaps the least ambiguous of valuation measures.*

*Stocks rose by a third and then fell all the way back within the following year. (J.T.)

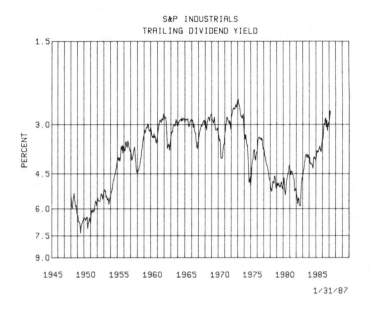

S&P INDUSTRIALS
TRAILING DIVIDEND YIELD

1/31/87

June 30, 1987

For the past five years the stock market has simply performed so much better than the businesses whose ownership it represents that it has built in a level of expectations for future performance that American businesses might be hard-pressed to deliver.

In the past five years the market has provided shareholder returns of 28% per year as measured by the Standard & Poor's 500 Stock Average, and over 30% on the Dow Jones Industrial Average. This is substantially higher than any five calendar-year period since 1930. Thus while corporate America has been chugging along generating 12% returns on equity in the past five years, its shareholders have enjoyed returns almost 2½ times as great. This has been made possible because, much like a closed-end investment company whose share-holders can earn returns far higher than the underlying portfolio when its shares are revalued from a discount to a premium, stockholders in American businesses have benefited from a massive revaluation of corporate equity. In the last five years stock prices have risen from 1.1× to 2.5× book value, from 8× to 25× trailing earnings and dividend yields have declined from over 6% to only 2.3%. This five-year period has seen a revaluation from historical record lows to record breaking highs. This process has been fueled by declining interest rates, reduced barriers to corporate takeovers and reorganizations, and a sharp increase in foreign investment in U.S. equities driven by a burgeoning trade deficit. However accustomed to it we all have become, this revaluation cannot be a sustainable source of continuing future returns. While the shares of a closed-end fund can for a time rise more rapidly than the value of its underlying portfolio this is ultimately a finite process. Similarly, the stock market cannot appreciate through revaluation forever. Just as closed-end fund stock market returns are ultimately harnessed to long-term portfolio returns, shareholders of corporate America cannot forever earn 2½× the returns earned by the operation of those businesses. That this has happened for five years now may make it seem a normal and continuing process, but it clearly is not.

Given the foregoing views, we are managing Source Capital's investment portfolio with an increased emphasis on liquidity and fixed-income securities, particularly those with short to intermediate maturities and a reduced emphasis on equities. As we have often stressed, we make our investment decisions based on our assessment of the attractiveness of individual securities, not on any preconceived notions of the future of stock prices generally. While we have found buying opportunities and have acted upon them, they have been more than offset by opportunities to sell. Given this view of the scarcity of attractive long-term equity investment opportunities and our willingness to wait for such opportunities to present themselves, it is almost inevitable that Source will continue to underperform a strong revaluation-driven stock market. In this vein, it is worth repeating the concluding comments from our 1983 First Quarter Report also written during a dynamic bull market advance: "Investing is inherently a long-term process involving decisions whose ultimate results must be measured over a period of years. It is easy to lose sight of this fact in the wake of very rapid short-term price movements. The following quote from the 1st Quarter Report of 1981 is particularly appropriate in this connection: 'Perhaps the most overlooked element in the investment process is time. The ability to wait—wait for an existing investment to mature, wait for a potential investment to become available at a reasonable price—often demands a degree of patience which is extremely difficult to sustain in the face of contrary interim market behavior.'*

December 31, 1987

With the sharp decline in stock prices, capped by The Crash on October 19, the remarkable five-year bull market which commenced in August of 1982 has apparently come to an end. It was an extraordinary end to an extraordinary rise and it was unique in a number of respects which are worthy of comment.

To begin with, this market advance began rather than ended with an explosion in the price of small speculative stocks. During its first year, from the summer of 1982 to the summer of 1983, the price of the average share on the American Stock Exchange was up over 140%. This price explosion in secondary stocks was the culmination of a trend of superior performance which commenced in 1975. It was accompanied by a booming new issue market and an explosion of trading on the American Exchange and in the Over-the-Counter markets, all classic signs of a speculative blowoff. While the broad market experienced a modest 15% correction during the first half of 1984, the correc-

*The crash of October 1987 occurred a few weeks later. (J.T.)

tion of these speculative excesses among small stocks was intense. During the remarkable advance in the ensuing three years, small stocks never regained center stage and investment interest was increasingly concentrated on large institutional blue chip stocks. In fact, this concentration of buying interest in major blue chip equities was so extreme that by late 1987, after four years of falling behind the blue chips, small stocks were as cheap *relative to the market* as they had been at the bear market bottom in 1974.

In addition to this early extinguishment of small stock speculation and subsequent relative price erosion in this market sector, the bull market was unusual in that the entire price rise representing more than a tripling of the Dow Jones Industrial Average took place with no more than a 15% increase in earnings from 1981 to 1987. As we expressed in our mid-year report, this bull market was made possible by "a massive revaluation of corporate equity. In the last five years stock prices have risen from 1.1× to 2.5× book value, from 8× to 25× trailing earnings and dividend yields have declined from over 6% to only 2.3%. This five-year period has seen a revaluation from historical record lows to record breaking highs." Never before had the market experienced such an extreme revaluation concentrated in such a short period of time.

Finally, the manner in which this five-year bull market ended represented perhaps its most uniquely distinguishing characteristic. Never before had stock prices fallen so far so quickly, culminated by the extraordinary circumstances of October 19th and 20th. It is our belief that all three of these phenomena— the erosion of interest in secondary stocks, the unrestrained explosion in valuations and the intensity of the decline—were in large measure related to the initiation of and broadening acceptance of listed option trading, particularly in stock index futures, and the broadening use of indexing and portfolio insurance which these instruments facilitated.

Portfolio insurance is a trading strategy devised by academicians designed to protect portfolios from major market declines. At some risk of offending proponents of this technique, I would suggest that it can be most clearly explained as amounting to a stop loss order. Thus, an investor who has purchased a stock at $10 a share and seen it appreciate to $20 may enter a stop loss order at $18, thereby protecting his profits in the event the stock falls to that level. As the price of the stock increases further he raises the stop loss order. By using stop loss orders in this fashion, an investor can ignore the issue of whether the stock is overvalued, thereby exposing himself to unlimited upside but always protecting against decline in excess of a predetermined amount. Portfolio insurance is nothing more than a more sophisticated use of large scale stop loss orders through which large institutional portfolios reduce equity exposure by selling stocks (or stock index futures) as prices decline past predetermined bench marks.

The proponents of portfolio insurance were extraordinarily successful marketeers, and this technique, which virtually did not exist at the start of the bull market in 1982, grew to encompass as much as $100 billion of institutional capital. While there were voices of skepticism raised that the very success of this technique in gaining adherents would ultimately insure its demise in practice, portfolio insurance was not really tested until October 19, 1987. Institutions which adopted portfolio insurance thought they were immune to market risk and thus were not concerned about the rising valuation structure of the market. They truly felt that they had the benefits of equity exposure without the corresponding risks. Thus, decisions to reduce equity exposure as valuations expanded and prices soared, were simply deferred or, more likely, not even considered. The normal pattern of selling in response to rapidly rising prices was to a significant degree preempted by the growing marketing success of portfolio insurance practitioners.

Of course, with the benefit of hindsight, we now know that portfolio insurance didn't work as advertised. The interesting question is whether portfolio insurance could ever have worked. The answer to that question is probably yes, provided that it was employed by only a limited number of market participants whose selling orders would not quickly overwhelm market liquidity. Even the most unsophisticated investor realizes that markets cannot accommodate an overwhelming unanimity of opinion. If everybody wants to sell, the only way buyers can be found to accomplish a trade is at a significant reduction in price. If our hypothetical investor has too much company with his stop loss order at $18, his sell order will not be executed at $18 but at some lower price. If the volume of sell orders is significant enough, intense enough, the price may be substantially lower than $18, at whatever level it takes to match buyers and sellers. For some reason this seemingly obvious fact (the law of supply and demand) was somehow ignored or considered strangely inapplicable to the sell orders generated by portfolio insurance programs. The avalanche of sell orders generated by predetermined portfolio insurance programs simply overwhelmed the liquidity of the marketplace on October 19, 1987. Judgment had been substantially suspended by the adoption of portfolio insurance techniques and the practitioners were forced by their own predetermined decision rules to continue selling, irrespective of price. This selling was initially focused primarily in the futures market but was quickly transmitted to the floor of the New York Stock Exchange through the arbitrage activities of program traders. The excessive valuations of last summer and fall simply evaporated in a matter of hours as prices overwhelmed all considerations of value. Thus, last summer's wildly excessive valuation levels were eliminated almost overnight rather than through an extended period of declining prices during which stocks seesawed ever lower until prices found some new level of equilibrium.

IV

Source Capital Portfolio and
Statistical Profile

Source Capital Portfolio, December 31, 1988

Issuer	Industry Classification	Number of Shares	Cost	Value
COMMON STOCKS				
Abbott Laboratories	Health Care	65,600	$ 2,955,992	$ 3,157,000
Banc One Corporation	Banking	151,925	3,240,265	3,380,331
Bandag, Incorporated	Producer Durable Goods	98,400	940,180	6,408,300
Bausch & Lomb Incorporated	Health Care	130,600	4,806,431	5,664,775
Bristol-Myers Company	Health Care	72,100	2,842,132	3,262,525
Burton Group PLC, The	Consumer Services—Retail	31,700	610,187	400,213
CPI Corp	Consumer Services—Retail	136,400	2,164,463	2,728,000
Capital Cities/ABC, Inc.	Communications & Information	9,900	2,289,481	3,586,275
Devon Group, Inc.*	Communications & Information	257,800	4,107,325	3,093,600
Donnelley (R.R.) & Sons Company	Communications & Information	88,800	2,895,766	3,074,700
Dreyfus Corporation, The	Financial Services	93,600	2,368,472	2,340,000
Emerson Electric Co.	Producer Durable Goods	100,600	2,824,684	3,043,150
First National Bank of Anchorage, The	Banking	3,501	3,102,960	4,726,350
First Wachovia Corporation	Banking	110,500	4,253,991	4,185,187
Fleetwood Enterprises, Inc.	Consumer Durable Goods	178,100	3,959,583	4,452,500
International Business Machines	Communications & Information	60,600	4,643,507	7,378,050
LADD Furniture, Inc.	Consumer Durable Goods	245,600	3,039,300	3,407,700
Liberty Homes, Inc. (Class A)	Consumer Durable Goods	70,500	634,500	502,313
Loctite Corporation	Materials	39,200	1,240,786	1,283,800
Loews Corporation	Multi-Industry	68,100	3,303,454	5,371,387
Lufkin Industries, Inc.	Energy	20,300	4,131,100	2,892,750
Marsh & McLennan Companies, Inc.	Insurance	143,200	8,038,754	8,055,000
Melville Corporation	Consumer Services—Retail	160,000	6,926,988	11,900,000
Mercantile Bankshares Corporation	Banking	100,000	3,180,252	3,550,000
Miller (Herman), Inc.	Producer Durable Goods	210,300	4,421,160	4,179,712
Morton Thiokol, Inc.	Materials	103,900	3,656,156	3,831,313
National Service Industries, Inc.	Multi-Industry	152,600	3,120,802	3,280,900
Petrolane Partners, L.P.	Energy	308,900	5,887,922	6,641,350
Pfizer Inc.	Health Care	71,700	3,780,734	4,149,637
Pittway Corporation	Multi-Industry	55,100	1,634,808	5,234,500
Times Mirror Company, The (Class A)	Communications & Information	117,900	3,863,319	3,875,963
Universal Furniture Limited	Consumer Durable Goods	43,000	633,563	800,875
VF Corporation	Consumer Non-Durable Goods	148,500	4,154,026	4,269,375
Wallace Computer Services, Inc.	Communications & Information	37,300	1,258,914	1,627,213
Weingarten Realty Investors	Real Estate Investment Trust	123,800	2,419,567	3,172,375
Zenith National Insurance Corp.	Insurance	247,930	4,163,353	4,338,775
Other Common Stocks			1,563,019	1,727,018
Total Common Stocks			$119,057,896	$144,972,912
PREFERRED STOCKS				
Federal Home Loan Mortgage Corporation ($2.50)	Financial Services	50,300	$ 2,455,234	$ 2,515,000
Other Preferred Stock			267,334	263,863
Total Preferred Stocks			$ 2,722,568	$ 2,778,863

Source Capital Portfolio, December 31, 1988   (continued)

Issuer	Industry Classification	Face Amount	Cost	Value
CONVERTIBLE SECURITIES				
Cetus Corporation—5¼% 2002	*Health Care*	$ 3,295,000	$ 1,891,300	$ 1,762,825
Diagnostic/Retrieval Systems, Inc.—8½% 1998	*Producer Durable Goods*	2,866,000	2,488,195	2,378,780
Genentech, Inc.—5% 2002	*Health Care*	3,100,000	1,962,750	1,697,250
Guilford Mills, Inc.—6% 2012	*Consumer Non-Durable Goods*	2,887,000	2,076,390	2,150,815
International Paper Company— 5¾% 2002	*Materials*	2,815,000	2,350,056	2,378,675
Magna International Inc.— 7% 1993	*Producer Durable Goods*	735,000	746,700	591,675
Rouse Company, The— 5⅞% 1996	*Construction & Real Estate*	2,400,000	2,078,500	2,448,000
Sage Energy Company—8½% 2005	*Energy*	1,400,000	1,050,000	882,000
St. Paul Companies, Inc., The—7½% 2000	*Insurance*	1,934,000	2,464,303	2,519,035
Seagate Technology, Inc.— 6¾% 2012	*Producer Durable Goods*	3,590,000	2,122,038	1,893,725
Total Convertible Securities			$ 19,230,232	$ 18,702,780
NON-CONVERTIBLE SECURITIES				
Federal Farm Credit Banks Consolidated Systems —14.70% 1991	*U.S. Government*	$ 5,000,000	$ 4,902,750	$ 5,571,900
Home Savings of America, F.A. —10% 2021	*Corporate*	1,053,500	1,053,540	1,009,390
Lear Petroleum Corporation —12⅝% 1997	*Corporate*	2,886,000	2,943,720	2,950,935
MSA Shopping Malls, Inc. —10.95% 1998	*Corporate*	4,100,000	3,945,141	4,012,875
Multimedia, Inc. (Series B) —0/16% 2005	*Corporate*	8,390,000	7,137,480	7,131,500
NRM Energy Company, L.P. —0% 1989	*Corporate*	11,950,000	11,688,676	12,189,000
Navistar Financial Corporation —7½% 1994	*Corporate*	1,400,000	971,600	1,247,750
—7⅝% 1993	*Corporate*	3,758,000	2,126,131	3,480,848
—8⅝% 1991	*Corporate*	1,081,000	1,022,236	1,039,111
SCI Holdings, Inc. —0% 1991	*Corporate*	2,700,000	1,966,673	1,940,625
—0% 1992	*Corporate*	8,000,000	5,084,989	5,110,000
—15% 1997	*Corporate*	5,700,000	6,426,750	6,334,125
Texaco Capital Inc. —8¼% 2000	*Corporate*	5,000,000	4,984,150	4,975,000
U.S. Treasury Notes —8⅛% 1998	*U.S. Government*	4,500,000	4,147,031	4,214,520
—9% 1993	*U.S. Government*	5,000,000	4,990,625	4,975,000
Zenith National Insurance Corp. —10¼% 1994	*Corporate*	2,000,000	1,736,111	1,970,000
Other Non-Convertible Securities			1,580,986	1,566,276
Total Non-Convertible Securities			$ 66,708,589	$ 69,718,855
Total Investment Securities			$207,719,285	$236,173,410

* Non-income producing security

Source Capital Statistical Profile of Principal Common Stock Holdings, December 31, 1988

	Fundamental Investment Data							Valuation Data			
	Earnings/Share		10-Yr. Growth		Total Debt % Capital	Ret. on Beg. Equity	Year-End Price	1987–88 Price Range	P/E Ratio	Price/ Book Value	Div. Yield
	1978	Last 12 Mos.	Growth Rate	Yrs. EPS Declined							
Abbott Laboratories	$ .62	$ 3.33	18%	0	28%	35%	$ 48	$43–52	14.5x	4.7x	2.5%
Banc One Corp.	.76	2.61	13	0	15	19	22	21–28	8.5	1.5	4.7
Bandag, Inc.	.85	4.68	19	1	34	53	65	53–67	13.9	6.8	1.4
Bausch & Lomb	1.27	3.27	10	1	24	17	43	33–48	13.8	2.2	2.3
Bristol-Myers	.77	2.88	14	0	11	26	45	38–47	15.7	3.7	4.4
Capital Cities/ABC	3.80	21.40	20	0	37	18	362	297–370	16.9	2.2	0.1
CPI Corp.	**	1.62	24*	1	0	27	20	17–22	12.3	2.7	2.0
Devon Group	**	1.33	**	1	22	20	12	9–15	8.8	1.6	0.0
Donnelley (R.R.) & Sons	.75	2.64	13	0	14	18	35	30–39	13.1	2.2	2.5
Dreyfus Corp.	.12	2.27	35	1	1	18	25	24–31	11.0	1.7	2.1
Emerson Electric	.98	2.31	9	0	23	20	30	27–36	13.1	2.4	3.7
Fed. Home Loan Mtg. Corp.	**	5.43	56*	0	39	35	50	46–52	9.2	2.5	5.0
First Nat. Bk. Anchorage	66.70	159.29	9	3	0	11	1330	1270–1370	8.3	0.9	2.3
First Wachovia	1.24	4.34	13	1	20	17	38	33–41	8.7	1.4	4.0
Fleetwood Enterprises	1.01	2.75	10	3	14	19	25	17–27	9.1	1.5	2.6
Int'l. Business Machines	5.32	9.27	6	4	18	15	122	104–130	13.1	1.9	3.6
LADD Furniture	**	1.32	46*	0	28	27	14	11–17	10.4	2.2	2.2
Loctite Corp.	1.03	2.65	9	2	19	25	33	27–39	12.4	2.8	2.7
Loews Corp.	1.21	7.79	21	1	30	22	79	62–83	10.2	2.2	1.3
Lufkin Inds. Inc.	10.94	5.12	(7)	6	0	4	135	130–190	26.4	1.0	5.9
Marsh & McLennan	1.23	4.09	13	2	26	37	56	45–60	13.8	5.4	4.4
Melville Corp.	1.76	6.40	13	0	9	24	74	53–77	11.6	2.7	3.5
Mercantile Bankshares	1.64	4.15	10	1	9	17	35	33–40	8.5	1.3	4.0

Miller (Herman)	.35	1.94	18	2	30	22	20	19–27	10.2	1.9	2.6
Morton Thiokol	.95	3.34	13	1	22	16	37	36–46	11.0	1.6	2.5
National Service Industries	.58	1.80	12	0	4	17	22	18–25	11.9	1.9	3.9
Pfizer Inc.	1.47	4.70	12	1	21	21	58	47–60	12.3	2.3	3.8
Pittway Corp.	4.75	8.35	3	6	22	13	95	73–100	11.4	1.3	1.9
Times Mirror Co.	1.04	2.28	8	2	36	20	33	29–40	14.4	2.6	3.0
Universal Furniture	.22	1.61	22	3	35	19	19	13–19	11.5	1.9	0.9
VF Corp.	.39	2.64	22	1	29	18	28	24–34	10.9	1.8	3.1
Wallace Computer	.74	3.15	15	0	9	17	44	35–45	13.8	2.1	1.8
Weingarten Realty	**	2.09	**	1	67	28	26	22–28	12.3	3.5	6.6
Zenith National Insurance	.54	2.15	15	2	10	16	17	14–22	8.1	1.1	4.6
Source Portfolio			14.0	1	20	19.0			11.5	2.0	3.1
Dow Jones Industrials			4.7	4	33	18.5	2168.57		11.1	1.9	3.8
S & P Industrials			7.4	3	37	19.5	321.26		12.0	2.1	3.0

*6-year growth rate
**Comparable data not available

V

Windsor Fund "Report Cards"

Windsor Fund 1981 "Report Card"

Industry Groups	Percent of Net Assets	S&P Group Percentage Change*	Performance of Meaningful Windsor Positions (In Order of Size)	Grade	Critique
Aluminum	4.8	−34.2	Reynolds Metals (−29.9), Kaiser Aluminum (−33.3)	D−	Very poor 1981 result—should be a real winner with economic recovery.
Apparel	4.1	−7.1	Interco (−3.6), Blue Bell (−9.8)	C	Average performances.
Banks	12.8	+11.7 (Non–New York City Banks) +29.2 (New York City Banks)	First Interstate Bancorp (+27.2), First Natl. Boston (+19.4), Ameritrust (−0−), Pittsburgh Natl. Corp. (+36.2), Phila. Natl. Corp. (−5.7), Seafirst Corp. (+32.3), Mercantile Bancorp (−1.9), Virginia Natl. Bankshares (+54.1), South Carolina Natl. Corp. (+32.9), Natl. City Corp. (−13.1), Bancorp Hawaii (+21.3), First Tennessee Natl. Corp. (+36.5)	A−	Finally paid off in big way—both concentration and selection, on balance, was excellent.
Conglomerates	2.5	−2.7	Northwest Industries (+67.4), Scott & Fetzer (+26.1)	A	Northwest, our oil well equipment participation, was "right on."
Consumer Durables (Household Appliances)	1.6	+12.6	Whirlpool (+30.7)	A	Excellent selection in lieu of autos; should be further heard from.
Containers (Metal & Glass)	1.7	+7.1	Anchor Hocking (−17.4)	D	Not our finest moment.
Finance (Personal Loans)	2.2	−10.7	Household International (−15.6)	D	Poor. Declining short-term interest rates should help in 1982.
Foods	6.4	+14.8	General Foods (+6.5), Dart & Kraft (+17.5), Consolidated Foods (+26.7)	B+	Good group, though General Foods behind the parade.

Sector	Weight	Return	Holdings	Grade	Comment
Insurance–Multi-Line	4.6	+22.3	Aetna Life & Casualty (+21.3), Travelers Corp. (+27.1)	A–	Workman-like Windsor result.
Media	1.1	+23.9	Washington Post (+25.7)	A	Good lesser-recognized growth choice plus fortuitous recent ABC purchase.
Oils	19.4	−19.0 (*Internatl.*) −17.5 (*Composite*)	Royal Dutch (−32.8), Exxon Corp. (−20.2), Gulf Oil (−9.7)	B+	Actually championship considering huge gain on Conoco, which was bought and sold during the year, and profits on heavy purchases at spring lows.
Paper	1.6	−8.1	Mead Corp. (−10.6)	C–	Another economic recovery participation.
Restaurants	4.3	+36.0	McDonald's (+58.2), Church's Fried Chicken (+2.9)	A	Outstanding McDonald's result plus other significant profit taking.
Retailing	5.8	+5.9	Melville Corp. (+4.0), U.S. Shoe (+103.8), K-Mart (−12.3)	A	Superb U.S. Shoe result; Levitz sold at large profit.
Shoes	0.4	+5.8	Brown Group (+29.1)	A	Our kind of grind-out.
Telephone	3.8	+20.7	AT&T (+19.6)	B+	Telephone an excellent big market cap stock.
Tire & Rubber	1.2	+4.4	Goodyear (+5.1)	B	Another auto substitute.
Trucking	1.3	+10.2	RLC Corp. (−30.4), Consolidated Freightways (+48.7)	A	Came of age, although RLC owes us a lot; Delta & Overnite sold at eye-catching gains.
Utilities–Electric	1.7	+9.4	Central & SouthWest (+10.9), Houston Industries (+11.1), Consolidated Edison (+37.8)	A–	Good selections in a positive group.

*Compares with overall S&P change of −4.4%

Windsor Fund 1984 "Report Card"

Industry Groups	Percent of Net Assets	S&P Group Percentage Change*	Performance of Meaningful Windsor Positions (In Order of Size)	Grade	Critique
Aluminum	1.0	−17.8	Reynolds Metals (−7.8)	C+	Bulk of position bought well in '84—pricing should improve.
Automobiles	8.5	+3.9	General Motors (+3.4)	A−	Good area relative to timely '84 purchases of both GM and Ford.
Banks	13.3	−9.9 (Non–New York City Banks) +10.8 (New York City Banks)	First Interstate (−9.5), J.P. Morgan (+18.3), Bank of Boston (+5.9), CoreStates Financial (+40.6), First Union (+18.9), Marine Midland (+21.3), Sovran Finl (+6.8), Mercantile Bancorp (+11.5), First Tennessee (+28.0), Bancorp Hawaii (−4.8), Central Bancshares (+12.4).	A−	Very good, other than First Interstate concentration.
Building & Construction	3.0	+3.3	Gifford-Hill (+12.8), Moore McCormack (−10.8)	C	All we need is decent cement pricing.
Computer & Business Equipment	0.3	−2.7	Xerox (−22.4)	C	Sold majority of position at $50.
Fertilizers	1.8	−3.8	International Minerals & Chemicals (−10.8)	D+	World fertilizer demand has to expand.
Insurance–Multi-Line	7.7	+2.8	Travelers (+16.1), Aetna (−1.7), Cigna (−18.6)	B−	Bulk of Cigna purchased advantageously in '84. Group should blossom now that 20%+ commercial rate increases are being realized.

Industry	%	Change	Holdings	Grade	Comment
Natural Gas Diversified	8.6	+0.8 (Pipelines)	Tenneco (−11.7), Panhandle Eastern (+2.8), InterNorth (−0−)	C+	Excellent profits taken in Transco and Pioneer. Owes us a fair bit, particularly Tenneco.
Oils	12.9	+15.4 (Oil Composite)	Royal Dutch (+14.2), Atlantic Richfield (+10.6), Exxon Corp. (+14.4), Amerada Hess (−7.1), Pennzoil Co. (+18.5)	B+	An excellent area in which we were about average.
Rails	1.9	−15.3	Norfolk Southern (−5.5)	C	Should do better as one billion dollar cash hoard is utilized.
Sweeteners	0.6	+1.5 (400 Industrials)	A.E. Staley (−24.4)	D−	Not our finest hour.
Telephone	12.6	+1.6 (S&P 500)	A.T.&T. (+13.5) Reconstructed	A	Stellar result. Sold new T well and built up rewarding BOC position—lofty dividend counts.
Utilities–Electric	8.5	−1.8	Texas Utilities (−1.9), Houston Ind. (−4.3), Central & SouthWest (+4.9), El Paso Electric (−18.3)	B−	Better than looks as part of position derived in '84 at good prices—also extraordinary dividend return.

*S&P 500 % Change = +1.6%

Windsor Fund 1985 "Report Card"

Industry Groups	Percent of Net Assets	S&P Group Percentage Change*	Performance of Meaningful Windsor Positions (In Order of Size)	Grade	Critique
Agricultural	1.2	+10.9 (Chemicals–Divers)	International Minerals & Chemical (+2.6)	C	Excellent Federal (broilers) sale and result partially offsets lackluster IMC performance.
Aluminum	1.0	−10.8	Reynolds Metals (−7.8)	D	Again a vale of tears, but inventories and operating rates have dropped, the Company has consolidated and rationalized facilities—1986 should exceed expectations.
Appliances	0.9	+5.7	Whirlpool (+0.9), Magic Chef (+49.4)	B+	Varied result but Magic Chef real coup.
Automobiles	10.5	−7.5	Ford (−1.1), General Motors (−16.7)	D	Ford actually better than it looks, as bought lower in size during year, but awful G.M. result cries out for compensatory 1986 contribution—we think autos will surprise in 1986, particularly bottom line relative to supposed dismal prospect.
Banks	13.3	+1.8 (Non–New York City Banks) +30.5 (New York City Banks)	First Interstate (+28.0), J.P. Morgan (+39.7), Bank of Boston (+37.7), Security Pacific (+5.3), Bancorp Hawaii (+39.1), Mercantile Bancorp (+30.1), Marine Midland (+29.4), First Tennessee (+31.5), CoreStates Financial (+36.2)	A	Consistently good numbers in major area.
Building & Construction	1.3	+18.3	Jim Walter (+28.9)	B+	Additionally aided by eye-catching Gifford-Hill virtual elimination.

Industry	% Change	Holdings	Grade	Comment
Insurance–Multi-Line	3.9	Travelers (+23.3), CIGNA (+56.4), Aetna (+36.0)	A	Insurance paid off in big way as extraordinary rate increases were garnered in commercial component of business.
Machinery	-9.2 (Trucks & Parts)	Cummins Engine (-13.4)	D	Both environment and pricing eroded relative to our perspective. However, fine company, poised for positive result assuming favorable industry backdrop.
Natural Gas Diversified	6.4	Tenneco (+4.5), Panhandle Eastern (-1.4), Columbia Gas (+17.4)	C–	Excellent InterNorth sales during year, but poor Tenneco and Panhandle result; both continue to owe us something.
Oils	14.3	Royal Dutch (+29.1), Exxon (+25.7), Atlantic Richfield (+40.4), Amerada Hess (+15.4)	A	Attention-getting across the board result in a decent area where we had big representation.
Recreational Vehicles	0.6	Fleetwood Enterprises (-15.9)	C	Fleetwood sold and repurchased during year advantageously—company profitability held up very well on declining volume. We need a favorable industry wind to our back.
Telephone	9.0	NYNEX (+17.0), U.S. West (+18.6), Southwestern Bell (+19.3), Ameritech (+25.4)	B+	Telephones were good again and we had large holding.
Transportation	1.7	Norfolk Southern (+24.7)	B+	Even better as a result of rewarding Yellow Freight sales.
Utilities–Electric	7.3	Texas Utilities (+7.5), Houston Ind. (+29.0), Central & SouthWest (+19.2), El Paso Electric (+10.7), Commonwealth Edison (+4.2)	B–	Somewhat better than industry result plus outstanding yields.

Oils change labeled (Composite).

*S&P 500 % Change = +14.3%

Windsor Fund 1986 "Report Card"

Industry Groups	Percent of Net Assets	S&P Group Percentage Change*	Performance of Meaningful Windsor Positions (In Order of Size)	Grade	Critique
Agricultural	0.4	+42.6 (Chemicals–Diversified)	International Minerals & Chemical (−33.7)	D−	Except for sale of 40% of position at decent price earlier in the year, an "F".
Aluminum	4.7	+214.2	Reynolds Metals (+47.0)	A	Good selection versus both market and industry.
Automobiles	15.5	+33.2	Ford (+85.1), General Motors (+6.6)	A−	Ford a real coup, unfortunately diluted by General Motors, though GM starting to make "right" decisions.
Banks	14.0	+18.3 (Non–New York City Banks) +30.0 (New York City Banks)	Citicorp (+17.0), First Interstate Bancorp (+8.2), Bankers Trust (+38.3), Security Pacific (+33.2), Bank of Boston (+54.3), J. P. Morgan (+61.3)	B+	Citicorp and First Interstate still expected to work out next year. Others did very well this year, and, in case of Bankers Trust, plenty of remaining potential.
Computers & Business Equipment	4.9	+6.8	International Business Machines (−4.9)	C−	Most of position purchased at knockdown prices during year.
Insurance	8.1	+13.5 (Multi-line)	CIGNA Corp. (−6.2), Travelers Corp. (−1.4)	C−	Some good sales earlier in the year, especially CIGNA and Aetna.
Natural Gas Diversified	6.0	+7.2	Tenneco (+7.6)	D+	Tenneco yield four points better than market fills in some of capital shortfall, plus excellent Panhandle sales during year.

Oils	13.7	+10.4 (Composite)	Atlantic Richfield (−13.6), Shell Transport (+31.2), Phillips Petroleum (−16.7), Royal Dutch (+38.8), Standard Oil (−5.1)	A−	84% of our oil position was in Exxon, Royal Dutch and Shell Transport—not only very good oil stocks, but good common stocks as well.
Savings & Loans	3.9	+59.5	Golden West Finl. (+50.5), Home Federal of San Diego (+14.1), Great Western Finl. (+51.4), H. F. Ahmanson (+74.9)	B+	Should be good equities to own next year also.
Telephone	4.2	+43.9	U.S. West (+38.2), Southwestern Bell (+37.3), Nynex (+50.3)	A	Excellent capital appreciation plus good yields as well.
Utilities–Electric	7.3	+33.6	Commonwealth Edison (+16.4), Houston Industries (+22.0), Texas Utilities (+19.7), El Paso Electric (+24.6)	C+	Good group but we underperformed across the board.

*S&P % Change = +28.5%

Windsor Fund 1988 "Report Card"

Industry Group	10/31/88 Percent of Net Assets	S&P Group Percentage Change*	Performance of Meaningful Windsor Positions (In Order of Size)	Grade	Critique
Aerospace/Defense	1.4	+23.8	Boeing (+68.0)	A+	Remarkable result; well researched.
Airlines	7.2	+26.6	AMR Corp. (+39.4), Delta Air Lines (+31.6), NWA, Inc. (+33.2)	A	Fine move in new area—fare increase case correct.
Automotive	22.2	+34.3	Ford Motor (+36.4), Chrysler Corp. (−0−), General Motors (+42.5)	A	Another eye-catching performance—Chrysler owes us a good bit.
Banks	16.0	+26.8 (Major Regional)	Citicorp (+24.1), Bankers Trust (+18.7), First Interstate Bancorp (+18.1), BankAmerica Corp. (+113.0), Bank of Boston (+4.2), Shawmut Natl. Corp. (+42.3), Security Pacific (+39.5)	A	Stunning recovery in BankAmerica; Large Citicorp and Bankers Trust holdings contributory; Security Pacific and Shawmut excellent.
		+12.6 (Money Center)			
Computer Systems	6.2	−6.6	International Business Machines (−0.1)	C−	Big ship slowly turning around.
Insurance	13.8	+0.6 (Multi-line)	CIGNA Corp. (−4.2), Aetna Life & Casualty (−1.5), Travelers Corp. (−0.3), USF&G Corp. (−1.2)	D	Quite disappointing area, but group health has turned and commercial P&C should have "soft" landing.
		−0.8 (Prop-Cas)			
Natural Gas	1.2	+34.0	Tenneco, Inc. (+14.7)	B−	O.K.—being eliminated.
Retail	1.8	+28.4**	Circuit City Stores (+115.1)**	A+	Very well-timed selection of premier retailer.

Savings & Loans	7.0	+2.2	H.F. Ahmanson (−4.6), Golden West Financial (+14.7), Home Federal of San Diego (+4.5), Great Western Financial (−1.5), CalFed (−12.9)	C	Industry chaos obliterates promise of "good guys"; FSLIC crisis should get resolved.
Telephone	1.5	+5.5	Telefonica de Espana (+17.5)	B	Fast-growing Spanish telephone company should get upgraded.
Utilities–Electric	8.4	+5.7	Commonwealth Edison (+15.8), Houston Industries (−7.5), El Paso Electric (−2.4)	C+	10% yields enhance total returns—Commonwealth and Houston rate increases should be resolved.

*S&P 500 % Change 10/31/87–10/31/88 = +10.8%. Capital change only.
**From purchase in fiscal 1988 to 10/31/88.

VI

Windsor Fund Portfolio

Windsor Fund Portfolio, October 31, 1988

	Shares	Market Value (000)
Aerospace (1.4%)		
The Boeing Co.	1,296,500	$ 84,110
Airlines (7.2%)		
[1]AMR Corp.	3,872,900	190,256
Delta Air Lines, Inc.	3,223,500	162,787
NWA Inc.	1,302,400	70,492
Group Total		423,535
Automotive (22.2%)		
*Chrysler Corp.	12,910,450	343,741
*Ford Motor Co.	12,270,300	631,920
*General Motors Corp.	4,072,800	339,570
Group Total		1,315,231
Banks (16.0%)		
Amsouth Bancorp	22,200	552
[1]BankAmerica Corp.	6,100,000	112,088
Bank of Boston Corp.	2,008,823	49,969
*Bankers Trust New York Corp.	5,374,180	204,891
*Citicorp	13,390,600	336,439
Citizens & Southern Corp.	142,800	3,784
First Fidelity Bancorp.	18,980	733
First Interstate Bancorp.	2,908,651	142,524
First Tennessee National Corp.	60,000	1,657
National City Corp.	170,900	5,490
National Westminster Bank ADR	375,300	10,837
Security Pacific Corp.	577,280	22,947
Shawmut National Corp.	1,213,400	32,610
Valley National Corp.	540,900	14,672
Wells Fargo & Co.	65,500	4,487
Group Total		943,680
Building & Construction (.7%)		
[1]Hovnanian Enterprises, Inc.	318,900	2,432
Kaufman & Broad Home Corp.	446,000	4,460
Lennar Corp.	525,000	9,384
MDC Holdings, Inc.	802,800	2,609
Ryland Group, Inc.	1,242,800	20,972
Group Total		39,857
Chemicals (.7%)		
Dow Chemical Co.	476,200	42,560

Windsor Fund Portfolio, October 31, 1988   (*continued*)

	Shares	Market Value (000)
Electric Utilities (8.4%)		
*Commonwealth Edison Co.	10,250,761	$ 329,306
El Paso Electric Co.	1,714,400	26,573
Houston Industries, Inc.	4,848,100	143,019
Group Total		498,898
Electronic Data Processing (5.8%)		
(1)Digital Equipment Corp.	1,550,000	148,800
*International Business Machines Corp.	1,596,600	196,182
Group Total		344,982
Home Furnishings		
Shaw Industries Inc.	24,100	548
Insurance (13.8%)		
*Aetna Life & Casualty Co.	5,096,286	256,725
*CIGNA Corp.	5,613,700	284,895
*Travelers Corp.	6,727,905	242,205
USF&G Corp.	1,112,245	33,646
Group Total		817,471
Metals (.3%)		
Phelps Dodge Corp.	400,000	19,000
Natural Gas Diversified (1.2%)		
ENSERCH Corp.	112,100	2,088
Tenneco, Inc.	1,408,903	71,326
Group Total		73,414
Oil (.9%)		
Amerada Hess Corp.	691,900	19,806
Phillips Petroleum Co.	575,600	11,584
USX Corp.	800,000	22,200
Group Total		53,590
Paper (.8%)		
Great Northern Nekoosa Corp.	1,260,000	48,825
Retail (1.8%)		
(1)Burlington Coat Factory	554,900	10,612
Circuit City Stores Inc.	2,155,500	91,070
Pier 1 Imports Inc.	190,900	2,148
Group Total		103,830

Windsor Fund Portfolio, October 31, 1988 (*continued*)

	Shares	Market Value (000)
Savings & Loan (7.0%)		
Ahmanson, H.F. & Co.	7,524,300	$ 127,913
American Savings Bank	310,000	5,115
[1]Bay View Federal Savings & Loan Assn.	295,000	5,531
CalFed Inc.	1,105,000	24,310
[1]Citadel Holding Corp.	302,900	12,040
Coast Savings & Loan Assn.	840,000	13,020
CrossLand Savings, FSB	900,000	14,513
First Federal of Michigan	173,400	2,536
GLENFED, Inc.	504,500	10,910
Golden West Financial Corp.	2,383,800	74,494
Great Western Financial Corp.	2,960,050	48,471
Home Federal Savings & Loan Assn. (San Diego)	2,015,900	52,665
Home Savings Bank (Brooklyn)	572,500	10,734
[1]SFFed Corp.	330,000	3,919
Washington Federal Savings & Loan Assn.	345,840	9,943
[1]Washington Savings Bank FSB	953	3
Group Total		416,117
Steel (.1%)		
Texas Industries, Inc.	187,961	5,850
Telephone (1.5%)		
Telefonica De Espana S.A. ADR	3,625,300	85,195
Miscellaneous (.7%)		
Cedar Fair Limited Partnership	654,200	6,460
Maritrans Partners Limited Partnership	578,200	5,710
Other (.5%)		31,170
Group Total		43,340
TOTAL COMMON STOCKS (Cost $4,631,105)		5,360,033

GOVERNMENT AND AGENCY OBLIGATIONS (3.9%)

	Face Amount (000)	
U.S. Treasury Notes		
8.875%, 2/15/96	$11,600	11,763
7.25%, 11/15/96	45,500	41,974
8.875%, 11/15/97	145,500	147,182
9.25%, 8/15/98	30,000	31,106
TOTAL GOVERNMENT AND AGENCY OBLIGATIONS (cost $225,686)		232,025

Windsor Fund Portfolio, October 31, 1988   (*continued*)

	Shares	Market Value (000)
TEMPORARY CASH INVESTMENTS (4.8%)		
Commercial Paper		
General Electric Capital Corp. 8.1%, 11/16/88	25,000	$ 24,831
Shearson Lehman 8.3%, 1/25/89	51,000	49,942
Repurchase Agreement		
Collateralized by U.S. Government Obligations		
in a Pooled Cash Account 8.15%, 11/1/88	$206,372	$206,372
TOTAL TEMPORARY CASH INVESTMENTS (Cost $281,145)		281,145
TOTAL INVESTMENTS (99.2%)		
(Cost $5,137,936)		5,873,203
OTHER ASSETS AND LIABILITIES (.8%)		
Other Assets		118,516
Liabilities		(71,762)
		46,754
NET ASSETS (100%)		
Applicable to 419,065,500 outstanding $.01 par value shares (authorized 1,000,000,000 shares)		$5,919,957
NET ASSET VALUE PER SHARE		$14.13

*Ten largest common stock investments representing 53.5% of net assets.
[1]Non-income producing securities.

VII

Extracts from the Acorn Fund Reports

June 30, 1975

Ochlocracy

For Acorn's official Bicentennial offering, we wish to revive a forgotten word used by our Founding Fathers. John Adams closed a letter to Abigail in April, 1776: "I am sure every good Politician would plot, as long as General Washington would, against Despotism, Empire, Monarchy, Aristocracy, or Ochlocracy." The first four forms of tyranny are familiar enough to everyone, but "ochlocracy" was completely unfamiliar to me, so I looked it up. The word, familiar enough to eighteenth century political scientists, even radicals like Adams, means "government by the mob or lowest of the people."

Alexis de Tocqueville, in 1835, looking at Andrew Jackson's frontiersmen battling the New England establishment, realized that, "There exists also in the human heart a depraved taste for equality which impels the weak to attempt to lower the powerful to their own level . . . liberty is not the chief and constant object of (a democratic nation's) desires; equality is their idol. . . ."

Irving Kristol, writing in the July, 1975 *Commentary,* reflects that, "All the classical political philosophers—Aristotle through Montesquieu—understood that the basic threat to a self-governing republic was the mobilization of organized greed (usually in the name of "equality") by ambitious and unscrupulous politicians . . . this is a debased vision of politics in a democracy."

Elizabeth Drew, quoting "A House Democrat" in "The Energy Bazaar" (*New Yorker,* July 21, 1975): "Congress is a very inadequate tool for doing the hard things. When you have an expanding economy and can give things away, Congress is splendid. But it doesn't want to do the hard things."

Two hundred years after John Adams' letter, despotism, empire, monarchy, and aristocracy are still familiar terms to us all. Our vigilance against them was proved again in the Watergate affair. Could it be that the fifth evil, ochlocracy, has remained a threat, so insidious that we have even forgotten its name? Are we slipping into a competitive populist giveaway by ochlocrats, or can our politicians, in the spirit of General Washington, do "the hard things" to balance budgets, cut energy consumption, and increase capital formation? After all the

311

work we went through to break away from British despotism, it would be unpleasant and ironic to copy the recent British slide into socialism, inflation, and stagnation.

June 30, 1976

The Spectator

The Acorn Fund is now six years old, a respectable 3% of our national history, and therefore is of age to join in the ubiquitous Bicentennial orgy of self-congratulation. Recitations of the events of 1776 have been done, and overdone, so we will go back another sixty years to one of the greatest, and surely the most graceful, sources of eighteenth-century social and political ideas.

The great American statesmen who built our Constitution all were affected in character and writing style by *The Spectator*, a series of essays written by Addison and Steele in 1711-12, printed in four pages several times a week, then republished in book form. Franklin in 1724, "bought it, read it over and over, and was much delighted with it. I thought the writing excellent, and wish'd if possible to imitate it." James Madison felt the moral tone of *The Spectator* "peculiarly adapted to inculcate in youthful minds, just sentiments, an appetite for knowledge, and a taste for the improvement of the mind and manners." Jefferson included the work on his list of literary works to be included in a young man's essential reading list.

The Spectator would be of interest for its witty comments on London life of the period, the fashions, theatre, literature and social history. The style of writing is spectacularly good—simple, direct, and elegant, without the pedantic element found later in the century in Johnson and Gibbon. These are some of the first writings addressed in large part to a specifically female audience, and can be read as one of the earliest advocates of Women's Rights.

The Spectator watched the change in English society from landed aristocracy, rural life, and the theological passions of the 17th century, as it was transformed into the great eighteenth-century London, where merchants were respected—a city urbane, anti-clerical, and scientific. This commercial revolution produced the men, ideas, and capital which became the Industrial Revolution, and was perhaps the ideological predecessor of the American Revolution. After all, Adam Smith published *Wealth of Nations* in 1776, too.

The new commercial classes of 1712 were the models for colonial lawyers, merchants and businessmen, such as Franklin, Adams, Hancock, Revere, Hamilton, and Madison—reasonable, practical lovers of liberty, and respecters of property.

> There are not more useful Members in a Commonwealth than Merchants. They knit Mankind together in a mutual Intercourse of good offices, distribute the gifts of Nature, find Work for the Poor, add Wealth to the Rich, and Magnificence to the Great.
>
> *—May 19, 1711*

Ben Franklin, in his role as Poor Richard, urging thrift, diligence, and temperance, certainly would have agreed also that—

There are very great Advantages in the Enjoyment of a plentiful Fortune. Indeed the best and wisest of Men, tho' they may possibly despise a good part of those Things which the World calls Pleasures, can, I think, hardly be insensible of that Weight and Dignity which a moderate Share of Wealth adds to their Characters, Counsels, and Actions.

—January 24, 1712

In 1711, the rising merchant class had to battle aristocratic privilege and mercantilist restrictions on free trade. Today, industrial leaders must contend with a host of government agencies. The newest crop, including the Environmental Protection Agency (EPA), the Occupational Safety and Health Act inspectors (OSHA), and the Consumer Product Safety Commission (CPSC), were all set up, with the best of intentions, to work on legitimate hazards to the environment, workers, and consumers. The horde of inspectors running about, enforcing directives written by inexperienced people, is expensive and disruptive to industry. The uncertainties associated with new product development are increased by this layer of bureaucracy, and the rate of innovation and growth of our country will be perceptibly slowed. One such case is the recent flu vaccine dilemma, which is too silly to discuss in prose.

The Swine Flu is bad for you,
But the new vaccine is in Catch-22.
The drug manufacturers cannot withstand
Threats of malpractice suits throughout the land.
Insurance companies won't quote a rate
For a risky new product just out of the gate.
While Congress, which ordered vaccine to be made
Will not authorize that these risks be repaid.
Please, Congressmen, think of your lung and your gut
And get this development out of the rut.
Consider the health of your nose and your mouth,
And get your minds off the parts further south.

Investing For Today

The Branches of the Oak endure all the Seasons of the Year, though its Leaves fall off in Autumn; and these too will be restored with the returning Spring.

—September 17, 1711

About the time *The Spectator* was written, James Watt and his friends discovered how to run machines using the energy of fossil fuels, and so created the modern world of technology. Our world is now seen to be critically dependent on an uninterrupted supply of energy. The Acorn Fund has positioned a major segment of the portfolio in the energy field, fuel producers, and also capital goods suppliers to the energy industry. In the latest quarter we bought some Tenneco Offshore convertible debentures, offering a major play in Gulf of Mexico gas while limiting our risks. We also added to our holdings of United Nuclear, an important uranium producer.

The shopkeeper of the eighteenth century has been replaced by mass merchandising methods and shopping centers. Acorn has invested in three successful developers of regional shopping centers. General Growth Properties, which builds shopping centers in the Midwest, was added to the list, and we added to our position in Ernest W. Hahn, a California-based developer.

The Spectator was printed on crude presses with handset type. Today, communications and information flow are as important as energy flow in the world. Television broadcasting and cable TV are a key portion of our portfolio. Cox Cable and American Television and Communications were bought in the second quarter; both are major factors in the cable television industry. In other areas of information processing, we added to positions in Incoterm, a maker of computer terminals, and MetPath, a clinical laboratory company serving hospitals and doctors throughout the country from a highly automated center in New Jersey.

This essay must end, for you are investors, rather than historians, and as *The Spectator* says:

A General Trader of good Sense, is pleasanter company than a General Scholar.

—March 2, 1711

September 30, 1976

Long-Term Trends

To make profits in the market long-term, we should try to identify very long-term trends that will provide places to put substantial percentages of our portfolios. The "efficient market hypothesis" states that earnings and prospects for the next quarter and next year are already reflected in the market price of institutional-quality stocks. One way to escape the "efficient market" box is to look forward to very long trends.

As previous examples of such trends, one could pick:

Xerox changing the office machinery industry,
The jet airplane changing the airline industry;
The air conditioner making possible the "New South";
The problems of the electric utility industry under inflation.

I propose that we examine two basic trends, moving in opposite directions. Neither is new, but they are so fundamental to the modern world that the trends will continue for a long time. We will talk about two common chemical elements.

Carbon

For the last two hundred years, the big news was cheap carbon. Carbon, as found in coal, oil, and natural gas, meant cheap energy. The harnessing of cheap carbon was called the Industrial Revolution. The transportation industry, the metals industry, the chemical industry, and the electrical industries all came into existence as a direct result of the availability of cheap carbon energy. It is no exaggeration to say that almost all of the industrial structure of the world, and all of the consumer household life of the industrialized world, is based on cheap energy. Even food is affected by fossil fuel! Much more fossil fuel energy is used in growing, transporting, processing and cooking foodstuffs than is contained in the nutritional energy of the food.

1973 marked the beginning of the end of cheap energy. Oil costs have more than quadrupled, as fossil fuel resources worldwide are being depleted and priced at higher levels. The end of cheap carbon marks a basic trend change which will persist for decades.

The key concept here is that the price of energy is rising, and will rise further. Therefore, one should invest in energy *producers*, and move out of investments in energy *users* who will be hurt by cost increases and energy shortages.

Silicon

Silicon is a very common element, but until twenty years ago it was of little importance as a pure material, although, of course, silicon is a major component of sand, clay, rocks, and glass. The only use for silicon metal listed in the 1953 *Handbook of Chemistry and Physics* was as an alloy for steel and aluminum. The discoveries in solid state physics changed all this, starting with transistors in 1948, and now delivering thousands of circuit elements on a tiny silicon chip. Mini-computers, the $10 calculator, the digital watch, and the TV "Pong" game attachments are important recent developments. Silicon technology is used to process information, and, today, information processing has become very cheap, and is getting cheaper. The big price drops in information and communication systems are still continuing. Cheap silicon devices have created a basic trend change which will affect investments for many years.

The key concept here is that the price of information and communication has gone down and will fall further. We should *invest* in information technology users, and *sell* companies obsoleted by the new technology.

Information and Energy

As carbon (energy) rises in price and silicon (information) drops in price, the world will substitute information for energy. For instance, if you are planning to drive to a party, by calling a friend on the telephone and arranging to take only one car, a unit of information has saved a unit of gasoline energy. When one can find a company that is using both energy-saving (or producing) technology and increasing its use of information technology, this can be a good investment.

The substitution of information for energy is a powerful and very general concept, and can be applied beyond the obvious constructive implications for energy producers and sophisticated electronics companies, such as Incoterm, Finnigan and MetPath.

For instance, shopping centers are good investments because the big covered-mall regional shopping center saves time and store-to-store driving energy by bringing dozens of stores into the same place. The most successful stores have been the users of information, in most cases televised advertising which builds national brand identification and chain store images.

December 31, 1977

Vertical Disjuncture Revisited

In April of 1973, when the "Favorite 50" growth stocks were selling at preposterously high prices relative to their dividends, earnings or book value, and most other stocks were trading at more reasonable prices, we wanted to dramatize this "two-tier" effect. Since the bank trust departments were among the leading advocates of "one-decision growth stock" investing, we conceived of the mock-mathematical idea of graphing the investment philosophy of each floor of a bank building. Because people on different floors of the building had sharply different ideas of what stocks were worth, we made a graph with the floors of the bank on the vertical axis, the price-earnings ratios appropriate to that floor on the horizontal axis, and called it the Theory of Vertical Disjuncture.

On the *third floor*, the loan officers were delighted to extend $30,000,000 in loans to APL Corp. (9 times 1972 earnings) for the purpose of expanding its rapidly growing and profitable business.

On the *twenty-fifth floor*, the directors of Wometco had just cleared a program to repurchase 125,000 shares of their own stock (the stock was at 12 times 1972 earnings).

On the *fortieth floor*, the president of the bank holding company had been talking about acquisitions; the Chase Manhattan with its own money went after

Dial Financial, a growing company with a fine record, which was selling on the New York Stock Exchange at 10 times 1972 earnings. Chase offered about 17 times earnings. (The merger attempt failed.)

Meanwhile, on the *ninth floor*, in the trust department, the money managers would not think of buying non-prestigious, temporarily unfashionable smaller companies like APL, Wometco, or Dial, even though they were listed on the New York Stock Exchange, had excellent records and good prospects, and were statistically cheap. The trust department preferred the prestigious growth stocks, even at historically high prices relative to earnings or book value. It was this vast difference in thinking (the ninth floor vs. the third, twenty-fifth and fortieth floors) that constituted the Vertical Disjuncture shown as the strange jiggle on the graph.

The Graph Inverts

For six representative growth stocks (Avon, American Home Products, K-Mart, Burroughs, Schlumberger, and Texas Instruments) the average change was as follows between December, 1972, and December, 1977:

Reported earnings	+162%
Dividends paid	+180%
Stock price	− 36%

The price-earnings ratio for the group fell from 48× to 13½× over the five years.

Since these deflowered Vestal Virgins were major components of almost all institutional portfolios, their price collapse gave *all* stocks a tarnished reputation. Today, we would redraw our graph as follows:

The businessmen discussing loans for expansion, making merger deals, or planning to buy in their own stock, still consider ten times earnings a fair price for an attractive company. However, the trust department (and all other investors, too) believe that stocks of attractive companies are worth only 5 to 8 times earnings. The curve of Vertical Disjuncture has over-corrected itself.

This means that many, many stocks are selling for less than it would cost to reproduce the assets that the stocks control. As a result, businessmen find they can buy good capital assets cheaper on Wall Street than by spending capital to build new plants, and so there is great activity in mergers and acquisitions. This frantic deal-making will continue until stocks rise to the value of their underlying assets. Most such acquisitions are taking place at prices roughly double the stock market price of these stocks. For example, Carborundum, Babcock & Wilcox, Cox Cable, and Incoterm were acquired at substantial premiums over the previous market price.

We believe that experienced industrial leaders are more reliable judges of company worth than institutional investors. Not only were portfolio managers wrong when they paid 40–60 times earnings five years ago, they are wrong again by being afraid to invest in good companies with growing earnings and growing dividends at 5–8 times earnings.

We believe that most stocks today are cheap, and when we look back three years from now, with inflation pushing consumer prices 15–20% higher than now, common stocks purchased now will reflect at least the same 15–20% rise in value.

December 31, 1978

Public-Sector Imperialism

For the last forty years at least, we have seen a transfer of real political power from business interests, the general public, and elected officials to an ever-increasing collection of bureaucrats. This has occurred in the United States at the federal, state and local level, and at about the same rate in most foreign countries as well. Today, there is a mood of reaction against the costs imposed on our economic system by the load of regulations and taxes these agencies have imposed. The article, "The Brusque Recessional," in *The Economist*, December 23, 1978, offers some hope for relief. In this piece by Norman Macrae the problem was named "public-sector imperialism."

The economic theory supporting tax reduction, as worked out by Professor Laffer, has received surprisingly wide notice. The Proposition 13 vote in California was the first major act of popular revolt against over-government, and has been of great benefit to the citizens of California so far. Can we reduce the role of our government? It will be a long war.

Energy Regulation

The bureaucracy is today firmly in control of the energy sector, both fuels and electricity. In the latest budget message, the Department of Energy is requesting $287 million for just "data-gathering activities." This money is needed to enforce the ridiculous government-imposed price control tangle in which the oil and gas industry is enwrapped. In turn, the industry will have to spend a multiple of the Department of Energy budget to supply all that data.

Every serious observer of the industry has realized that we must switch electrical generating capacity away from oil to coal and nuclear. This is now made more clear by the revolution in Iran, which instantaneously collapsed our entire Mideastern policy and opens wide our energy debate. However, at a time when the utility industry must use less oil and should be encouraged to expand at a rapid rate, both coal and nuclear plants are being stalled by an overlapping network of dilatory federal, state and judicial regulatory bodies. Arthur Hailey (*Airport*) has just written *Overload,* an entertaining but well researched book on utility problems, with a lot more sex than this report.

The regulatory thicket is costing each of us, as electricity users, many hundreds of dollars. This occurs through three mechanisms. First, plant design costs and legal costs are way too high. In 1960, a nuclear plant took 500,000 man-hours to design; a similar, but more standardized, plant now takes 3,500,000 man-hours, adding perhaps $60,000,000 to design costs. Second is the delay in completion due to extended licensing procedures, so that 12 to 14 years is the time required to build a plant. It could be done in about six years. The third factor, inflation (also government-induced), interacts with the delay time to grossly inflate the final costs. One industry source estimates that just a three-year delay adds $450,000,000 (28%) to the cost of a plant assuming 8½% cost inflation. In the case of the troubled Seabrook nuclear plant, the added cost to each household in New Hampshire is estimated at $1,300. That's a lot of money to pay for superfluous regulation.

Selby's Law

Consumers Power Co. of Michigan built their first nuclear plant starting in 1960. The job took three years. In 1968, they announced a nuclear plant, joint with Dow, to be completed in 1975, with an estimated cost of $400 million. That project has been delayed time and again, and is now seven years late, with a new cost estimate of $1.67 billion, quadruple the original figure. Mr. Selby, President of Consumers Power, and a nuclear engineer, says, "I assure you that I will never allow Consumers Power to embark on another project like Midland without a high degree of confidence in the licensing process. Today that confidence does not exist." Mr. Selby is 57 years old, so his eight years before retirement is now less than the twelve years needed to build a nuclear plant. If he authorizes a project, he will have his life made miserable by innumerable public hearings, but his successor will get to open the new plant.

Nobody wants to start a project for which he does all the work and somebody else gets the benefit. I proclaim Selby's Law in his honor: "When the time to build a plant exceeds the likely tenure in office of the responsible executive, to hell with it."

March 31, 1981

Tennis Balls and Cannonballs

Here is a terrific bit of tennis trivia for use at your next cocktail party: Why do tennis players keep score in such a funny way (15, 30, 40, game) instead of 1, 2, 3, 4? The answer comes from the siege of Harfleur in 1415. The English King Henry V, in his foolish attempt to grab France, attacked Harfleur. His army included a siege train of three stone-firing artillery pieces, which were rated by the size of the stone, respectively a 15 pounder, 30 pounder and a 40 pounder.

That bit of lore is from *East and West*, by C. Northcote Parkinson, famous for Parkinson's Law, but also Raffles Professor of History at the University of Malaya. As it turned out, the invention of artillery affected other things besides tennis. For instance, guns destroyed the feudal system and allowed European powers to conquer most of the rest of the world. By the end of the nineteenth Century, Great Britain and the other Western powers ruled over most everybody, but now they don't. Why not?

Professor Parkinson believes that the crucial year in this century was 1905, when two very significant events occurred. First, the defeat of the Russian fleet by the Japanese at Tsushima marked the first time that an Asian power had defeated a European power in several centuries. Secondly, the British chose to cut their naval budget in favor of social welfare following the defeat of the Conservatives in the 1905 election.

> Lloyd George became Chancellor of the Exchequer. In his speech made when presenting the budget of 1909, he said that his additional taxes were to wage implacable warfare against poverty and squalor. These taxes were, in fact, highly significant, comprising both a new supertax, and far heavier death duties. As the revolutionary H.M.S. *Dreadnought* had been launched in 1906, starting an armament race in which Britain had only the smallest lead, some increases in taxation might have been thought inevitable. But it was not on the Navy that the money was to be spent. More of it was to go for old age pensions, which were quite expensive in theory and far more expensive in practice. And the most significant thing about this socialist legislation was—for our present purpose—its looking to the past. Spent on education or health, the money would have done something for the rising generation. Spent on armaments, it might have averted the First World War or at least shortened its duration. Instead, its purpose was more sentimental—the care of the old. Only in a country with a slackened momentum could such an emphasis have been possible.

It may have crossed your mind that a similar train of events has been occurring in the United States over the last several decades. We have increased social welfare and allowed our defense effort to lag, from the most humane motives. Meanwhile, the Soviets and their allies have been using their relatively greater military, naval, and air power to achieve their aims by direct military means. A recent list of victims would include: Soviet Union—Afghanistan,

Ethiopia, South Yemen; Cuba—Angola; Syria—Lebanon; Libya—Chad; and Vietnam—Cambodia.

One does not have to actually invade another country to achieve one's political aims. In the Polish confrontation, the Soviets and their satellites merely massed a couple of dozen divisions on "maneuvers" in order to make their point.

We applaud the efforts of President Reagan and his administration to restore the military power of the United States. If the Soviet Union and its satellites believe they have military superiority, they will continue their aggressions until we are forced to fight or abandon our vital interests, and such a war, as in Vietnam, demands a terrible price in lives and money. One can argue that there should be no real conflict between defense expenditures and social welfare, for, as politicians from Lloyd George to the Ayatollah Khomeini have found out, without the ability to defend your country, pensions have no value.

Sloshing with Martinis

Why, in the sixteenth through nineteenth centuries, did Britain, France, Holland, Russia, and Spain conquer most of America, Africa, and Asia instead of Turkey or China conquering Europe? That sounds like a silly question, for everyone remembers the British Army, led by Errol Flynn in red jacket and pith helmet, easily massacring little brown men dressed in towels. In "Fuzzy-Wuzzy", Kipling paid tribute to the brave but primitive Sudanese, "We sloshed you with Martinis, an' it wasn't 'ardly fair." (This metaphor needs explaining too. The battle did not take place in the Officers' Club; the British rifle was manufactured by a firm named Martini.) However, the cannon which won the world for the Europeans was not at all a European development. Probably gunpowder was invented in China, and the Chinese built cannon in 1356. The Ottoman Turks were the world leaders in siege artillery in the fifteenth and sixteenth Century, using their guns to capture Constantinople in 1453, Hungary in 1526.

Two centuries later, the Turkish Empire had decayed from a position as number one power on earth to "The Sick Man of Europe." One symptom of its decay was high inflation. Lord Kinross, in *The Ottoman Centuries*, quotes a Turkish writer of 1584, who complained that the high-quality silver coinage of the Empire had been debased until it was "as light as the leaves of the almond tree and as worthless as drops of dew."

Parkinson thinks that the advantage in military ability of the European powers lay in the evolution of the "literate soldier" who could enforce the complex drill and discipline needed to work firearms effectively. The ensigns and sergeants of Europe were members of an educated lower-middle class which had no counterpart in Asia, so Europe ruled the world until Asian education and culture was restructured on the European model.

Today, everyone has learned the best technical tricks that were once exclusively European. Japanese and Israeli electronics, Korean, Malayan, and Taiwanese mass production are up to world standards. Militarily, no one wants to mess with the Vietnamese, let alone the Chinese. Economically, the Arabians have first call on the world's wealth.

December 31, 1981

Easier Questions, Please

My children have been complaining about the tough questions on their final exams. When one realizes that he is unable to answer the hard questions of life, or the difficult dilemmas of investing, one can do what students cannot do and ask for some easier questions. In this report, we discuss the easiest questions we could think up.

Why Is It Dark at Night?

In 1826, Wilhelm Olbers asked the world's silliest question: "Why is the sky dark at night?" He argued, from thermodynamic principles, that in a steady-state universe the stars would shine as much light into the solar system as the sun radiates out of it, so that the night sky would be as bright as daylight. In fact, for many decades nobody could resolve this question, which was named Olber's Paradox. It turns out the answer hinges on the fact that the universe must be expanding, but this expansion was not accepted by science until Hubble's discovery of the "red shift" recession of distant galaxies in the 1920's. The "silly question" predicted the expanding universe a century earlier, but scientific opinion was not ready to accept the answer.

Our objective as long-term investors is to compute a rational value for a stock which differs from investor opinion. Since we will be disagreeing with conventional wisdom, our selection will look silly for a while, but if the analysis is correct, market opinion eventually will shift in our favor. Acorn was able to identify systematically undervalued groups such as the real estate stocks in 1975 and the bank stocks in 1980.

Which Way Is Up?

Another classic dumb question is "Which way is up?" That is no problem for people, for people are big and affected strongly by gravity. For small creatures, gravity loses its primacy, so flies can easily walk on the ceiling. Bacteria are buffeted by Brownian motion in their watery environment, so that gravity is too weak a force to help a bacterium navigate. The resourcefulness of nature was demonstrated when Blakemore in 1975 discovered several species of bacteria with tiny chains of magnetite crystals inside each single cell, so that they can follow the lines of magnetic dip to navigate downward. These built-in magnets give their hosts a "sixth sense" to help them survive in their no-gravity world. Since these bacteria can only live where there is a low concentration of oxygen, the ability to move away from the high-oxygen concentration in surface water is a valuable adaptative mechanism.

Acorn Fund tries to find the special companies with the built-in magnets which can give them an edge over the average company. The engineering genius of Seymour Cray, the real estate expertise of Rouse or Ira Koger, and the management skills at Northwest Industries give these companies their little magnets.

Why Did the Egyptians Lie?

The Italian philosopher Giambattista Vico was a marvelous transitional figure between Renaissance and modern thought. His "New Science" pioneered the use of philology and etymology in historical criticism. As he studied the documents of the earliest civilizations, he ran into a question of chronology. Egyptian historical records were continuous from 4200 B.C. or earlier, but Vico "knew for sure" that Noah's flood wiped out Egypt in 2332 B.C. Therefore, to him it was a logical consequence that the Egyptians must have fudged the books. Vico was forced to seek psychological causes for his deduced Pharaonic mendacity.

Of course, we now know that Egyptian chronology was correct, leaving Vico with nothing but the honor of writing erroneous psychohistory 150 years before Freud popularized the genre. One can't blame Vico for staying with his orthodox belief in literal biblical chronology; he was a professor at the conservative University of Naples in the 1740's, and a novel theory could have brought him before the Papal Inquisition. Nevertheless, Vico provides us with an example of careful analysis based on faulty premises, resulting in an erroneous conclusion.

The United States is in a serious recession today, and economists and journalists are constantly criticizing the Federal Reserve Board and the Treasury for their roles in causing or curing the slump. In our opinion, the belief that domestic monetary policy is the sole factor in economic health is analysis based on a faulty premise. We believe that the entire world has been in a recession for three years, triggered by the trebling of oil prices by the OPECers after the Iranian Revolution following the quadrupling of prices in the few years preceding. The most diligent efforts of the U.S. government and the rhetoric of our Presidential candidates have had exactly the same results as those of Mrs. Thatcher or Mr. Mitterand—nothing in particular. Only a look at the whole world is going to enable one to understand what's going on. One conclusion we reach from a world-wide analysis is that there is no visible reason to expect a vigorous recovery to begin any time soon, even though most U.S. experts expect a turn up beginning in the next couple of months. Acorn is holding a high percentage of its assets in reserves (high-grade commercial paper).

June 30, 1983

Augustine's Laws

Norman R. Augustine has written a marvelous book called *Augustine's Laws* (American Institute of Aeronautics and Astronautics (AIAA), New York, 1982) based on his career in the aerospace industry as engineer and executive for both industry and the Department of Defense. He is now president of Martin Marietta Denver Aerospace and president of the AIAA. As an important participant in the aircraft procurement system, he understands the delays, waste, and inefficiencies in the procurement process—while still believing in his company and his country. The result was a book that I wish I could have written, funny and serious at the same time. Using his engineering skills, he uses graphs of real data to generate "laws". For instance, after graphing the probability distribution of cost overruns on research and development contracts, he came up with Augustine's Law of Apocalyptic Costing:

> Ninety percent of the time things will turn out worse than you expect. The other ten percent of the time, you had no right to expect so much. (Law III)

This law is a clear relative of Murphy's Law, "If anything can go wrong, it will," but Augustine's law is of obvious value in security analysis. Any market forecaster who thinks he can find a group of stocks with long-term earnings growth trends of 30% per year should remember this law, as well as the citation from Cicero's speech to the Roman Senate:

> It seems to me that no soothsayer should be able to look at another soothsayer without laughing.

Extrapolation

Mr. Augustine uses extrapolation to prove up many of his laws. (Extrapolation takes past data, defines a trend, and pushes the trend into the future. If the data points are 2, 4, 6, 8, then extrapolation would extend the series 10, 12, 14.) For instance, a logarithmic plot, government employees as a percentage of total employees vs. time, rises from 0.2% in 1770 to 4% in 1900 and 12% in 1980. An extension of the trend line shows that in 2060, the line will hit 100%, so that:

> By the time of the Nation's Tricentennial, there will be more government workers than there are workers. (Law XLI)

The cost of aircraft can be plotted similarly. From the Wright Brothers to the F-18, fighter aircraft have quadrupled in price every four years. Since the total defense budget has grown at a slower rate, extrapolating both lines suggests the Final Law of Economic Disarmament:

> In the year 2054, the entire defense budget will purchase just one tactical aircraft. This aircraft will have to be shared by the Air Force and Navy 3½ days each per week except for leap year, when it will be made available to the Marines for the extra day.

The extrapolation of any growth trend for a long enough time span will give rise to this sort of ironic contradiction. For instance, the foreign debt of non-oil producing developing nations rose from $80 billion in 1971 to $520 billion currently, an 18% growth rate. A sum growing at 18% per year will double in four years. Should we extrapolate these foreign debts to one trillion dollars in 1987? No way! The arithmetic shows that one cannot extend a growth trend for a very long time without generating impossibly large numbers. Don't try to extend the last twelve months gain in the stock market for another two years, or figure that Cray Research can extend sales gains equal to the 67% per year of their last five years.

Augustine quotes Thucydides on the perils of expecting easy success, which could be a warning to present day speculators:

> . . . their judgment was based more on wishful thinking than on sound calculation of probabilities; for the usual thing among men is that when they want something they will, without any reflection, leave that to hope, while they will employ the full force of reason in rejecting what they find unpalatable.

Software Growth Inevitable

Software is like entropy. It is difficult to grasp, weighs nothing, and obeys the Second Law of Thermodynamics; i.e., it always increases. (Law XVI)

The data show that the number of lines of software code needed for a complex system has been growing by a factor of ten every ten years. The demand to expand software has been driven by faster, cheaper computers, which are able to run bigger programs than before. This helps software contractors, such as Computer Sciences and Planning Research. Software costs have not come down, so programming efficiency is a problem today. An answer is application development software to help programmers write programs faster. Applied Data Research and Pansophic (bought for Acorn in July) are leaders in this business.

Quality vs. Quantity

Why are small companies more innovative on average than large? Why can a mutual fund organization with a few good analysts match the performance of much larger organizations with many analysts? Augustine presents data for the productivity of football players, authors, and staff officers to show that a small number of hotshots do much of the work, and adding more bodies doesn't improve results much. Only 25% of the police produce 50% of the arrests in Washington, D.C., just as 25% of RAF pilots in World War II shot down half of the enemy planes downed.

> One-tenth of the people involved in a given endeavor produce at least one-third of the output, and increasing the number of participants merely serves to reduce the average performance. (Law XIX)

One Seymour Cray can be more productive than a dozen engineers at a competitor's facility.

June 30, 1986

WILL YOUR REPORT GET READ?

General Wang Yang-Ming, a thousand years ago, writing a book on military strategy for the Imperial army, wrote: "To know and not to act is not to know."

The job of an analyst involves knowing a whole lot of neat stuff about industries and companies, but his job is only done well if he causes other people to act. Buy-side analysts have to generate Buy and Sell ratings (there is also a Hold rating, but it is not clear what Hold means) and then portfolio managers act on these ratings to modify their portfolios. Sell-side analysts have to generate revenues for their firms in one of three ways: commissions on trades, underwriting business, and fixed payment ("third party" research).

Both sell-side and buy-side analysts perform a marketing function. It is obvious that sell-side analysts come in with a salesman, and are part of a marketing team. It is also true, but less obvious, that buy-side analysts must do selling, too. To convert knowledge into action, a buy-side analyst must sell an idea to the portfolio managers at his institution, and this selling job may be just as tough as that faced by a sell-side analyst peddling to that institution from outside.

Too Much Paper

How does my firm handle research material? My firm is Harris Associates, a medium-sized investment counseling firm running about $2.5 billion in assets, evenly split between individual and institutional money. We have 6 portfolio managers and 9 security analysts. As you would expect, our sell-side friends have made us a good customer of the U.S. Post Office. As the firm has grown, the amount of research we get into our mail room has grown in spectacular fashion. The body of research material far exceeds anyone's ability to read it. Our mail room sorts the material and publishes a daily index. On the June 6 list, the index ran 4 full double-column pages and a little on page 5, which is about 400 separate items.

Each analyst and portfolio manager gets a copy of the index each day, and marks the items he or she wants to see. The mail room then delivers those reports. One must be careful not to order so many items that the whole day is spent just in studying reports!

In summary, we have a lot of people, a lot of input, and a few systems to fight clutter, but not enough. We are undoubtedly typical of a whole lot of institutions today. If you have a suggestion on how to improve our report-handling system, we would love to hear it.

Style

I have stressed how the user of your reports is overwhelmed with material. You have to grab his attention in order to get your report in the "5% pile" which actually gets read and will help boost your firm's brokerage allocation. Your report must be clear and interesting.

Clarity can be enhanced by the use of standardized formats, so I know where to find the cash flow exhibit in your firm's reports. A summary at the front of the report will help. A table of contents is good in a long report. Spreadsheets are fine, but label the rows and columns very clearly. Try to figure out how to include some graphs (pertinent to the report and well-labelled) even if it is just a Mansfield price chart. If you can add diagrams, pictures, or cartoons, great. An economic forecaster, Siff, Oakley & Marks, always includes some cartoons in their material, sometimes *The Wizard of Id*, sometimes drawn by one of their own staff people. I can tell you that the cartoons get read first.

Humor, vivid writing, and clear style are very helpful. Strategists such as Barton Biggs at Morgan Stanley and Eric Miller at DL&J are reasonable and thoughtful people, but their high reputation is due in large part to their witty and incisive writing style. If your own writing is still stuck at the high school junior level, you have two things that will help. One is to practice writing conscientiously, just as you would do practice questions for a CFA (Chartered Financial Analyst) exam. This means a lot of time and work, so it is impractical. The second method is a short-cut—plagiarism. You ought not to take another analyst's work, but you can use quotations to brighten up your own sludge pile of dreary prose. To use quotes, you first need a pile of them, so start a file called "Quotes", and when you see a good one, put it in the file. When you use a quote, it is nice to use it correctly, but many people do use quotations out of context, which is fair, or change a few words, which isn't fair, but who is to know? The last rule on quotes is to tell who said it. If you can't remember who said it, the rule is: say it was John Maynard Keynes if it is about money, and Mark Twain if it is not about money.

Have I left you with the impression that style is more important than substance? Good—it is, if you are trying to get to the top of our profession. Every analyst makes some good forecasts and some bad forecasts, but wit gets remembered, and so a well-written report is more likely to get the reader to take action than is a dull report. "The world is full of accurate, boring, underpaid drudges."* We are CFA's, not accountants, so let's be interesting characters.

Editing

Two parts of a good report are (1) timeliness and (2) candor. We know that candor is the first casualty, so that when Wall Street sell-side analysts should tell you to Buy or Sell, the ratings they put into print are Buy Right Now, Buy Pretty Soon, and Buy On Dips. It's like reading a Communist newspaper—any adjective less upbeat than "superior" is code for a disaster.

Candor and timeliness both get destroyed when you send the draft of your report to the company for "factual editing". You know perfectly well that you can check items you are not sure of over the phone in a few minutes. Having the company edit your report is submitting to censorship, dullness and delay.

*J. M. Keynes, *"Mark Twain's Cambridge Year."*

The good stuff gets crossed out, and the report gets stalled while the stock goes up from 15, where it was a buy, to 21 on publication date, which is a half-point from the top price the stock will see for the next two years.

Analysts are supposed to be critics of corporations. They end up being public relations spokesmen for them. What a waste!

Evaluating Management

Most of us agree that evaluating corporate management is an essential part of the analyst's job. This evaluation is not always done as well as it might be. For instance, if you sent your report to the company for "editing", you have asked the movie director to write the review of his own movie, so forget it.

Some analysts rely on corporate statistics and ratios to judge management. These count, but a high return on equity may mean that this management's predecessors had the sense to get into a good business, and the current incumbents haven't been there long enough for their wrecking job to show up in the numbers. Businesses like broadcasting or soft-drink bottling tend to have high margins without requiring management genius, while a farm equipment manufacturer may prove superb management by not being broke already.

There is a logical fallacy here, if you judge a management by its numbers and then pay more for the stock because of "good management". This is what bridge players call "double-counting" face cards.

So, what are my definitions of your definition of good management? Here are two:

1. Good management is what an analyst says a company has in the next-to-last paragraph of his report.

Most of the time, the analyst means that he has found a glib management, so that the CFO is willing to tell him some titillating detail—monthly sales figures, for instance. A taciturn management will not be considered as good, and may not even get written up at all.

One example of glib management was the chairman of a large Midwestern bank. He built a spectacular new bank building to replace a dowdy old building, then outfitted the new headquarters with a plush directors' room with two slide projectors and big leather chairs with calculators built into the armrests. It worked—the bank P/E doubled in a couple of years, until 1973 came along and everyone found out that the bank was up to its femur in bad loans.

2. Good management is a company with three up quarters in a row!

What Do Research Users Want?

We want two categories of information, the contradictory and the impossible. By contradictory, we mean data that is timely but well-confirmed, reports that are detailed but brief, analysts who are wired in to management but objective, information that is crucial but not "inside", and so on.

By impossible, we want you to supply us with stock ideas which will outperform the market on a risk-adjusted basis; every academic test of brokerage reports says that this has never happened for the entire output of a large brokerage firm for any length of time.

What Will Research Users Settle For?

Experience suggests we will settle for what we are getting now. We will settle for journalism, bringing us up to date on recent events such as sales, earnings, and new products. We will settle for file stuffers, stacks of paper on big dull companies that we can point to post-disaster to prove that you didn't see it coming either, so how could we? We will settle for bald earnings forecasts, without mention of risk or alternative scenarios, which we will plug into our valuation models to set us up for next quarter's unpleasant surprise. We will settle for detailed statistical dissection of historical data that would pass a CFA II test, but deals with a past irrelevant to the company's future. We will try to decipher the output of the Lotus-Eaters with fold-out spreadsheets but no understanding of what the people in the business actually do. We will look at publicity releases for past or future underwritings masquerading as objective research in the hope of pulling a raisin of truth out of six inches of manure. We will settle for reports that tell us about an industry but ignore the existence of Japanese and Korean competition.

This will enable us to continue to be over-confident and over-fed customers, over-informed by overworked and overpaid analysts who overstate potential and overlook the obvious.

VIII

The Acorn Fund Portfolio

The Acorn Fund Portfolio, December 31, 1988

Number of Shares or Principal Amount		Value (000)
COMMON STOCKS AND OTHER EQUITY-LIKE SECURITIES—94.9%		
	INFORMATION GROUP—28.9%	
	Broadcasting/Publishing/Cellular Phone—8.3%	
210,000	LIN Broadcasting Corporation(b)	$ 15,015
390,000	Telephone and Data Systems, Inc.	10,676
220,000	Mobile Communications Corporation of America, Class A(b)	6,572
500,000	Westwood One, Inc.(b)	4,750
130,000	New York Times Company, Class A ...	3,494
300,000	IDB Communications Group, Inc.(b)(c)	2,700
55,000	Cellular Communications, Inc.(b)	1,443
6,250	Metro Mobile CTS, Inc., Class A(b) ...	272
50,000	Metro Mobile CTS, Inc., Class B(b) ...	2,100
		47,022
	Marketing Services/Software—3.5%	
280,000	Systematics, Inc.	8,750
320,000	Information Resources, Inc.(b)	3,200
220,000	Pansophic Systems, Incorporated	3,080
400,000	ADVO-System, Inc.(b)	1,900

Number of Shares or Principal Amount		Value (000)
	Aerospace—1.1%	
170,000	Precision Castparts Corp.	$ 4,675
170,000	Avantek Inc.(b)	808
120,000	Datum Inc.(b)	540
40,000	Moog Inc., Class A	325
		6,348
	Distribution—1.2%	
152,000	Richardson Electronics, Ltd.	3,002
156,000	Bell Industries, Inc.	2,282
100,000	Pioneer-Standard Electronics, Inc.	925
27,000	Anthem Electronics, Inc.	280
		6,489
	Office Supplies and Forms—3.3%	
430,000	New England Business Service, Inc. ..	9,998
245,000	Sanford Corporation	6,676
67,000	Dennison Manufacturing Company	1,666
		18,340
	Consumer Electronics—2.4%	
295,000	InterTAN, Inc.(b)	10,399

Shares	Company	Value (000)
55,000	Telecredit, Inc.	1,856
200,000	Scientific Software-Intercomp, Inc.(b)(c)	650
340,000	Precision Target Marketing, Inc.(b)(c)	43
		19,479

Health Care—3.3%

Shares	Company	Value (000)
273,000	Hillenbrand Industries, Inc.	8,361
180,000	New England Critical Care, Incorporated(b)	3,960
135,000	Molecular Biosystems, Inc.(b)	2,092
56,000	Westmark International(b)	1,512
150,000	Biotech Research Laboratories, Inc.(b)	1,050
$1,000,000	Lifetime Corporation, 10% Cv. Deb., 11/1/91	850
145,000	Syncor International Corporation(b)	689
59,000	Gish Biomedical, Inc.(b)	354
		18,868

Computer Systems—5.8%

Shares	Company	Value (000)
470,000	Howtek Inc.(b)(c)	7,402
80,000	Cray Research, Inc.(b)	4,860
256,000	SCI Systems, Inc.(b)	3,808
370,000	The Ultimate Corp.(b)	3,469
200,000	Evans & Sutherland Computer Corporation(b)	3,200
250,000	Network Systems Corporation(b)	2,750
179,000	Triad Systems Corporation(b)	2,394
370,000	Daisy Systems Corporation(b)	2,359
302,000	Key Tronic Corporation(b)	1,510
205,000	Reliability Incorporated(b)	999
		32,751

Shares	Company	Value (000)
175,500	Harman International Industries Incorporated(b)	2,961
125,000	Lowrance Electronics, Inc.(b)	313
		13,673
	Information Group—Total	162,970

CONSUMER GOODS AND SERVICES—17.1%

Food—3.5%

Shares	Company	Value (000)
185,000	Culbro Corporation	6,568
201,000	McCormick & Company Incorporated	5,578
424,500	National Pizza Company(b)	4,033
185,000	A & W Brands, Inc.(b)	3,423
		19,602

Retail—3.2%

Shares	Company	Value (000)
230,000	Zayre Corp.	5,865
200,000	CML Group, Inc.(b)	3,525
140,000	The Neiman-Marcus Group, Inc.	2,363
270,000	Dairy Mart Convenience Stores, Inc.(c)	2,329
180,000	Spiegel, Inc., Class A	1,598
110,000	Town & Country Corporation, Class A(b)	1,100
75,100	Intermark, Inc.	1,023
		17,803

Carpets—0.6%

Shares	Company	Value (000)
80,000	Shaw Industries, Inc.	1,880
120,000	Galaxy Carpet Mills, Inc.(b)	1,725
		3,605

The Acorn Fund Portfolio, December 31, 1988   (continued)

Number of Shares or Principal Amount		Value (000)
	Recreational Vehicles—2.1%	
260,000	Harley-Davidson, Inc.(b)	$ 6,598
270,000	Thor Industries, Inc.(c)	3,578
310,000	Cruise America, Inc.(b)(c)	1,628
		11,804
	Entertainment and Leisure—4.4%	
588,000	Carnival Cruise Lines, Inc.	9,114
380,000	International Game Technology(b)(c)	8,503
380,000	United Gaming, Inc. (formerly Gaming and Technology, Inc.)(b)	3,135
260,000	Divi Hotels, N.V.	2,275
90,000	San Juan Racing Association, Inc.(b)	1,159
30,000	Caesars New Jersey, Inc.(b)	630
28,000	Sands Regent(b)	315
		25,131
	Other—3.3%	
230,000	The Stride Rite Corporation	6,153
204,000	Newell Companies, Inc.	5,763
115,000	Oil-Dri Corporation of America	2,645
132,000	CPI Corp.	2,624
215,000	View-Master Ideal Group, Inc.(b)	753
280,500	American Nursery Products, Inc.(b)(c)	605
		18,543
	Consumer Group—Total	96,488

Number of Shares or Principal Amount		Value (000)
	Chemicals—1.2%	
80,000	Raychem Corporation	$ 2,800
141,000	Lilly Industrial Coatings, Inc.	2,432
114,000	Cambrex Corporation(b)	1,653
		6,885
	Other—2.3%	
385,000	Willcox & Gibbs, Inc.(c)	6,497
182,000	Expeditors International of Washington, Inc.(b)	2,844
108,000	America Filtrona Corporation	2,808
53,200	LSI Lighting Systems Inc.	725
		12,874
	Industrial Group—Total	59,752
	FINANCE GROUP—10.0%	
	Banks—4.0%	
230,000	Wilmington Trust Co.	6,153
290,000	Puget Sound Bancorp	5,365
112,500	First American Corporation	2,489
77,000	First Security Corporation	1,906
74,000	Union Planters Corporation	1,850
60,000	First Hawaiian Inc.	1,785
104,000	Riverside National Bank(b)	1,118
19,000	Baker Boyer Bancorp(b)	665

INDUSTRIAL GOODS AND SERVICES—10.6%

Machinery and Metal Processing—4.3%

Shares		Value
400,000	Worthington Industries, Inc.	9,000
171,000	Mine Safety Appliances Company	7,268
106,500	Nordson Corporation	4,952
175,000	Washington Scientific Industries, Inc.(c)	1,444
90,000	Stevens Graphics Corporation, Class A(b)	945
35,000	Stevens Graphics Corporation, Class B(b)	359
		23,968

Auto Parts—0.4%

Shares		Value
78,500	Douglas & Lomason Company	1,452
160,000	Jason Incorporated(b)	1,000
		2,452

Forest Products and Construction—0.9%

Shares		Value
160,000	T J International, Inc.	3,960
120,000	U.S. Intec, Inc.(b)	750
8,900	Greif Bros. Corporation, Class A	376
157,500	Lakewood Forest Products Ltd.	128
		5,214

Waste Disposal—1.5%

Shares		Value
180,000	Wellman, Inc.	6,728
150,000	Rollins Environmental Services, Inc.	1,631
		8,359

Shares		Value
31,325	F & M Bancorporation	470
92,400	Suburban Bankshares, Inc.(b)	370
		22,171

Savings & Loans—1.4%

Shares		Value
160,000	Washington Mutual Savings Bank	2,240
75,000	North Fork Bancorp	1,378
125,000	Heart Federal Savings and Loan Association	1,188
100,000	Webster Financial Corporation	1,075
50,000	Peoples Westchester Savings Bank(b)	988
90,000	United Savings Bank(b)(c)	765
53,500	Washington Federal Savings & Loan Association	415
		8,049

Insurance—2.3%

Shares		Value
196,000	Colonial Life & Accident Insurance Company, Class B	6,076
262,000	Baldwin & Lyons, Inc., Class B	3,897
100,000	United Fire & Casualty Company	3,013
		12,986

Other—2.3%

Shares		Value
338,259	Baker, Fentress & Company	6,723
240,000	United Asset Management Corporation	3,300
145,000	Cash America Investments, Inc.(b)	1,577
92,500	First Financial Caribbean Corporation(b)	1,226
43,000	Workers' Compensation Medical Centers, Inc. (formerly Electronic Financial Systems, Inc., Class A)(b)	22
		12,848
	Finance Group—Total	56,054

The Acorn Fund Portfolio, December 31, 1988   (continued)

Number of Shares or Principal Amount		Value (000)
REAL ESTATE—8.0%		
884,000	The Rouse Company	$ 21,216
245,000	Rockefeller Center Properties, Inc.	4,808
275,000	Sizeler Property Investors, Inc.(c)	4,056
94,700	Forest City Enterprises, Inc., Class A	3,800
154,700	Forest City Enterprises, Inc., Class B	6,401
120,000	Weingarten Realty Investors	3,075
722,000	The Koger Company, 8% Real Estate Appreciation Notes, 6/1/00	964
72,500	Property Trust of America	707
	Real Estate Total	45,027
ENERGY—3.8%		
Cogeneration—1.8%		
255,000	Thermo Electron Corporation(b)	5,196
$4,000,000	Catalyst Energy Development Corporation, 7.25% Cv. Sub. Deb., 6/1/06	2,290
3,580,000	Catalyst Energy Development Corporation, 7.75% Cv. Sub. Deb., 7/1/02	1,665
285,000	Catalyst Thermal Energy Corporation	926
		10,077

Number of Shares or Principal Amount		Value (000)
$2,000,000	Jardine Strategic Holdings Limited, 6½%, Cv. Cum. Pref.	$ 1,530
700,000	Jardine Strategy Holdings Limited	870
1,500,000	Johnson Electric Industrial Manufactory, Limited	1,316
1,500,000	Dairy Farm International Holdings Ltd.	1,153
700,000	The Wharf (Holdings) Ltd.	794
1,000,000	Video Technology International (Holdings) Limited	519
900,000	Mandarin Oriental International Limited	516
2,500,000	Café de Coral Group Limited	330
2,500,000	Lafé Holdings Limited	243
		22,118
Latin America—0.2%		
4,000,000	Teléfonos de México, S.A. de C.V.	1,125
Singapore/Malaysia/Thailand—3.7%		
193,000	The Thailand Fund	3,809
500,000	Singapore Airlines Limited	3,784
$2,700,000	Keppel Corporation Limited, 4% Cv. Bond, 7/13/97	2,511
1,000,000	Malaysian Airlines System Berhad	2,453
200,000	The Thai Fund, Inc.	2,350
500,000	Genting Berhad	1,416
1,000,000	Far East-Levingston Shipbuilding Limited	1,143

Electric Utilities—1.0%

Shares	Security	Value
200,000	PSI Holdings, Inc.(b)	2,775
75,000	The Empire District Electric Company	2,081
60,000	St. Joseph Light & Power Company	1,215
		6,071

Oil & Gas—1.0%

Shares	Security	Value
275,000	Seagull Energy Corporation(b)	4,228
500,000	Oceaneering International, Inc.(b)	1,281
		5,509
	Energy Group—Total	21,657

FOREIGN SECURITIES—16.5%

Europe—4.7%

Shares	Security	Value
290,000	Esselte Business Systems Inc.	8,736
5,000,000	Blue Arrow PLC	7,493
300,000	Waterford Stock Units	4,350
240,000	The France Fund, Inc.	2,310
600,000	British & Commonwealth Holdings PLC	2,221
400,000	Boddington Group PLC	1,177
125,000	Marston, Thompson & Evershed PLC	375
		26,662

Hong Kong—3.9%

Shares	Security	Value
1,813,626	Swire Pacific Limited "A"	4,414
3,500,000	The Hongkong Land Company Limited	4,125
2,700,000	Cathay Pacific Airways Limited	3,217
1,900,000	Television Broadcasting Ltd. (formerly HK-TVB Limited)	3,091
720,000	City Development Limited	1,049
150,000	Malayan Breweries Ltd.	873
400,000	Jurong Shipyards Ltd.	680
750,000	Genting International Ltd.(b)	386
200,000	Sembawang Shipyard Limited	358
		20,812

Japan—1.8%

Shares	Security	Value
300,000	Dai-Tokyo Fire & Marine Insurance	3,122
240,000	The Nippon Fire & Marine Insurance Co., Ltd.	2,114
35,000	Shin-Etsu Polymer Co., Ltd.	1,805
130,000	The Koa Fire & Marine Insurance Co., Ltd.	1,697
30,000	Komori Printing Machinery Co., Ltd.	968
50,000	Takasago Thermal Engineering Co., Ltd.	520
		10,226

Canada—1.5%

Shares	Security	Value
220,000	Dofasco Inc., Class A	4,843
400,000	FPI Limited	3,355
		8,198

Israel—0.7%

Shares	Security	Value
490,000	Teva Pharmaceutical Industries Limited	3,369
80,500	Elron Electronic Industries Limited(b)	272
		3,641
	Foreign Group—Total	92,782

	Value
Total Common Stocks and Other Equity-Like Securities—94.9%	534,730
(Cost: $451,554,000)	

The Acorn Fund Portfolio, December 31, 1988   (continued)

Number of Shares or Principal Amount	Value (000)
FIXED INCOME—1.8%	
¥1,200,000,000 Canadian Government Euro-Yen, 6.125%, 2/20/91	$ 9,963
(Cost: $10,083,000)	
MONEY MARKET INSTRUMENTS—3.4%	
Yield 7.76% to 9.50%	
Due—January, 1989 to February, 1989	
General Motors Acceptance Corporation	
. . . .	10,000
Ford Motor Credit Company	4,000
BarclaysAmericanCorporation	3,000
United States Treasury Bills	2,468
	19,468
(Cost: $19,468,000)	

Number of Shares or Principal Amount	Value (000)
Total Investments—100.1%	
(Cost: $481,105,000)	$ 564,161
FUTURES—0.0%	
80 Short, Standard and Poor's 500 Stock Index Futures, Expiration March 17, 1989	(71)
70 Long, Kansas City Value Line Index Futures, Expiration March 17, 1989 .	208
	137
LIABILITIES, LESS CASH AND OTHER ASSETS—(0.1%)	(840)
TOTAL NET ASSETS—100%	$563,458

Notes

(a) At December 31, 1988, net unrealized appreciation of $83,004,000 for federal income tax purposes consisted of gross unrealized appreciation of $125,137,000 and gross unrealized depreciation of $42,133,000; cost for federal income tax purposes was $481,157,000.

(b) Nonincome producing security.

(c) On December 31, 1988, the Fund held the following percentages of the outstanding shares of the companies listed below:

American Nursery Products, Inc.	7.7%	Dairy Mart Convenience Stores, Inc.	6.5%
International Game Technology	7.4%	IDB Communications Group, Inc.	6.1%
Sizeler Property Investors, Inc.	7.4%	Cruise America, Inc.	5.6%
United Savings Bank	7.4%	Scientific Software-Intercomp, Inc.	5.5%
Howtek Inc.	7.1%	Thor Industries, Inc.	5.3%
Washington Scientific Industries, Inc.	7.1%	Precision Target Marketing, Inc.	5.1%

The cost and value of investments in affiliates at December 31, 1988 was $37,362,000 and $36,622,000, respectively. Dividends received from affiliates during the year ended December 31, 1988 amounted to $511,000.

IX

Harvard Management Company Portfolio

Harvard Management Company
General Investment Summary, June 30, 1988

	Amount (000)	Percent
Cash and short-term reserves	$644,176	13.9
Fixed Income:		
Intermediate and long-term bonds	1,171,669	25.3
Funds under discretionary		
management*	33,489	0.7
Intermediate and long-term bond futures	216,856	4.7
Total fixed income	1,422,014	30.7
Equities:		
Selected issues	1,069,522	23.1
Funds under discretionary		
management*	178,067	3.8
Index issues	694,080	15.0
Index futures and options	192,780	4.2
	2,134,449	46.1
Private placements	787,863	17.0
Total equities	2,922,312	63.1
All others—net	(359,687)	(7.7)
Total	$4,628,815	100.0%

*These categories are fixed-income and equity investments managed by independent advisors. At June 30, 1988, Harvard Management Company utilized one outside manager for fixed-income securities and six outside managers for equity securities.

Harvard Management Company
Distribution of Private Placement Portfolio
By Investment Type, June 30, 1988

	Amount (000)	Percent
Real Estate	$142,335	18.1
Venture Capital:		
Partnerships	190,997	24.2
Direct investments	116,627	14.8
Total venture capital	307,624	39.0
Leveraged buyouts	162,508	20.6
Special situations	101,125	12.9
Oil and gas	74,271	9.4
	$787,863	100.0%

Harvard Management Company
General Investments Major Equity Holdings, June 30, 1988

	Market Value	
	Non-indexed Holdings (000)	Indexed Holdings (000)
International Business Machines	$25,475	$28,405
The Henley Group	49,350	
Philip Morris Companies, Inc.	20,994	7,347
Student Loan Marketing Association (voting and non-voting) (A)	28,286	
The Dow Chemical Company	20,901	6,616
Digital Equipment Corporation	21,252	5,583
Exxon Corporation	6,806	18,590
Property Capital Trust (A)	23,083	
General Motors Corporation	10,817	9,663
NYNEX Corporation	12,015	5,093
Middle South Utilities, Inc.	15,873	1,099
BellSouth Corporation	8,600	7,783
General Electric Company	904	15,071
Dimensional Fund Advisors, Inc. (B)		15,753
The Boeing Company	11,750	3,325
CMS Energy Corporation	14,907	
Bankers Trust New York Corp.	13,875	1,014
The Dun and Bradstreet Corporation	11,298	3,261
Ford Motor Company	10,650	3,674
Fiserv, Inc.	13,230	
Pacific Telesis Group	8,365	4,750
Delta Airlines	11,897	1,040
The Upjohn Company	10,400	2,304
Outboard Marine Corporation	12,119	260
Wells Fargo and Company	11,281	926
Oracle Systems Corporation	12,095	
United Technologies Corp.	10,010	2,017
The Stride Rite Corporation	11,750	
BayBanks, Inc.	11,588	
Navistar International Corporation	10,884	670
Federal National Mortgage Association	11,528	
UST Inc.	10,675	705
Warner Lambert	9,485	1,809
Kimberly-Clark Corporation	9,300	1,910
Kansas City Power & Light	11,068	
Baxter International, Inc.	9,169	1,828
Waste Management, Inc.	7,810	3,156
Minnesota Mining & Manufacturing Co.	5,280	5,656
American Telephone & Telegraph		10,633
Amoco Corp.	1,819	8,461
Melville Corporation	8,921	1,345
Kerr-McGee Corporation	9,300	753
Murphy Oil Corporation	9,960	
E.I. duPont de Nemours & Company	1,393	8,387
Champion International Corporation	8,309	1,463

Harvard Management Company
General Investments Major Equity Holdings, June 30, 1988   *(continued)*

	Market Value	
	Non-indexed Holdings (000)	Indexed Holdings (000)
Canadian Pacific Limited	$ 9,625	$
Consolidated Freightways	9,000	534
Bank of New England Corp.	9,335	
Salomon Inc.	8,025	1,289
PepsiCo, Inc.	5,588	3,583
American Television & Communications	9,090	
JWP, Inc.	9,000	
Merck & Co., Inc.		8,612
Inco Limited	6,500	1,827
Raytheon Company	6,270	1,881
Warner Communications, Inc.	6,337	1,699
USX Corporation	4,772	3,191
Norton Co.	7,735	190
Tele-Communications, Inc. Class A	6,903	848
Eastman Kodak Company	1,810	5,711
The New York Times Company	6,885	597
Henley Manufacturing Corp.	7,150	
Commonwealth Edison Company	4,900	2,240
Govett Atlantic Trust PLC (Pound sterling denominated)	6,883	
Shorewood Packaging Corporation	6,868	
New England Business Service, Inc.	6,795	
Stratus Computer, Inc.	6,670	
State Street Boston Corporation	6,572	
Deere & Company	5,382	1,187
Chief Automotive Systems, Inc.	6,521	
Wal-Mart Stores Inc.		6,422
Johnson & Johnson	1,191	5,231
Atlantic Richfield Company		6,384
Consolidated Rail Corporation	4,883	1,018
Yellow Freight Systems, Inc. of Delaware	5,700	194
Bolt Beranek and Newman, Inc.	5,827	
Washington Post Company	5,724	
Agency Rent-A-Car, Inc.	5,712	
The Procter & Gamble Co.	853	4,836
Long Island Lighting Co.	5,550	
Continental Illinois Corporation	5,500	
Ames Department Stores, Inc.	5,458	
Hewlett-Packard Co.		5,452
Burlington Northern Inc.	3,506	1,900
Coca Cola Enterprises Inc.		5,335
Sears Roebuck & Co.		5,273

Harvard Management Company
General Investments Major Equity Holdings, June 30, 1988   *(continued)*

	Market Value	
	Non-indexed Holdings (000)	Indexed Holdings (000)
Raychem Corporation	$ 5,224	$
Bell Atlantic Corp.		5,218
Columbia Pictures Entertainment, Inc.	5,179	
Super Valu Stores, Inc.	4,370	633
Tenneco Inc.	2,149	2,832
Harley-Davidson, Inc.	4,957	
Healthvest	4,918	
Halliburton Company	3,525	1,375
Rubbermaid Incorporated	4,253	631
BankAmerica Corporation	4,050	825
Caterpillar, Inc.	2,229	2,615
Teradata Corporation	4,822	
Duquesne Systems Inc.	4,813	
GTE Corp.		4,746
American Information Technologies Corporation		4,741
Electra Investment Trust (Pound sterling denominated)	4,725	
First Union Corporation	4,675	
Atlantic Southeast Airlines, Inc.	4,669	

(A) Equity securities held in the private placement portfolio.
(B) Index fund of smaller publicly traded companies weighted by market capital.

X

Fidelity Magellan Fund Portfolio

Fidelity Magellan Fund Portfolio, March 31, 1988

	Shares	Value		Shares	Value
COMMON STOCKS—94.4%					
AEROSPACE AND DEFENSE—1.3%					
AAR Corp.	268,000	$ 6,398,500	International Minerals & Chemicals Corp.	460,000	$ 19,320,000
Boeing Co.	1,020,000	47,430,000	Lawter International, Inc.	486,666	6,144,158
CERBCO, Inc. Class A	69,200	276,800	Linear Films, Inc.†	75,000	993,750
Frequency Electronics, Inc.†	16,300	167,075	Loctite Corp.	95,500	3,461,875
General Dynamics Corp.	75,000	3,975,000	Lubrizol Corp.	650,000	24,456,250
Kaman Corp. Class A	230,400	3,974,400	MacDermid, Inc.	20,000	490,000
Lockheed Corp.	60,000	2,655,000	Melamine Chemicals Inc.†	77,600	873,000
Logicon, Inc.	45,000	1,012,500	Minnesota Mining & Manufacturing Co.	280,000	16,100,000
Martin Marietta Corp.	210,000	9,345,000	Monsanto Co.	200,000	16,125,000
Maxwell Laboratories, Inc.†	6,300	72,450	Morton Thiokol, Inc.	40,000	1,695,000
Moog Inc. Class A	54,100	635,675	NOVA, an Alberta Corporation Class A	1,860,000	17,328,950
Northrop Corp.	161,000	4,809,875	Olin Corp.	20,000	1,012,500
Orbit Instrument Corp.†	150,000	825,000	Pennwalt Corp.	35,000	1,872,500
Photronics Corp.†	16,000	64,000	Petrolite Corporation	30,000	855,000
Precision Castparts Corp.	79,500	2,941,500	Polysar Energy & Chemical Corp.†	1,520,000	26,783,327
Raytheon Co.	10,000	665,000	Quantum Chemical Corp.	466,000	42,173,000
S.P.I.—Suspension & Parts Industries Ltd.†	40,000	45,000	Raychem Corp.	190,000	9,571,250
Solitron Devices, Inc.†	20,000	132,500	S.A.Y. Industries, Inc.†	60,000	142,500
TRW Inc.	90,000	4,432,500	Solvay	29,000	9,415,854
UTL Corp.†	100,000	787,500	Union Carbide Corp.	915,924	21,295,233
United Industrial Corp.	95,000	1,353,750	Valspar Corp.	10,000	270,000
United Technologies Corp.	350,000	13,650,000	Vista Chemical Co.	440,000	23,265,000
Zero Corp.	120,000	1,770,000			549,787,420
		107,419,025			
			Iron and Steel—0.9%		
BASIC INDUSTRIES—14.3%			Allegheny Ludlum Industries Inc.†	7,500	181,875
Chemicals and Plastics—6.5%			Armco Inc.†	630,000	7,166,250
AEP Industries Inc.†	50,000	462,500	Bethlehem Steel Corp.†	1,800,000	37,125,000
AGA AB Series B	70,000	2,144,498			
Air Products & Chemicals, Inc.	60,000	2,692,500			

	Shares	Value
Akzo N.V.	82,000	4,553,598
American Cyanamid Co.	330,000	16,830,000
ARCO Chemical Co.	522,900	15,883,087
Aristech Chemical Corp.	350,000	10,150,000
Ausimont Compo N.V.	420,000	11,235,000
Avery International Corp. NB	202,500	4,606,875
BOC Group	400,000	2,791,279
Bayer AG	90,000	14,307,692
Bayer AG (warrants 1994)†	14,000	1,068,476
Bayer AG (warrants 1995)†	7,000	453,152
Borden Chemicals & Plastics L.P.	320,000	4,760,000
Cabot Corp.	224,000	8,064,000
Calgon Carbon Corp.	19,000	793,250
Cambrex Corp.†	203,200	3,200,400
Ciba Geigy Ltd. PC†	1,000	1,355,609
Dexter Corp.	150,700	3,899,362
Dow Chemical Co.	720,000	58,680,000
du Pont (E.I.) de Nemours & Co.	100,000	8,087,500
Engelhard Corp.	4,400	85,800
Envirodyne Industries, Inc.†	505,000	10,478,750
Ferro Corp.	80,000	2,240,000
Freeport-McMoRan Resource Partners LP	448,100	9,074,025
GAF Corp.	10,000	541,250
Georgia Gulf Corp.	82,300	5,339,212
Goodrich (B.F.) Company	250,000	12,000,000
Grace (W.R.) & Co.	604,900	15,122,500
Great Lakes Chemical Corp.	85,000	4,930,000
Hercules Inc.	112,000	5,586,000
Himont Inc.	40,000	1,580,000
Hoechst AG ORD	55,000	8,700,452
Hoechst AG (warrants 1993)†	32,000	2,809,049
Hoechst Group (warrants)†	9,000	687,420
Hyponex Corp.†	20,000	145,000
IMC Fertilizer Group Inc.	518,300	15,613,787
Imperial Chemical Industries ADR	470,000	35,191,250

	Shares	Value
Birmingham Steel Corp.	110,000	3,052,500
Eastmet Corp.††	100,000	150,000
Fansteel Inc.	48,000	588,000
Inland Steel Industries, Inc.	240,000	7,440,000
Intermet Corp.	75,000	937,500
Lukens, Inc.	37,500	1,410,937
Material Sciences Corp.†	8,800	149,600
National Intergroup, Inc.	280,000	5,285,000
New Jersey Steel Corp.	150,000	3,037,500
Nucor Corp.	167,100	6,913,762
Steel of West Virginia Inc.†	108,300	1,001,775
Wheeling Pittsburgh Steel Corp.†	122,600	1,226,000
Wilton Enterprises, Inc.†	90,000	348,750
Worthington Industries, Inc.	10,000	201,250
		76,215,699

Nonferrous Metals—1.8%

	Shares	Value
Alcan Aluminum Ltd.	145,000	3,949,952
Aluminum Co. of America	550,000	23,925,000
AMAX, Inc.†	25,000	503,125
ASARCO Inc.	490,000	11,147,500
ASARCO Inc. (warrants)†	187,300	2,153,950
Cleveland Cliffs Inc.	180,000	3,465,000
Commercial Metals Co.	40,400	1,105,950
Cyprus Minerals Co.†	20,000	475,000
Falconbridge Ltd.†	225,000	4,146,918
Hanna (M.A.) Co.	79,300	2,230,312
Inco Ltd.	1,200,000	29,043,623
Kaisertech Ltd.†	80,000	990,000
Magma Copper Co. Class B†	20,000	122,500
Noranda Inc.	376,000	7,082,268
Pechiney C.I.P.†	100,000	3,574,921
Phelps Dodge Corp.	500,000	20,250,000
Reynolds Metals Co.	770,000	33,398,750
Yuba National Resources, Inc.†	90,000	180,000
		147,744,769

Fidelity Magellan Fund Portfolio, March 31, 1988, *continued*

	Shares	Value
Packaging and Containers—0.4%		
Anchor Glass Container Corp.	335,000	$ 5,653,125
Constar International, Inc.	193,600	3,533,200
Heekin Can, Inc.†*	165,000	4,248,750
Liqui-Box Corp.	38,000	1,216,000
Sealed Air Corp.	120,000	5,295,000
Shorewood Packaging Corp.†	142,400	1,886,800
Triangle Industries, Inc.	360,000	10,260,000
		32,092,875
Paper and Forest Products—4.7%		
Bohemia Inc.	190,000	2,707,500
Boise Cascade Corp.	140,000	6,160,000
Bowater Inc.	860,000	28,487,500
Bunzl plc†	1,200,000	3,507,959
Champion International Corp.	700,000	23,625,000
Consolidated Bathurst Inc. Series A	417,000	5,912,017
Consolidated Papers, Inc.	40,000	2,680,000
English China Clays Public Ltd. Co. ADR	60,000	1,312,500
Federal Paper Board Co., Inc.	482,250	17,412,250
Georgia-Pacific Corp.	740,000	28,767,500
Great Northern Nekoosa Corp.	550,000	22,481,250
IP Timberlands, Ltd.	39,700	863,475
International Paper Co.	585,000	23,765,625
James River Corp. (VA)	840,000	21,210,000
Jefferson Smurfit Corp.	62,600	3,474,300
Jefferson Smurfit Group Ltd.	10,000	71,667
Louisiana-Pacific Corp.	233,400	7,264,575
MacMillan Bloedel Ltd.	35,000	545,833
Mead Corp.	820,000	30,135,000
Nortek, Inc.	7,000	$ 68,250
Polly Peck International plc	3,110,000	15,367,505
Prospect Group, Inc. (stapled stock)	172,000	1,118,000
Sequa Corp. Class A	196,900	12,946,175
Standex International Corp.	27,000	452,250
Teledyne, Inc.	62,000	20,033,750
UNC Inc.	465,000	3,836,250
		136,534,410
CONSTRUCTION AND REAL ESTATE—1.5%		
Building Materials—1.1%		
AFG Industries Inc.	15,000	489,375
Amre Inc.	155,900	3,001,075
CalMat Co.	40,000	1,740,000
Clairson International Corp.†	240,000	1,740,000
Desoto, Inc.	40,900	1,237,225
Dravo Corp.	10,000	130,000
Florida Rock & Tank Lines Inc.†	20,000	285,000
GIANT Group, Ltd.†	40,000	845,000
Ideal Basic Industries Inc.†	63,000	181,125
Lafarge Coppee†	4,000	771,898
Lafarge Corp.	190,000	3,063,750
Masco Corp.	125,000	3,296,875
Morgan Products, Ltd.†	180,000	3,757,500
Owens-Corning Fiberglas Corp.†	2,530,000	50,916,250
RPM, Inc.	6,000	98,250
Sherwin-Williams Co.	70,000	1,951,250
Siam Cement Group	30,000	2,407,422
Sikes Corp. Class A	90,000	911,250
Southdown, Inc.	124,800	5,179,200

	Shares	Value
Pentair Inc.	10,000	285,000
Pope & Talbot, Inc.	163,600	3,312,900
Rayonier Timberlands L.P. Class A	373,400	6,861,225
Scott Paper Co.	1,579,000	57,633,500
Stone Container Corp.	1,040,000	29,900,000
Svenska Cellulosa Aktiebolaget ADR	1,000	57,356
Temple-Inland Inc.	320,000	14,680,000
Union Camp Corp.	660,000	22,027,500
WTD Industries, Inc.†	172,000	2,021,000
Westvaco Corp.	500,000	13,562,500
Weyerhaeuser Co.	205,000	7,943,750
Willamette Industries, Inc.	232,000	10,614,000
		399,282,682
TOTAL BASIC INDUSTRIES		1,205,123,445

CONGLOMERATES—1.6%	Shares	Value
Artra Group Inc.†	32,000	576,000
Brascan Ltd. Class A	700,000	15,524,361
Canadian Pacific Ltd. ORD par $5.00	820,000	15,445,372
Crane Co.	215,000	6,611,250
Emhart Corp.	140,000	3,062,500
Greyhound Corp.	5,500	163,625
Gulf & Western Inc.	40,000	3,130,000
Hanson Trust plc ORD	1,350,000	3,157,163
Henley Group Inc.	470,000	10,633,750
IC Industries, Inc.	57,300	1,919,550
IFI Privilege	10,000	137,832
ITT Corp.	82,800	3,694,950
Insilco Corp.	79,759	1,525,390
Intermark Inc.	194,400	2,089,800
Itel Corp. (New)†	570,000	10,687,500
Litton Industries, Inc.†	35,000	2,870,000
Mark IV Industries, Inc.†	124,900	1,483,187

	Shares	Value
St. Lawrence Cement Inc. Class A	114,800	1,197,431
Texas Industries, Inc.	44,300	1,478,512
U.S. Intec, Inc.†	4,100	28,700
Waxman Industries, Inc.	247,100	2,810,762
		87,517,850

Construction—0.3%	Shares	Value
Blount Inc. Class A	256	3,424
Blount Inc. Class B cv	9,000	118,125
Bonneville Pacific†	112,400	857,050
CRS Sirrine Inc.	2,500	41,562
Clayton Homes, Inc.†	197,000	1,994,625
Conner Corp.††	10,000	5,000
Fischbach Corp.†	5,000	43,125
Fleetwood Enterprises, Inc.	10,000	200,000
Fluor Corp.†	50,000	912,500
General Development Corp.†	215,000	3,440,000
Hovnanian Enterprises, Inc.†	10,000	100,000
Kasler Corp.†	20,000	180,000
Kaufman & Broad, Inc.	205,500	2,774,250
LVI Group, Inc.†	33,800	109,850
Leisure & Technology, Inc.†	10,000	50,000
Lennar Corp.	45,000	821,250
Liberty Homes, Inc. Class A	70,000	682,500
Liberty Homes, Inc. Class B	56,000	504,000
Morrison-Knudsen Co., Inc.	20,000	745,000
NVRyan L.P. Units Ltd.	40,000	205,000
Ocilla Industries, Inc.†	39,000	53,625
PSE Inc.	17,400	78,300
Philips Industries, Inc. (Ohio)	240,000	5,010,000
Ryland Group, Inc.	15,000	234,375
Standard-Pacific L.P.	620,000	5,735,000
Writer Corp.†	17,000	25,500
		24,924,061

Fidelity Magellan Fund Portfolio, March 31, 1988, *continued*

	Shares	Value		Shares	Value
Real Estate—0.0%			Haverty Furniture Companies,		
Avatar Holdings Inc.†	9,000	$ 191,250	Inc. Class A	13,000	$ 152,750
Hong Kong Land Co., Ltd. ADR	90,000	88,868	Heilig-Meyers Co.	6,900	118,162
Johnstown American			LADD Furniture, Inc.	94,900	1,565,850
Companies†	185,200	138,900	Lincoln Foodservice Products,		
Koger Co.	8,601	216,100	Inc.†	68,000	493,000
Major Realty Corp.†	9,000	100,125	Ohio Mattress Co.	60,000	900,000
Patten Corp.	10,000	66,250	SSMC Inc.†	20,000	582,500
Southmark Corp.	375,000	1,125,000	Toro Co.	130,000	2,372,500
		1,926,493	Union Special Corp.	18,800	488,800
			Universal Furniture Ltd.	895,400	14,102,550
Real Estate Investment Trusts—0.1%			Welbilt Corp.†	116,200	2,004,450
American Health Properties Inc.	31,800	580,350	Windmere Corp.†	2,500	47,187
Dial Real Estate Investment Trust					29,246,224
Inc.	55,000	1,038,125			
Health Care Property Investors,			**Textiles and Apparel—0.8%**		
Inc.	34,300	943,250	Chatham Manufacturing Co.	3,000	159,000
Health Care REIT, Inc.	55,789	1,011,173	Cherokee Group†	60,000	495,000
Healthvest	203,000	4,034,625	Crystal Brands, Inc.	200,000	4,850,000
Meditrust	67,800	1,347,525	Delta Woodside Industries Inc.†	111,000	1,165,500
Prime Motor Inns Ltd.	84,800	1,505,200	Dixie Yarns, Inc.	5,000	93,750
Weingarten Realty, Inc.	25,300	635,662	Fruit of the Loom Inc. Class A†	995,000	5,845,625
		11,095,910	Guilford Mills, Inc.	22,800	627,000
			Hartmarx Corp.	55,000	1,457,500
TOTAL CONSTRUCTION			Horizon Industries, Inc.†	50,000	250,000
AND REAL ESTATE		125,464,314	Hyde Athletic Industries, Inc.†	2,500	17,500
			Interco Incorporated	12,800	537,600
DURABLES—6.9%			Interface Flooring Systems, Inc.	510,000	5,992,500
Autos, Tires, and Accessories—5.7%			Kellwood Co.	35,700	1,048,687
Bandag Inc.	29,100	1,858,762	L.A. Gear Inc.†	20,000	505,000
Chrysler Corp.	4,149,000	97,501,500	Liz Claiborne, Inc.	90,000	1,440,000
Danaher Corp.†	188,000	2,185,500	NIKE, Inc. Class B	130,000	2,892,500
Eagle-Picher Industries, Inc.	500	14,875			

Security	Shares	Value
Eaton Corp.	15,000	1,237,500
Echlin Inc.	150,000	2,493,750
Federal-Mogul Corp.	9,200	353,050
Ford Motor Co.	5,095,000	217,174,375
General Motors Corp.	580,000	41,470,000
Genuine Parts Company	120,000	4,575,000
Goodyear Tire & Rubber Co.	1,050,000	66,806,250
J.P. Industries, Inc.†	75,500	1,377,875
Jaguar plc ADR	310,000	1,646,875
Jiffy Lube International, Inc.†	125,000	1,437,500
Michelin Class B	6,000	176,184
Modine Manufacturing Co.	30,000	540,000
Navistar International Corp.	810,000	5,265,000
NEOAX, Inc.†	152,400	1,428,750
Pep Boys—Manny, Moe & Jack	245,000	3,276,875
Peugeot Citroen, SA	1,000	163,450
Pullman Co. (The)	180,000	1,057,500
Saab-Scania Akteibolaget	27,000	831,759
Sealed Power Corp.	5,000	183,125
Standard Motor Products, Inc.	50,000	762,500
Sudbury Holdings, Inc.†	3,000	24,000
TBC Corp.†	510,000	6,757,500
Volkswagen AG	19,000	2,733,936
Volvo Aktiebolaget Class B	250,000	14,254,104
Western Auto Supply Co.†	145,000	2,718,750
Wickes Companies Inc. (New)†	35,000	336,875
		480,643,120
Household Durables—0.4%		
Bush Industries Inc.†	16,800	434,700
Chicago Pacific Corp.	41,000	1,640,000
Easco Hand Tools Inc.†	59,500	669,375
Emerson Radio Corp.†	10,000	31,250
Haverty Furniture Companies, Inc.	297,400	3,643,150
Oshkosh B'Gosh, Inc. Class A	20,700	543,375
RSI Corp.†	118,965	1,070,685
Reebok International Ltd.	520,000	7,930,000
Salant Corp.†	30,000	382,500
Salem Carpet Mills, Inc.†	80,000	500,000
Shaw Industries, Inc.	376,300	6,961,550
Stride Rite Corp.*	948,000	21,685,500
Timberland Co. Class A†	166,300	2,536,075
Unifi, Inc.†	35,000	765,625
VF Corp.	52,800	1,610,400
		71,362,872
TOTAL DURABLES		581,252,216
ENERGY—6.6%		
Coal—0.0%		
Addington Resources, Inc.†	15,000	326,250
Pyro Energy Corp.†	48,000	222,000
		548,250
Energy Services—0.7%		
Atwood Oceanics, Inc.†	23,000	322,000
Baker Hughes Inc.	350,000	6,256,250
Bolt Tecnology Corp.†	105,000	183,750
Computalog Grearhart Ltd.†	240,000	972,170
Daniel Industries, Inc.	75,000	693,750
Dresser Industries, Inc.	115,000	3,608,125
Gearhart Industries, Inc.†	20,000	17,500
Geo International Corp.†	80,000	420,000
Halliburton Co.	465,000	15,751,875
Helmerich & Payne, Inc.	69,000	1,578,375
Kaneb Services, Inc.†	9,400	21,150
Lone Star Technologies, Inc.	170,000	2,847,500
Lufkin Industries, Inc.	600	96,000
McDermott International, Inc.	252,000	4,977,000
N L Industries, Inc.	10,000	66,250

Fidelity Magellan Fund Portfolio, March 31, 1988, *continued*

	Shares	Value		Shares	Value
Energy Services—*continued*			Norsk Hydro a.s. ADR	672,100	$20,667,075
Noble Drilling Corp.†	165,319	$909,254	North Canadian Oils, Ltd.†	77,900	1,230,647
Nowsco Well Service Ltd.	171,000	2,147,284	North European Oil Royalty Trust	290,000	4,712,500
Ocean Drilling & Exploration Co.†	20,000	385,000	Occidental Petroleum Corp.	120,000	3,150,000
Oceaneering International Inc.†	607,600	1,898,750	Park-Ohio Industries, Inc.	150,000	900,000
Offshore Logistics, Inc.†	15,000	39,375	Pennzoil Co.	176,200	13,325,125
Parker Drilling Co.†	116,300	479,737	Phillips Petroleum Co.	915,000	15,555,000
Petroleum Helicopters, Inc.†	27,000	249,750	Plains Petroleum Co.	14,000	365,750
Petroleum Helicopters, Inc. (non vtg.)†	89,500	827,875	Poco Petroleums Ltd.	690,000	6,707,986
Production Operations Corp.	10,500	53,812	Presidio Oil Co. Class A	80,000	460,000
RPC Energy Services, Inc.†	266,900	1,467,950	Ranger Oil Ltd.†	9,000	51,038
Reading & Bates Corp.†	35,000	70,000	Renaissance Energy Ltd.†	350,000	4,607,686
Rowan Companies, Inc.†	23,000	163,875	Royal Dutch Petroleum Co. (10 gldr)	500,000	59,562,500
Schlumberger Ltd.	255,000	8,765,625	Seagull Energy Corp.†	157,000	2,433,500
Scientific Software Corp.†	29,000	148,625	"Shell" Transport & Trading Co., plc (NY shares)	60,000	4,657,500
Service Fracturing Co.†	42,400	227,900	Snyder Oil Partners Ltd.*	970,000	8,851,250
Tidewater Inc.†	110,000	715,000	Sun Energy Partners, L.P.	264,400	4,164,300
Tucker Drilling Co., Inc.†	63,500	404,812	Sun Inc.	13,700	820,287
Zapata Corp.†	20,000	62,500	Tenneco Inc.	225,000	9,590,625
		56,828,819	Texaco Canada Inc.	10,000	280,511
			Texaco Inc.†	650,000	31,200,000
Oil and Gas—5.9%			Total Petroleum (North America) Ltd.	40,000	631,911
Amerada Hess Corp.	440,000	13,090,000	Transco Explorations Partners, Ltd.	144,700	958,637
Amoco Corp.	200,000	14,675,000	USX Corp.	1,715,000	49,520,625
Anadarko Petroleum Corp.	20,000	490,000	Unimar Co., Indonesian (Participating Certificate)*	888,400	5,885,650
Apache Corp.	36,000	288,000	Union Exploration Partners, Ltd.	98,600	1,528,300
Apache Petroleum Co.	59,000	206,500			
Asamera Inc.	100,000	951,917			
Ashland Oil, Inc.	15,000	956,250			
Atlantic Richfield Co.	700,000	58,800,000			

Shares		Value
290,200	Beard Oil Co.†	4,425,550
53,500	Bogert Oil Co.†	642,000
20,735	Bonanza Oil & Gas Ltd.†	50,394
199,228	Bow Valley Industries, Ltd.	2,279,819
340,000	British Petroleum plc ADR	20,145,000
139,500	British Petroleum plc (warrants)†	1,133,437
20,000	British Petroleum Canada Inc.	332,158
48,000	Canada Northwest Energy Ltd.†	631,911
60,000	Chevron Corp.	2,790,000
1,259,800	Conquest Exploration Co.†	3,621,925
	Crown Central Petroleum Corp.	
80,500	Class A	1,388,625
100,000	Elf Aquitaine	4,793,240
	Enserch Exploration Partners,	
349,500	Ltd.	3,800,812
10,000	Ensource Inc.†	80,000
220,000	Enterprise Oil plc	1,398,280
625,000	Exxon Corp.	26,250,000
4,500	Falcon Oil & Gas, Inc.†	12,937
20,757	Forest Oil Corp.†	311,355
	Freeport-McMoRan Energy	
11,500	Partners Ltd.	163,375
310,000	Gulf Canada Corp.	4,238,059
119,500	Hamilton Oil Corp.	3,077,125
63,000	Imperial Oil Ltd. Class A cv	3,024,061
20,000	Kelley Oil and Gas Partners, Ltd.	250,000
170,000	Kerr-McGee Corp.	6,205,000
15,000	Louisiana Land & Exploration Co.	487,500
38,000	Mark Resources Inc.†	296,309
229,900	Maxus Energy Corp.	1,609,300
25,000	Mesa Limited Partnership	325,000
750,000	Mobil Corp.	33,187,500
80,000	Murphy Oil Corp.	2,520,000
277,000	Norcen Energy Resources Ltd.	4,235,728
120,000	Norsk Hydro a.s.	3,759,615
530,000	Unocal Corp.	20,802,500
84,000	Wiser Oil Co.	1,449,000
		500,994,085
	TOTAL ENERGY	558,371,154

FINANCE—16.1%

Banks—6.5%

Shares		Value
80,000	Allied Irish Bank	328,918
15,000	Baltimore Bancorp	230,625
15,000	Banc One Corp.	363,750
10,000	Banco Popular de Puerto Rico	282,500
47,085	Bancorp Hawaii, Inc.	2,354,250
	BancTEXAS Group Inc. par	
200,000	$0.01†	325,000
400,000	Bangkok Bank	5,283,319
26,666	Bangkok Bank (rights)†	245,803
700,000	Bank of Boston Corp.	16,362,500
966,044	Bank of New England Corp.	27,049,232
14,000	Bank of New Hampshire Corp.	329,000
250,400	Bank of New York Co., Inc.	7,856,300
	Bank of San Francisco Holding	
60,000	Co.†	240,000
1,225,000	BankAmerica Corp.†	13,321,875
700,000	Bankers Trust New York Corp.	21,875,000
1,350,000	Barclays plc ORD	12,017,591
50,000	Barnett Banks Inc.	1,637,500
35,000	BayBanks, Inc.	1,461,250
27,500	Boatmen's Bancshares Inc.	996,875
700,000	Chase Manhattan Corp.	17,587,500
20,818	Chemical New York Corp.	447,587
1,960,000	Citicorp	37,240,000
181,100	Citizens & Southern Corp.	4,504,862
	Colorado National Bankshares,	
50,300	Inc.†	603,600
35,000	Comerica Inc.	2,213,750

Fidelity Magellan Fund Portfolio, March 31, 1988, *continued*

	Shares	Value		Shares	Value
Banks—*continued*			**Insurance—3.0%**		
Community Bank System Inc.	15,000	$ 251,250	Aetna Life & Casualty Co.	400,000	$ 17,550,000
Continental Illinois Corp.	712,500	2,582,812	American Family Corp.	44,700	726,375
CoreStates Financial Corp.	580,000	23,345,000	American Home Shield Corp.†	36,700	233,962
Crestar Financial Corp.	33,000	833,250	American Income Life Insurance Co. *	877,200	10,087,800
Dominion Bankshares Corp.	139,646	2,513,628	American International Group, Inc.	140,000	7,507,500
Equimark Corp.†	35,000	450,625	Aon Corp.	90,000	2,272,500
Fifth Third Bancorp	200,200	7,057,050	Berkley (W.R.) Corp.	150,000	3,600,000
First of America Bank Corp	200,000	9,300,000	CIGNA Corp.	100,000	4,675,000
First Bank System, Inc.	375,000	8,156,250	Capital Holding Corp.	129,500	3,804,062
First Chicago Corp.	95,000	2,256,250	Chubb Corp. (The)	170,000	9,647,500
First Empire State Corp.	204,500	10,506,187	Continental Corp. (The)	85,000	3,208,750
First Fidelity Bancorporation	1,160,000	41,905,000	Corroon & Black Corporation	20,000	612,500
First Pennsylvania Corp.†	70,000	735,000	FGIC Corp.	502,900	8,234,987
First Tennessee National Corp.	51,200	1,382,400	First American Financial Corp.	50,000	1,337,500
First Union Corp.	460,000	8,912,500	First Executive Corp.†	3,555,000	45,770,625
First Virginia Banks, Inc.	235	5,786	First Executive Corp. (warrants)†	148,500	445,500
Fleet/Norstar Financial Group Inc.	520,002	12,480,048	General Re Corp.	580,000	27,767,500
Fourth Financial Corp.	11,800	230,100	Guaranty National Corp.	460,000	3,105,000
Guaranty Bancshares Corp. *	136,000	884,000	Hanover Insurance Co.	65,000	1,543,750
Huntington Bancshares Inc.	126,657	2,976,439	I.C.H. Corp.†	436,600	3,110,775
KeyCorp.	230,200	4,949,300	Independent Insurance Group, Inc. (non vtg)	14,800	481,000
Landmark Bancshares Corp.	25,683	337,089	Kemper Corp.	1,191,976	27,415,448
Lloyds Bank plc	1,400,000	6,970,655	Liberty Corp. (The)	105,377	4,741,965
MNC Financial Inc.	204,923	9,375,227	Lincoln National Life Corp.	55,000	2,530,000
Manufacturers Hanover Corp.	150,000	3,712,500	MBIA Inc.	612,400	9,798,400
Manufacturers National Corp.	315,588	13,096,902	Mercury General Corp.	59,000	811,250
Mellon Bank Corp.	75,400	2,120,625	Milwaukee Insurance Group Inc.†	10,000	102,500
Mercantile Bancorporation Inc.	51,000	1,122,000	NAC Re Corp.†	85,000	2,018,750
Mercantile Bankshares Corp.	9,201	328,935			
Merchants National Corp.	12,700	304,800			
Meridian Bancorp, Inc.	20,000	380,000			

Company	Shares	Value
Merrimack Bancorp Inc. (Mass.)	110,000	907,500
Michigan National Corp.	25,200	1,121,400
Midland Bank plc	500,000	3,611,689
Midlantic Corp.	430,000	18,920,000
Morgan (J.P.) & Co. Inc.	291,509	9,692,674
Multibank Financial Corp.	10,198	244,752
NBD Bancorp, Inc.	440,000	15,015,000
National City Corp.	500,000	15,000,000
National Westminster Bank plc	970,000	10,244,751
National Westminster Bank plc ADR	100,000	3,200,000
North Fork Bancorporation, Inc.	83,000	1,660,000
Northern Trust Corp.	380,000	16,387,500
Norwest Corp.	65,000	2,746,250
PNC Financial Corp.	144,500	5,617,437
Planters Corp.	9,000	139,500
Puget Sound Bancorp	9,000	173,250
Security Bancorp, Inc. (Mich.)	9,000	255,375
Security Pacific Corp.	320,000	9,520,000
Shawmut National Corp.	553,300	12,587,575
Signet Banking Corp.	133,158	3,861,582
Society Corporation	467,500	15,836,562
Southeast Banking Corp.	436,531	10,804,142
Southtrust Corporation	15,000	322,500
Sovran Financial Corp.	65,407	2,281,069
State Street Boston Corp.	40,000	945,000
Suburban Bank Corp.	5,000	95,000
SunTrust Banks, Inc.	260,000	5,460,000
Thai Farmers Bank	19,000	269,153
Union Planters Corp.	116,300	3,023,800
United Banks of Colorado, Inc.	30,000	435,000
United Financial Banking Cos. Inc.†	31,854	278,722
Wells Fargo & Co.	190,000	9,927,500
Wilmington Trust Company	450,000	13,275,000
		548,479,878

Company	Shares	Value
New York Marine & General Insurance Co.†	130,000	1,950,000
Nobel Insurance Ltd.	8,000	40,000
North East Insurance Co.†	131,000	204,687
Old Republic International Corp.	44,310	1,019,130
Provident Life & Accident Insurance Co. of America Class B	98,700	1,961,662
Reliance Group Holdings, Inc.	110,000	687,500
Republic American Corp.	200,000	3,075,000
Seibels Bruce Group, Inc.	16,033	196,404
Skandia†	10,000	234,873
Skandia International Holding Co. AB†	7,000	177,516
St. Paul Companies, Inc. (The)	355,000	15,442,500
Trilon Financial Corp. Class A	160,000	2,235,993
UNUM Corp.	160,000	3,360,000
United Insurance Companies, Inc.	92,000	1,495,000
USLICO Corp.	70,000	1,443,750
Williams (A.L.) Co.†	925,000	14,453,125
Zenith National Insurance Corp.	200,000	4,100,000
		255,218,039
Other Finance—4.1%		
American Express Co.	3,030,000	73,098,750
Cash America Investments Inc.	10,000	160,000
City Investing Co. Liquidating Trust	420,000	1,680,000
Commercial Credit Co.	160,000	4,140,000
Federal National Mortgage Assn.*	6,170,000	198,211,250
Federal National Mortgage Assn. (warrants)†*	668,900	4,682,300
First Trust Co.†	23,600	41,300
Green Tree Acceptance, Inc.	90,000	1,451,250
International Lease Finance Corp.	800,000	13,500,000

Fidelity Magellan Fund Portfolio, March 31, 1988, *continued*

	Shares	Value
Other Finance—*continued*		
Leucadia National Corp.†	160,000	$ 1,880,000
Lomas Mortgage Corp.	107,000	2,206,875
NorthEastern Mortgage Co., Inc.†	4,900	9,187
Phoenix American Inc.†	26,731	80,193
Primerica Corp.	535,000	15,916,250
Student Loan Marketing Association (non vtg.)	325,000	24,456,250
		341,513,605
Savings and Loans—2.2%		
Ahmanson (H.F.) & Co.	109,200	1,583,400
American Savings Bank, FSB*	344,000	4,816,000
Anchor Savings Bank†	314,300	1,846,512
Apple Bank for Savings†	148,000	4,144,000
Banking Center	70,000	813,750
Bankworcester Corp.	16,000	220,000
Bay View Federal Savings & Loan Assn.†	46,300	810,250
Binghamton Savings Bank (The)	135,000	1,890,000
CalFed Inc.	342,200	8,726,100
Charter One Financial Corp.†	200,300	1,652,475
Citizens Savings Bank FSB†	3,900	37,050
Co-Operative Bank of Concord	25,000	306,250
Coast Savings & Loan Assn.	190,000	3,230,000
Collective Federal Savings & Loan Association	24,000	228,000
Commercial Federal Corp.†	9,000	103,500
Crestmont Federal Savings & Loan Assn.†	170,000	1,997,500
CrossLand Savings, FSB*	735,000	9,738,750
Home & City Savings Bank†	98,000	$ 1,886,500
Home Federal Savings & Loan Assn. (San Diego)	381,300	9,246,525
Home Federal Savings & Loan Assn. (Upper East Tennessee, Johnson City)	142,700	2,461,575
Home Savings Bank (Brooklyn, N.Y.)	410,000	5,945,000
Imperial Corp. of America	20,000	227,500
Landmark Savings Assn.	113,100	593,775
Loyola Capital Corp.†	5,200	55,250
Maryland Federal Savings & Loan Association†	34,000	340,000
Merchants Capital Corp. Class A	163,500	817,500
Metropolitan Federal Savings & Loan Association†	90,000	2,497,500
Metropolitan Financial Corp.	230,900	2,135,825
Montclair Savings Bank	30,000	506,250
New Bedford Institution for Savings	33,100	529,600
New York Bancorp Inc.†	104,200	794,525
One Bancorp	164,700	2,408,737
Onondaga Savings Bank†	91,300	490,737
Pacific First Financial Group	90,000	1,170,000
Parkvale Savings Association†	79,000	553,000
People's Savings Bank FSB Monroe, Michigan†	15,000	140,625
People's Bancorp Worcester Inc.	59,000	966,125
People's Heritage Bank	89,200	1,627,900
People's Savings Bank of Brockton (Mass.)†	112,100	938,837

	Shares	Value
Cumberland Federal Savings & Loan Association*	205,200	2,462,400
D & N Savings Bank FSB	83,500	668,000
Dime Savings Bank of New York, FSB†	459,300	7,922,925
Dime Savings Bank of New York	10,000	132,500
Eliot Savings Bank†*	166,900	1,543,825
Excel Bancorp	240,000	2,970,000
Family Mutual Savings Bank†	199,700	2,046,925
Fidelity Federal Savings & Loan Assn.	65,000	1,746,875
First American Bancorp Inc.	470,000	5,581,250
First American Savings, F.A.*	185,000	2,543,750
First Essex Bancorp Inc.	60,000	480,000
First Federal Bank of Connecticut	30,000	483,750
First Federal Savings Bank of Puerto Rico†	179,400	1,480,050
First Northern Savings & Loan Association	2,000	29,500
First Woburn Bancorp Inc.	65,000	650,000
Firstfed Financial Corp.†	5,000	79,375
FirstFed America, Inc. Honolulu†*	239,300	2,811,775
Framingham Savings Bank	90,000	1,125,000
Germantown Savings Bank†	55,300	511,525
Gibraltar Financial Corp.	10,000	40,000
GLENFED Inc.	649,300	14,041,112
Golden West Financial Corp.	44,500	1,190,375
Great American First Savings Bank	80,000	1,030,000
Great Country Bank	90,000	1,755,000
Great Lakes Bancorp., FSB	144,000	2,628,000
Great Western Financial Corp.	450,000	6,018,750
Greater New York Savings Bank	482,600	3,378,200
Grove Bank For Savings	43,000	440,750
Heritage Bank for Savings	76,000	940,500
Ponce Federal Bank, FSB	93,000	825,375
Portsmouth Bankshares Inc.†	5,000	54,375
Provident Bancshares Corp.	74,000	860,250
Raleigh Federal Savings Bank†	126,800	1,252,150
Richmond Hill Savings Bank	140,000	2,835,000
Rochester Community Savings Bank	80,000	1,030,000
Roosevelt Federal Savings & Loan Association*	340,000	3,272,500
San Francisco Federal Savings & Loan Association†	274,000	3,767,500
Society for Savings Bancorp Inc.	8,300	150,437
Somerset Savings Bank	339,400	4,030,375
Southold Savings Bank†	87,500	1,815,625
St. Paul Bancorp Inc.	30,000	330,000
Standard Federal Bank†	993,200	8,069,750
TCF Banking & Savings, FA†	210,000	1,995,000
Talman Home Federal Savings & Loan Association	340,000	2,635,000
Unionfed Financial Corp.	500	6,500
Vanguard Savings Bank	60,000	615,000
Warren Five Cents Savings Bank†	10,000	81,250
Washington Federal Savings & Loan Association	49,720	1,342,440
Washington Mutual Savings Bank	52,000	760,500
Webster Financial Corp.	115,000	1,265,000
Western Federal Savings Bank*	90,000	1,417,500
		183,620,462

Securities Industry—0.3%

	Shares	Value
Bear Stearns Cos. Inc.	15,000	193,125
Colonial Group, Inc. Class A	80,500	945,875
Dreyfus Corp.	150,000	4,368,750
Eaton Financial Corp.†	80,000	510,000
Eaton Vance Corp.	62,300	1,370,600

Fidelity Magellan Fund Portfolio, March 31, 1988, *continued*

	Shares	Value		Shares	Value
Securities Industry—*continued*			Inmed Corp.†	15,000	$ 33,750
First Boston, Inc.	45,000	$ 1,057,500	Johnson & Johnson	236,000	18,732,500
First Capital Holdings Corp.†	70,000	385,000	Marquest Medical Products, Inc.	18,500	138,750
Franklin Resources, Inc.	49,000	863,625	McKesson Corp.	181,100	5,840,475
Hallwood Group Inc.	150,000	2,287,500	Medtronic, Inc.	73,000	6,597,375
Investor AB B Free	5,000	188,920	Mentor Corp.	265,800	2,691,225
Merrill Lynch & Co., Inc.	50,000	1,181,250	Moore Medical Corp.†*	243,700	4,081,975
Morgan Stanley & Co., Inc.	95,500	5,897,125	Novametrix Medical Systems Inc.†	7,000	50,750
Oppenheimer Capital L P unit limited partnership	2,000	22,250	Omnicare, Inc.†	140,000	1,015,000
PaineWebber Group Inc.	120,000	1,950,000	Pall Corp.	75,000	2,250,000
Providentia Forval Series B	5,000	146,370	Puritan Bennett Corp.	1,800	43,650
Royal Business Group, Inc.†*	113,000	395,500			86,252,574
Salomon Inc.	87,000	1,892,250			
Schwab, Charles Corp. (New)†	20,000	147,500	**Medical Facilities Management—0.5%**		
Shearson Lehman Brothers Holdings, Inc.	120,000	2,160,000	American Health Companies Inc.	193,000	3,474,000
United Asset Management Corp.	150,000	1,856,250	Beverly Enterprises	81,544	591,194
		27,819,390	Charter Medical Corp. Class A	75,000	2,306,250
TOTAL FINANCE		1,356,651,374	Community Psychiatric Centers	380,000	8,312,500
			Continental Medical Systems†	64,100	657,025
HEALTH—4.6%			Forum Group, Inc.	40,000	160,000
Drugs and Pharmaceuticals—3.1%			Health South Rehabilitation Corp.†	160,000	1,920,000
ALZA Corp.†	420,000	10,972,500	Healthcare Intl., Inc. Class A†	10,000	30,000
Amgen Inc.†	10,000	322,500	Hospital Corp. of America	200,000	6,200,000
Beecham Group plc ADR	70,000	1,190,000	Humana Inc.	294,000	7,644,000
Beecham Group plc ORD	140,000	1,201,381	Maxicare Health Plans, Inc.†	840,000	1,785,000
Bristol-Myers Co.	565,000	23,235,625	Medical Care International, Inc.†	157,500	1,122,187
CDC Life Sciences Inc.†	75,000	1,473,447	National Health Care Systems, Inc.†	55,000	22,343
Centocor Inc.†	65,700	1,905,300	National Heritage Inc.	237,700	1,188,500
Collagen Corp.†	35,000	205,625	National Medical Enterprises, Inc.	280,000	6,055,000
Elan Corp. plc ADR†	50,000	587,500			

	Shares	Value
Genetics Institute, Inc.†	90,900	2,067,975
Glaxo Holdings plc ADR	175,000	3,215,625
Glaxo Holdings plc ORD	80,000	1,493,711
Immunex Corp.†	5,000	69,375
Lilly (Eli) & Co.	330,000	27,720,000
Lilly (Eli) & Co. (warrants)†	80,000	2,220,000
Marion Laboratories, Inc.	250,000	4,937,500
Medco Containment Services, Inc.	160,000	2,240,000
Merck & Co., Inc.	420,000	65,730,000
Schering-Plough Corp.	620,000	30,302,500
Sigma Aldrich Corp.†	5,000	218,750
SmithKline Beckman Corp.	260,000	13,845,000
Squibb Corp.	175,000	11,331,250
Upjohn Co.	1,110,000	32,190,000
Warner-Lambert Co.	340,000	24,395,000
Wellcome plc†	180,000	1,503,896
		264,574,460

Medical Equipment and Supplies—1.0%

	Shares	Value
Abbott Laboratories	125,000	5,859,375
Alco Health Services Corp.	80,000	1,440,000
Animed, Inc.†	196,500	307,031
Applied Bioscience International Inc.†	49,000	710,500
Bard (C.R.), Inc.	100,000	3,987,500
Bausch & Lomb Inc.	50,000	2,200,000
Baxter Travenol Laboratories, Inc.	868,000	19,964,000
Becton, Dickinson & Co.	90,000	5,017,500
Bergen Brunswig Corp. Class A	40,000	1,065,000
Bioassay Systems Corp.†	55,000	6,875
COBE Laboratories, Inc.†	5,000	116,250
Concept, Inc.†	5,000	66,250
Healthco International, Inc.†	176,425	3,307,968
Hillenbrand Industries, Inc.	23,800	728,875

	Shares	Value
PacifiCare Health Systems, Inc.†	30,000	240,000
Safeguard Health Enterprises, Inc.†	74,500	372,500
Salick Health Care, Inc.†	33,000	437,250
United HealthCare Corp.†	510,000	2,486,250
Westworld Community Healthcare, Inc.†	281,000	210,750
		45,214,749
TOTAL HEALTH		396,041,783

INDUSTRIAL MACHINERY AND EQUIPMENT—3.1%

Electrical Equipment—0.7%

	Shares	Value
AMP Inc.	100,000	4,775,000
Besicorp Group Inc.†	150,000	93,750
Charter Power Systems Inc.	143,800	916,725
Computer Products, Inc.†	320,000	640,000
Dynamics Corp. of America*	310,000	7,091,250
Emerson Electric Co.	15,000	455,625
General Electric Co.	840,000	33,915,000
Hubbell (Harvey), Inc. Class B	85,500	2,874,937
Intermagnetics General Corp.†	20,000	97,500
Optrotech Ltd.†	17,500	109,375
Sensormatic Electronics Corp.	96,500	880,562
Specialty Equipment Cos. Inc.†	81,900	1,832,512
Stanford Telecommunications, Inc.†	28,600	328,900
Vertex Communications Corp.†	33,600	88,200
Vitronics Corp.†	25,000	65,625
Willcox & Gibbs Inc.	21,600	437,400
Zenith Electronics Corp.†	75,000	1,396,875
		55,999,236

Industrial Machinery and Equipment—1.8%

	Shares	Value
American Hoist & Derrick Co.†	170,000	1,317,500
Bearings, Inc.	26,000	1,332,500
CMI Corp.†	5,000	15,625

Fidelity Magellan Fund Portfolio, March 31, 1988, *continued*

	Shares	Value		Shares	Value
Industrial Machinery and Equipment—*continued*			Caesars World, Inc.†	708,800	$ 17,011,200
Caterpillar, Inc.	300,000	$ 18,712,500	Capital Cities/ABC, Inc.	18,200	6,215,300
Cooper Industries, Inc.	640,000	37,520,000	Carnival Cruise Lines Inc.		
Deere & Co.	365,000	16,835,625	Class A	2,310,000	31,185,000
Designatronics Inc.	25,007	100,028	Cedar Fair LP	840,600	7,880,625
Donaldson Company, Inc.	50,000	2,106,250	Centel Cable Television Co.		
Dover Corp.	5,000	311,250	Class A	148,500	3,749,625
Enfield Ltd.	750,000	3,797,542	Century Communications Corp.†	60,000	1,065,000
Goulds Pumps, Inc.	10,000	187,500	Circus Circus Enterprises, Inc.†	500,000	14,000,000
Graco Inc.	500	16,687	Club Med Inc.	68,300	939,125
Hafslund†	38,000	3,197,115	Columbia Pictures Entertainment		
Harnischfeger Corp.	460,000	9,085,000	Inc.†	22,080	171,120
Imo Delaval Inc.	315,000	11,733,750	Comcast Corp. Class A	140,000	3,500,000
Ingersoll-Rand Co.	100,000	3,875,000	Comcast Corp. Class A (Special)	160,000	3,640,000
Interlake Inc.	146,268	6,289,524	Disney (Walt) Co.	50,000	2,956,250
Kennametal Inc.	60,864	2,092,200	Financial New Network, Inc.†	125,000	718,750
Keystone International, Inc.	227,500	4,038,125	Four Seasons Hotels Inc. (sub.		
Les Industries Charan Inc.†	631,000	2,095,916	sh. vtg.)	280,000	4,083,119
MLX Corp.†	47,324	136,056	Golden Nugget, Inc.†	10,000	108,750
Milton Roy Co.	96,300	1,191,712	Granada	700,000	4,185,033
Monarch Machine Tool Co.	2,100	48,562	Great American Communications	23,800	273,700
Newcor, Inc.	5,000	36,875	Holiday Corp.	550,000	14,368,750
Nordson Corp.	47,700	1,812,600	Hong Kong TVB	35,000	63,285
Parker-Hannifin Corp.	20,000	725,000	Infinity Broadcasting Corp.†	70,000	1,487,500
Regal-Beloit Corp.	91,200	2,416,800	Jones Intercable Investments LP		
Rheometrics, Inc.†	37,200	279,000	Class A†	119,200	1,698,600
Rule Industries, Inc.†	20,500	158,875	Jones Intercable, Inc.	4,000	50,500
S.K.F. B Free	8,000	318,611	King World Productions, Inc.†	364,300	6,967,237
Thermo Electron Corp.†	5,000	84,375	La Quinta Motor Inns L.P.	5,000	69,375
Timken Co.	80,000	5,850,000	La Quinta Motor Inns, Inc.	40,000	505,000
Tokheim Corporation	90,800	2,111,100	Marriott Corp.	180,000	5,310,000

Name	Shares	Value
Trinova Corp.	130,000	4,095,000
Varity Corp.†	1,700,000	5,508,968
		149,433,171
Pollution Control—0.6%		
Browning-Ferris Industries, Inc.	205,000	5,330,000
Chemical Waste Management Inc.	380,000	9,880,000
Commodore Environmental Services Inc.†	10,000	16,875
Control Resource Industries, Inc.†	30,000	176,250
Environmental Treatment & Technologies Corp.†	10,000	148,750
Laidlaw Transportation Ltd.	620,000	10,799,203
Ogden Corp.	30,200	913,550
Pacific Nuclear Systems, Inc.†	10,000	65,000
Rollins Environmental Services, Inc.	264,000	5,874,000
Waste Management, Inc.	330,000	11,508,750
Weston (Roy F.), Inc.†	31,000	534,750
Wheelabrator Technologies Inc.†	110,000	2,213,750
Zurn Industries, Inc.	66,100	1,379,837
		48,840,715
TOTAL INDUSTRIAL MACHINERY AND EQUIPMENT		254,273,122
MEDIA AND LEISURE—5.8%		
Leisure—2.6%		
Adelphia Communications Class A†	64,000	1,104,000
Aircoa Hospitality Services, Inc.	140,000	805,000
American Television & Communications Corp.†	620,000	15,965,000
Barris Industries, Inc.†	175,000	1,771,875
Cablevision Systems Corp.†	80,000	2,740,000
Midwest Communications Corp.†	40,000	190,000
Prime Motor Inns, Inc.	85,000	3,315,000
Reeves Communications Corp.†	50,000	275,000
Rogers Communications, Inc. Class B†	199,731	5,279,074
Tele-Communications, Inc. Class A†	748,000	19,822,000
Turner Broadcasting System Inc. (warrants)†	99,000	643,500
Turner Broadcasting System Inc. Class A	180,000	2,745,000
Turner Broadcasting System Inc. Class B†	199,900	3,048,475
United Artists Communications, Inc.†	84,000	2,436,000
United Cable Television Corp.	60,000	1,995,000
Viacom Inc.†	290,000	6,597,500
Warner Communications Inc.	480,000	14,640,000
Westwood One, Inc.†	76,700	1,744,925
		217,320,193
Publishing—2.2%		
Affiliated Publications, Inc.	190,000	11,780,000
Gannett Co., Inc.	240,000	8,550,000
Gibson Greetings, Inc.	60,000	945,000
Grolier, Inc.†	200,000	4,875,000
Harcourt Brace Jovanovich, Inc.	320,000	2,560,000
Houghton Mifflin Co.	103,100	3,776,037
International Thompson Organization Ltd.	1,200,000	13,367,363
Knight-Ridder, Inc.	15,500	623,875
MacMillan, Inc.	15,000	855,000
Mcclatchy Newspapers Inc. Class A	45,000	736,875
Maclean Hunter Ltd. Class X cv	359,000	6,689,347
Media General, Inc. Class A	140,000	5,740,000

Fidelity Magellan Fund Portfolio, March 31, 1988, *continued*

	Shares	Value
Publishing—*continued*		
New York Times Co. (The) Class A	325,600	$ 9,645,900
Pulitzer Publishing Co.	20,000	680,000
Southam Inc.	620,000	11,050,352
Thomson Newspapers Ltd. Class A (part cv)	620,000	14,566,372
Time Inc.	445,000	37,936,250
Times Mirror Co. (The)	370,100	12,583,400
Torstar Corp. Class B	980,000	21,634,871
Tribune Co.	195,000	7,215,000
Washington Post Co. Class B	53,700	11,733,450
		187,544,092
Restaurants—0.6%		
Bob Evans Farms Inc.	30,000	525,000
Buffets Inc.†	1,800	24,300
Church's Fried Chicken, Inc.	28,000	192,500
Collins Food International, Inc.	440,000	6,270,000
Cracker Barrel Old Country Store, Inc.	80,000	1,520,000
Dunkin' Donuts Inc.	283,700	6,454,175
Karcher (Carl) Enterprises†	64,000	992,000
Marcus Corp.	23,000	356,500
McDonald's Corp.	520,000	22,620,000
Piccadilly Cafeterias, Inc.	95,000	1,306,250
Ryan's Family Steak Houses, Inc.†	83,200	613,600
Sbarro, Inc.†	340,300	5,700,025
Sizzler Restaurants International, Inc.†	131,000	2,227,000
Skipper's, Inc.	33,200	211,650

	Shares	Value
Foods—0.7%		
Archer-Daniels-Midland Co.	935,000	$ 18,816,875
Borden, Inc.	150,000	7,781,250
Castle & Cooke, Inc.†	25,000	584,375
Colorado Prime Corp.†	3,500	45,062
Conagra, Inc.	73,400	1,899,225
Dreyer's Grand Ice Cream, Inc.†	24,000	357,000
FPI Ltd.	240,000	2,916,513
General Mills, Inc.	55,000	2,612,500
Gerber Products Co.	7,100	286,662
Goodmark Foods, Inc.†	20,000	235,000
Hudson Foods, Inc.	36,500	296,562
I B P Inc.	5,000	73,125
Kraft, Inc.	15,000	802,500
Michael Foods Inc.	35,500	807,625
Quaker Oats Co.	56,000	2,597,000
Ralston Purina Co.	43,400	3,070,550
Rymer Co. (The)†	88,200	1,036,350
Sara Lee Corp.	210,000	8,452,500
Stokeley USA, Inc.	80,000	450,000
Tasty Baking Co.	205,000	3,997,500
Tootsie Roll Industries, Inc.	106,970	3,021,902
Universal Foods Corp.	73,781	2,194,984
Wilson Foods Corp.†	84,000	1,071,000
		63,406,060
Household Products—0.9%		
Avon Products, Inc.	5,000	121,250
Clorox Co.	65,000	2,039,375
Colgate-Palmolive Co.	425,000	18,221,875
Lancaster Colony Corp.	5,000	80,000
Paterson Zochonis	40,000	239,144

TW Services Inc.	75,000	1,284,375
Uno Restaurant Corp.†	100,400	953,800
Vie de France Corp.	60,000	255,000
		51,506,175
Toys and Leisure Durables—0.4%		
American Land Cruisers, Inc.†	104,700	837,600
Baldwin Piano & Organ Co.†	50,000	612,500
Brunswick Corp.	920,000	21,505,000
Chris-Craft Industries, Inc.†	300,000	5,212,500
Coachmen Industries, Inc.	20,000	155,000
Coast R.V., Inc.†	162,400	913,500
Hasbro, Inc.	15,000	215,625
Mattel, Inc.†	16,500	113,437
Thor Industries, Inc.	10,000	117,500
View-Master Ideal Group, Inc.†	19,000	114,000
		29,796,662
TOTAL MEDIA AND LEISURE		486,167,122
NONDURABLES—4.4%		
Beverages—1.0%		
A & W Brands†	321,700	4,503,800
Anheuser-Busch Companies, Inc.	455,000	14,503,125
Canadaigua Wine Co. Class A†	27,300	341,250
Coca-Cola Bottling Co. Consolidated	74,000	2,146,000
Coca-Cola Company (The)	240,000	9,180,000
Coca-Cola Enterprises Inc.	950,000	14,012,500
General Cinema Corp.	230,000	3,766,250
Heineken NV ADR	5,000	336,250
PepsiCo, Inc.	324,000	11,340,000
Seagram Co. Ltd.	450,000	23,240,974
		83,370,149
Premark International, Inc.	225,200	6,812,300
Procter & Gamble Co.	260,000	20,247,500
Stanhome Inc.	306,000	11,322,000
Unilever plc (Amer. shares)	40,000	1,420,000
Unilever NV (NY shares)	220,000	12,980,000
		73,483,444
Tobacco—1.8%		
Americus Trust for Philip Morris†	129,100	2,307,662
B-A-T Industries plc ADR	80,000	630,000
Loews Corp.	645,000	46,117,500
Philip Morris Companies, Inc.	570,000	51,086,250
RJR Nabisco, Inc.	735,000	38,128,125
UST Inc.	399,000	11,970,000
		150,239,537
TOTAL NONDURABLES		370,499,190
PRECIOUS METALS—0.5%		
De Beers Consolidated Mines Ltd. ADR	2,400,000	25,800,000
Lonrho Ltd. ORD	2,500,000	11,033,099
Minorco ADR	280,000	3,780,000
		40,613,099
RETAIL AND WHOLESALE—5.7%		
Apparel Stores—0.6%		
Allison's Place†	115,000	129,375
Baker (J.) Inc.	400,000	3,750,000
Brown Group, Inc.	76,500	2,658,375
Burlington Coat Factory Warehouse Corp.†	453,500	7,199,312
CML Group, Inc.†*	434,400	8,579,400
Charming Shoppes, Inc.	16,300	209,862
Dress Barn, Inc.†	20,000	245,000

Fidelity Magellan Fund Portfolio, March 31, 1988, *continued*

	Shares	Value
Apparel Stores—*continued*		
Evans, Inc.	150,000	$ 712,500
Fur Vault, Inc.	390,000	975,000
Gantos, Inc.†	60,000	720,000
Gap, Inc.	20,000	417,500
Limited, Inc. (The)	140,000	2,730,000
Melville Corp.	114,600	7,434,675
Merry-Go-Round Enterprises, Inc.†	180,000	1,822,500
Petrie Stores Corp.	30,000	607,500
S & K Famous Brands, Inc.†*	150,200	1,483,225
Syms Corp.†	843,000	9,273,000
United States Shoe Corp.	65,000	1,332,500
		50,279,724
Appliance Stores—0.2%		
Circuit City Stores, Inc.	309,100	8,577,525
First Family Group, Inc.†	5,000	15,000
Handleman Co. (Del.)	100,000	2,850,000
Intertan Inc.†	88,800	1,898,100
Sound Warehouse Inc.†	1,000	11,500
Trans World Music Corp.†	115,000	2,587,500
		15,939,625
Drug Stores—0.1%		
Rite Aid Corporation	213,700	8,147,312
General Merchandise Stores—3.0%		
Ames Department Stores, Inc.	250,000	3,875,000
Best Products Co., Inc.†	36,000	418,500
C V N Companies, Inc.†	150,000	2,306,250
Campeau Corp.†	512,000	9,229,148
Carson Pirie Scott & Co. (New)	285,000	3,811,875

	Shares	Value
Boys Markets Inc.†	210,000	$ 2,572,500
Cullum Companies, Inc.	40,000	670,000
Delhaize Freres	64,000	8,458,715
Great Atlantic & Pacific Tea Co., Inc.	59,500	2,037,875
Lucky Stores, Inc.	214,000	10,165,000
Mayfair Super Markets, Inc. Class A†	16,500	313,500
Nash Finch Co.	35,000	805,000
Provigo Inc.	140,000	1,176,732
Pueblo International Inc.	20,000	500,000
Rykoff-Sexton, Inc.	53,100	1,407,150
Super Food Services, Inc.	129,900	3,036,412
		33,016,925
Retail, Miscellaneous—1.4%		
Advanced Marketing Services Inc.†	109,900	1,648,500
Bercor, Inc.†*	287,000	645,750
CSS Industries, Inc.†	126,000	1,464,750
Casey's General Stores, Inc.†	21,500	322,500
Child World Inc.†	200,000	2,750,000
Circle K Corp. (The)	710,000	8,963,750
D.O.C. Optics Corp.†	25,000	175,000
Designcraft Industries, Inc.†	10,000	51,250
Fabricland Inc.	20,000	207,500
General Building Products Corp.†	6,000	36,000
General Host Corp.	414,000	3,881,250
Grossmans Inc.†	365,000	2,783,125
Gruen Marketing Corp.†	14,500	152,250
Hancock Fabrics Inc.	174,000	2,827,500
Hechinger Co. Class B cv	121,500	2,035,125

	Shares	Value
Carter Hawley Hale Stores, Inc.	510,000	5,163,750
Consolidated Stores Corp.†	146,000	693,500
Costco Wholesale Corp.†	430,000	6,020,000
Dart Group Corp. Class A	19,700	1,457,800
Dayton Hudson Corp.	25,000	946,875
Dillard Department Stores, Inc.	60,000	2,205,000
Family Dollar Stores, Inc.	73,100	877,200
Federated Department Stores, Inc.	29,500	2,138,750
Gottschalks Inc.†	422,000	5,433,250
Hills Department Stores, Inc.†	310,200	3,024,450
K mart Corp.	850,000	28,368,750
Luria (L.) & Son, Inc.†	33,400	350,700
May Department Stores Co. (The)	200,000	6,975,000
Mercantile Stores Co., Inc.	395,400	16,903,350
Neiman-Marcus Group, Inc.	215,000	2,902,500
PACE Membership Warehouse, Inc.†	255,100	2,040,800
Penney (J.C.) Co., Inc.	365,000	17,748,125
Pic 'N' Save Corp.†	795,000	12,620,625
Price Co. (The)†	530,000	19,875,000
Sears, Roebuck and Co.	569,000	20,341,750
Service Merchandise Co., Inc.	520,000	3,835,000
TJX Companies Inc.	783,100	13,606,362
Wal-Mart Stores, Inc.	463,000	13,021,875
Ward White ORD	80,000	488,851
Warehouse Club, Inc.†	9,000	20,250
Wholesale Club, Inc. (The)†	193,500	749,812
Woolworth (F.W.) Co.	960,000	43,440,000
Zayre Corp.	200,000	4,250,000
		255,140,098

Grocery Stores—0.4%

	Shares	Value
Albertson's, Inc.	45,000	1,299,375
Argyll	100,000	371,541
Bildner (J.) & Sons Inc.†	125,000	203,125

	Shares	Value
Home Depot, Inc. (The)	885,000	21,240,000
Initio, Inc.†	216,000	378,000
Jan Bell Marketing Inc.†	167,200	2,048,200
Jewelmaster, Inc.†	30,000	127,500
Kay Jewelers Inc.	237,875	3,181,578
Lionel Corporation†	21,500	91,375
Michaels Stores, Inc.†	5,000	29,375
Michigan General Corp.††	289,000	14,449
Moore-Handley, Inc.†	68,000	272,000
National Convenience Stores Inc.	78,000	643,500
NuVision, Inc.†*	160,000	1,160,000
Paxton (Frank) Co. Class A	15,000	219,375
Payless Cashways, Inc.	56,000	819,000
Pier 1 Imports Inc.	760,000	6,460,000
QVC Network Inc.†	16,000	144,000
Spiegel Inc. Class A	103,700	998,112
Sunbelt Nursery Group, Inc.†	22,300	103,137
Town & Country Jewelry Manufacturing Corp.	13,500	94,500
Toys "R" Us, Inc.†	1,295,000	44,515,625
Tuesday Morning, Inc.†	6,000	38,250
Uni Marts Inc. Class A	130,690	914,830
WNS, Inc.†	20,000	95,000
Williams-Sonoma, Inc.†	147,000	2,940,000
		114,472,056
TOTAL RETAIL AND WHOLESALE		476,995,740

SERVICES—2.5%
Printing—0.6%

	Shares	Value
AM International, Inc.	110,000	453,750
Esselte AB ORD Series B	600,000	17,564,459
Esselte Business Systems Inc.	200,000	7,975,000
Nashua Corp.*	578,300	18,144,162
Paris Business Forms, Inc.†	61,600	431,200
Reynolds & Reynolds Co.	35,000	743,750

Fidelity Magellan Fund Portfolio, March 31, 1988, *continued*

	Shares	Value
Printing—*continued*		
Rockaway Corp.	207,200	$ 1,838,900
United Stationers Inc.	28,800	612,000
Varitronic Systems Inc.†	6,000	87,000
Wallace Computer Services	13,300	553,612
		48,403,833
Services—**1.9%**		
ADT Ltd.	6,469,565	12,811,679
ADVO-Systems, Inc.†	54,000	317,250
AIFS, Inc.†*	262,600	1,280,175
Agency Rent-A-Car, Inc.†	75,000	1,425,000
Anacomp, Inc.†	955,600	8,361,500
Blue Arrow	3,000,000	6,393,539
CPI Corp.	399,000	7,780,500
CUC International, Inc.†	295,000	7,227,500
Corrections Corp. of America†	9,500	59,375
Ecolab Inc.	36,000	918,000
FCA Intl. Ltd.	229,000	1,669,703
Foote Cone & Belding Communications, Inc.	17,600	902,000
Interpublic Group of Companies, Inc.	48,700	1,613,187
Kinder-Care Learning Centers, Inc.	1,124,000	12,645,000
La Petite Academy, Inc.†*	800,000	14,200,000
Lex Service Group plc	1,910,000	12,067,570
Mickelberry Corp.	20,000	107,500
National Education Corp.†	445,000	10,624,375
National Guardian Corp.†	252,800	1,769,600
National Service Industries, Inc.	32,300	726,750
Omnicom Group Inc.	12,000	241,500

	Shares	Value
American Management Systems, Inc.†	136,700	$ 1,982,150
Amplicon Inc.†	43,000	559,000
Ashton-Tate Corp.†	150,000	4,125,000
Businessland, Inc.†	410,000	3,433,750
Capital Associates Inc.†	150,000	806,250
Cognos Inc.†	10,000	71,900
Comdisco, Inc.	685,000	14,470,625
Computer Associates International, Inc.†	165,000	4,516,875
Computer Entry Systems Corp.†	3,000	17,250
Computer Factory, Inc.†	45,000	551,250
Computer Horizons Corp.†	64,000	656,000
Continental Information Systems Corp.†	481,500	3,671,437
Continuum Co., Inc.†	10,000	125,000
Duquesne Systems, Inc.†	4,000	83,000
Epsilon Data Management, Inc.†	7,500	78,750
First Financial Management Corp.†	227,000	6,980,250
Fiserv, Inc.†	32,600	684,600
General Motors Corp. Class E	95,000	3,657,500
Gerber Scientific Inc.	620,000	11,005,000
HBO & Co.	20,000	180,000
Hospitality Capital Corp. (New)†	49,000	12,250
ISI Systems Inc.	5,000	60,625
Inacomp Computer Centers, Inc.†	89,700	661,537
Information Science Inc.†	27,300	20,475
Intelogic Trace, Inc.†	219,000	684,375
Interleaf, Inc.†	70,000	1,233,750
Lotus Development Corp.†	30,000	705,000
MacNeal-Schwendler Corp.	93,200	1,712,550

Pronet Inc.†	25,000	143,750
Robert Half International Inc.	19,200	388,800
Roto-Rooter, Inc.	210,000	4,410,000
Saatchi & Saatchi plc	675,000	5,155,852
Saatchi & Saatchi Co. plc. ADR	242,100	5,507,775
Service Corp. International	1,530,000	35,763,750
ServiceMaster Ltd. Partnership	25,000	646,875
Seven Oaks Intl., Inc.	10,000	85,000
Thrifty Rent-A-Car Systems Inc.†	77,000	1,212,750
United Tote, Inc.†*	116,000	1,015,000
Wilfred American Educational Corp.	93,700	456,787
		157,928,042
TOTAL SERVICES		206,331,875

TECHNOLOGY—9.1%

Communications Equipment—0.2%

Data Switch Corp.†	170,000	1,402,500
Digital Microwave Corp.†	20,000	310,000
Dynatech Corp.†	10,000	222,500
Excelan Inc.†	10,000	122,500
Geonex Corp.†	14,000	52,500
ICOT Corp.†	45,000	202,500
Network Systems Corp.†	245,200	2,084,200
Plantronics, Inc.	188,000	3,313,500
Regency Electronics, Inc.	30,000	138,750
Synercom Technology, Inc.†	10,000	40,000
3Com Corp.†	261,500	5,099,250
Tellabs, Inc.†	28,000	409,500
Vodavi Technology Corp.†	100,000	412,500
		13,810,200

Computer Services and Software—1.9%

AGS Computers, Inc.†	60,000	1,027,500
ASK Computer Systems, Inc.†	295,000	3,613,750
Adobe Systems Inc.†	60,000	1,860,000
Management Science America, Inc.†	17,400	106,575
Mentor Graphics Corp.†	190,000	5,035,000
Microsoft Corp.†	60,000	3,390,000
Morino Associates, Inc.†	18,000	288,000
NEECO, Inc.†	190,300	2,236,025
On-Line Software Intl., Inc.†	71,800	744,925
Oracle Systems Corp.†	745,000	12,106,250
Pansophic Systems, Inc.	380,000	6,365,000
Policy Management Systems Corp.†	190,000	4,465,000
Prime Capital Corp.†	108,000	486,000
SEI Corp.†	445,000	7,342,500
SHL Systemhouse Inc.†	160,000	2,317,009
SafeCard Services, Inc.	190,000	1,377,500
SofTech, Inc.†	77,600	446,200
Software Publishing Corp.†	360,000	5,265,000
Sterling Software, Inc.†	40,000	330,000
Structural Dynamics Research Corp.	23,000	310,500
SunGard Data Systems Inc.†	354,400	6,024,800
Systematics, Inc.	55,000	1,732,500
Systems Software Associates Inc.†	73,500	1,065,750
Telecredit, Inc.	75,000	2,962,500
Telerate, Inc.	1,380,000	26,220,000
Worlco Data Systems, Inc.†	75,000	93,750
Wyland Services, Inc.†	15,000	33,750
XL/DataComp, Inc.†	50,000	1,100,000
		161,091,933

Computers and Office Equipment—3.9%

Adage, Inc.†	90,000	78,750
Adaptec Inc.†	100,000	662,500
Amdahl Corp.	64,000	2,136,000
Apollo Computer Inc.†	130,000	1,852,500

Fidelity Magellan Fund Portfolio, March 31, 1988, *continued*

	Shares	Value		Shares	Value
Computers and Office Equipment—*continued*			Anthem Electronics, Inc.†	346,466	$ 3,681,201
Apple Computer, Inc.	910,000	$ 36,400,000	Arrow Electronics, Inc.†	65,000	487,500
Applied Magnetics Corp.†	217,000	3,390,625	Avnet, Inc.	226,000	5,480,500
Atari Corp.†	20,000	140,000	BRIntec Corp.†	88,000	484,000
C-3 Inc.†	65,900	914,362	Burr-Brown Corp.†	240,500	3,547,375
Commodore International Ltd.†	103,300	1,058,825	CTS Corp.	23,200	545,200
Computer & Communications			Corcom, Inc.†	115,000	517,500
Technology Corp.†	11,500	71,875	Cypress Semiconductor Corp.†	160,000	1,780,000
Control Data Corp.†	115,000	3,004,375	Diceon Electronics, Inc.†	39,500	1,125,750
Cray Research, Inc.†	10,000	796,250	Ducommun Inc.	65,000	292,500
Data I/O Corp.†	70,000	437,500	Electromagnetic Sciences, Inc.†	20,000	255,000
Data Translation, Inc.†	25,000	281,250	Hadco Corp.†	10,000	57,500
Digilog Inc.†	2,500	10,000	Integrated Device Technology,		
Digital Equipment Corp.†	540,000	56,295,000	Inc.†	175,000	2,406,250
EMC Corp. (Mass)†	714,400	10,805,300	Intel Corp.†	1,660,000	48,762,500
Genicom Corp.†	210,000	1,811,250	Linear Technology Corp.†	7,000	73,500
GTECH Corp.†	57,700	750,100	Marshall Industries†*	737,000	12,068,375
Honeywell Inc.	5,000	321,250	Matrix Science Corp.	30,000	345,000
Hutchinson Technology Inc.†	4,000	45,000	Methode Electronics, Inc. Class A	183,000	1,052,250
Intelligent Systems Master LP	5,200	20,800	Micron Technology, Inc.†	100,000	1,787,500
International Business Machines			Microsemi Corp.†	270,500	1,690,625
Corp.	855,000	91,912,500	Molex, Inc.	53,500	2,126,625
MAI Basic Four, Inc.	9,500	168,625	Motorola, Inc.	500,000	21,875,000
MSI Data Corp.†	22,900	558,187	National Semiconductor Corp.†	1,530,000	17,403,750
Maxtor Corporation†	275,000	3,781,250	Pioneer-Standard Electronics,		
Micropolis Corp.†	172,000	4,063,500	Inc.	69,400	598,575
MiniScribe Corp.†	170,000	1,785,000	Premier Industrial Corp.	15,300	436,050
NCR Corp.	90,000	5,186,250	Richardson Electronics, Ltd.†	14,500	282,750
National Micronetics Inc.†	10,000	29,375	Rogers Corp.	48,900	1,259,175
Perception Technology Corp.†	45,000	213,750	Sheldahl, Inc.†	15,000	91,875
Pitney Bowes, Inc.	515,000	22,981,875	Silicon General, Inc.†	25,000	90,625
Pyramid Technology Corp.†	8,400	88,200	Silicon Systems, Inc.†	115,000	1,552,500

Company	Shares	Value
Reuter, Inc.†	77,200	810,600
Summagraphics Corp.†	10,000	100,000
Sun Microsystems, Inc.†	80,000	2,860,000
Tandem Computers, Inc.†	80,000	1,430,000
Tandy Corp.	225,000	9,450,000
Telxon Corp.	8,400	168,000
Tempest Technologies Inc.†	122,900	891,025
Teradata Corp.†	268,000	4,556,000
Triad Systems Corp.†	160,000	1,700,000
Unisys Corp.	1,350,000	44,043,750
Valid Logic Systems Inc.†	105,000	459,375
Western Digital Corp.†	64,000	952,000
WICAT Systems, Inc.†	66,000	165,000
Xerox Corp.	143,569	7,591,210
XSCribe Corp.†	36,000	121,500
		327,350,484

Electronic Instruments—0.2%

Company	Shares	Value
Applied Materials, Inc.†	180,000	4,590,000
BMC Industries, Inc.†	105,700	673,837
Core Industries, Inc.	30,000	412,500
GenRad, Inc.†	100,000	912,500
KLA Instruments Corp.†	175,000	3,193,750
Kulicke & Soffa Industries, Inc.†	20,000	185,000
LTX Corp.†	10,000	155,000
Maxim Integrated Products Inc.†	105,000	630,000
Nanometrics Inc.†	20,000	55,000
Reliability Inc.†	24,000	105,000
Silicon Valley Group, Inc.†	215,000	1,612,500
Varian Associates, Inc.†	21,100	548,600
VeeCo Instruments Inc.	5,000	75,000
		13,148,687

Electronics—2.1%

Company	Shares	Value
AVX Corp.†	145,000	2,338,125
Advance Circuits, Inc.†	126,700	443,450
Advanced Micro Devices, Inc.†	20,000	220,000

Company	Shares	Value
Sprague Technologies Inc.†	10,000	101,250
Standard Microsystems Corp.†	225,000	1,265,625
Texas Instruments Inc.	595,000	27,741,875
Thomas & Betts Corp.	62,500	3,281,250
Tyler Corp.	207,300	2,772,637
Unitech plc	120,000	445,850
Vishay Intertechnology, Inc.†	1,700	45,050
Wyle Laboratories	441,400	3,972,600
Xicor, Inc.†	280,000	2,310,000
		177,094,663

Photographic Equipment—0.8%

Company	Shares	Value
Eastman Kodak Co.	1,660,000	67,437,500
Polaroid Corp.	110,000	3,465,000
		70,902,500

TOTAL TECHNOLOGY 763,398,467

TRANSPORTATION—4.5%
Air Transportation—1.8%

Company	Shares	Value
AMR Corp.†	293,500	12,620,500
Alaska Air Group, Inc.	100,000	1,687,500
Allegis Corp.	100,000	8,325,000
Command Airways, Inc.†*	45,000	360,000
D.N.L.†	100,000	1,866,986
Delta Air Lines, Inc.	720,900	36,856,012
Expeditors International of Washington, Inc.†	194,100	3,251,175
Federal Express Corp.†	140,000	6,492,500
Intertrans Corp.†	206,800	1,990,450
KLM Royal Dutch Airlines	545,000	10,355,000
Metro Airlines, Inc.†	10,000	40,000
Midway Airlines, Inc.†	280,000	3,465,000
NWA Inc.	310,000	13,485,000
Northern Air Freight Inc.	45,100	298,787
PWA Corp.†	541,000	8,656,173
Ports of Call, Inc.†	54,000	351,000

Fidelity Magellan Fund Portfolio, March 31, 1988, *continued*

	Shares	Value
Air Transportation—*continued*		
Southwest Airlines Co.	170,000	$ 2,911,250
Sunworld International Airways, Inc.†	69,000	21,562
Texas Air Corporation†	755,000	9,626,250
Tiger International, Inc.†	218,500	3,113,625
Trans World Airlines, Inc.†	36,500	1,040,250
USAir Group, Inc.	770,000	28,393,750
		155,207,770
Railroads—1.7%		
Burlington Northern Inc.	400,000	27,250,000
CNW Corp.	105,000	2,283,750
CSX Corp.	1,425,000	43,106,250
Consolidated Rail Corp.	970,000	29,706,250
GATX Corp.	180,000	8,235,000
Harmon Industries, Inc.	3,100	18,987
MidSouth Corp.†	1,500	32,250
Norfolk Southern Corp.	330,000	8,992,500
Trinity Industries, Inc.	200,000	5,875,000
Union Pacific Corp.	280,000	17,850,000
		143,349,987
Shipping—0.5%		
American President Companies, Ltd.	200,700	5,895,562
Bergesen Group Class A	115,000	9,030,448
Bergesen Group Class B	135,000	10,384,614
Bonheur†	40,000	935,897
Bulk Transport†	140,000	2,800,000
Ganger Rolf†	40,000	945,512
Gotaas-Larsen Shipping Corp.	170,000	4,845,000
International Shipholding Corp.†	28,500	498,750

	Shares	Value
Scientific-Atlanta, Inc.	10,000	$ 146,250
Securicor Group ORD	50,000	247,065
Securicor Group Class A	150,000	596,918
Security Services ORD	550,000	2,199,075
Shaw Cablesystems Ltd. Class B cv	434,700	2,905,391
Vanguard Cellular Systems Inc.†	20,000	425,000
		64,677,413
Electric—1.8%		
American Electric Power Co., Inc.	40,000	1,085,000
CMS Energy Corp.†	1,420,000	23,430,000
Central & South West Corp.	5,000	157,500
Central Maine Power Co.	137,800	2,325,375
China Light & Power Co. Ltd.	1,684,500	4,061,110
Commonwealth Edison Co.	618	16,686
Eastern Utilities Associates	31,794	786,901
El Paso Electric Co.	220,000	3,547,500
General Public Utilities Corp.	1,855,000	57,968,750
Hong Kong Electric Holdings Ltd.	3,936,000	3,987,482
Houston Industries, Inc.	5,000	152,500
Kansas City Power & Light Co.	80,000	2,140,000
Kansas Gas & Electric Co.	115,000	2,271,250
Long Island Lighting Co.†	550,000	4,881,250
Middle South Utilities, Inc.†	2,350,000	22,618,750
Minnesota Power & Light Co.	235,000	5,493,125
Montana Power Co.	15,000	495,000
New York State Electric & Gas Corp.	4,500	97,312
Niagara Mohawk Power Corp.	105,000	1,351,875
Northeast Utilities	145,000	2,863,750
PacifiCorp	50,000	1,706,250

	Shares	Value
Maritrans Partners LP	112,700	1,028,387
Overseas Shipholding Group, Inc.	143,400	3,047,250
Sea Containers Ltd.	200,000	4,425,000
Twin City Barge, Inc.‡	68,000	4,250
Vard†	5,000	87,339
		43,928,009

Trucking—0.5%

	Shares	Value
Arkansas Best Corp.	65,000	877,500
Builders Transport, Inc.†	25,000	306,250
Carolina Freight Corp.	35,000	896,875
Consolidated Freightways, Inc.	30,000	888,750
Courier Dispatch Group, Inc.†	70,600	229,450
MNX Inc.†	40,000	355,000
P.A.M. Transportation Services, Inc.†	10,000	30,000
RLC Corp.	330,000	2,887,500
Roadway Services, Inc.	35,000	1,111,250
Ryder Systems, Inc.	865,000	25,193,125
Werner Enterprises, Inc.	33,000	470,250
XTRA Corp.	309,700	9,600,700
Yellow Freight System, Inc. of Delaware	10,000	286,250
		43,132,900
TOTAL TRANSPORTATION		385,618,666

UTILITIES—5.9%

Cellular—0.8%

	Shares	Value
BCE Inc.†	73,500	1,027,160
General Instrument Corp.	190,000	5,890,000
LIN Broadcasting Corp.†	395,000	20,688,125
LPL Investment Group Inc.†	184,500	2,214,000
Metro Mobile CTS, Inc.†	290,000	9,570,000
Mobile Communications Corp. of America Class B†	125,000	3,328,125
Racal Electronics Ltd. ORD	3,880,000	15,440,304

	Shares	Value
Public Service Co. of Indiana, Inc.†	525,000	6,759,375
Sierra Pacific Resources	30,300	662,812
Union Electric Co.	33,000	767,250
United Illuminating Co.	10,000	202,500
		149,829,303

Gas—0.6%

	Shares	Value
Coastal Corp. (The)	794,000	22,331,250
Enron Corp.	45,000	1,648,125
ENSERCH Corp.	190,000	3,443,750
Equitable Resources Inc.	91,300	3,127,025
K N Energy, Inc.	12,500	214,062
MAPCO Inc.	71,800	3,706,675
Petrolane Partners L.P.	560,000	10,710,000
Southwestern Energy Co.	257,900	4,964,575
Texas Eastern Corp.	20,000	625,000
Transco Energy Co.	10,000	286,250
Valero Energy Corp.†	300,000	1,950,000
Williams Companies (The)	65,000	1,787,500
		54,794,212

Telephone Services—2.7%

	Shares	Value
American Telephone & Telegraph Co.	595,000	16,065,000
Ameritech Corp.	135,000	11,677,500
Bell Atlantic Corp.	165,000	10,910,625
BellSouth Corp.	5,000	193,750
Century Telephone Enterprises, Inc.	189,850	4,675,056
Communications Satellite Corp.	30,000	877,500
Compania Telefonica Nacional de Espana, SA ADR	910,000	20,816,250
Contel Corp.	550,000	18,287,500
GTE Corp.	80,000	2,850,000
MCI Communications Corp.†	705,000	7,843,125

Fidelity Magellan Fund Portfolio, March 31, 1988, *continued*

	Shares	Value
Telephone Services—*continued*		
NYNEX Corp.	315,000	$ 20,278,125
Pacific Telesis Group	2,250,000	64,125,000
Southern New England Telecommunications Corp.	228,200	11,438,525
Southwestern Bell Corp.	570,000	20,662,500
Telefonica Nacional De Espana (New) ORD	20,719	159,096
Telefonos De Mexico, S.A. ADR	22,800,000	4,275,000
Telephone & Data Systems, Inc.	157,000	3,826,875
U.S. West, Inc.	105,000	5,499,375
United Telecommunications, Inc.	232,600	6,570,950
		231,031,752
TOTAL UTILITIES		500,332,680
TOTAL COMMON STOCKS (Average Cost $7,795,659,705)		7,951,087,682
PREFERRED STOCKS—0.7%		
CONVERTIBLE PREFERRED STOCKS—0.6%		
BASIC INDUSTRIES—0.3%		
Iron and Steel—0.2%		
Bethlehem Steel Corporation $2.50	190,000	4,940,000
Bethlehem Steel Corporation $5.00	160,300	8,475,862
		13,415,862
Nonferrous Metals—0.1%		
Phelps Dodge Corp. $3.00	110,000	6,242,500
TOTAL BASIC INDUSTRIES		19,658,362

	Shares	Value
Securities Industry—0.0%		
First Capital Holdings Corp. $2.0625	85,000	$ 1,466,250
TOTAL FINANCE		8,861,875
INDUSTRIAL MACHINERY AND EQUIPMENT—0.0%		
American International Group, Inc. $2.00 exchangeable	62,000	1,162,500
RETAIL AND WHOLESALE—0.0%		
Retail, Miscellaneous—0.0%		
Wholesale Club, Inc. (The) $2.125	63,600	954,000
SERVICES—0.0%		
Leasing and Rental—0.0%		
Xtra Corp. $1.9375 Series B	42,300	1,120,950
Services—0.0%		
Hawley Group 36 pence†	400,000	2,640,399
TOTAL SERVICES		3,761,349
TECHNOLOGY—0.0%		
Computers and Office Equipment—0.0%		
Unisys Corp. $3.75 Series A	29,000	1,754,500
Electronics—0.0%		
Advanced Micro Devices, Inc. $0.30	20,000	700,000
TOTAL TECHNOLOGY		2,454,500
TRANSPORTATION—0.0%		
Shipping—0.0%		
Sea Containers Ltd. $4.125	34,700	1,561,500

CONGLOMERATES—0.1%

	Shares	Value
Hanson plc 10%	800,000	1,765,295
Itel Corp. $3.375 Class B, Series C	51,700	2,559,150
		4,324,445

CONSTRUCTION AND REAL ESTATE—0.0%
Construction—0.0%

	Shares	Value
Magnet & Southern $5.625	8,000	12,673
Perini Corp. $2.125	43,300	1,001,312
		1,013,985

DURABLES—0.1%
Autos, Tires and Accessories—0.1%

	Shares	Value
Lamson & Sessions Co. $2.0625 Series I exchangeable	24,000	720,000
Navistar International Corp. $6.00 Series G	46,000	2,288,500
		3,008,500

ENERGY—0.0%
Oil and Gas—0.0%

	Shares	Value
Seagull Energy Corp. $2.25 Series A	17,000	463,250
Tosco Corp. $2.375 Series E	59,100	2,002,012
		2,465,262

FINANCE—0.1%
Insurance—0.1%

	Shares	Value
First Executive Corp. $1.5625 Series G	403,000	6,548,750
Integrated Resources, Inc. $4.25	25,000	846,875
		7,395,625

UTILITIES—0.0%
Gas—0.0%

	Shares	Value
Valero Energy Corp. $2.0625	138,600	2,494,800
TOTAL CONVERTIBLE PREFERRED STOCKS		51,721,078

NONCONVERTIBLE PREFERRED STOCKS—0.1%
ENERGY—0.1%
Oil and Gas—0.1%

	Shares	Value
Mesa Limited Partnership preference A	80,000	1,000,000
Snyder Oil Partners Ltd. preference A	139,700	2,514,600
		3,514,600

NONDURABLES—0.0%
Foods—0.0%

	Shares	Value
Swift Independent Packaging Corp. adj. rate Series A	30,000	213,750

RETAIL AND WHOLESALE—0.0%
Apparel Stores—0.0%

	Shares	Value
Dylex Limited Partnership Class A	15,000	118,483

Retail, Miscellaneous—0.0%

	Shares	Value
Pier 1 Imports, Inc. $0.25	65,790	180,922
TOTAL RETAIL AND WHOLESALE		299,405

TRANSPORTATION—0.0%
Air Transportation—0.0%

	Shares	Value
Texas Air Corp. 12.00%	70,000	428,750
Texas Air Corp. $6.50	53,000	192,125
		620,875

Fidelity Magellan Fund Portfolio, March 31, 1988, *continued*

	Shares	Value
Shipping—0.0%		
Sea Containers Ltd. $2.10	9,199	$ 155,233
Sea Containers Ltd. $2.10 Series 1982	21,751	361,610
		516,843
TOTAL TRANSPORTATION		1,137,718
UTILITIES—0.0%		
Electric—0.0%		
Long Island Lighting Co. $3.31 Series T	37,600	1,123,300
Long Island Lighting Co. $3.50 Series V	30,800	935,550
Long Island Lighting Co. $4.25 Series U	11,100	373,237
Public Service Co. of New Hampshire $11.24‡	19,000	109,250
Public Service Co. of New Hampshire $13.80‡	65,000	390,000
		2,931,337
Gas—0.0%		
Yankee Companies, Inc. $1.15	21,800	21,800
TOTAL UTILITIES		2,953,137
TOTAL NONCONVERTIBLE PREFERRED STOCKS		8,118,610
TOTAL PREFERRED STOCKS (Average Cost $66,036,725)		59,839,688

	Principal Amount	Value
HEALTH—0.1%		
Drugs and Pharmaceuticals—0.0%		
Bio Technology General Corp. sub. sr. notes 7½%, 4/15/1997	200,000	$ 120,000
Medical Facilities Management—0.1%		
Forum Group, Inc. sub. s.f. deb. 6¼%, 8/15/2011	1,500,000	1,245,000
National Medical Enterprises, Inc. sub. liquid yield option notes 0%, 12/4/2004	9,000,000	2,655,000
		3,900,000
TOTAL HEALTH		4,020,000
INDUSTRIAL MACHINERY AND EQUIPMENT—0.0%		
Electrical Equipment—0.0%		
Computer Products Inc. sub. deb. 9½%, 5/15/1997	300,000	216,000
MEDIA AND LEISURE—0.1%		
Entertainment—0.1%		
Comcast Corp. sub. notes 0%, 1/15/1995	8,000,000	5,280,000
NONDURABLES—0.0%		
Foods—0.0%		
Allegheny Beverage Corp. sr. sub. s.f. deb. 9½%, 9/1/2010	1,400,000	868,000
Dreyer's Grand Ice Cream, Inc. sub. s.f. deb. 6½%, 6/1/2011	1,000,000	670,000
		1,538,000

CORPORATE BONDS—0.2%

CONVERTIBLE BONDS—0.2%

BASIC INDUSTRIES—0.0%

Chemicals and Plastics—0.0%

Park Electrochemical Corp. sub. s.f. deb. 7¼%, 6/15/2006	1,400,000	1,372,000

CONGLOMERATES—0.0%

UNC Inc. sub. deb. 7½%, 3/30/2006	2,400,000	1,836,000

CONSTRUCTION AND REAL ESTATE—0.0%

Real Estate—0.0%

Southmark Corp. sub. s.f. deb. 8½%, 1/15/1998	2,800,000	1,064,000

DURABLES—0.0%

Autos, Tires, and Accessories—0.0%

Sudbury Holdings, Inc. sub. s.f. deb. 7½%, 4/15/2011	500,000	415,000
Wickes Companies, Inc. s.f. deb. 12%, 1/31/1994	39,500	39,500
		454,500

Household Durables—0.0%

Grant Industries Inc. sub. s.f. deb. 8½%, 6/1/2003	1,249,000	674,460
TOTAL DURABLES		1,128,960

ENERGY—0.0%

Oil and Gas—0.0%

Varco International Inc. deb. 10%, 1/15/2007	500,000	1,000,000

FINANCE—0.0%

Banks—0.0%

Mellon Bank Corp. sub. cap. notes 7¼%, 9/1/1999	500,000	405,000

RETAIL AND WHOLESALE—0.0%

Apparel Stores—0.0%

CML Group, Inc. sub. deb. 7½%, 7/1/2012	1,800,000	1,494,000
Petrie Stores Corp. sub. s.f. deb. 8%, 12/15/2010	400,000	424,000
		1,918,000

SERVICES—0.0%

Service Corp. International sub. s.f. deb. 6½%, 4/15/2011	500,000	550,000

TRANSPORTATION—0.0%

Air Transportation—0.0%

America West Airlines, Inc. sub. deb. 7¾%, 8/1/2010	400,000	196,000

Railroads—0.0%

Trinity Industries, Inc. liquid yield option notes 0%, 11/23/2001†	3,400,000	1,432,250
TOTAL TRANSPORTATION		1,628,250
TOTAL CONVERTIBLE BONDS		21,956,210

NON-CONVERTIBLE BONDS—0.0%

CONSTRUCTION AND REAL ESTATE—0.0%

Building Materials—0.0%

GIANT Group, Ltd. sub. notes 14½%, 4/15/1995	800,000	800,000

Real Estate—0.0%

Miller H. & Sons sub. deb. 11%, 10/1/1989	52,100	50,277
TOTAL CONSTRUCTION AND REAL ESTATE		850,277

Fidelity Magellan Fund Portfolio, March 31, 1988, *continued*

	Principal Amount	Value
INDUSTRIAL MACHINERY AND EQUIPMENT—0.0%		
Pollution Control—0.0%		
Waste Management, Inc. sub. liquid yield option notes 0%, 1/21/2001†	2,000,000	$ 1,220,000
NONDURABLES—0.0%		
Beverages—0.0%		
Seagram (Joseph E.) & Sons, Inc. liquid yield option notes 0%, 3/15/2006†	5,000,000	1,343,750
TRANSPORTATION—0.0%		
Air Transportation—0.0%		
Continental Airlines Corp. sub. deb. 11%, 9/2/1996	1,422,400	1,072,276
UTILITIES—0.0%		
Electric—0.0%		
Public Service Co. of New Hampshire deb. 17½%, 10/15/2004‡	2,500,000	971,875
TOTAL NON-CONVERTIBLE BONDS		5,458,178
TOTAL CORPORATE BONDS (Average cost $30,998,577)		27,414,388

	Units	Value
UNITS—0.1%		
ENERGY—0.0%		
Oil & Gas—0.0%		
Unit Corp. (3 common & 1 warrant)†	141,000	$ 881,250
SERVICES—0.1%		
Sun Distributors LP (1 depositary receipt Class A & 1 depositary receipt Class B)	412,800	3,715,200
TOTAL UNITS (Average Cost $5,054,429)		4,596,450

	Maturity Amount	Value
SHORT-TERM OBLIGATION—4.6%		
Investments in repurchase agreements (U.S. Treasury obligations), in a joint trading account dated 3/31/1988:		
At 6.50% due 4/1/1988	9,001,625	9,000,000
At 6.49% due 4/4/1988	374,894,190	374,624,000
		383,624,000
TOTAL INVESTMENTS—100.0% (Average Cost $8,281,373,436)		$8,426,562,208

†Non-income producing.
††Non-income producing; issuer filed petition under Chapter 11.
*Affiliated company: represents ownership of at least 5% of the voting securities of the issuer.

XI

Picking a Winning Fund*

Michael D. Hirsch explains the growth of mutual funds and discusses how to select funds in an orderly fashion. It is, of course, not enough to buy the recent best performers. That way you may tie on to the end of one fad after another. He instances the 44 Wall Street Fund, for example, which was the top fund in 1975 and the worst in 1984.

Mr. Hirsch recommends making selections from funds with consistently superior records, and staying with them for some time. Out of more than 1,000 funds, he starts by reducing the list of candidates to several dozen.

An important step omitted in the book is how to do that conveniently. *Forbes* publishes a sensibly devised "honor roll" every summer in its mutual fund issue, but the list has a high turnover: 25% to 30% a year. Mr. Hirsch himself uses a service put out by CDA Investment Technologies Inc. of Silver Spring, Md., which supplies a list of funds with superior three-year performance records. The longer-term records come from the funds themselves.

Then, you have to get to know the individual managers. (Mr. Hirsch uses the infelicitous term "personalization.") That's easy for the heavy hitter, but Mr. Average Investor will tend to receive a dose of slick PR from the shareholder relations department. Mr. Hirsch, however, suggests specific questions to ask (and recheck periodically) that the fund is bound to answer, even if through an underling. Is the fund run by a committee or by a star? (Mr. Hirsch favors stars.) How long has the star been there? (Mr. Hirsch favors at least three years, and preferably more than five.)

If a key manager leaves, or changes his winning technique, one should reconsider the choice. Mr. Hirsch cites a highly disciplined "relative strength" manager—in fact George Chestnutt—whose performance collapsed when he fell in love with Kirby Oil, one of his largest holdings, ignoring its market deterioration. Anyway, after this screening, perhaps 30 or 35 funds will remain as interesting candidates, from which you make the final picks.

Mr. Hirsch next recommends a series of a priori allocations: fixed income,

*From a review by John Train in the April 17, 1987, *Wall Street Journal* of "Multi-fund Investing" by Michael D. Hirsch, Manager of Republic National Bank's investment division.

aggressive growth, stable growth and so on. The book suggests that one should vary these allocations according to circumstances. I'm not so sure. All too likely, most retail-fund buyers will be chasing frothy equities at the top and be out of the market, petrified with fear, at the bottom. The average reader would be better off rarely varying the allocations significantly.

Anyway, my guess is that at the end of all this the average reader who really does what Mr. Hirsch advises should indeed improve his life somewhat, on balance.

I have examined Mr. Hirsch's own record, and it would seem that net of costs he is slightly ahead of the averages in balanced funds, and more or less even in equity funds. Other fund counselors may be less successful. By the nature of entrepreneurial swarming, fund consultants should eventually proliferate until their collective value-added is negative. On the other hand, if you only break even with one you've still saved time and gained systematic diversification, although you know less about your actual holdings.

Can a larger, experienced investor do better with funds? My experience is that it takes not much more work to find a consistently successful company than a consistently successful fund. The substantial investor should consider funds primarily for specialized purposes, such as particular countries or industries.

Index

379